Public Administration in C

Brief Edition

Paul Barker

University of Western Ontario

THOMSON

NELSON

Australia   Canada   Mexico   Singapore   Spain   United Kingdom   United States

THOMSON
NELSON

Public Administration in Canada, Brief Edition
by Paul Barker

Associate Vice President, Editorial Director:
Evelyn Veitch

Editor-in-Chief, Higher Education:
Anne Williams

Executive Editor:
Cara Yarzab

Acquisitions Editor:
Bram Sepers

Senior Marketing Manager:
Lenore Taylor-Atkins

Developmental Editor:
MY EDITOR

Photo Researcher and Permissions Coordinator:
Donna Dudinsky

Senior Content Production Manager:
Tammy Scherer

Production Service:
International Typesetting and Composition

Copy Editor:
Rodney Rawlings

Proofreader:
Tara Tovell

Indexer:
Robert Swanson

Production Coordinator:
Ferial Suleman

Design Director:
Ken Phipps

Interior Design:
Katherine Strain

Cover Design:
Brenda Barratt

Cover Image:
© Jennifer Hewitson/Images.com

Compositor:
International Typesetting and Composition

Printer:
Thomson/West

COPYRIGHT 2008, 1999
by Nelson, a division of Thomson Canada Limited.

Printed and bound in the United States
1 2 3 4 09 08 07 06

For more information contact Nelson, 1120 Birchmount Road, Toronto, Ontario, M1K 5G4. Or you can visit our Internet site at http://www.nelson.com

Statistics Canada information is used with the permission of Statistics Canada. Users are forbidden to copy this material and/or redisseminate the data, in an original or modified form, for commercial purposes, without the expressed permissions of Statistics Canada. Information on the availability of the wide range of data from Statistics Canada can be obtained from Statistics Canada's Regional Offices, its World Wide Web site at http://www.statcan.ca, and its toll-free access number 1-800-263-1136.

ALL RIGHTS RESERVED. No part of this work covered by the copyright herein may be reproduced, transcribed, or used in any form or by any meansgraphic, electronic, or mechanical, including photocopying, recording, taping, Web distribution, or information storage and retrieval systems without the written permission of the publisher.

For permission to use material from this text or product, submit a request online at www.thomsonrights.com

Every effort has been made to trace ownership of all copyrighted material and to secure permission from copyright holders. In the event of any question arising as to the use of any material, we will be pleased to make the necessary corrections in future printings.

Library and Archives Canada Cataloguing in Publication Data

Barker, Paul, 1953-
    Public administration in Canada / Paul Barker.—Brief ed.

Updated and brief ed. of: Public administration in Canada : a text / Kenneth Kernaghan, David Siegel. 4th ed. 1999.

Includes bibliographical references and index.

ISBN-13: 978-0-17-625137-6
ISBN-10: 0-17-625137-5

    1. Public administration—Canada. 2. Canada—Politics and government. I. Kernaghan, Kenneth, 1940- . Public administration in Canada. II. Title.

JL108.B37 2006   351.71
C2006-905986-1

Contents

Preface

The purpose of this book is to provide a brief and updated version of Kernaghan and Siegel's *Public Administration in Canada: A Text*. The case for an update is easy to make, for the last edition of the text was published nearly a decade ago. This updating, however, still leaves large parts of the previous edition untouched, which means that many of the words and ideas of Kernaghan and Siegel remain within the text. As for the relative brevity of the text, the belief was that some might benefit from a more concise presentation of public administration in Canada. The shortening was accomplished mostly by the omission of chapters, but a few chapters were also either condensed or combined with others (and a new one was added). The philosophy guiding the creation of this brief edition was to provide a close-up view of the operation of public administration in Canada. This brief edition of *Public Administration in Canada* seeks to give the reader a sense of what it means to be a public servant in the governments of Canada.

This book basically follows the same structure of the earlier editions:

- Part 1 offers an introduction to the study of public administration in Canada. Chapter 1 investigates the meaning of public administration, looks at the environment of the public service, and tries to make the reader sensitive to some of the key issues and themes in Canadian public administration. Chapters 2 through 4 examine the various theories or schools of thought on the structure and operation of organizations and how they relate to the practice of public administration in Canada. Chapter 2 deals with the early theorists of bureaucracy, which include Weber, Taylor, Gulick, and Urwick. Chapter 3 traces the evolution of humanist theories from their beginnings to contemporary theories of employee participation, while Chapter 4 (the only entirely new chapter) reviews the work on the new public management.
- Part 2 moves from the theories of organizations to the actual structures of government used to deliver services and regulate the economic and social processes in Canada. Chapter 5 focuses on central agencies and the most commonly employed organizational form, namely the operating department. Chapter 6 discusses Crown corporations, and Chapter 7 deals with independent regulatory agencies. Chapter 8 examines an interesting and relatively new development in Canadian public administration which is the rise of new organizational mechanisms in government that fall under the category of alternative service delivery.
- Part 3 develops a framework for examining interactions between public servants found in the basic organizational forms and other actors in the Canadian political process. Chapter 9 outlines the framework for considering the type and nature of these interactions, and discusses some of the values that appointed officials and the other actors pursue in their relations with one another. Chapter 10 concentrates on two values, accountability and integrity, that are particularly important to the behaviour of public servants in their relations with others.
- Part 4 addresses the aforementioned interactions, and in so doing reflects some of the themes enumerated in the first chapter (the power of bureaucracy, the crowded nature of the world of public administration, the changing relationship between the minister and senior officials). Chapter 11 examines the relations of the bureaucracy with senior

political actors in cabinet, while Chapter 12 shifts the focus to interactions within and between departments and other agencies. Chapters 13 and 14 consider interactions between public servants and the legislature and the courts respectively, and Chapter 15 endeavours to offer an understanding of intergovernmental administrative relations. Part 4 ends with a review of relations that sometimes receive little attention, namely those between appointed officials and nongovernmental actors (pressure groups, the media, interested public, and extraparliamentary wing of political parties).

- Part 5 concludes the text with an examination of the two of major tasks associated with the management of organizational resources in the public sector. In other words, this last part gives the reader a better view of public servants in action. Chapters 17 and 18 deal with the management of human resources, with the first of the two chapters discussing the emergence of the merit principle and the structure of the human resource management system, and the second assessing efforts at the federal level to provide for a more representative bureaucracy. The final two chapters address the difficult challenge of managing the country's financial resources. Chapter 19 discusses the various aspects of budgeting in government, which can be considered the first step in the financial management process. Chapter 20 examines the remaining steps in the attempt to ensure that the public finances are managed soundly.

The text contains some features that seek to further the learning process. The Bibliography at the end of the book is divided by chapter, so that students can, if they wish, pursue matters discussed in any given chapter. A Glossary is also provided at the end of the text, with each entry accompanied by the page on which the term is first discussed. Boldfaced terms in the text refer to the Glossary. For the most the chapters are self-contained, so users of the text may read the chapters in the order they prefer. However, the book is best studied in the chapter order used in the text.

I am indebted to the previous authors, Kenneth Kernaghan and David Siegel, for their dedication and commitment to the earlier editions. As stated previously, the text's structure and many of their words were mostly retained. A note of thanks also goes to these reviewers for their comments and suggestions:

Christopher Stoney, Carleton University
Evert Lindquist, University of Victoria
Andres Perez, University of Western Ontario
Thomas Klassen, York University

— P.B.

1

Introduction to
Public Administration

1

What Is Public Administration?

This is an exciting period in the field of public administration in Canada. As in other parts of the world, governments in Canada are being challenged to respond to such forces as rapid social change, the emergence of a global economy, startling advances in information technology, and the public's insistence on a more open and participative decision-making process. But some public servants might use a less charitable term than "exciting" to describe this period. To appreciate this sentiment, we have only to imagine developing policies for the modern family or dealing with the many implications of the Internet. Being a public servant means engaging in very difficult work, with failure always just around the corner. This period in public administration is also troubling because the forces of change have rearranged the manner in which those in government carry out their duties. The work of public administration in Canada was once largely limited to public servants and their political superiors, producing a village-like setting in which roles and expectations were clear and certain and issues were handled without elaborate rules and procedures.[1] But the refusal of the world to remain the same has ended this stable and at times comfortable existence. Technology and a more aggressive media now make public servants much more open to the public, and various bodies—interest groups, new investigative entities, the courts—have emerged to play a larger role in the shaping of government actions. Traditional organizational forms and procedures must also make room for different ways of formulating and delivering services.

Despite these disruptions and changes, public servants remain centrally involved in public administration. They are expected to devise appropriate solutions to societal challenges, in part through efforts to reinvent, rethink, reshape, and revitalize government in general and the public service in particular. Though the disruptions and difficulties apparent in public administration are unsettling, they also present public servants with opportunities unavailable until now. This chapter serves as an attempt to lay a foundation for understanding the increasingly fascinating and complex world of public administration by examining its role and development in the Canadian context.

Importance and Meaning of Public Administration

During this century, and especially since the beginning of World War II, there has been an enormous expansion in the activities of Canadian governments. The growth of responsibilities in all spheres of Canadian government—federal, provincial, and municipal—has a great impact on the daily lives and future prospects of Canadian citizens. The degree of happiness and prosperity or misery and poverty experienced by Canadians is affected by the countless decisions made each day by our governments. The range of governmental activities includes the traditional functions of administration of justice, conduct of external relations, and defence of the country, as well as newer responsibilities such as health care, environmental protection, and scientific research. Federal public servants control and inspect air traffic; protect coastal waterways against pollution and overfishing; guard prisoners in penitentiaries and rehabilitate offenders; protect our health and safety by inspecting food, water, air, and medicine; issue millions of cheques annually to seniors and needy Canadians; help unemployed Canadians find jobs; and support science, technology, and the delivery of foreign aid.

The two major areas of government activities are the provision of services and the enforcement of regulations. The service functions include the delivery of mail, the maintenance of roads and highways, and the administration of grants and loans. Among the regulatory functions are the prevention of unsafe workplaces, the support of Canadian culture, and the enforcement of fair housing and employment regulations. In order to carry out these and other responsibilities as effectively as possible, governments are actively engaged in research on matters ranging from the inspection of food and drugs to scientific and medical concerns. Virtually every government department and agency is involved in research related to its service or regulatory functions. Research activities are a costly but essential component of the total responsibilities of government.

Few Canadians are aware of the importance and the magnitude of their governments' operations. Canadians, like citizens of other countries, tend to be conscious of only those government activities that affect them directly and significantly. Many important functions of government, such as the preservation of internal law and order or the administration of justice, are taken for granted unless the services are discontinued or disrupted for some reason. Half a century ago, governments in Canada rested content with the provision of security and basic public services. Today, even though many political leaders aspire to limit the size of the public sector, governments involve themselves in all facets of the lives of Canadians.

These extensive and pervasive activities of Canadian governments have a great deal to do with public administration. Public administrators play a large role in formulating and implementing policies to fulfill their government's service and regulatory responsibilities. These responsibilities are performed through what is known as the public bureaucracy or bureaucracy, which is an organizational system for achieving government objectives.[2] Elected representatives, especially political executives (e.g., cabinet ministers, city mayors), participate actively in the making of public policies. However, we shall see in later chapters that public servants (also called civil servants, government employees, *appointed* officials, or bureaucrats) have considerable influence on the content of these policies and make most of the decisions required to implement them. Thus, while a recurring theme in this book is the importance of relations between the political and bureaucratic realms of government, the role of the bureaucracy is the major focus.

The Meaning of Public Administration

"Public administration" is a term more easily explained than defined. This fact has not discouraged several scholars from trying to capture its meaning in a single sentence.

| Box 1.1 | What Is Public Policy? |

Definitions and discussions of public administration often contain references to **public policy** (or **policy**). The term means an action or decision made by the government to address a particular problem. A policy of government might be to help individuals attend postsecondary institutions or ensure that all residents have access to medically required care. Often the term is accompanied by reference to **program**, which means a set of activities used to carry out the policies of government. Grant and loan programs might be employed to assist entry into university, or a fully government-financed health system may be set up to make certain that no resident goes without necessary health care services.

Source: Ivan L. Richardson and Sidney Baldwin, *Public Administration: Government in Action* (Charles E. Merrill Columbus, Ohio:, 1976), 3; John M. Pfiffner and Robert Presthus, *Public Administration*, 5th ed. (Ronald Press New York:, 1967), 7.

Typical one-sentence definitions of public administration include "the study and practice of the tasks associated with the conduct of the administrative state" and "the coordination of individual group efforts to carry out publc policy."[3] A more ambitious attempt at defining public administration sees it as the "use of managerial, political, and legal theories and processes to fulfill legislative, executive, and judicial governmental mandates for the provision of regulatory and service functions for the society as a whole or for some segments of it."[4] These definitions indicate the scope and purpose of public administration, but they are incomplete in their coverage and very general in their wording. The emphasis in these and most other definitions of public administration is on the implementation of policy; there is insufficient recognition of the role of bureaucrats in the formulation of programs and policies. These definitions also contain abstract words and terms that tend to leave the reader with more questions than answers. For example, what are the tasks associated with the conduct of the administrative state? What are the relationships between bureaucrats and such institutions as legislatures, executives, and courts? What is distinctive about organization and management in public administration as opposed to private administration? This book provides answers to these and many other questions about public administration.

The terms "public administration" and "public bureaucracy" are often used interchangeably, but they do not mean the same thing. Public administration refers to a field of practice (or occupation) and to a field of study (or discipline). Public bureaucracy is the system of authority, people, offices, and methods—in other words, an organizational form—that government uses to achieve its objectives. It is the means by which the practice of public administration is largely carried on; it is also the main focus of the study of public administration. We use the term public administration to refer to its practice unless we indicate otherwise by specific reference to its study. Thus, this book is devoted to studying the practice of public administration as that practice is conducted through the system known as public bureaucracy. However, at this point it is important to recognize that public bureaucracy, the central element in public administration, is undergoing a critical review and that we are moving toward the examination of new types of administrative structures. It is also important to always recall that the consideration of bureaucracy includes not only the investigation of the behaviour or internal operation of bureaucratic forms but also the relations between bureaucracy and other elements in the political process. With all this in mind, a workable definition of public administration is that it deals with "the public, civil, or civic service, including all matters of concern within itself, all matters which impinge on it, and all matters on which it impinges."[5] The definition fixes on the public or civil service—other terms for the public bureaucracy—and also notes that public administration goes beyond the inner workings of bureaucratic agencies and structures.

Public Administration Versus Private Administration

The meaning of public administration can be clarified by comparing it with private (or business) administration. There is, in fact, much that is similar in the two sectors. Administration in all organizations involves cooperative group action. Moreover, all large organizations, whether they are government departments, hospitals, universities, labour unions, factories, or commercial enterprises, must provide for the performance of such functions of general management as planning, organizing, staffing, and budgeting. There are, however, many distinguishing factors in the administration of public sector organizations, and these differences have important implications for the study and practice of public administration. At the very least, these differences suggest the need for caution in transferring practices and technologies from private sector organizations to public sector organizations.

The first and most frequently cited difference is that the overall mission of public administration is service to the public, whereas the primary raison d'être of private administration is profit, or what is often described as "the bottom line." The service orientation of public administration results from the need for bureaucrats to assist elected politicians to respond to public demands and requirements for government services. Private administration is profit-oriented because the survival of private sector organizations ultimately depends on making a profit.

It is commonly argued that a second difference, following directly from the service-versus-profit distinction, is that public administration operates less efficiently than private administration. Governments are not oriented toward a single goal such as profit maximization; rather, they typically must satisfy several goals simultaneously, some of which may conflict with one another, and some of which cannot even be stated openly. In this complex environment, it is not surprising that governments sometimes do things that would not stand the test of businesslike principles. It is also suggested that since government departments receive their funds largely through annual appropriations from the public treasury, they do not have to worry about profits; thus, they have less incentive to cut costs and operate efficiently. Business organizations are motivated to operate efficiently because they must compete in the marketplace; most government operations, however, are monopolistic (e.g., the police) so that the public does not have a choice among competing organizations for the delivery of services. Another consideration is that politicians are concerned, first and foremost, with winning public support. The public judges politicians by their public personae and policy initiatives, not by how well they manage their departments. Thus, many politicians do not expend a great deal of effort in managing their departments well or in rewarding public service managers who do. Politicians want public servants who provide good policy advice and who keep them out of trouble.

A third difference between public and private administration is the greater emphasis in the public sector on accountability. This arises in part from the fact that all of us are forced to contribute financially to government and thus we expect some say over its operation and or at least an indication that matters are being handled properly. The typical government monopoly of government over the provision of services also leads to greater demands for accountability because recipients of the services have nowhere else to go. Parents with children at private schools can always turn to an alternative, but those in the public school system usually have no choice. For these parents, there is an incentive to take a greater interest in the operation of the public function.[6] More generally, in the private sector accountability is mostly confined to pleasing shareholders, whereas in the public sector theoretically the entire population has a stake.

A fourth difference between public and private administration is that the human resources management system is much more complicated and rigid in government than in private sector organizations. In general, it is harder both to hire and to fire government employees. In the public sector, the merit system of hiring and promoting employees includes several criteria that go well beyond the idea of technical proficiency. To promote sensitivity and responsiveness to the needs of a certain minority group, for example, the government may hire a person from that group who is not as well qualified as other candidates in terms of education and experience. The complexity and inflexibility of human resources management systems also result from the general emphasis on accountability and the need to demonstrate that the required procedures have been properly established and followed.

Fifth, and finally, the public nature of public administration requires that much of it be conducted in a fishbowl of publicity. Many government deliberations are conducted behind closed doors but, compared to the private sector, many more government decisions are subjected to public scrutiny. Most of the work of private sector managers "is internal and far removed from public view," but "the public sector is fair game for anyone."[7] The media, for one, pays a great deal more attention to the trials and tribulations of ministers and their officials than they do to the goings-on in business life. Front-page headlines are more likely to reveal some inefficiency in government than they would comparable developments in the private sector. One implication of this reality is the greater emphasis in the public sector on such considerations as responsiveness and accountability.

Two major characteristics of government account in large part for the differences between public and private administration: (1) the vast scope and complexity of government activities and (2) the political environment within which these activities are conducted. Given these considerations, the issue of whether public or private administration is more efficient is not the most relevant concern. The critical question is whether public administration is conducted as efficiently as can reasonably be expected. We shall see at various points in this book that governments are actively engaged in reforms to increase their efficiency, effectiveness, and responsiveness by such means as improved service to the public and the reduction of rules and regulations.

It is important to avoid exaggerating the differences between public and private administration. In the private sector, many organizations are extremely large and complex, and most of them are influenced by the broad political environment that requires that they consider many factors other than the bottom line. Private sector organizations are being required to be much more open about their activities and to follow the public sector's lead in such areas as employment equity and pay equity.

The Study of Public Administration

The systematic study of public administration in North America is a relatively recent development. In the United States, the study of the field is generally acknowledged to date from 1887 with the publication of Woodrow Wilson's essay, "The Study of Administration."[8] Although no single date or publication marks the beginning of the study of public administration in Canada, there are several noteworthy developments in the evolution of the formal study of Canadian public administration.

Several of the 23 volumes of *Canada and Its Provinces*, written by A. Shortt and A.G. Doherty and published in 1914, covered aspects of public administration and public bureaucracy in Canada. In 1918, the first work focusing on a particular problem in Canadian public administration was written by two scholars from the United States.[9] The earliest general work in the field was R. MacGregor Dawson's *The Civil Service of Canada*, published in 1929.[10] In 1936 Luther Richter and R.A. Mackay established the

Box 1.2 Educational Route to Careers in Public Administration

A variety of arrangements exists for the master's-level education of aspiring public servants. Programs leading to a Master of Public Administration (M.P.A.) degree, or to a degree in political science or public sector management, are available in departments of political science or in schools or faculties of administrative studies. However, the most common route to an M.P.A. is through one of the several specialized schools of public administration that have grown rapidly during the past 25 years in Canada. These schools offer an interdisciplinary approach with a professional emphasis. Programs are designed to accommodate students proceeding directly from their bachelor's degree as well as mid-career public servants. The schools require a similar group of core courses (e.g., government structure and organization, policy formulation, quantitative methods, applied economics, the management process in government, and public sector financial management and accounting) and a range of elective courses in specialized areas such as local government administration and intergovernmental relations.

first degree program in Canadian public administration at Dalhousie University. Carleton College (now Carleton University) graduated students with a Bachelor of Public Administration degree in 1946, and the university's School of Public Administration was established in 1952. However, it was not until the early 1950s that a group of academic scholars emerged and a more broad-based literature in public administration started to develop. *Canadian Public Administration*, the scholarly journal devoted to the study of the subject, commenced publication in 1958.

The academic study of public administration began to flourish in the late 1960s. In fact, progress in the study of Canadian public administration since 1970, as measured by research, publications, teachers, and programs, has been greater than in all the preceding years combined. This increased attention to research and teaching in public administration is largely due to the growth of the operations, expenditures, and size of the federal, provincial, and municipal bureaucracies. It also coincided with the expansion of Canadian universities and colleges, which were thereby able to devote more resources to teaching and research in public administration.[11]

Environment and Size of Public Administration

Environment of Public Administration

Public administration is greatly influenced by the broad environment within which it is conducted. Aside from the political and legal setting of public administration, discussed in detail elsewhere in this book, some of the more important environmental influences of today are globalization, technological change, political culture, the financial position of governments, and the legacy of past attempts to reform the public service.

Globalization

"The death of distance" and the "borderless world" are phrases used in the attempt to convey the essence of globalization. Once, we defined ourselves territorially, but globalization turns the whole planet into a "single social space" producing a sense of "simultaneity."[12] To its limit, globalization means that everything that happens does so to everybody and at the same time. For many, globalization is identified with its economic dimension, which is the movement from a world of distinct economies to a global economy characterized by worldwide markets for investment, production, distribution, and consumption. This in fact is a key element of globalization, and it forces national governments and their bureaucratic agents to be creative in order to remain competitive in the new global marketplace and to guard industries and individuals against the some-times harsh effects of globalization.[13] Economic globalization also puts a premium on governments' ability to act quickly, so there is pressure to make decision making in the public sector more flexible and open to new ways of organizing itself.

Globalization also has a cultural dimension that puts at risk national cultures as it acts to establish common beliefs and values on a worldwide basis. For governments eager to preserve the cultural uniqueness of their countries, this cultural aspect of glob-alization represents a tremendous challenge. In Canada, regulatory agencies try to pro-vide for Canadian content in our various cultural products, but the Internet, iPods, satellite radio, and the 500-channel universe tear away at these efforts. Threats of global warming and signs of widespread damage to the ecosystem demonstrate that globaliza-tion also has an environmental dimension, and this too—as with the other dimensions of globalization—requires governments to act differently. In this instance, the challenge is for governments to coordinate their efforts to ensure that we do not seriously hurt or even destroy the planet.

Technological Change

Advances in technology represent another force influencing the work of government and their public services. New computing and information processing technology facilitate better access to government services and make it simpler for citizens to communicate with their governments. Frontline workers in government are now better able to produce decisions because of the easy availability of information, a development that makes public services more sensitive to the needs of the citizenry. Technology also makes pos-sible services—efficient highway tolling, for example—that were only a few years ago thought quite impossible. "E-government," the term applied to government increasingly reliant on electronic devices, makes government faster, more innovative, and more effec-tive. In some instances, e-government reduces to a digital reality, able to offer services and information without the need for bricks and mortar.

But technology also produces problems for public administration. New technology which involves the processing and sharing of information holds great potential for inva-sions of privacy. Scientific advances, especially in the area of health care, also present governments with difficult decisions. Technology also threatens to overwhelm us and our governments; email messaging makes governments go faster, but it may also clog the arteries of the public sector with its mass of information. A more prosaic concern is that we may lack the personnel necessary to set up and maintain this new technology.

Political Culture

A third force is the changing political culture in Canada and other developed countries. Political culture refers to the values, beliefs, and attitudes we hold about political life, and surveys reveal that people are less confident in government (and non-government institutions as well). These same surveys also reveal a heightened interest in politics and participation in irregular types of political behaviour. Altogether, the findings sug-gest that people, including Canadians, are not as willing to accept public authority as in the past and wish for new ways of interacting with their elected and appointed officials. There has been, as Nevitte writes, a "decline of deference" in the political cultures of the developed world.[14] Higher levels of education and affluence, the disappointing perfor-mance of governments, and shifting constitutional arrangements (the Charter of Rights and Freedoms in Canada's case) have all put forward in an attempt to explain this shift in attitudes about politics. For public administration, a major implication of this change is that governments must consult more widely and in a more varied fashion with the interested public. People are clearly unhappy with the both the level and the type of

Chapter 1 / What Is Public Administration?

traditional interactions with government. Another implication is that existing organizational structures in government are unacceptable and that bureaucratic forms in particular need to be fixed.[15]

Financial Position

The final two decades of the 20th century witnessed difficult financial times for many governments. Public spending on various programs and services often exceeded available revenues, a development that led to large budget deficits and burgeoning public debts. Governments responded with a variety of actions to reduce public obligations and restore fiscal health to the Treasury. The actions included elimination of programs, trimming of transfers to other governments, privatization of public corporations, and reductions in the number of public servants. Today, many governments have managed to successfully address their earlier fiscal troubles, but they remain committed to greater efficiency and effectiveness in government. An important part of this effort is to make the machinery of government function in a more timely and sensitive fashion.

Demography

The impact of demographic factors on the public service is becoming increasingly important. One demographic factor with significant implications for public administration is the changing age composition. The percentage of Canadians over sixty-five years of age is estimated at a little above 13 percent and is projected to rise rapidly after about 2012 when the first baby boomers turn sixty-five. As the number of elderly persons increases, so will their needs for health, housing, and community services. There will be a growing requirement for different orders of government and different administrative units within each order to find the financial and human resources to meet these needs. Another demographic factor worthy of special mention is the greatly increased participation of women in the labour force, which has implications for the provision of child care services and other family-related programs. Sixty years ago, only about one-fifth of prime-aged women (twenty-five to forty-four years) in Canada held a job, but now that figure has risen to over 80 percent. Finally, such countries as Canada are becoming increasingly multicultural through shifting patterns of immigration. Governments will have to become more sensitive to the possibility of shifting preferences in a more culturally varied society, and understand as well that the public service will have to become a more appealing workplace in order to attract talented representatives of visible minority groups.

Legacy of Past Reforms

A force specific to public bureaucracies in Canada is the legacy of past efforts at reforming the public service.[16] In the early 20th century, the merit principle succeeded in uprooting the practice of making patronage appointments to the civil service, which set the stage for the application of bureaucratic expertise and knowledge to difficult public policy problems. It also provided the grounds for workable and mutually beneficial relations between individual ministers and their senior advisors. For a period of time, reform efforts were few in number, but in the 1960s demands arose for a restructuring of the bureaucracy in the direction of giving public managers more autonomy. This in turn was quickly followed by a series of reforms directed at instituting rational procedures and systems for budgeting and decision making at highest levels. Notwithstanding these and other changes, there were indications of poor morale in the federal public service, which precipitated additional proposals for reforming the public sector. However, economic difficulties, growing deficits, and rising public debt assumed some prominence, and support both in and outside government for reform fell as perceptions of bureaucratic power grew. But more long-term forces gave support for the recent creation of new bureaucratic forms, and these came to be identified with a theory of organizational behaviour called the new public management. At the same time, the public service realized that a more complicated web of relations had replaced the simple arrangement or bargain between ministers and their bureaucratic advisors.

The legacy of this story of public sector reform is that there is the recognition for change in the public service, but that this change is difficult to achieve. The story also suggests that the reform has to be undertaken in an environment in which the place of the public service in the political process itself is changing.

Size of the Public Service

In Canada, expansion in the scope and complexity of government activities since the end of World War II has been accompanied by substantial growth in public expenditure and in the number of government employees. In 1950, total government expenditures as a percentage of the gross domestic product was 21.3 percent, which meant that federal, provincial, and local spending represented about 20 cents for every dollar spent in Canada. Over half a century later, the percentage had risen, in 2004, to 41.5 percent, a doubling of the size of government measured by its expenditures measured against the total wealth of the country. Over this same time period, spending of the federal government remained fairly stable, increasingly only marginally from 11 percent of GDP in 1950 to 12.6 percent in 2004. But provincial spending has grown quite dramatically, going from 5.5 percent in 1950 to 18.3 percent in 2004 (the remaining percentage taken up by local spending and public pension outlays).[17] The increase in expenditure by the ten provincial governments combined resulted from the growing revenue available to the resource-rich provinces and the increased demand for provincially provided services, particularly in the areas of education, health care, and social services. However, we must remember that the federal government represents the largest single government in terms of expenditures, for the provincial percentages constitute the spending of ten separate governments.

The increase in total expenditure at all levels of Canadian government has resulted in a large number of public employees required to carry out increased government responsibilities. In 2005, slightly over three million people were working in the public sector in Canada, with nearly one-half million of these people employed in federal departments and agencies and the remaining number working at the provincial and local levels or in hospitals, schools, and other bodies funded through public revenues.[18] The total of three million represents about one-fifth of the total labour force, which means that one in five people are employed in some kind of public agency or institution in Canada. These people are also employed in a wide variety of occupations. In the federal public service, for example, there are six occupational categories—executive management, scientific and professional, administrative and foreign service, technical, administrative support, and operational—and each of these categories encompass a variety of occupational groups. For instance, the scientific and professional category has 29 groups, which include actuarial science, auditing, chemistry, library science, psychology and social work.[19] Clearly, a wide variety of job opportunities is available to those who aspire to become Canadian public servants.

Another point in relation to the public service in Canada is that the complex and technical nature of government operations has brought about a significant qualitative change in the public service. Especially over the past few decades, jobs in the managerial, professional, and technical occupational categories have increased while those in the traditional clerical and operational categories have declined. One result of this trend is that students must not only spend a longer time in school to obtain the education necessary for appointment to the public service, but also return to school in later years to keep informed about new developments affecting their jobs and to upgrade their skills.

Issues and Themes

As stated earlier, public bureaucracy is an organizational form with people, offices, and procedures, and one of the challenges in the study of public administration is to become informed about these qualities of bureaucracy. Another challenge is to be aware of some of the major issues and themes inherent in the field of public administration; in the study of public administration, there is always a danger of getting lost in all the details and neglecting the larger picture. The following are some of the issues and themes that we should keep in mind when undertaking our examination of public administration in Canada in this book.

Power of the Bureaucracy. A lasting issue in the study of public administration is the power and influence of appointed officials in government. In a democracy, the intent is for elected officials to make the important decisions and to properly represent the wishes of the electorate; they are the ones who ensure that the preferences of the citizenry shape government actions. But there is a concern that the expertise and experience of public servants along with the sheer size of the public service put at risk democratic practices. Many bureaucrats, especially those at the senior levels, are highly educated and have received extensive training in order to carry out their jobs. On the other hand, most elected officials, while educated, have received little or no training for their specific duties. In this situation, the "'political master' finds himself in the position of the 'dilettante' who stands opposite the 'expert.'"[20] Appointed officials also usually have a long tenure in the public service, which enables them to set up networks and to acquire an appreciation of how things get done in the political system. Alternatively, most politicians come and go at a fairly rapid pace; in fact, the quick turnover of elected officials in Canadian politics is a major concern. And then there is the matter of size. At the federal level, there are nearly a half-million federal public servants working in one capacity or another. When it comes to politicians, there are usually thirty or so in cabinet, a little over three hundred in the House of Commons, and a small number of ministerial assistants in central agencies and individual departments. Accordingly, any study of public administration, such as this text, concentrates on establishing mechanisms to control the power of the bureaucracy. Few, if any bureaucrats, aspire to wrest power away from political officials, but the aforementioned qualities of bureaucracy—the expertise, the experience, and the size—may work in this direction.

The Right Organizational Form. Bureaucracy is the term used to describe organizational forms and processes found in government. Historically, bureaucracy has assumed a precise shape in which a hierarchical arrangement of superiors and subordinates carry out their duties in accordance with a precise set of rules and procedures. Bureaucracy has also at times been used to describe the various processes that tie together appointed officials with other players in the political process. This set of bureaucratic forms and processes have served Canada and other countries quite well, because they help contribute to the efficient and equitable delivery of services to the citizenry. However, there has been a continuous effort to locate new organizational forms—some scholars called these "post-bureaucratic" forms—that allow public servants to fully exploit their talents and government to meet the increasingly varied and complex demands of society.[21] Some of the proposals include less hierarchy and fewer rules and procedures, and seemingly all try to provide the proper motivation to public servants. In a way, there is a quest to find the one right organization for the task at hand. This quest extends, albeit in a less determined way, to processes involving public servants and others participating in the formulation and administration of government programs and policies. The processes relate to such matters as cabinet approval of departmental proposals, financial management of public resources, and intergovernmental collaborations in the making of public policy. As with bureaucratic forms, there is a desire to make these processes more workable.

Crowded World of Public Administration. At one time, the activities of public servants were quite simple and straightforward. In their individual departments, they would administer programs and assist the minister in devising new ideas for consideration by cabinet. As mentioned earlier, life was similar to a comfortable existence in a village, but all that has changed. The activities of public servants now include numerous relations with newly prominent players in the political process. Appointed officials now must interact with the media, pressure groups, and interested members of the public, and they also have to be aware of the rising influence of the judiciary. Relations with other government have also become more visible and a larger part of the bureaucrat's life. Even interactions between public servants have become more evident, as departments find they must deal with other departments more and more to get things done. All in all, the village has become a bustling city.

End of the "Bargain." Essential to public administration has been the relationship between ministers and public servants. The relationship has amounted to a kind of bargain in which public servants acted as loyal and professional advisors to elected officials in return for anonymity and secure employment in the public service. For many scholars of public administration, this bargain was a big part of the foundation for good government in Canada. But there are signs that the bargain is beginning to crumble. Increasingly, ministers are unwilling to protect the anonymity of public servants and at times seek to place the blame on public servants when things go wrong. Fearing that appointed officials may wield too much power, ministers are also more prone to seek advice from those outside the public service. Public servants feel hurt by these actions, and sincerely ponder the causes of this seeming betrayal. Do they truly deserve to be singled out in the front pages of national newspapers, or humiliated when ministers slight their advice and turn to so-called experts outside of government? Bureaucrats feel themselves at times to be the jilted party in a failed relationship that once worked so well.

Competitive Relations. It is often assumed that the actions and relations of public servants and others in the political process are connected to the goal of serving the citizenry; all of the participants have basically the same conception of the public interest. The result is that we see public administration as an effort on part of the participants to work together to achieve some agreed-upon outcomes. An example of an outcome in the public interest would be the fair and effective delivery of government services. But an examination of public administration sometimes reveals a different dynamic at play, one which sees public servants competing with each other and with others in the political process in the pursuit of differing values and interests. With this conceptualization, the policies of government more often than not represent the compromises that inevitably arise out of the bargaining inherent in this competitive atmosphere. It is this quality that sometimes makes government policies appear more a product of a committee than of a rational entity. This way of looking at government and public administration also means that hierarchy may have less influence than typically believed; in the competition, formal superiors—the bosses—may merely represent another set of players forced to play against others.

Conclusion

The discussion in this chapter of the meaning, the importance, and the environment of public administration provides a basis for an examination of public administration in Canada. This examination, as outlined in the Preface, begins in the following chapters with a consideration of the theories of organizations in order to better understand the behaviour and structure of bureaucratic forms. It then moves to look at the specific organizational structures used to deliver public services and regulate the behaviour of Canadians, which include departments, Crown corporations, independent regulatory agencies, and alternative service delivery mechanisms. The study of public administration must not slight the relations of bureaucratic structures with others in the political process, so the text next considers the significant interactions in public administration. The examination ends with an appreciation of two of the major duties of public servants, namely the management of people and money. For the most part, the investigation of public administration in this book focuses on the federal government, but at times the relevant actions of provinces and territories are analyzed.

1. Donald J. Savoie, *Breaking the Bargain: Public Servants, Ministers, and Parliament* (Toronto: University of Toronto Press, 2003), 66–69.

2. Strictly speaking, *public bureaucracy* refers to the operation of bureaucracy in government, while *bureaucracy* refers to its operation in any sector (private, public, nonprofit). But often the two are both used to refer to bureaucracy in the public sector, which will be the practice in this text.

3. Ivan L. Richardson and Sidney Baldwin, *Public Administration: Government in Action* (Columbus, Ohio: Charles E. Merrill, 1976), 3; John M. Pfiffner and Robert Presthus, *Public Administration*, 5th ed. (New York: Ronald Press, 1967), 7.

4. David H. Rosenbloom, *Public Administration: Understanding Management, Politics, and Law in the Public Sector* (New York: Random House, 1986), 6.

5. Robert F. Adie and Paul G. Thomas, *Canadian Public Administration: Problematical Perspectives*, 2nd ed. (Scarborough: Prentice-Hall Canada, Inc., 1987), 2.

6. James Q. Wilson, *Bureaucracy: What Government Agencies Do and Why They Do It* (New York: Basic Books, 1989), 348.

7. Donald J. Savoie, *Thatcher, Reagan, Mulroney: In Search of a New Bureaucracy* (Toronto: University of Toronto Press, 1994), 134.

8. Reprinted in Peter Woll, ed., *Public Administration and Policy* (New York: Harper & Row, 1966), 15–41.

9. H.S. Villard and W.W. Willoughby, *The Canadian Budgetary System* (New York: Appleton, 1918).

10. R. MacGregor Dawson, *The Civil Service of Canada* (Oxford: Oxford University Press, 1929). For a discussion of Dawson's views on the role of the public service, see Ken Rasmussen, "The Administrative Liberalism of R. MacGregor Dawson," *Canadian Public Administration* 33(1) (spring 1990): 37–51.

11. Jonathan Malloy argues, however, that the downsizing of government in the 1990s has led recently to less interest at universities in public administration. See Jonathan Malloy, "The Next Generation? Recruitment and Renewal in the Federal Public Service," in G. Bruce Doern, ed., *How Ottawa Spends 2004–2005: Mandate Change in the Paul Martin Era* (Montreal & Kingston: McGill-Queen's University Press, 2004), 287.

12. Leslie A. Pal, *Beyond Policy Analysis: Public Issue Management in Turbulent Times*, 3rd ed. (Toronto: Thomson Nelson, 2006), 46.

13. Kenneth Kernaghan, Brian Marson, and Sandford Borins, *The New Public Organization* (Toronto: The Institute of Public Administration of Canada, 2000), 5.

14. Neil Nevitte, *Decline of Deference: Canadian Value Change in Cross-National Perspective* (Peterborough: Broadview Press, 1996).

15. Savoie, *Breaking the Bargain*, 85.

16. Kernaghan, Marson, and Borins, *The New Public Organization*, 8–10.

17. Karin Treff and David B. Perry, *Finances of the Nation 2005: A Review of Expenditures and Revenues of Federal, Provincial and Local Governments of Canada* (Toronto: Canadian Tax Foundation, 2006), B10.

18. Statistics Canada, "Public Sector Employment, Wages and Salaries." Available at www40.statcan.ca/l01/cst01/govt54a.htm. Accessed July 2, 2006.

19. Public Service Human Resources Management Agency of Canada, *Employment Equity in the Federal Public Service 2003–04* (Ottawa: Her Majesty the Queen in Right of Canada, 2005), 25–27.

20. H.H. Gerth and C. Wright Mills, eds., *From Max Weber: Essays in Sociology* (New York: Oxford University Press, 1958), 232.

21. See, for example, Kernaghan, Marson, and Borins, *The New Public Organization*, 3.

2

Public Administration and Organization Theory: The Structural Foundation

The study of public administration revolves around the careful consideration of government bureaucracy. This means that we investigate the basic structures that constitute the bureaucratic organizations in government and their interactions with other bodies in the political process. It also means taking a close look at some of the essential duties of public bureaucracies. But an important first step in pursuing an appreciation of public administration is the examination of theories of organizations, which is the concern of the remaining chapters in Part 1. These theories grapple with the challenge of offering clear and accurate descriptions of organizational forms. They also put forward suggestions for enhancing the performance of organizations and ensuring that services are provided more fairly and efficiently. Above all, theories of organization offer us the framework for better explaining the behaviour or operation of various structures that may arise in public administration.

Many theories have been developed in the attempt to understand organizations. In this chapter, we study the first modern efforts to provide theories and models about the processes and structures of bureaucracy. The chapter examines the pioneering work of Max Weber on the features of traditional bureaucratic organizations as well as his thoughts about the place of bureaucracy in society and government. Frederick Taylor was another early student of organizations, and his endeavour to discover the one best way to organize the workplace is discussed. The chapter also considers the influential thinking of Luther Gulick and Lyndall Urwick on organizations. Such important and well-known terms of organizational analysis as "span of control" and "line and staff functions" receive a great deal of attention in the scholarly efforts of these two individuals. All together, the theories addressed in this chapter represent the foundation of organization theory.

Max Weber and Classical Bureaucratic Theory

It would be difficult to locate the first bureaucratic organization, but the first person who systematically studied the emerging phenomenon of **bureaucracy** was Max Weber, who was born in 1864. Weber was a brilliant German scholar who sought to examine bureaucracy in the context of authority in any society. For Weber, there were three sources of authority, each distinguished on the basis of their claim to legitimacy. Under traditional authority, the right to rule or exercise authority is legitimated by such factors as heredity, religious beliefs, or divine right. Charismatic authority is based on the outstanding personal characteristics of an individual—for example, Jesus, John F. Kennedy, Hitler. Finally, legal or rational authority is legitimated by rules and regulations obeyed by both the rulers and ruled. In this last system, "obedience is owed not to a person—whether a traditional chief or charismatic leader—but to a set of impersonal principles."[1] Each type of authority is associated with a different administrative arrangement, and the usual organizational system under legal authority is bureaucracy.

The Characteristics of Weberian Bureaucracy

Weber's empirical study of the German bureaucracy suggested to him that the modern bureaucratic form consisted of a number of related characteristics. When these characteristics were combined in the same organization, the result was what he called the pure or "ideal-type" bureaucracy (see Figure 2.1).[2] The main components of bureaucracy, which Weber believed generated a high level of efficiency, were as follows.

Hierarchical Structure. As Figure 2.1 shows, a bureaucratic organization is arranged in a series of superior–subordinate relationships, at the pinnacle of which is one—and only one—superior. This can also be described as **unity of command**, which means that for each position in the hierarchy, there is only one supervisor. The clear line of authority produced by unity of command was one reason Weber felt that bureaucracy was more efficient than previous forms of organization, but there were also other reasons for his belief.

Specialization of Labour. The purpose of the hierarchical structure was to allocate responsibilities to subordinates in a clear and unambiguous fashion. This division of responsibilities was significant because a person could become very efficient when able to

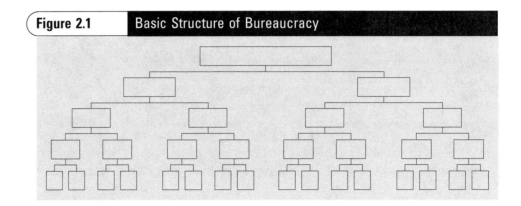

Figure 2.1 Basic Structure of Bureaucracy

concentrate on a specific job. Specialization of labour, however, is not enough if the employees are not qualified to learn to perform the work.

Employment and Promotion Based on Merit. In earlier times, people often obtained organizational positions through either heredity or outright purchase. Obviously, this method of staffing provided no guarantee that the person in a particular position was the best person for the job or even a competent one. Without some assurance of competence, no organization could operate efficiently. In the German bureaucracy that Weber studied, employment and promotion based on an objective test of merit provided this assurance and thus increased the efficiency of operation.

Full-Time Employment. An important principle related to employment based on merit was that employment in the bureaucracy was the full-time activity and major source of income of the official. This ensured that the official would develop allegiance to the bureaucracy and that the bureaucrat's hierarchical superior could exercise real *control* over the day-to-day activities of the official. The superior needed effective control to force the subordinate to abide by organizational regulations in carrying out duties. This led to another important characteristic of modern bureaucracy.

Decisions Based on Impersonal Rules. Bureaucrats are bound by certain rules in dealing with the public. These rules are impersonal in the sense that they apply equally to all clients in similar situations. Bureaucrats cannot substitute their own set of rules for those legitimately proclaimed by superiors. If a particular benefit is to be provided without regard to race or religion, then a member of the bureaucracy would risk severe penalties if he or she allowed personal prejudice to affect the decision made. This reliance on impersonal rules increases confidence in the bureaucracy by establishing a regime of certainty in dealings.

Importance of Written Files. The significance of these rules makes written files very important. If the bureaucrat must prove that he or she has abided by the rules in making decisions, then he or she must maintain written records, first, of the rules themselves, and second, of all decisions made and the rationale for those decisions. It is worth noting here that the bureaucrat's allegiance to the rules takes precedence over allegiance to her or his superior. A superior can exercise judgment in an area that is unclear under the rules, but he or she cannot order a subordinate to violate those rules.

Bureaucratic Employment Is Separate from the Individual Bureaucrat's Private Life. This is a recognition of both the autonomous nature of the bureaucracy as an organization and the fact that the bureaucrat does not own his or her position and the rights that go with it. Bureaucrats possess a great deal of authority. In the case of members of a government bureaucracy, this could be highly coercive authority. However, it is always clear that the power is attached to the position rather than to the individual. This distinction was not always clear among members of the monarch's retinue in pre-bureaucratic times. An obvious result of this division is that the bureaucrat is not permitted to obtain any personal gain, other than a fixed salary, from his or her position.

Weber's Views on Bureaucracy

Weber seems to have had a rather difficult love–hate relationship with this new organizational form called bureaucracy. As a serious scholar, he documented the characteristics of the German bureaucracy as he saw them without favourable or critical comment. Beyond that, though, he appears to have been of two minds about bureaucracy. On the one hand, he argued that bureaucracy was the most efficient method of organization:

> The fully developed bureaucratic apparatus compares with other organizations exactly as does the machine with the non-mechanical modes of production. Precision, speed, unambiguity, knowledge of the files, continuity, discretion, unity, strict subordination, reduction of friction and of material and personal costs—these are raised to the optimum point in the strictly bureaucratic administration . . . .[3]

On the other hand, Weber foresaw many of the problems familiar to anyone who interacts with bureaucratic organizations. Weber understood that the technical superiority of bureaucratic officials might put them in a position to overwhelm leaders of the organization—elected officials, for instance, might be unable to stand up to their appointed officials in government. More ominously, he feared that the bureaucratic values of order and security might prevail over those which we cherish and see as essential to an open, thriving community. For Weber, a central challenge for any society was to propose practices that can oppose the "machinery" of bureaucracy and "keep a portion of humanity free from this pigeon-holing of the spirit, from this total domination of the bureaucratic ideal."[4]

In his views on bureaucracy, Weber touched upon the crucial aspects of bureaucracy that still confound us today. It does seem to be the most efficient way of arranging a large number of offices and accomplishing complex, repetitive tasks. No company, no government, no organization of any kind it appears can afford to be without a bureaucratic form. But we also condemn the impersonal, mind-numbing aspects of its operation. Since the advent of bureaucracy in modern times, attempts have been made to find viable alternatives.

Criticisms of Weber

There have been many criticisms of Weber and his work on bureaucracy. A major line of criticism is that Weber dwelt too much on the structural aspects of bureaucracy and not enough on the human side of the organization. It is suggested that because Weber viewed bureaucrats as mere cogs in the mechanism, he overstated the impact of the organization on the worker and overlooked the effect of the worker on the organization. Employees, for instance, may pursue goals that are inconsistent with the professed aims of the organization but that satisfy their particular needs. More generally, informal systems of authority may emerge and effectively displace the formal systems—subordinates become the bosses and the bosses the subordinates. A related criticism is the claim that rational bureaucratic structures may produce irrational or inefficient outcomes. For instance, the emphasis on rules, which are designed as means, may become the ends of the organization. Bureaucrats seek strict compliance with the rules even though such action might be detrimental to servicing customers or recipients of a government service. The well-known term "red tape" arises from this excessive obedience to requirements and regulations as does the reluctance of bureaucracies to consider changes in their operation.

Others criticize Weber because of perceived internal inconsistencies in his model of bureaucracy. The model relies on professional or expert decision making to ensure efficiency, but it is possible that superiors may lack the knowledge to make the best decision. The dilemma for the subordinate becomes whether to report to the ill-informed boss or seek out someone with requisite knowledge—a clear violation of hierarchy and the principle of unity of command. Still others contend that bureaucracy is simply outmoded as a form of organization. It is argued that modern trends such as rapid change and the increasing professionalization of the workforce make bureaucracy obsolete. To be productive, organizations require fewer rules, less hierarchy, and employees free to innovate and meet the challenges of an increasingly complex and competitive world.[5]

Surprisingly, even a cursory look at Weber's points out some obvious problems. A hierarchical organization can soon produce so many levels that it becomes difficult to operate within the firm or government or to comprehend its overall structure. The emphasis on a strict division of labour increases the chances that workers will become bored with doing the same activity every day. It is also easy to require that people be hired and promoted on merit, but measuring merit can be difficult—especially in organizations that wish to build a workplace broadly representative of the society it serves. Full-time employment also appears to ignore the cost advantages of part-time or casual workers, and a government agency can effectively choke on the presence of too many files.

As will be seen later in the text, contemporary theories of organization aim to avoid the pitfalls of Weber's bureaucratic structures. In fact, one group of influential Canadian researchers employ the term "post-bureaucratic organization" to describe their preferred model.[6] However, we must be careful not to see Weber's bureaucracy as an "organizational dinosaur."[7] It provides insights into the workings of organizations and constitutes part of the repertoire of administrative forms available for structuring organizations. Moreover, some contend that bureaucracy and its qualities of hierarchy, specialization, and standardization represent a necessary condition for achieving sound management in government.[8]

Frederick W. Taylor and Scientific Management

Max Weber was a philosopher who could stand at arm's length from organizations and describe in broad terms their general characteristics. By contrast, Frederick Winslow Taylor, born in 1856, was a mechanical engineer who began his career working as a technician on the factory floor and spent much of his later life in either a supervisory or an advisory capacity dealing with problems of production management. His major concern was the proper arrangement of the human and mechanical resources of the factory so as to minimize waste, particularly waste of workers' time.

Taylor's experience in the factory showed him that a great deal of slacking off or "soldiering" was taking place. He posited two reasons for this behaviour. One was what he regarded as the natural tendency of employees to do as little work as possible. The second was that work was sometimes arranged in such an awkward manner that no reasonable human being, regardless of how ambitious or honest, could physically perform what was expected by superiors. Since soldiering constituted the squandering of a resource, it was important for management to end it. Taylor argued that the resulting increased productivity would benefit both employers and employees.

The employee's natural tendency toward soldiering might be eliminated if the employer used scientific principles rather than informal calculations to determine an employee's appropriate workload. Some soldiering was caused by the employee's rational reaction to the method of piecework payment that was prevalent in Taylor's time. Employees knew that in the short run they could earn more by working hard and producing above standard, but they realized that in the long run this was counterproductive, because employers simply raised the standard. It was therefore better to work at a steady pace and receive adequate pay than to be a "rate-buster." The problem was that employers had no idea what an employee could do in an average shift. Thus, most employers used unscientific rules to establish standards and so did not have the confidence of their employees. The obvious solution to the problem was to establish scientific standards based on the proven physical capacities of workers and then refrain from adjusting those standards arbitrarily.

Taylor's usual approach to establishing these scientific standards was to select employees who performed a particular task exceptionally well (e.g., moving the most pig iron, shovelling the most coal). A trained management employee would then carefully scrutinize the actions of these employees, watching and timing their every movement. This was the beginning of the time-and-motion study that has stirred so much controversy on factory floors. The purpose of these studies was to learn the ideal method of performing a particular task from the most efficient employees. This is the "one best way" employed by Frank and Lillian Gilbreth and popularized with humorous effect by their children in the book and movie *Cheaper by the Dozen*.[9] When the best set of physical motions was determined, it was the responsibility of managers to teach this technique to all employees.

The second cause of soldiering was the simple inability of workers to maintain the pace expected of them because of how the work was organized. Taylor pointed out that workers could be more productive if management took greater care in organizing the work. He put particular emphasis on such factors as determining the optimal working rhythm necessary to maximize output. The next time you are working in the garden or shovelling snow it might be useful to know that, according to Taylor, the greatest tonnage per day can be shovelled when the worker moves twenty-one pounds on each shovel-load.[10]

Taylor felt that it was important to have a clear division of duties between management and labour. It was the job of management to select employees for specific jobs in a scientific manner so that the physical and mental characteristics of the individual fit the job. It was then the role of management to teach labourers the optimum way to perform their duties. For the labourers, their job was to supply strong backs.

Taylor also emphasized the importance of financial factors as a motivating force. However, he rejected the crude principle of piecework, because he knew that workers could easily manipulate the standard. Instead, he singled out the best workers for the privilege of working in a higher-paid group. By examining their actions as described above, he was able to determine in a scientific manner how much work should be accomplished. In one experiment, workers who had met the standard in their previous day's work were given white slips at the beginning of their next shift, while those who had not were given yellow slips. Those receiving yellow slips obviously did not understand fully how their job should be done, so it was the responsibility of management to provide additional training. The consistent receipt of yellow slips would cause one's return to the lower-paid gang.[11] This was Taylor's method of using financial incentives without the drawbacks identified with piecework.

Some writers suggest that Taylor showed a lack of concern for the workers. It is clear that he viewed management as very enlightened and workers in a rather condescending manner. However, Taylor did strive for harmony between management and workers and was sensitive to the need not to alienate unions. He always argued that cooperation was the best way to maximize productivity—but one gets the impression that it would be cooperation on management's terms. Furthermore, he strongly opposed overworking employees in sweatshop conditions. Although this might well have been more for reasons of productivity than humanity, it was still a fairly radical idea for his time.

Taylor's main contribution to organization theory was his emphasis on the scientific approach to work management—the "one best way"—and his emphasis on the important role of management in organizing the work. But there were certain problems with how Taylor's ideas were implemented. In some cases, management used time-and-motion studies to attempt to extract the maximum possible production from workers. This led to worker resistance to the entire concept. The idea of the narrow subdivision of work into its smallest components created monotony, which led to further worker unrest.

The ideas of Weber and Taylor are significant because they had a great influence on management thinking at one time, and because their influence can still be detected in some mechanistic aspects of organization theory. However, their approaches have been challenged by newer forms of organization. Their ideas made more sense when applied to large factories where workers assembled products manually but less sense in knowledge-based organizations. However, before these problems became evident, their ideas were tried in a number of places, including the Canadian federal government.

The Canadian Experience—From Patronage to Merit

The Canadian federal government gradually began adopting some of Taylor's ideas to speed up the move from a patronage-based public service to a merit-based one, thus simultaneously moving toward the Weberian concept of bureaucracy.

The Civil Service Commission (CSC) was established in 1908 to act as guardian of the merit principle. The CSC was the outgrowth of a number of reports indicating that the prevalence of **patronage** appointments in the Canadian civil service was having a detrimental impact on its efficiency. The CSC began the process of entrenching the merit principle by administering competitive examinations to applicants for government positions. But the CSC soon discovered that a serious problem existed because the duties of specific positions were not usually well defined. Without a clear description of duties, creating a meaningful competitive examination was problematic.

Gradually the powers and responsibilities of the CSC evolved, until in 1918 it was given the power to make appointments to positions and to reorganize departments, whether this was sought by the department or not. This legislation seemed to be influenced by officials of the CSC, who were in turn influenced by the principles of scientific management that were so prevalent at the time.[12]

The commissioners and the executive secretary of the CSC hired the American consulting firm of Arthur Young & Co. to introduce the principles of scientific management into the Canadian federal government. The exercise began with the systematic description and classification of 50,000 positions. The positions had to be described in great detail because this was the starting point for the mechanistic process of matching the person possessing the proper qualifications with the appropriate position. The next step was to be a sweeping reorganization of the entire governmental bureaucratic apparatus, streamlining and reducing the number of departments and agencies. Obviously, the idea of government reform is not as new and radical as some think.

Arthur Young & Co.'s involvement became bogged down in a series of problems and, as a result, the reorganization did not occur. The sole, but significant, result of the exercise was an extensive and systematic classification of all government positions. The **scientific management** approach to job classification made it possible to match, in a mechanical fashion, the skills required in a particular job with the skills possessed by a given person. When the match was complete, presumably the process would be like pushing a plug into a wall socket—an automatic perfect connection that would last until it was unplugged. But not everyone was impressed by the neatness of this arrangement. It worked well with positions that required specialized knowledge. A chemist or engineer could easily be placed in the appropriate position. More difficult would be finding the best person for administrative or managerial jobs in which the necessary skills and aptitudes were not so easily discovered.[13]

At roughly the same time that Taylor and consultants such as Arthur Young were concerned with the classification and arrangement of individual jobs, there was a movement afoot to consider broader theoretical questions of the appropriate overall structure of organizations.

Gulick and Urwick and the Scientific Theory of Organization

In the United States in the 1930s, the President's Committee on Administrative Management spurred a great deal of interest by trying to develop a scientific theory of organization. Taylor's work dealt with how to organize work on the factory floor, but Luther Gulick and Lyndall Urwick were concerned with developing broader theories about the ideal structure for any organization. Their concerns were span of control and the proper alignment of related functions.

Span of Control

Span of control refers to the number of subordinates who report to one supervisor. There has long been controversy about what that ideal number should be. As Figure 2.2 shows, the smaller or narrower span provides for better control of employees.

However, a span of control that is too narrow can lead to too many supervisors and too much overhead. As Figure 2.2 also shows, a wider span of control avoids these problems and makes communication both up and down the organization considerably easier. But the cost of widening the span of control is the loss of close supervision. Managers now have more subordinates to look after. A dilemma thus presents itself:

> Small spans of control may appear to tighten control for the superior–subordinate relationship, but they loosen the overall control of the organization by extending the number of levels and thereby making the top that much more removed from the bottom. To cut down on the number of levels will reduce the distance between top and bottom, but the resulting increase in the span of control at each level will lessen the control that each level can maintain.[14]

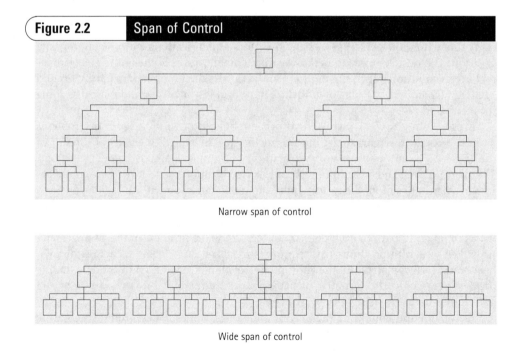

Figure 2.2   Span of Control

Narrow span of control

Wide span of control

The question of the appropriate span of control is still answered much as it was in Gulick and Urwick's time. It depends on the interaction of several things:

- The nature of the work supervised (routine procedures allow for a broader span of control, but supervision of several heterogeneous activities requires a narrower span of control)
- The level of training of the subordinates
- The extent of geographical decentralization of the work
- The overall stability of the organization[15]

Empirical research supports the belief that these four factors largely determine the span of control. However, it also suggests that the weight or importance of these factors differs depending on the level in the hierarchy of the organization. Instability, for instance, may matter more in shaping the span of the control at the lower levels of the organization than it does at the upper levels. Research shows as well that the span of control does indeed have an effect on the productivity or performance of an organization.[16]

The continuing significance of span of control can be seen in such recent catch phrases as "flattening the hierarchy" and "removing layers of management". A flatter hierarchy will lead to increased spans of control. This can be seen as a cost-saving move, because fewer managers are required. But it can also be justified on several other grounds. Reducing the number of levels between the top and the bottom of the organization decreases the isolation of those at the top and ensures that they will be more in touch with the organization's environment. It also reflects the fact that contemporary workers are much better trained than previous generations and workplaces are more mechanized. Both of these factors reduce the level of detailed supervision needed.

Organization of Duties

Aside from span of control, Gulick and Urwick were concerned with the problem of the ideal arrangement of duties within the organization. They argued that the process of organizational design should work simultaneously from the top down and from the bottom up.[17] When working from the top down, the primary criterion was to limit the span of control. Gulick reflected the conventional wisdom of the time that the senior executive should not have more than three direct subordinates. Working from the bottom up, the important factor was to combine homogeneous activities to facilitate coordination and supervision. The analyst then simply built in both directions until the two were joined.

When working from the bottom up, it was important to have an appropriate definition of homogeneity. The definition suggests that people doing similar work ought to be grouped together, but on further analysis this idea is difficult to apply. Gulick suggested that each worker could be characterized in four different ways:

1. The major *purpose* he or she serves, such as furnishing water, controlling crime, or conducting education
2. The *process* he or she uses, such as engineering, medicine, carpentry, stenography, statistics, or accounting
3. The *persons* or things he or she deals with or serves (immigrants, veterans, aboriginal peoples, forests, mines, parks, orphans, farmers, automobiles, the poor)
4. The *place* where he or she renders the service (Toronto, Vancouver, Quebec City, St. Pius X High School)[18]

In designing an organization, employees who had all four things in common would be grouped together in the same organizational unit. If an employee was different in one category—for example, if he or she worked in a slightly different location—that would

Chapter 2 / Public Administration and Organization Theory

Figure 2.3 Organization of Activities

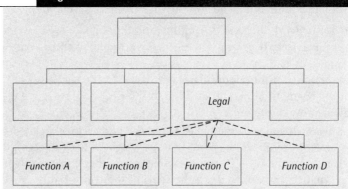

Organization by process

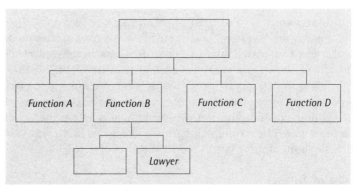

Organization by purpose

suggest he or she ought to be in another unit, but Gulick emphasized the importance of applying pragmatism and judgment to individual cases. Where employees had only one or two things in common, they would likely be in separate units. The question remains as to which of the four should be the dominant organizing principle.[19]

This problem occurs in a very practical way when deciding how to arrange the legal services function in a large, multi-function organization. Figure 2.3 illustrates two ways in which legal services may be organized. The upper half of the figure depicts an organization with one legal department containing all lawyers, who would then provide service to other departments. This is an example of an organization based on process. If, instead, the lawyers are divided and assigned to the units that handle the programs, as in the lower half of Figure 2.3, organization by purpose is being used. At first glance, one arrangement seems to have as many advantages and disadvantages as the other. Gulick admitted that the lack of empirical evidence made serious discussion difficult, but he did suggest some of the pros and cons of each method.[20]

It is difficult to resolve this question of the best method of organization. In general it can be said that governments are most often organized by purpose. There are departments for health, education, labour, and other purposes. But some governments also have departments with a special mandate to look after the unique problems of a particular area. In some cases, these "place" departments actually deliver services provided by the "purpose" departments in designated area, and in others they act as coordinating bodies. There is usually some tension between this "place" department and the traditional "purpose" departments over their appropriate roles.

Staff and Line Functions

Gulick also dealt with the activities of the executive. He argued that words like "administration" and "management" had lost their specific meaning. He felt that the job of the executive could be summed up by the acronym POSDCORB, which stood for planning, organizing, staffing, directing, coordinating, reporting, and budgeting activities. Carrying out all these functions as part of managing a complex organization became very difficult, particularly as each of these functions was becoming more complex in itself. Urwick noted that one way many organizations were dealing with this problem was by the use of separate line and staff functions.[21] A **line** function is directly involved in producing and distributing the goods or services provided by the organization. A classic example would be the manufacturing section of an industrial organization. Some typical examples in government would be public health nurses, social workers, or officers dealing directly with social assistance claimants. A **staff** function is a function that aids, advises, and supports the employees providing the line function, usually without dealing directly with the clients or output of the organization. The obvious examples are human resources management, accounting, and legal services.

When organizations are structured in this typical line–staff manner, the organization chart resembles Figure 2.4. Ideally, the two functions work together closely to further the objectives of the organization. The staff units can provide specialized advice to the line units about handling unusual situations. This means that line officers can concentrate on their standard repetitive tasks and do not have to be trained to cope with every eventuality. Another function frequently provided by staff employees is specialized record keeping. Again, this relieves the line officers of the responsibility for a specialized task and allows them to concentrate on their major function. Thus, one would expect a smooth, complementary relationship between these two functions, and this is the case in many organizations.

When problems do crop up in the line–staff relationship, they usually concern the question: Is the staff function a *service* or a *control* function? If the answer to the question is ambiguous, there can be serious problems. In some cases the staff department will render advice that the line department would rather not hear or act upon. Line officials might argue that to carry out their duties appropriately, they cannot be constrained by

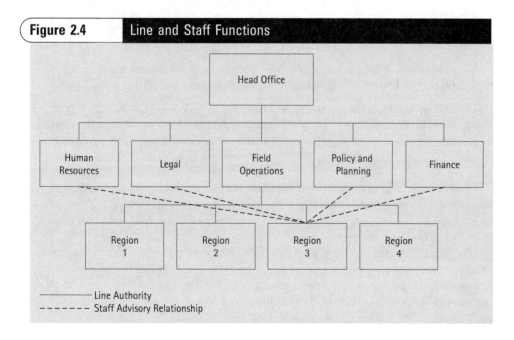

Figure 2.4   Line and Staff Functions

Head Office

Human Resources | Legal | Field Operations | Policy and Planning | Finance

Region 1 | Region 2 | Region 3 | Region 4

——— Line Authority
- - - - - Staff Advisory Relationship

the whims of some group that does not fully understand the operation of the organization. The line manager may also point out the amount of profit or units of production that her or his unit has contributed to the organization and ask rhetorically how much the staff units have contributed. But the staff official might respond that his or her advice is essential to avoiding legal problems or to hiring the best possible people.

Organizations usually try to resolve possible difficulties between line and staff officials by establishing clear lines of authority and procedures to be followed in particular cases. These procedures seldom anticipate every circumstance. Obviously, both line and staff functions are important in an organization. How well they work together is frequently what separates good organizations from those that limp along from one crisis to the next.

Gulick and Urwick contributed to the theory of organizational behaviour by synthesizing and disseminating other people's ideas. Nevertheless, these two men made a valuable contribution both by forcing people to think about management in a systematic manner, and in beginning to set out certain principles—many of which are still seen as beneficial guides to action today. However, not everyone treated these scientific principles with reverence.

Herbert Simon and the Proverbs of Administration

Herbert Simon is a prolific writer on many topics of administration. One of his most widely quoted passages deals with the scientific principles of administration:

> It is a fatal defect of the current principles of administration that, like proverbs, they occur in pairs. For almost every principle one can find an equally plausible and acceptable contradictory principle. Although the two principles of the pair will lead to exactly opposite organizational recommendations, there is nothing in the theory to indicate which is the proper one to apply.[22]

One example of this kind of problematic pair of proverbs is "Look before you leap" and "He who hesitates is lost." If the so-called scientific principles of management could be seen to have similar flaws, their validity would be in doubt.

Simon gives the juxtaposition of these two principles as an example:

> Administrative efficiency is supposed to be enhanced by limiting the number of subordinates who report directly to any one administrator to a small number—say six....

> Administrative efficiency is enhanced by keeping at a minimum the number of organizational levels through which a matter must pass before it is acted upon.[23]

Obviously, an organization cannot have it both ways. Earlier in this chapter, Figure 2.2 illustrated how a narrow span of control always results in a large number of layers in the organization. A truly scientific principle of management would not allow this dilemma. If one must exercise judgment and discretion in achieving a blend of the two rules, the rules are not very scientific.

Simon saves most of his attack for the idea of organizing by purpose, process, people, or place. He points out that not only is the overall idea contradictory in that one of the four must take precedence, but that the concepts themselves are fuzzy and that some of them shade into one another.

The rebuttal might be made here that Simon is being too fussy. The principles are simply guides to action; they are considerations to be taken into account before acting, to be used to shape our judgment and guide our discretion. This defence might be valid, but the crucial point remains evident: if judgment and discretion are so important in applying these principles, can they really be called "scientific"?

Simon's solution recognizes this point. He argues that these ideas should not be discarded because all have real value in certain cases. The challenge is to find the proper combination of them to work in different cases. To accomplish this, he argues that good empirical work on the efficiency of existing organizations is needed more than additional theories.

Decentralization and Deconcentration

Gulick and Urwick's discussion of methods of organization opened the way for a serious discussion of decentralization of government services, a very important issue in a country as large and heterogeneous as Canada. The size and diversity of most provinces and even some of our larger cities make it an issue for provincial and municipal governments as well.

An important distinction must be made between decentralization and deconcentration. The difference between the two lies in the amount of real decision-making authority vested in the outlying unit. **Decentralization** suggests a placing of real discretionary authority in the outlying unit. In some cases, this might mean that the unit will also be physically removed from the centre to facilitate an understanding of local conditions; but physical dispersal is not a prerequisite for decentralization. **Deconcentration**, on the other hand, suggests a physical dispersal of members of the organization with only very limited delegation of decision-making authority.

Obviously, the line between the two is sometimes unclear. Even in deconcentration, there is virtually always some limited amount of discretion given to field officials, just as in decentralization there are always some kinds of decisions that can only be made after consultation with head office. Sometimes authority to deal with matters of an operational nature will be decentralized, while matters of a policy or program nature will be retained within the control of head office.

The large size and diversity of Canada causes Canadians to think of decentralization in terms of the physical dispersal of operating units. This is an appropriate use of the term, but it has a more general meaning as well. Geographic decentralization is decentralization by place, but decentralization can also be based on any of Gulick and Urwick's other classical methods of organization—process, purpose, or people.[24] Even an organization with all of its divisions located in the same building can be decentralized if real decision-making authority is vested in each of the separate units.

The large majority of federal-government employees in regular government departments work outside the national capital region of Ottawa and Hull. These employees are located across the vast expanse of Canada in field units that vary greatly in purpose, size, and organization. This deconcentration of the federal government's operations is essential to the successful development and implementation of its policies and programs. The present balance in each department or agency between the number and level of employees at headquarters and in the field is a culmination of more than a century of political, administrative, economic, and geographical factors. In the earliest days of the Canadian federation, it was necessary to establish outposts for such government services as the post office and customs. The subsequent geographical dispersal of the public service is a government response to the challenge of providing a broad range of services to a population that is spread across a large country. Virtually all government departments now have field units, although the size of these units varies enormously.

Whether this dispersal represents decentralization or deconcentration, the problem remains the same. There must be a balance between accountability to rules specified in head office and responsiveness to regional needs. Officials in the field always feel pulled between the two. On the one hand, the rules and procedures set out by head office must be followed. On the other hand, field workers are sufficiently close to clientele in their everyday work to perceive situations in which an injustice is being done when the general rule is applied without sensitivity. The pressures to bend the rule are sometimes irresistible.

From the standpoint of head office, the problem is to maintain mechanisms to ensure that officials in the field are complying with head office rules and procedures without unnecessarily restricting the freedom of field officials to be responsive to local conditions. After all, it is these officials who are closest to the situation and are most knowledgeable about what should be done. However, they cannot be given carte blanche to do whatever they like without regard to the overall objectives of the department.

Specific approaches to departmental decentralization in Canada will be discussed later in the text, but at this point it is important to consider the general form that decentralization or deconcentration can take. In any organization serving a large geographic area, there must be some form of decentralization. Oversimplifying somewhat, this decentralization can take one of two forms. Figure 2.5 illustrates the two possibilities for an organization carrying out two different functions across the country.[25] The upper half illustrates decentralization by place. This style of decentralization is more likely to be true decentralization rather than deconcentration. In this case there is one main office in each region and that office is subdivided on the basis of the two functions. This kind of structure will tend to improve coordination between the two functions within each region. Because of this ease of coordination and because of the orientation toward place, the regional office of this kind of organization is likely to be highly responsive to the needs of its geographic area. The advantages of this form

Figure 2.5 Two Types of Organizational Structures

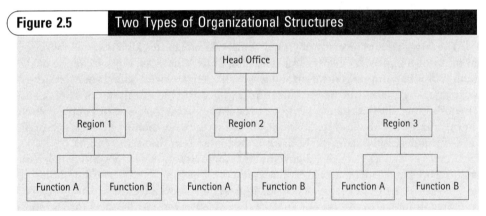

Organization by place

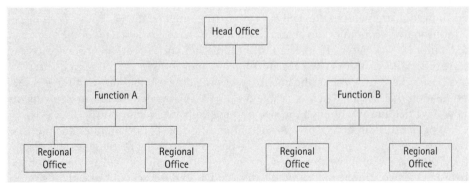

Organization by purpose

of organization include good coordination within each region and responsiveness to regional needs. The disadvantages include possible departures from national objectives and a complex form of organization.

The lower half of Figure 2.5 illustrates decentralization based on purpose, although this same form could also apply to decentralization based on process or people. This form is more likely to result in deconcentration than decentralization. In this case, the primary division is by purpose, with the senior managers responsible for each function remaining in head office. Within each branch there is a subdivision by region, although the geographic areas covered by the regions are not necessarily the same for each branch. This reflects the fact that some programs might be more important in certain areas of the country than in others. Because each branch and each regional office specialize in providing only one function, it is relatively easy to ensure uniformity of administration across the entire country without the awkward organizational structure required in the case of decentralization by place.

The advantages of this style of organization are the simpler form of organization and the uniformity of program administration across the country. Its disadvantages are a lack of coordination of the programs at the regional level and a weaker responsiveness to regional needs.

The best style of organization depends on the nature of the programs to be delivered and the need for regional responsiveness. If good coordination between programs at the regional level and a greater sensitivity to regional needs is important, then the preferable style is decentralization by place. An example of this kind of program would be one aimed at regional economic development. Uniform administration across the country is less important than responsiveness to local conditions. In some cases, the uniform administration of a program across the country is more important than regional sensitivity. When this occurs, deconcentration by program would be preferable. The word "deconcentration" is used here because if there is uniformity of administration across the country, then by definition there will be little scope for decision making within each region. An example of this kind of organization would be a tax collection organization where fairness and equity demand that the same rules apply to everyone in the country.

Conclusion

Weber and Taylor, and even Gulick and Urwick later, viewed good management as devising an optimal organizational structure to maximize output. They took little account of the needs and desires of the workers themselves. In these early theories, the worker is just like any other interchangeable machine part to be moved at the whim of management in order to create a better organizational chart. Taylor, in particular, seemed to view the worker as simply an extension of the machine. Gradually a different approach to management emerged—one that took a more human and humane view of the worker.

1. Peter Blau and Richard W. Scott, *Formal Organizations* (San Francisco: Chandler, 1962), 32.

2. The phrase "ideal-type" has a particular meaning in this context. It is not "ideal" in the sense of "perfect" or "cannot be improved upon"; rather, it suggests that Weber's characterization is a polar or extreme description that probably does not exist exactly in the real world. For a good explanation of this, see Michael M. Harmon and Richard T. Mayer, *Organization Theory for Public Administration* (Boston: Little, Brown, 1986), 71–74, 83.

3. Max Weber, *Economy and Society: An Outline of Interpretative Sociology*, Volume 2, Guenther Roth and Claus Wittich, eds. (Berkeley: University of California Press, 1978), 973.

4. Weber quoted in David Beetham, *Bureaucracy*, 2nd ed. (Minneapolis: University of Minnesota Press, 1996), 55.

5. A discussion of the criticisms of Weber can be found in Martin Albrow, *Bureaucracy* (London: The Macmillan Press, 1970), 54–61.

6. Kenneth Kernaghan, Brian Marson, and Sandford Borins, *The New Public Organization* (Toronto: The Institute of Public Administration of Canada, 2000) 3.

7. Johan P. Olsen, "Maybe It Is Time to Rediscover Bureaucracy," *Journal of Public Administration Research and Theory* 16 (2005): 1.

8. Peter Aucoin, "The Design of Public Organizations for the 21st Century: Why Bureaucracy Will Survive in Public Management," *Canadian Public Administration* 40(2) (summer 1997): 290–306.

9. Frank B. Gilbreth, Jr. and Ernestine Gilbreth Carey, *Cheaper by the Dozen* (New York: Thomas Y. Crowell, 1948).

10. Fredrick Winslow Taylor, *The Principles of Scientific Management* (New York: W.W. Norton, 1967), 65.

11. Ibid., 67–68.

12. J.E. Hodgetts, William McCloskey, Reginald Whitaker, and V. Seymour Wilson, *The Biography of an Institution: The Civil Service Commission of Canada, 1908–1967* (Montreal: McGill-Queen's University Press, 1972), ch. 4.

13. R. MacGregor Dawson, "The Canadian Civil Service," *Canadian Journal of Economics and Political Science* 2 (August 1936): 293.

14. Robert I. McLaren, *Organizational Dilemmas* (Chichester, U.K.: John Wiley & Sons, 1982), 45–46.

15. Luther Gulick, "Notes on the Theory of Organization," in Luther Gulick and L. Urwick, eds., *Papers on the Science of Administration* (New York: Augustus M. Kelley, 1969), 7–9.

16. See Kenneth J. Meier and John Bohte, "Span of Control and Public Organizations: Implementing Luther Gulick's Research Design," *Public Administration Review* 63(1) (January/February 2003): 61–70.

17. Gulick, "Notes on the Theory of Organization," 11–12.

18. Ibid., 15. (Emphasis in original.)

19. Ibid., 31–32.

20. Ibid., 21–30.

21. Lyndall Urwick, "Organization as a Technical Problem," in ibid., 47–88.

22. Herbert Simon, *Administrative Behavior* (New York: The Free Press, 1957), 20.

23. Ibid., 26.

24. McLaren points out that decentralization can occur in several dimensions. *Organizational Dilemmas*, ch. 2.

25. McLaren's enlightening treatment takes a slightly different approach, but deals with the same issues. *Organizational Dilemmas*, 12–17.

3

Public Administration and Organization Theory: The Humanistic Response

The early theories of organization represented an important first step in the scientific understanding of organizations. They offered a model of bureaucracy and put forward ways of making people more productive. However, the work of Weber, Taylor, and Gulick and Urwick also provided the stimulus for a new theoretical perspective on organizations. Whereas the initial work on organizations emphasized formal structures and the significance of rules, this new view took more notice of informal structures and the need for greater flexibility and autonomy in the workplace. The humanist perspective, a term applied to this new view, also had a different appreciation of the nature of human beings. The early theorists saw the worker at times as a little more than a cog in a machine, easily replaceable and controllable through various devices. But for the humanist the employee constituted a complex individual who could achieve a high level of productivity with the application of the appropriate motivation. The only thing that really had to be done was to free the employee of the shackles of bureaucracy and nurture an environment conducive to innovative behaviour.

This chapter traces the emergence of the humanist perspective with an examination of the first group of theories to challenge the more mechanist view of organizations and their inhabitants. These theories came to be known as organizational humanism and include the work of Mary Follett, Chester Barnard, and Abraham Maslow. The chapter also considers more recent work on humanism— called participatory management—that seeks to build upon the earliest attempts to challenge the model of bureaucracy. These theories, which encompass the efforts of Peter Drucker, W. Edwards Deming and others, tried to correct the failings of organizational humanism and in so doing establish a more sound understanding of organizations and a better basis for effecting greater productivity in the workplace.

Organizational Humanism

Just as scientific management bore the imprint of production engineers such as Frederick Taylor, **organizational humanism**, or the **human relations school**, bore the imprint of the social psychologists. Taylor focused on what *should* happen in the factory to maximize production. The organizational humanists focused instead on what *actually* happened on the factory floor. Their findings seem rather unspectacular now, but they totally upset scientific management theorists. They found that in addition to the formal system of authority through which management controlled workers, there was an informal system of worker control that was in some cases more powerful than the formal system. The informal system was characterized by the network of friendships, workplace banter, and informal sanctions that occur in every work setting. The devastating impact that this finding had on the scientific management theory was obvious. Taylor and his disciples might continue to set their standards, but workers would simply not comply with them if it meant the ostracism frequently accorded the "rate-buster." This meant that Taylor's emphasis on scientific principles to set the work pace and on financial incentives to improve productivity was somewhat misplaced. While these factors had some value, it was becoming clear that another route to increased productivity lay with the informal system.

Mary Parker Follett

One of the first people to understand the importance of the informal system was not a conventional researcher but a very perceptive student of human nature. Mary Parker Follett, born in 1868, did not study organizations systematically in the ordinary sense, but she did use every opportunity to discuss organizational questions with everyone from senior executives to factory workers. From these discussions, she developed a number of important ideas.

Her basic philosophy stemmed from the fact that she rejected the conventional use of raw power in organizations. She felt that its use was either futile or, in some cases, totally counterproductive. Instead, she focused on two related concepts—circular response and integration.

She rejected the biological concept of unidirectional stimulus–response relationships as inapplicable in the human setting. Instead, she emphasized shared interaction.[1] *Circular response* means no one unilaterally acts on someone else; rather, people interact with one another in ways that influence both parties. It was this view that caused her to reject the idea of power as a one-way street. *Integration* referred to the need to combine diverse elements into a useful whole. In some ways, this could be seen as simply a restatement of the old idea of division of labour, but Follett realized that integration was a dynamic concept and not simply the static arrangement of slots on an organizational chart. She understood that conflict would inevitably develop in any organization because of the existence of circular response and the informal organization.

It was, however, the particular genius of Follett's contribution that she recognized and held fast to the notion that the process of change that generates conflict also provides the opportunity for the further changes necessary to resolve that conflict. Each solution contains the seeds of new differences, but these differences also contain the seeds of new solutions. What they need is freedom to grow within a milieu of intelligent and sympathetic cultivation.[2] This latter point was a very important one for Follett. She frequently emphasized the significance of executives exercising *leadership* rather than *wielding power*. She felt that the way to motivate employees was through a rational appeal to a person's higher instincts rather than a reliance on fear or threats.

Roethlisberger and Dickson and the Hawthorne Experiments

The beginnings of the human relations school are usually traced to an experiment conducted with workers at the Hawthorne Works (near Chicago) of Western Electric in 1924. The idea was to test the impact of different levels of lighting on employee productivity. The experiments were organized and conducted by an industrial psychologist from Harvard, F.J. Roethlisberger, and a Western Electric management employee, William J. Dickson. They were later joined by another Harvard professor, Elton Mayo.[3]

The experimenters assumed that improving physical working conditions by increasing levels of lighting would increase productivity. The research was poorly designed and the results inconclusive. One problem the researchers encountered was that production tended to move erratically up or down without much regard to changes in the level of lighting. The experimenters had to discard their original hypothesis, because the ambiguity of the results indicated that the physical conditions surrounding work did not have the paramount influence assumed.

The Hawthorne experiment was followed by a series of experiments that tested the impact of many other changes in physical conditions in the workplace. Again, the results were ambiguous. This caused experimenters to think about a characteristic of the experiments that they had not considered previously. In every case, the tests were conducted using a group of people who were selected from the workroom, moved to a special place, and singled out for a great deal of consideration from researchers. This led experimenters to focus on the *Hawthorne* or *sympathetic observer effect*—the idea that workers given special attention will experience an increase in morale, which will lead to greater productivity.

This finding has been criticized widely over the years.[4] Some critics have pointed to the poor design of the research, while others have argued that the research findings do not support the conclusions usually drawn from them. Nevertheless, the ideas flowing from the Hawthorne studies "have had a significant effect on the field of organizational behavior."[5]

Chester Barnard and the Importance of Cooperation

Chester Barnard was a career business executive, born in 1886, who rose to become president of the New Jersey Bell Telephone Company. In 1938, after his retirement, he wrote his landmark work *The Functions of the Executive*.[6] His crucial idea was that an organization is a cooperative system held together by a good communication system and by the continuing desire of individual members to see the organization thrive.

Members of the organization make *contributions* to it, but only when they receive adequate *inducements* to encourage them to continue to do so. It is important to balance contributions and inducements. If inducements exceed contributions, business failure will result because the organization is too free with its resources. However, if inducements are inadequate, workers will cease making contributions and business failure will result. The essence of good management is maintaining a balance between these two. The inducements offered to workers could be in the form of monetary rewards, but Barnard felt that other forms of inducement such as loyalty, good working conditions, and pride in both the work and the organization were probably more effective.

Barnard tried to be sensitive to the needs of workers, but his basic attitude to workers was somewhat patronizing. The title of his book—*The Functions of the Executive*—probably says it all. He felt that workers were rather docile, uninspired creatures who depended on leadership to accomplish anything. It was the responsibility of the executive to establish good communication systems that would in turn instil the appropriate company spirit in employees.

Chapter 3 / Public Administration and Organization Theory

He recognized that there was an informal organization that could thwart the desires of management; however, he argued that it was the responsibility of management to use the idea of cooperation to harness that informal system for the benefit of the organization. This idea is still found in the argument that job interviews are an important part of the hiring process, not because they disclose specific job skills, but because they can indicate whether the prospective employee's personality fits with the organization's culture.[7]

Abraham Maslow's Hierarchy of Needs

Scientific management focused on the idea of monetary rewards as an incentive for good work performance. Maslow argued that this was too simplistic. He said that people are motivated by a hierarchy of five categories of needs ranging from the physiological to self-actualization. He believed that a person will first be motivated by a desire to satisfy the most basic physiological needs, but as these are satisfied, the person will strive to meet the next level of needs, and so on up the hierarchy. As an employee attains each succeeding level in the hierarchy, he or she will no longer be motivated by rewards directed at the more basic needs. As shown in Figure 3.1, the five levels in the **hierarchy of needs** are as follows:

1. Physiological—food, shelter, clothing, sex, and sleep
2. Safety—security, stability, freedom from fear
3. Belongingness and love—friendship, love, membership in some community
4. Esteem—achievement, competence, independence, prestige, status
5. Self-actualization—self-fulfilment, attaining ultimate goals in life[8]

Maslow's contention was that there is no "one best way" to motivate employees. Instead, management must be sensitive to the fact that workers have a variety of needs beyond the simple need for money. Thinking about employee needs such as self-esteem and self-actualization posed serious problems for managers who were accustomed to thinking in simple piecework terms.

A discussion of Maslow's complex theory of motivation appears in almost every management textbook, and it is the basis for most participative management philosophy. It also seems to strike a more responsive chord than the simpler, one-dimensional approach of the scientific management school. It agrees with the usual observation that different people, and even the same person, are motivated by different factors at different times.

Despite the widespread repetition of Maslow's ideas, contemporary scholars have taken issue with it. Some of the concepts (especially self-actualization) are poorly defined, and operationalizing the theory for purpose of scientific testing has been

Figure 3.1	Maslow's Hierarchy of Needs

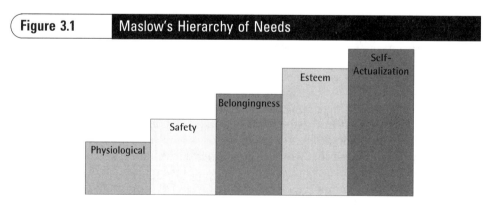

Source: A. H. Maslow, *Eupsychian Management* (Homewood, Ill.: Dorsey Press, 1965), 55–56.

Table 3.1	Theory X and Theory Y Assumptions
THEORY X	**THEORY Y**
Employees dislike work and will make every attempt to avoid it.	Employees see work as being natural as rest or play.
Employees must be cajoled or threatened to get them to work.	Employees willingly perform work if committed to the objectives.
Employees will shirk responsibilities and must be told what to do.	Employees can learn to take on and even seek responsibility.
Most workers seek security above all and display little ambition.	The capacity to solve organizational problems is widely dispersed.

challenging. Even Maslow himself had some reservations about these ideas, but they have been repeated so often that they have taken on a life of their own.[9]

Douglas McGregor's Theory X and Theory Y

Regardless of caveats to Maslow's theory, McGregor built on his ideas and related them to the attitudes of individual managers.[10] He noted that some managers simply do not trust or respect their employees. He felt that this reflected a group of assumptions about human nature, which he called **Theory X**. This theory depicts people as seeking to do as little work as possible and who must be threatened and closely supervised to ensure that they will do the necessary work. Others managers, however, hold a more optimistic view of their subordinates, which can be captured in **Theory Y**. This theory claims that work is a natural activity—not something to be avoided—and that employees will be quite productive if given the opportunity to reach their potential. There is no need for controls and close supervision. Table 3.1 lists the assumptions underlying these two perspectives on human nature.

McGregor's basic message was that employees react differently depending on how they are treated. If managers convey the impression that they believe their employees are Theory X types of workers, the workers will likely meet those expectations. Conversely, managers who treat employees in a Theory Y manner will likely be more successful. On the basis of their perception of workers, these managers will delegate responsibility, enlarge the duties of their employees, and nurture a more consultative style within the organization.

There are a number of similarities between Maslow's and McGregor's thinking. The most obvious is that they both have a very positive view of human nature. They argue that workers can be positively motivated without recourse to threats, but that this requires a certain amount of understanding and sensitivity on the part of managers. Another major similarity is that both theories seem intuitively correct but are difficult to test empirically. In fact, neither has been widely tested, although they are widely discussed in the management literature.

Box 3.1	Summary of the Principles of Organizational Humanism
• Respect for workers as complex human beings with diverse sets of needs • Distrust of simple, one-dimensional theories of motivation	• Recognition that the informal organization can be as instrumental as the formal one in setting work rules

Criticisms of Organizational Humanism

There have been many criticisms of the philosophy of the human relations school. The most significant are based on the idea that the presumed community of interest between workers and management does not exist. Thus, the entire human relations concept is a method to manipulate employees to behave in the interests of management.

It is obviously in management's interest to extract as much work as possible from employees. This is the profit motive. However, it is in the employees' interest to restrict their output to what they can do in physical comfort. Employees are also aware that the amount of work to be done is usually finite and that their reward for working hard might be a layoff slip when the work is completed. When one views the workplace in this way, the cooperation treasured by the organizational humanists is somewhat elusive.

Critics charge that this is precisely the point where the theories developed by the organizational humanists become important. How does management convince workers to behave in the best interests of management rather than in their own best interests? The human relations response is to establish a feeling of caring and unity in the workplace that can then be used to manipulate employees. Critics like to point to one aspect of the work done at Hawthorne that involved hiring 300 employees to wander the factory floor and listen to complaints of other employees. Management never did anything about the complaints and never intended to do anything; the sole purpose of this action was to create the impression that management actually cared about workers and to maintain control of employees.

> In the end, therefore, the human relations approach to management proves to be simply another technique for managerial control. Although the human relations approach provides a recognition of the human factors in organizational life, it ultimately treats these as just another set of inducements to be manipulated in the pursuit of managerial control. Where conflicts arise between the individual and the organization, managers are admonished to resort to their hierarchical authority. Ultimately, this approach remains simplistic and unfulfilling and, in any case, hardly leads toward a true alternative to the rational model of administration. Though appearing humanistic, the human relations approach may simply be more subtle.[11]

The human relations approach was also criticized from the opposite perspective by production-conscious managers. They were concerned that this school was too employee-centred. Their criticism was that in its revulsion from scientific management, it tipped the balance too far in the other direction. Some derisively referred to human relations as "country club" management, meaning that the ideal workplace ought to resemble a country club. Others suggested that for human relations, the "one best way" was employee satisfaction rather than concern for production.

In the face of this criticism from both sides, organizational humanism had to evolve. The next step was a cluster of ideas that attempted to meet both kinds of criticisms. These varying concepts can be loosely grouped under the heading of participatory management.

Participatory Management

Gradually it became accepted that there was an innate tension and conflict in the workplace. This tension could revolve around general issues such as rates of pay and speed of the production processes, or specific issues such as the attitude of a particular supervisor or the quality of food served in the lunchroom. Organizational humanism tried to cover over this tension by in effect bribing employees to accept management views. The participatory theories held that the tension could be controlled and directed, but probably not totally eliminated, by allowing workers a real decision-making role in the workplace.

There are many approaches to **participatory management**. Peter Drucker is one of the early proponents of participatory management. His view of organizations stood Weber's views of bureaucracy on their head.[12] Drucker argued that the very characteristics that Weber saw as such powerful engines of *efficiency*—bureaucracy, hierarchical structures, and specialization—were in fact powerful forces for *misdirection*. Drucker felt that in large organizations managers and employees became too involved in their own specialty and had a tendency to emphasize this at the expense of the overall good of the organization. For example, if the purchasing department emphasizes buying at low prices rather than the high quality of the product or security of supply, the production department can suffer precisely because the purchasing department is doing its job well—at least, in the view of people in that department. Thus, it frequently happens that inefficiency and misdirection occur because of hierarchy and specialization of labour. The problem is the inability to focus on the overall organizational goal; the solution is a more participatory form of management that would allow managers to have a broader view of the organization and a clearer understanding of its overall goals. Two recent and important approaches to participatory management are discussed here—organization development and total quality management.

Organization Development

Organization development (OD) is based on the idea that all organizations tend to become rigid or "frozen." While the organization remains rigid, the environment around the organization changes, and this has serious consequences. Usually, conditions gradually deteriorate until a serious crisis occurs, which causes either radical restructuring or even the collapse of the organization. The purpose of OD is to locate the barriers to change and to show the organization how to engage in planned, goal-directed change and not directionless evolution or radical revolution.

Organization development recognizes that all organizations have a history that creates an organizational culture.[13] In some cases this can be a good thing, but in many it is not. This history, or culture, develops as a result of the organization's past successes and failures. For example, when someone responds to a new proposal by saying, "We can't do that because we tried something like it ten years ago and it didn't work," history is at work. The fact that something similar was unsuccessful ten years earlier might or might not be relevant now, but in many cases this kind of argument will carry the day. When the culture or history of an organization has this kind of negative influence, it is referred to as "drag."

Practitioners of OD warn that the patterns and procedures that create drag are merely symptoms of a more serious underlying problem in the organization's culture. It is pointless to change these patterns and procedures—merely the manifestations of the basic problems—without also changing the underlying culture. Such changes would meet strong resistance, and inappropriate new patterns could possibly be imposed on an unfriendly environment.

There are many practitioners of OD, and each has a slightly different approach. However, they share a belief in a general three-phase approach—unfreezing, moving or changing, and refreezing.[14] The unfreezing stage involves identifying current dysfunctional behaviour and helping the organization to "unlearn" that behaviour. In the second phase, the improvements needed are identified and implemented. The third stage

Chapter 3 / Public Administration and Organization Theory

Figure 3.2   Approach of Organization Development

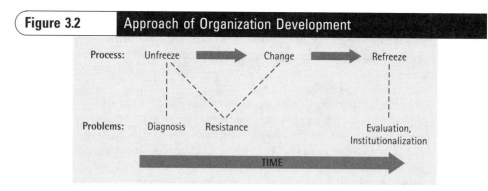

Source: Gary Johns and Alan M. Saks, *Organizational Behaviour,* 6th ed. (Toronto: Pearson Education Canada, Inc., 2005). Reprinted with permission by Pearson Education Canada Inc.

involves refreezing the organization with its new behaviour in place so that the organization does not unconsciously revert to the old behaviour. Figure 3.2 offers a visual representation of the three stages.

Total Quality Management

Total quality management (TQM) was the next approach to participatory management. It was popularized in North America in the 1980s and early 1990s as a response to the Japanese system of management. Its leading proponent was W. Edwards Deming.[15]

Deming's work began before World War II in the United States with the development of statistical process control (SPC) to improve production quality. This involved using various statistical techniques to identify and correct deviations from the ideal quality production standard. After the war, he became disillusioned with the way American companies were using his philosophy, because they tended to view the statistical techniques as an end in themselves and did not incorporate thinking about quality into their overall management and organizational culture. When he was given the opportunity to teach his technique to Japanese business leaders after the war, he did not repeat this mistake. He emphasized to them that they must make quality the overall focus of their organizational culture.[16] The Japanese learned this lesson very well.

The basic difference between the American and the Japanese approach to quality can be illustrated by an example from the auto industry. The somewhat exaggerated stereotype suggests that the American auto industry focused on production rather than quality. This meant producing the maximum number of cars and then employing a separate quality control group to detect and repair problems after the cars were built. The Japanese approach was to put less emphasis on the raw speed of construction and make every employee responsible for quality control of her or his aspect of the work. Thus, the cars took longer and cost more to build in the first place, but there was greater assurance that the job was done properly the first time and less expense involved in the later correction of errors. The guiding principle of TQM is "Get it right the first time."[17]

The basic tenet of TQM is eliminating quality control as a separate function, and instead making every employee responsible for quality and giving each a role in designing production processes to ensure maximum quality.[18]

TQM has been defined as

a broad-scale approach to changing an organization's entire culture to focus on establishing and maintaining high standards of quality, especially with respect to meeting "customer" expectations. The key of TQM is to serve the "customer," whether the "customer" is internal to the organization or someone outside.[19]

The important point of this definition is that TQM involves the creation of an entire organizational culture based on concern for both quality and production.

> Contrary to conventional wisdom in the United States, quality and productivity were not to be traded off against each other. Rather, productivity was a by-product of quality and of doing the job right the first time....[20]

As with most new management processes, there are a number of different ways this technique can be implemented. One method of establishing TQM in the public sector focuses on three basic components:

1. Working with suppliers to ensure that the supplies utilized in the work processes are designed for your use
2. Continuous employee analysis of work processes to improve their functioning and reduce process variation
3. Close communication with customers to identify and understand what they want and how they define quality[21]

Another important aspect of TQM is that it focuses on how the organization relates to its environment. It recognizes that quality is largely a function of how well the organization works with both its suppliers and customers in the larger environment.

Criticisms of the Participative Approach

One of the criticisms frequently levelled at the participative approaches is that they require a huge commitment of resources on the part of the organization, and that they are so disruptive that they can lead to rather lengthy periods of turmoil. The basic principle of the approach is that virtually all employees of the organization must become involved and, in some cases, for fairly lengthy periods. This level of participation imposes a heavy internal cost on the organization. Moreover, there is usually a psychological cost to the organization from undergoing this kind of radical surgery. Even though the actual organizational changes themselves can be planned in an incremental and minimally disruptive manner, the rumour mill that always works full time in these situations can hurt morale.

The obvious response to this criticism is that the end result is worth the short-term trauma, and this has often proven correct. However, given the cost and turmoil engendered in the short run, management's frequent reluctance to become fully involved in a participative management exercise is understandable.

Many of the criticisms of the concept of participative management echo those directed against the organizational humanists. There seems to be a lingering concern that the process is not really and truly participative but is guided—not to say manipulated—by management. "Frederick Taylor was satisfied if he could control the physical movements of the workers; OD wants their hearts, souls, and minds."[22]

While organizational humanism and participative management stress concern for the whole person, they both focus on the person as a worker, with less concern for the non-work-related aspects of the person's life. For example, it is not difficult to determine how they would view an employee who refused to work more than forty hours a week, even though it meant passing up a promotion, because the person wanted to spend more time with her or his family or take part in other activities.

As mentioned above, this stands more as a criticism of the manner in which the process has been applied in certain cases than a basic criticism of the process itself. But it does raise a difficult conundrum. In a true hierarchical setting, those at the pinnacle of the hierarchy have authority over those at lower levels. Some things have not changed since Weber. Given this fact, is real participation possible?

Participative Management in the Public Sector

There is a particular set of problems with the use of participative management in the public sector. The most serious concern is whether a bottom-up participative approach to decision making is consistent with the principle of instilling final responsibility for activities of a department with the minister. A second concern arises when it is suggested that "participation" should extend beyond employees and allow clients who are affected by the agency to be involved in the decision-making process. Few would argue with the right of clients to have a voice in the consultation process. However, this must be limited because clients of a particular service constitute a special interest group whose perspective on an issue might be at odds with the broader public interest.

In practice, the concern for top-down accountability has often won out over bottom-up participation. At the risk of generalizing, it seems that few government agencies give more than lip service to participatory management. However, this does not preclude certain kinds of OD or TQM approaches that are geared more to operation of the agency than basic public policy decision making. Robert T. Golembiewski, a recognized expert on OD in the public sector, has argued that there are particular problems with the use of OD in the public sector, and that these problems result in a "lower batting average" in the success of OD in the public sector. After an extensive review of the literature on OD attempts, he arrives at the conclusion that "the 'lower batting average' is still pretty high."[23] The next section reviews the Canadian experience with participative management.

The Canadian Experience

In the previous chapter, the status of scientific management in the federal government was considered. In this chapter, many other styles of management have been discussed, but there has been no comment on their impact on Canadian governments. The reason is quite simple—they seem to have had little impact.[24] It might be unfair to say that absolutely nothing of the organizational humanist school filtered into the Canadian public sector. Since the human relations school is, in large part, a prescription for changes in the actions of individual managers, it is possible that certain managers followed the advice of the organizational humanists without any system-wide documentation of the practice. But it is correct to conclude that overall its influence was minimal. Throughout the time of the organizational humanists, Canadian governments continued to exhibit rigid hierarchies, inflexible job classification structures, and the other trappings of scientific management.

When the participatory style of management came into full flower, it found easier acceptance. Many government organizations in Canada have espoused the TQM concept or similar participatory approaches under a variety of different names.[25] TQM thinking underlay much of the federal government's PS2000 program in the late 1980s and similar initiatives in several provinces.[26] TQM could become even more important as government organizations face pressures to be more efficient. It should enable government organizations to find ways of working smarter and ensuring that quality of service to clients remains high.

These various reforms have probably produced a higher quality of management, but they have also created problems. While new innovations have been implemented, few of the trappings of the older systems have been discarded. The entire arrangement is reminiscent of an old European building with a basic structure from one era and many additions, each bearing the architectural style of the era in which it was added. There is nothing wrong with each separate part, but the total building creates a rather unusual overall impression. For example, total quality management and team-building exercises that emphasize flexibility, empowerment, and cooperation have been combined with lengthy, complex job descriptions that emphasize rigidity and differentiation of duties.

More Theoretical Developments

While such practical changes as OD, TQM, and other managerial reforms were being introduced into the Canadian scene, progress continued in the theoretical study of organizations. Many of these new approaches represented significant improvements in organization theory, but they basically constituted a continuation of the attack against mechanist thinking in organizational behaviour.

Katz and Kahn's Open Systems Approach

One such theory is **open systems theory**.[27] Some sociologists and social psychologists such as Robert Merton, Talcott Parsons, Daniel Katz, and Robert L. Kahn became disenchanted with the earlier organizational theories because they put too much emphasis on activities of individuals within organizations and on the activities of the organization as a monolithic body, without consideration of the environment within which the organization operated. They criticized this kind of thinking as the "closed system" approach, because, in their eyes, it considered the organization only as a closed system and not as a part of its environment. For example, both Weber and Taylor, in their work, assumed incorrectly that the organization's environment was "regulated and stabilized in such a way that one [could], analytically, ignore the environment when describing, dissecting, and manipulating the system."[28]

Followers of the open systems approach were influenced by biological models that dealt with both the internal organization of organisms and how they interacted with their environment. Natural scientists did this by thinking in terms of inputs-through-puts-outputs-feedback. To continue to exist, any organism must receive certain inputs from its environment. It then converts these to outputs that, through feedback, help it to attain more inputs. In the case of simple, one-cell organisms, this means capturing some nourishment and converting it to energy, which it uses to move about to capture more nourishment. Human beings operate on the same principle, only with a more complex interaction system. They need nourishment, shelter, and psychic encouragement, which they convert to work effort that can be sold for cash or traded to satisfy such needs as food, shelter, and psychic encouragement.

The open systems theorists felt that organizations could be approached in the same manner (see Figure 3.3 on page 44). Organizations need inputs in the form of labour power, raw materials, and so forth. These are then converted to finished products or outputs, which are sold for cash so that more inputs can be purchased. Not-for-profit organizations do not follow exactly the same cycle in that their products are usually not sold, but they still must produce an acceptable level of output so that some organization, such as a government, will provide inputs to them. Katz and Kahn argued that successful organizations arrange the input-throughput-output process so as to reverse the normal entropy to which living organisms are subject. Entropy is the process through which organisms are subject to deterioration. In complex physical systems, as the system becomes larger, the individual parts of the system become more disorganized until they are no longer able to sustain the organization as a whole. At this point, the system perishes.

A successful organization overcomes this process by developing *negative entropy*, which is the process of importing and storing more energy than it expends. This allows the organization to expand and to survive in difficult times by drawing on the stored

Figure 3.3 | Open Systems Approach to Organizations

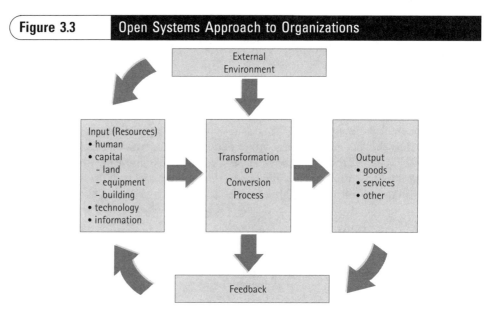

reserve.[29] This stored reserve could take several forms. An obvious one is cash and other hard assets, but some other forms of stored energy could be the trust and goodwill of important people or a high-quality management team.

The crucial lesson for managers in open systems theory is that all organizations are a part of their environments. Earlier thinkers such as Frederick Taylor and, to a lesser extent, the organizational humanists attempted to see the organization as a closed system unaffected by its environment. The open system concept reminds managers that, in addition to managing the internal aspects of their organization, they must also be sensitive to the rapidly changing environment that affects such things as the acceptance of their product, their relationship with their clientele, and the attitudes of their employees.

The next theory we discuss continues the open system approach and focuses on how an organization must fit in with its environment.

Contingency Theory

Contingency theory was first developed in a systematic fashion in the 1960s. Its basic premise is "There is no one best way to organize," but "Any way of organizing is not equally effective."[30] Instead, contingency theory suggests that the best way to structure an organization is contingent on a number of factors affecting the organization. The most commonly cited factors are "the task environment of the organization, the technology used within the organization, and the organization's size."[31] The task environment of an organization consists of its clients or customers, competitors, suppliers, regulatory agencies, and, in the case of public organizations, the legislature that established them and provides their funding. Some organizations face a task environment that is uncertain and rapidly changing. These organizations must be very flexible and able to change as rapidly as their environment. Other task environments are considerably more stable and organizations operating in them can become a little complacent.

Technology refers to *"the process by which an organization converts inputs into outputs."*[32] In a manufacturing environment, this is the assembly line or other mechanism used to produce the finished product. However, service organizations and even organizations producing such ephemeral products as "policy advice" also have production processes.

Where a technology is very routine and repetitive, such as an assembly line, the organization can have a very broad span of control because problems are not likely to occur, and when they do, there is usually a prearranged solution. Where the production process is less highly specified, such as in a policy advice unit, the span of control must be considerably smaller, because each new task is different from previous tasks and superiors and subordinates must work closely together.

The size of the organization also has an impact on its organizational structure. In very small organizations, the chief executive is in daily contact with all her or his subordinates and everyone understands by tradition what is to be done. As organizations become larger, layers of hierarchy are established, and written job descriptions and standard operating procedures are required to delineate responsibilities.

One of the strengths of contingency theory is that, unlike many of the other theories that have been discussed, it is a dynamic approach to organization. Managers must be aware that there is no "one best way" to organize their operation. The structure that was highly successful last year might be a dismal failure with the changed conditions of the new year. The need to adjust to the rapidly changing environment is a challenge to all modern organizations.

Theories of Motivation

Earlier ideas of motivation were rather simplistic. Bosses simply told workers what to do and they did it—or were fired. Henry Ford is purported to have said that the best incentive for an employee is the presence of unemployed workers outside the factory gate. Traditional forms of motivation based on punishment have fallen into disuse for a number of reasons. The strength of unions and recent changes in labour laws to protect workers have reduced the unilateral power that employers once had to discipline employees. However, evidence indicates that motivation by fear of punishment is not very efficient anyway. Negative forms of motivation might well motivate employees to do just enough to avoid being disciplined. The result might be a continual game of employees trying to find out how much they can "get away with" before they are disciplined. This might then lead to management continually imposing new controls and restrictions as employees find ways of circumventing them. Positive methods of motivating people are probably much more effective.

Chris Argyris's maturity–immaturity theory represents one development in the attempt to better understand the significance of motivation in organizations. He points out that all social organizations are composed of individuals and a formal structure, but that tensions inevitably develop because there is a basic incongruence between the behaviour pattern of mature individuals and the needs of the formal organization. He suggests that the characteristics of a mature individual are, among others, self-determination, increased independence, self-awareness, a longer-time perspective, and a deepening interest in stimulating challenges. He goes on to point out that formal organizations are based on such principles as task or work specialization, chain of command, unity of direction, and span of control.[33] Most of these principles require not mature but immature behaviour on the part of the individual. For example, mature individuals capable of complex behaviour and interested in challenges are placed in jobs that require boring, repetitive actions. "[O]rganizations are willing to pay high wages and provide adequate seniority if mature adults will, for eight hours a day, behave in a less than mature manner!"[34]

It is quite rational for employees to react negatively when confronted with this situation. They might simply leave the organization. Or they might stay and become apathetic and/or establish an informal work group that has a detrimental effect on production. Or they might resolve to work their way up the organizational ladder because the incongruity between personality and organizational demands is less pronounced at the higher levels.

In a later work, Argyris presents some tentative suggestions for resolving this basic incongruity.[35] He suggests that organizations of the future will emphasize the pyramidal organizational structure less and recognize that there are other, less formal structures in place that are also important. He strongly supports a form of job enlargement that would ensure that employees develop a greater understanding of, and concern for, the activities of the entire organization, rather than only their narrow portion of it. This should be supplemented by employees meeting in small groups to discuss problems and possibilities for improvement. He argued that autocratic leadership styles should be replaced by situational approaches to leadership—different types of employees and situations call for different leadership styles. Control mechanisms should be oriented less toward detecting transgressions and more toward helping individuals achieve greater "self-responsibility and psychological success."[36]

Frederick Herzberg is another who has examined closely the importance and complexity of motivation in the workplace. Herzberg sought to test the conventional wisdom that the factors that cause *satisfaction* in the work environment are simply the reverse of those that cause *dissatisfaction*. Frederick Herzberg tested this assumption by asking a number of employees to describe work occurrences that led to satisfaction and dissatisfaction. In many cases, the factors causing satisfaction were very different from those causing dissatisfaction.[37] For example, a feeling of achievement tended to satisfy workers, but its absence did not make them dissatisfied; it simply reduced their satisfaction. Conversely, company policy and administration were a frequent source of dissatisfaction, but correcting problems in this area merely lessened dissatisfaction; it did not increase satisfaction.

Herzberg referred to the factors that led to dissatisfaction as "hygiene" factors, because "they act in a manner analogous to the principles of medical hygiene. Hygiene operates to remove health hazards from the environment of man. It is not curative; it is, rather, a preventive."[38] Herzberg labelled the factors that led to satisfaction "motivators," because they had a highly positive effect on people's feelings about their job. Figure 3.4 lists motivators and hygiene factors, and also shows how Herzberg's views differed from traditional ones on satisfaction and dissatisfaction.

Herzberg noted a very interesting difference between the hygiene and motivating factors. The hygiene factors all relate to the general work environment, while the motivating factors are all intrinsic to the nature of the job itself. The implications of Herzberg's theory for management are clear: the general work environment should be pleasant enough to avoid dissatisfaction, but any major improvements in motivation can be made only through changes in the nature of the job itself.

The theories of both Argyris and Herzberg focused on the ability to improve motivation through careful job design. However, two experts in job design, Richard Hackman and Greg Oldham, remind us that sometimes the problem is not with the nature of the job itself. They emphasize the need for proper selection and training techniques to ensure that there is a good fit between the person and the job.[39]

> When people are well matched with their jobs, it rarely is necessary to force, coerce, bribe, or trick them into working hard and trying to perform the job well. Instead, they try to do well because it is rewarding and satisfying to do so.[40]

However, the job itself must be reasonably attractive. A number of different approaches to improving job designs have been tried. "Job rotation" involves keeping the job descriptions for all positions the same, but shifting the people who fill the position. This could be done for only a half-day at a time or for a few weeks. It adds some variety to an employee's workday and may increase an employee's sense of

Figure 3.4 | Herzberg's Motivation and Hygiene Factors

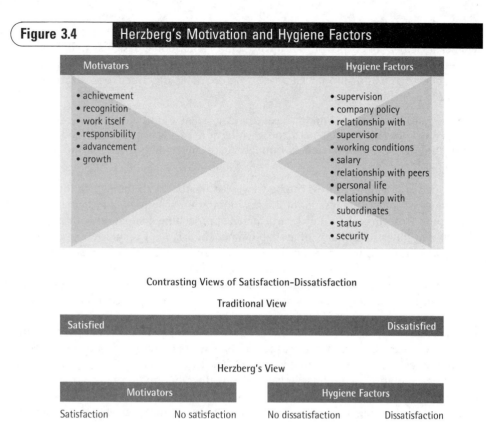

Source: Stephen P. Robbins, Mary Coulter, and Nancy Langton, *Management*, 8th Canadian Edition (Toronto: Pearson Education Canada, Inc., 2006), 381. Reprinted with permission by Pearson Education Canada Inc.

accomplishment and responsibility if he or she knows how to do several jobs instead of just one. "Job enlargement" tries to relieve the boredom in a job by expanding the size of the job. Instead of spending all day simply examining and filing forms, an employee might also be responsible for working at a counter and helping members of the public fill out forms. Having broader responsibilities and being able to see more of the total process should increase an employee's sense of belonging and accomplishment. "Job enrichment," or "vertical job loading," is a variant of job enlargement proposed by Hackman and Oldham, Argyris, and Herzberg, among many others. Herzberg, in particular, emphasized the importance of expanding jobs not just by arbitrarily adding more duties but by considering the needs of the mature employee. He pointed out the difference between "horizontal job loading," which means simply loading a person with more work, and vertical job loading, which means expanding the job through such means as eliminating controls, introducing more precise and demanding tasks, and setting out a specified area of work in which an employee is assigned new responsibilities.[41]

Emergent View Process

The organization theories discussed to this point have been based on the idea that managers have a great deal of control in making decisions about organizational structure, and that they always exercise that control in a rational manner and after extensive evaluation of alternatives. An alternative view suggests that organization design should be seen "as an emergent process, partially under the manager's control and partially beyond control.... [Managers are] partly proactive and partly reactive, capable of influencing organization design but not being the dominant influence."[42] This idea recognizes that external constraints play an important role in influencing organizational design, but that there is a significant element of chance or luck involved in organizational design as well.

One of the first discussions of this idea was an article colourfully titled "A Garbage Can Model of Organizational Choice."[43] This article described organizations as "organized anarchies."

> The organization operates on the basis of inconsistent and ill-defined preferences. It can be described better as a loose collection of ideas than as a coherent structure; it discovers preferences through action more than it acts on the basis of preferences.[44]

The decision-making process can be viewed as a garbage can into which four items are thrown. One item represents problems looking for solutions, another solutions looking for problems, and a third participants approaching a situation with different interests and different amounts of available time. The last item is choice opportunities or occasions when organizations are forced to take some action. These items are thrown into the can randomly and stirred about. Thus, problems do not always precede solutions. In some cases, solutions that have not yet discovered a problem are available. In any particular situation, the decision made is a function not of cold, rational logic but of the arbitrary way these four elements are thrown into and stirred about in the garbage can. For example, decisions are frequently influenced by the particular people who attend a key meeting. Thus, a bout of the flu or a flat tire that prevents a particular person from attending a meeting can determine what decision is made.

But one should not go too far in emphasizing the randomness of decision making. Managers have the legal and effective authority to make decisions and they do use rational processes in making those decisions. The significance of the emergent process view is that it recognizes that managers face certain uncontrollable factors in making decisions and that they do sometimes temper their rationality with impulse and irrational bias in making decisions.

Conclusion

The history of organization theory begins with the mechanistic views of Weber and Taylor and progresses to the considerably more humanistic perspectives of the social psychologists and organizational development specialists. Both organizational humanism and participatory management rejected the notion that the employee was merely a cog in a machine. The humanistic perspective also rejected the simple structure and rationality of bureaucracy—the organization and its employees were more complicated than depicted in the early theories of organizations. However, the humanist school of thought would not be the last word on organizations.

1. Mary Parker Follett, *Creative Experience* (New York: Peter Smith, 1951), ch. 3; Mary Parker Follett, *The New State* (Gloucester, Mass.: Peter Smith, 1965), 25–26.

2. Mary Parker Follett, *Dynamic Administration: The Collected Papers of Mary Parker Follett*, eds. Elliot M. Fox and L. Urwick (London: Pitman, 1973), xxv.

3. Their work is described in great detail in Roethlisberger and Dickson's book, *Management and the Worker* (Cambridge, Mass.: Harvard University Press, 1964).

4. Two of the more trenchant critics are Charles Perrow, *Complex Organizations: A Critical Essay* (Glenview, Ill.: Scott, Foresman, 1972), 97–106; and Amitai Etzioni, *Modern Organizations* (Englewood Cliffs, N.J.: Prentice-Hall, 1964), 39–49. A good overview of many of the critical articles can be found in Michael M. Harmon and Richard T. Mayer, *Organization Theory for Public Administration* (Boston: Little, Brown, 1986), 96–102.

5. John B. Miner, *Organizational Behavior: Foundations, Theories, and Analyses* (New York: Oxford University Press, 2002), 35–36.

6. Chester Barnard, *The Functions of the Executive* (Cambridge, Mass.: Harvard University Press, 1962).

7. Glenn Bassett, "From Job Fit to Cultural Compatibility: Evaluating Worker Skills and Temperament in the '90s," *Optimum* (1) (summer 1994): 11–17.

8. Abraham H. Maslow, *Motivation and Personality* (New York: Harper & Row, 1970), ch. 4.

9. A.H. Maslow, *Eupsychian Management* (Homewood, Ill.: Dorsey Press, 1965), 55–56.

10. Douglas McGregor, *The Human Side of Enterprise* (New York: McGraw-Hill, 1960), chs. 3 and 4 and passim.

11. Robert B. Denhardt, *Theories of Public Organization* (Pacific Grove, Calif.: Brooks/Cole, 1984), 97.

12. Peter F. Drucker, *The Practice of Management* (New York: Harper & Row, 1954).

13. A good, complete discussion of the concept of organizational culture is found in Florence Heffron, *Organization Theory and Public Organizations* (Englewood Cliffs, N.J.: Prentice-Hall, 1989), ch. 7.

14. This terminology was first used by one of the founders of organization development, Kurt Lewin, in "Frontiers in Group Dynamics," *Human Relations* 1(1) (1947): 34.

15. Deming's simultaneously insightful and folksy approach to management improvement is well illustrated in his major work, *Quality, Productivity, and Competitive Position* (Cambridge, Mass.: Massachusetts Institute of Technology, Center for Advanced Engineering Study, 1982).

16. Marshall Sashkin and Kenneth J. Kiser, *Putting Total Quality Management to Work* (San Francisco: Berrett-Koehler Publishers, 1993), ch. 1.

17. Joseph R. Jablonski, *Implementing Total Quality Management: An Overview* (San Diego: Pfeiffer & Company, 1991), 7.

18. Armand V. Feigenbaum, "Linking Quality Processes to International Leadership," in Frank Caropreso, ed., *Making Total Quality Happen* (New York: The Conference Board, 1990), 4.

19. Robert B. Denhardt, *Public Administration: An Action Orientation* (Pacific Groves, Calif.: Brooks/Cole Publishing Company, 1991), 316.

20. David A. Garvin and Artemis March, "A Note on Quality: The Views of Deming, Juran, and Crosby," in *Unconditional Quality* (Boston, Mass.: Harvard Business School Press, 1991), 18. For a more complete discussion of this issue, see Deming, *Quality, Productivity, and Competitive Position*, ch. 1.

21. Steven Cohen and Ronald Brand, *Total Quality Management in Government* (San Francisco: Jossey-Bass Publishers, 1993), 18.

22. Heffron, *Organization Theory and Public Organizations*, 161.

23. Robert T. Golembiewski, *Humanizing Public Organizations* (Mt. Airy, Md.: Lomond Press, 1985), 61.

24. V. Seymour Wilson, "The Influence of Organization Theory in Canadian Public Administration," *Canadian Public Administration* 25 (winter 1982): 553–54.

25. Denis Martin, "Culture and Client Service at the Department of Fisheries and Oceans," *Optimum* 24 (winter 1993), 99–104; "Un ministère qui se donne des airs de PME," *Le Devoir*, October 2, 1992; Tom Rankin and Archie Gardner, "New Forms of Work Organization in the Federal Public Service: The Case of CFB Shearwater/UNDE Local 80409," *Optimum* 24 (spring 1994), 25–36.

26. Brian Marson, "Building Customer-Focused Organizations in British Columbia," *Public Administration Quarterly* 17(1) (spring 1993): 30–41.

27. One of the best discussions of the open systems is Saeed Rahnema, *Organization Structure: A Systemic Approach* (Toronto: McGraw-Hill Ryerson, 1992).

28. Michael M. Harmon and Richard T. Mayer, *Organization Theory for Public Administration* (Boston: Little, Brown, 1986), 162.

29. Daniel Katz and Robert L. Kahn, *The Social Psychology of Organizations* (New York: John Wiley & Sons, 1966), ch. 2.

30. Jay Galbraith, *Designing Complex Organizations* (Reading, Mass.: Addison-Wesley, 1973), 2.

31. Daniel Robey, *Designing Organizations*, 3rd ed. (Homewood, Ill.: Richard D. Irwin, 1990), 26. See also Saeed Rahnema, *Organization Structure: A Systemic Approach*.

32. Robey, *Designing Organizations*, 28. Emphasis in original.

33. Chris Argyris, *Personality and Organization: The Conflict Between System and the Individual* (New York: Harper & Row, 1957), 50–51 and ch. 3.

34. Ibid., 66.

35. Chris Argyris, *Integrating the Individual and the Organization* (New York: John Wiley & Sons, 1964).

36. Ibid., 275.

37. The results of this research were reported in detail in Frederick Herzberg, Bernard Mausner, and Barbara Bloch Snyderman, *The Motivation to Work* (New York: John Wiley & Sons, 1959). A more elaborate discussion and further verification of the theory is contained in Frederick Herzberg, *Work and the Nature of Man* (Cleveland: The World Publishing Company, 1966).

38. Herzberg et al., *The Motivation to Work*, 113.

39. J. Richard Hackman and Greg R. Oldham, *Work Redesign* (Reading, Mass.: Addison-Wesley, 1980), ch. 2.

40. Ibid., 71.

41. Frederick Herzberg, "One More Time: How Do You Motivate Employees?" *Harvard Business Review* 46 (January/February 1968): 59–62.

42. Robey, *Designing Organizations*, 38.

43. Michael D. Cohen, James G. March, and John P. Olsen, *Administrative Science Quarterly* 17(1) (March 1972): 1–25.

44. Ibid., 1.

4

Public Administration and Organization Theory: The New Public Management

In the 1970s governments in many of the Western democracies appeared to be living beyond their means as public spending began to outstrip available public revenues. At the same time, the confidence of the public in the effectiveness and value of public services was declining; it seemed that many citizens believed that government policies and programs failed in their many purposes and fell short of the level of quality expected of public agencies. The advent of a globalizing world also translated into a belief that national governments had to be that much more effective in order to compete with other nations in a world that was becoming smaller and smaller. There was as well an uneasy feeling among those close to government that public servants exercised too much influence in making policy. Elected officials, not appointed ones, were supposed to take the lead in formulating government initiatives.

All of these forces created a greater sense of urgency for new thinking about government and its organizations and eventually helped give birth to a new theoretical perspective on organizations called the **new public management (NPM)**. As with the theories of bureaucracy, scientific management and humanism, this new theory sought to provide a sound description and explanation of the behaviour of organizational forms. It also delved into the normative issue of how organizations should be structured for the purpose of achieving effectiveness. But it differed from the preceding theories because it focused mostly on organizations in government. Excessive government spending, declining faith in public programs, the spectre of globalization, and concerns of excessive bureaucratic power supplied fertile ground for a theoretical view centred on the public sector and its shortcomings. The theoretical thrust of NPM was that public bureaucracies had to become less rule-bound and more inclined toward participating in a competitive environment in which government employees would be given a great deal more autonomy and flexibility. New public management also looked to a more strict division of responsibilities, whereby elected officials looked after policy and appointed officials tended to the implementation and management of public policies. With this orientation, NPM amounted to an attack on the structural or mechanist foundations of organization theory in public administration. The new public management was more kind to its immediate predecessor, because it borrowed quite liberally from the ideas of the humanistic perspective. If fact, in some respects NPM was just another aspect or element of the school of participatory management. However, it went beyond humanism in its attempt to locate a more theoretically sound perspective on organizations and their operation in the public sector.

In this chapter, we examine the theoretical tenets of the new public management and the various scholars and writers who contributed to the development of this theory. Some of the contributions more directly address the issue of organizations within the public sector, but all are identified with the effort to provide a new viewpoint on organizations that ultimately came to be known as the new public management. The chapter also summarizes the elements of NPM in an attempt to bring together the common threads in the relevant writings, and looks at the criticisms directed at this theory of government organization and behaviour. Finally, the chapter reviews the application of this new perspective in Canada and speculates on the future of organization theory in public administration and the possible place of new public management in this future.

Theoretical Foundations of the New Public Management

The works and texts arising from the new public management are heavy on prescription and recommend to government what they *should* do in order to reform their organizational apparatuses. Nevertheless, some theoretical propositions about the nature and operations of organizations underlie these prescriptions and give some intellectual muscle to this perspective on organizations. One of the propositions is the claim that "career public servants are not primarily motivated by the public interest in good government but by the promotion of their own individual or collective self-interests."[1] More subtle versions of the proposition contend that appointed officials still focus on the public interest but seek to provide their own interpretations of it. However, in all instances the government bureaucrat can be likened to the rational or self-seeking consumer depicted in economic theory, eager to satisfy his or her preferences in the most economical way. Some companion claims to this basic belief include the assertion that the self-interests of appointed officials or their perceptions of the public interest may clash with those of elected officials. For instance, the latter may want to cut spending in response to the wishes of the electorate, but the interest of bureaucrats in maximizing the size of departmental budgets may frustrate movement in this direction. This theoretical perspective, which is called **public choice theory**, also asserts that public servants often get their way with politicians and their constituents.[2] The kinds of recommendations for organizational reform following from this perspective include more competitive relations within the public sector to counter the will of public servants and the transfer of administrative duties to entities existing outside of government.

The second theoretical proposition is identified with the school of thinking typically called **managerialism**.[3] Leaning on humanist thinking, managerialism contends that the essence of any large organizational form is not the Weberian ideal-type of bureaucracy. Rather, it is an entity that posits a few basic organizational objectives while providing employees with the autonomy and motivation to achieve these objectives. Managerialism is rooted in practices found in the private sector, but it is assumed that it can be applied to the public sector on the grounds that both sectors amount to large, complex organizations. Thus, managerialism envisions an uprooting of the traditional practice of public administration with its many levels of hierarchy and close attention to established procedures and practices. In some eyes this transformation is symbolized by the substitution of the term "management" for "administration." The latter term "conjures up images of rules, regulations and lethargic decision-making processes"; the former term "implies a decisiveness, a dynamic mindset and a bias for action."[4]

In their application, these theoretical underpinnings of the new public management do not always receive equal attention. In some countries, public choice theory has been emphasized and the result has been reforms consistent with this theoretical perspective. In other countries, such as Canada, managerialism has mostly been the inspiration for efforts at reforming the public sector.

The new public management has arisen from the work of a number of theorists of organizations. The following provides a summary of some of the more important of these studies.

In Search of Excellence

In 1982, Thomas Peters and Robert Waterman published a book that would resonate with those looking to break away from the strictures of traditional organization theory and find an entirely new way to manage public organizations. *In Search of Excellence* examined a number of well-run American companies in order to determine the qualities that make for success. Though Peters and Waterman focused on the private sector, many believed their findings had implications for the public sector as well. These findings represented part of the continuing assault against the traditional bureaucratic forms in the field of organization theory. The two authors argued that the rationalism inherent in bureaucracy missed "all of that messy human stuff" that contributed to productivity and high achievement.[5] They also urged, however, managers to go beyond practices associated with the human relations school of thought and other theorists who were part of the first wave of attack against the early mechanists. The excellence school borrowed heavily from the work of McGregor, Barnard, and other humanists, but also argued that we must recognize even more clearly the "limits of rationality" and the consequent benefit of doings things that are seemingly irrational. Peters and Waterman wanted managers to think in terms of "product champions," "skunk works," the "technology of foolishness," and other phrases and practices foreign to most organizations and their members.[6]

In Search of Excellence discovered a number of attributes common to successful companies, many of which went on to influence theorists and practitioners of public management (see Table 4.1). Well-managed firms had a close relationship with their customers and had developed a near-obsession with providing high-quality services and products. The emphasis was not on cost, technology, or the internal operation of the company, but on the needs of the customer. These same firms also provided their employees with the autonomy to support innovative and entrepreneurial activities within the company.

Table 4.1	Attributes of Excellence

1. *Bias for action.* A preference for moving on ideas and avoiding endless discussion of proposals
2. *Staying close to the customer.* Garnering insights from customers and meeting their every need
3. *Autonomy and entrepreneurship.* Giving people the freedom to be innovative
4. *Productivity through people.* Recognizing that employees are the organization's most valuable asset
5. *Hands-on, value-driven.* Making clear what the organization stands for and communicating this message to all
6. *Stick to the knitting.* Staying with what you do best
7. *Simple form, lean staff.* Limiting the administrative layers and having few at the top
8. *Simultaneous loose-tight properties.* Stressing the company's central values while maximizing employee autonomy

Source: Adapted from Thomas J. Peters and Robert H. Waterman Jr. *In Search of Excellence: Lessons from America's Best Run Companies* (New York: Harper & Row, 1982).

In this type of organizational environment, "champions" naturally emerged to take the lead in the development of new and exciting products. "Productivity through people" constituted a further attribute and was in some ways at the heart of any high-performing firm. As Peters and Waterman wrote, "if you want productivity and the financial reward that goes with it, you must treat your workers as your most important asset."[7] There were other attributes, but the one that most influenced public-management theorists was the somewhat awkwardly phrased "simultaneous loose-tight properties," because it nicely summed up the philosophy of excellence. Success meant that companies needed a core set of values and practices that would be followed with almost religious fervour; these were the tight properties of an organization. However, success also meant giving employees the opportunity to achieve their potential and not to be tied down by rules. Beyond the foundational beliefs of the company, employees could do just about anything they wanted in the pursuit of satisfying the core aims of the organization.

The work of Peters and Waterman elicited a great deal of criticism. Some, like Peter Drucker, thought it "a book for juveniles" that ignored the full complexity of organizations.[8] Another criticism centred on the fact that some of the so-called excellent companies identified in the book have failed to maintain their high level of performance, suggesting that there was more to success than embracing the eight principles of excellence. Even one of the authors of *In Search of Excellence* later expressed some doubts about the value of the supporting research and admitted that the excellence principles might be insufficient for achieving good results.[9] Despite all of these criticisms, surveys revealed that *In Search of Excellence* had greatly influenced the thinking of managers in public organizations.

Well-Performing Government Organizations

In a report for Canada's Office of the Auditor General, Otto Brodtrick sought to determine the attributes of well-performing organizations in government. Brodtrick first identified a group of successful government agencies and organizations at the federal level, and then investigated the causes of their high level of performance. The intent and methods of the study parallelled those of *In Search of Excellence*, save for the fact that the focus was directly on government. The key to success, the study found, was the ability to transcend the traditional organizational structure:

> When we considered our findings, we reached an overall conclusion: the well-performing organizations have been able to move "beyond bureaucracy." One may say that they have moved from being public bureaucracies to being public enterprises, if we construe the term bureaucracy to mean red tape and unresponsiveness, and if we characterize public enterprise by innovation, responsiveness and productivity.[10]

Brodtrick determined that four overall qualities were essential to overcoming the dead hand of bureaucracy. One was the "emphasis on people" and the ability of well-performing government agencies to challenge and motivate their employees. People in these organizations were given the opportunity to act independently and to operate in an environment that stresses success and not a fear of failure. Brodtrick also found that "participative leadership"—and not authoritarian or coercive leadership—contributed to the effectiveness of government bodies. "The leaders envision an ideal organization, define purpose and goals, then articulate these and foster commitment in their people."[11] "Innovative work styles" also represented an important element of sound management in government. This meant organizations able to learn and to solve problems as a natural part of their activities, and to be self-sufficient and not dependent on orders and commands from those outside the organization. Lastly, Brodtrick determined that the well-performing public organizations "focus strongly on the needs and preferences of their clients" and "derive satisfaction from serving the client rather than the bureaucracy."[12]

In his study, Brodtrick also tried to discover the process by which organizations acquire the attributes of a well-performing organization. He found that an organization and its employees had to recognize the need for improvement in order to become successful. Sometimes a crisis would lead to the emergence of this mindset, and other times a new opportunity offered the necessary motivation for change. Interestingly, members of well-performing organizations were often unaware of putting in place any plan for pursuing improvement—they just did it. Similarly, once started, the process of improvement moved forward without real direction. People in well-performing organizations seemed to act without any conscious deliberation, a sign that in these agencies the need for improvement was instinctive and deeply entrenched.

Reinventing Government

David Osborne and Ted Gaebler's *Reinventing Government* (originally published 1992) had a large influence on thinking about public management. As the title suggests, the book had the ambitious aim of changing the way government worked. Though directed at the behaviour of the public sector in the United States, the work of Osborne and Gaebler spoke to those in other countries wishing to reform their own public services. The two authors felt that the bureaucratic form in most instances had outlived its usefulness and that a new form—a kind of entrepreneurial government—was imperative if government were to meet the challenges of the day. The public sector had to think of contracting out services, it had to offer more choice to citizens, it had to develop less controlling budget systems, and it had to eliminate many of its rules and procedures. In short, government had to reinvent itself.

In their book, Osborne and Gaebler made their argument about the need for change through a series of case studies illustrating the wisdom of their approach. One case study examined an aspect of reinventing government that related to the provision of a more competitive environment in the public sector. A few years ago, the city of Phoenix believed it could save money by requiring its garbage collection department to compete with private collectors over the right to pick up the city's refuse. In the first couple of years, the department lost out to the private interests, who were able to put forward more attractive bids. However, eventually the department regained its responsibility for garbage collection through the introduction of new and more efficient practices and equipment. The result of the competitive process was that the city of Phoenix was able to provide better garbage collection services at a lower cost. For the authors of *Reinventing Government*, this was just one instance of how entrepreneurial government overcame the lethargy of traditional bureaucratic practices.

As with the other authors considered so far in this chapter, Osborne and Gaebler reduced their thinking to a set of principles or prescriptions, which included:

- Conceive government as largely responsible for providing overall direction and rely on innovative partnerships with the private and nonprofit sectors to carry out public programs and services.
- Encourage competition among government agencies and between public and private suppliers of services in order to take advantage of the benefits available in any competitive situation (lower cost and higher quality).
- Measure the performance of government agencies and concentrate on the outcomes of government action rather than the actions or inputs of government.
- See recipients of government services as customers and focus on the provision of quality services through the availability of choice.

Chapter 4 / Public Administration and Organization Theory

- When feasible, decentralize agency operations and embrace a participatory form of management.
- Earn revenues wherever possible, and use mission statements—to direct and drive the organization.[13]

At first glance, reinventing government appeared to mean nothing more than government adopting the practices of business. But Osborne and Gaebler knew that important differences separated the public and private sectors; government could not be "run like a business." However, it was possible for government to be more entrepreneurial without becoming a business. The problem, for the two authors, was not government, but the fact that we had the *wrong kind of government.*[14] The principles of *Reinventing Government* would serve to fix this problem. Notwithstanding this distinction between the reinvented public sector and the private sector, the two authors still emphasized the use of competition and market-based thinking in structuring organizational arrangements for government. As with other proponents of the new public management, they touted the advantages of managerialism and wanted to make sure that it was appreciated that we could learn from the private sector.

At the time of the publication of *Reinventing Government*, Michael Barzelay published a study called *Breaking Through Bureaucracy* that recommended government become a "customer-driven service organization."[15] The implications of this recommendation mirrored many of those associated with entrepreneurial government: visualize the citizen as customer, focus on results or outcomes, create a competitive environment, provide choice, and empower employees at the street level.

Robert Denhardt and the Pursuit of Significance

As with other proponents of a different method of organizing the public sector, Robert Denhardt saw the need to move away from the bureaucratic form and toward a new way of managing. He also had a list of qualities that made up the new way, some of which were similar or even identical to those in comparable lists seeking to capture the essence of the new public management. Empowerment and shared leadership and serving the public were two such qualities. But on the basis of his research of organizational change in Canada, Great Britain, Australia, and the United States, Denhardt claimed that public servants were engaged in a "pursuit of significance" in which they strive to have an impact in their work.[16] The primacy of private interest, which can be found in some of the other works on new public management (e.g., competition), is replaced by the preeminence of meaning and significance. Thus, Denhardt emphasized in his work the importance of "a commitment to values," which meant that the mission statement and the beliefs contained in the statement became vital to the organization. Similarly, Denhardt included in his list "a dedication to public service." This quality also revealed a public servant who goes beyond competition and innovation and toward a commitment to the special place and importance of the public service in a democratic society.[17]

Denhardt appreciated that reference to a commitment to values or a dedication to the public service may appear soft compared to some of the other models and theories of new public management. Osborne and Gaebler's dashing entrepreneurial manager may seem more appropriate—and certainly more attractive—than a public servant who merely subscribes to values. But Denhardt belongs in the group of theories of new public management, because he emphasized an important part of this new approach. Recently, Denhardt authored (with his wife) a book that builds upon his earlier ideas and puts forward the model of the "New Public Service."[18] This model emphasizes the importance of respecting people, servicing the citizenry, and constructing the public interest through deliberations between government and the community. With this book, Denhardt sees himself explicitly rejecting most of the core elements of the new public management and providing a new perspective on public organizations. At the end of this chapter, we too shall consider the future of the new public management and whether a new paradigm in organization theory is in the making.

The New Public Organization

Kenneth Kernaghan, Brian Marson, and Sandford Borins recently proposed a new structural model for government called the "new public organization."[19] The three authors are reluctant—unlike some of the other authors considered in this chapter—to see their proposal as a new paradigm in thinking about public management or as being appropriate to all government agencies. They understand that no "magic pill" exists for addressing the complexities and problems of the public sector.[20] Nevertheless, they are eager to move government away from the bureaucratic form and toward something quite different. Table 4.2 (on page 58) outlines their thinking on the shift and compares the qualities of the bureaucratic organization with those of the new public organization or **post-bureaucratic organization**.

As the table shows, the bureaucratic structure looks first to its own needs, whereas the new public organization is citizen-oriented. Also, performance and accountability in bureaucracy are examined in light of how well the worker complies with the rules and follows the stipulated processes, but the value of the employee in the new public organization is measured according to results achieved. Bureaucracy is a risk-averse entity, unwilling to take chances and fearful of mistakes, while the new public organization knows that beneficial change and innovative requires taking chances. To make another comparison, an agency with a bureaucratic structure typically holds a monopoly over delivery of its services; the post-bureaucratic agency operates in a competitive environment with the private sector. As may be noted, the post-bureaucratic organization reflects the two theoretical propositions underlying the new public management. Managerialism can be seen in the advocacy of decentralized structures, the participative leadership, and the people-centred orientation; the emphasis on results, competition, and the accumulation of revenue all follow from the public choice perspective.

As with many of the other scholars writing about developments in organizational theory, Kernaghan and his colleagues use examples or cases to make clearer their particular model. The Canadian Passport Office was once an operating division within a traditional department at the federal level in Canada. But in 1990 it was given a greater degree of autonomy and allowed to function almost like a private commercial operation. With this newfound freedom, the office became more efficient and better attuned to the needs of those wishing to use its services. It speeded up processing of passport applications, empowered its employees with additional training, and collaborated with Canada Post to make it easier for citizens to submit their applications and to receive express delivery of their passports. With these developments, the Passport Office had become a post-bureaucratic organization. Another case involves Prince Edward Island's Department of Agriculture and Forestry. In the 1990s, the department set out six major goals, attached to each of which was a performance measure and methods for measuring movement toward meeting the goal. This results-oriented approach, an essential quality of the post-bureaucratic organization, led to higher levels of both client and staff satisfaction while contributing to the preservation of the cost-effectiveness of the organization.

The authors of *The New Public Organization* stress the benefits of their organizational approach, but they are careful to concede that the new public organization form is not for all public service agencies. Bodies that rely on rules for good performance—immigration departments, for instance—may be well advised to stay with the traditional bureaucratic form. More generally, the nature of the organization and the duties it

Table 4.2	From Bureaucratic to Post-bureaucratic Organization

CHARACTERISTICS OF BUREAUCRATIC ORGANIZATION	CHARACTERISTICS OF POST–BUREAUCRATIC ORGANIZATION
POLICY AND MANAGEMENT CULTURE	
Organization-Centred	**Citizen-Centred**
Emphasis on needs of the organization itself	Quality service to citizens (and clients/stakeholders)
Position Power	**Participation Leadership**
Control, command, and compliance	Shared values and participative decision making
Rule-Centred	**People-Centred**
Rules, procedures, and constraints	An empowering and caring milieu for employees
Independent Action	**Collective Action**
Little consultation, cooperation, or coordination	Consultation, cooperation, and coordination
Status Quo–Oriented	**Change-Oriented**
Avoiding risks and mistakes	Innovation, risk-taking, and continuous improvement
Process-Oriented	**Results-Oriented**
Accountability of process	Accountability for results
STRUCTURE	
Centralized	**Decentralized**
Hierarchy and central controls	Decentralization of authority and control
Departmental Form	**Non-departmental Form**
Most programs delivered by operation departments	Programs delivered by wide variety of mechanisms
MARKET ORIENTATION	
Budget-Driven	**Revenue-Driven**
Programs financed largely from appropriations	Programs financed as far as possible on cost-recovery basis
Monopolistic	**Competitive**
Government has monopoly on program delivery	Competition with private sector program delivery

Source: Kenneth Kernaghan, Brian Marson, and Sandford Borins, *The Public Organization* (Toronto: Institute of Public Adminstration of Canada, 2000), 3.

carries out will determine whether the agency in question can make the transition. Nevertheless, the forces of globalization, technology, financial constraints, and a political culture that is less deferential to government are pushing more and more government agencies toward the post-bureaucratic form. Even those departments whose functions seemingly call for the traditional bureaucratic form—for example, departments with the duty of preserving the security of the nation—may benefit from reforms along the lines found in the new public organization.

Elements of NPM

Any attempt to point to the essential elements of the new public management can be frustrating. The frustration emerges in part from the fact that no two lists of qualities are the same, which has led some to argue that the new public management is similar to an "empty canvas" on which we can paint anything we wish.[21] The frustration is also a product of the fact that elements of this new perspective may appear incompatible or even contradictory. It may seem strange that managers are given a large amount of flexibility while the government department requires its employees to pay careful respect to closely held organizational values and practices. It might even be claimed that new public management fails to represent anything really new, that it simply borrows from more traditional theories of organizational humanism and participatory management. Despite all these concerns, the preceding survey of texts and studies on new managerial behaviour suggests that it is possible to give a listing of the core qualities and that such an exercise is worthy of some consideration.[22]

1. **Autonomy and managerial flexibility.** A key element of the new public management is the belief that the modern public organization requires fewer rules and more autonomy and flexibility. The public servant of today is highly educated and capable of innovative actions—rules thus serve only to limit unnecessarily appointed officials and deny society important gains in productivity. It is also assumed that in some cases the appointed official is motivated to offer the best service possible; the modern civil servant, as Denhardt claims, desperately wishes to be significant and acts accordingly. The self-seeking public servant of public choice theory still exists, but he or she must make room for his more publicly minded counterpart. More generally, people simply work better in a setting of limited controls.

2. **Performance measurement.** Another important quality of the new public management is the insistence that the performance of public servants be measured. The traditional evaluative approach has been to determine whether public officials faithfully carried out their duties and responsibilities. In other words, the focus has been on processes. But the new public management shifts attention away from these processes toward the actual impact of bureaucratic behaviour on society. Outcomes now become central to the evaluative exercise, because we believe that this gives a better indication of productivity and effectiveness. The fact that the new public management promises greater flexibility also means that there are fewer rules upon which to assess performance. A new way of gauging the contributions of employees has to be found, and that way is performance management.

3. **Citizen-centred delivery of services.** All governments profess to serve the nation's citizenry, but the new public management puts special emphasis on ensuring that the quality of services to taxpayers is high. To reinforce this notion, some proponents of new public management use the term "client" or "customer" in the belief that the term "citizen" insufficiently conveys the commitment of the new public management to providing high-quality programs and policies. This particular element also means that the services in question are services that the electorate actually wants, so citizens may participate in the determination of the most appropriate services.

4. **Openness to competition.** The new public management contends that public agencies should be receptive to competitive arrangements both within government and between the public and private sectors. Too often government agencies fail

because of monopolistic conditions that inhibit innovation and encourage the inefficient supply of public services. For some proponents of the new view of public management, the struggling school systems of Western democracies with their neighbourhood schools symbolize the absence of choice in government programs and the need to find more competitive arrangements. An openness to competition implies as well that government bodies may realize responsibility for some public services should be transferred to the private sector.

5. **Shared values.** The effect of many aspects of the new public management is to decentralize operations and to provide public servants with a great deal of discretion. The focus on shared values tries to balance this effect and provide overall direction for employees of a public agency. The shared values, if properly formulated, also motivate organizational members and instil in them a sense of the organization's mission.

6. **Focus on managing.** Implicit in many discussions of the new public management (and explicit in some) is the belief that public servants should concentrate on managing and leave policy-making to elected officials. The desired arrangement in the new public management is a clear division between politics and administration. Such an arrangement pushes public servants to the area in which they hold considerable expertise and also ensures that elected officials determine the priorities of government. As in the private sector, the head executive issues the orders and the managers carry them out.

Criticisms of NPM

The new public management has many supporters who believe that this school of thought holds the key to understanding public organizations. We have only to see the work completed on the topic to appreciate this point. However, this theory of organizations has its detractors, who believe that many of the aforementioned elements of the new public management are unable to survive critical scrutiny.

Some who have studied NPM claim that greater managerial autonomy and flexibility increases the chances of a loss of accountability. Ministers, who are ultimately responsible for the actions of government, might now find it difficult to oversee the actions of their appointed subordinates. Private sector leaders may be able to suffer a decline in accountability, but such is not the case for senior political officials. Political officials are also reluctant to leave administration solely to the appointed officials, because ministers simply like to be in direct contact with voters, and also wish to be seen to be at the forefront of some important accomplishments.[23] Eventually, the combination of a sense of loss of accountability and a desire to be involved in administration may lead political leaders to develop new rules and requirements. The new public management thus succeeds only in returning us to the typical bureaucratic form.

One of the most criticized aspects of NPM is the claim that performance measurement (and the companion concept of **performance management**) is and should be central to the operation of the modern public organization. Such a stance may misinterpret the nature of most public services and the implications of this fact for the measurement of performance. As Carroll and Dewar say, "governments tend to be left with the messy, complex, and difficult jobs—and the messy, complex, and difficult results are harder to define and measure."[24] Also, the purposes of a government program or service are often multifaceted, so it is sometimes difficult to interpret the meaning or importance of some performance scores. A school program may do well on standardized tests, but parents may be more interested in safety or accessibility.[25] Performance measurement, critics say, also pays insufficient attention to the nature of the government environment. Because of political considerations, only a small amount of useful information may be made available, and that information may be ignored by those seeking to establish

Box 4.1   Savoie Versus Borins

The best debate on the new public management so far has involved two prominent Canadian scholars, Donald Savoie and Sandford Borins. The two combatants pulled few punches. Savoie claimed that NPM constituted a "flawed concept" in its attempt to apply business principles and practices to government. For Savoie, the private and public sectors were similar only in insignificant ways. Borins countered that Savoie misunderstood the new public management and referred to an earlier work of Savoie's that revealed a more sympathetic appreciation of this perspective. Undeterred, Savoie responded that Borins supplied no real arguments for his position and was no better than a preacher trying to sell some "old time religion." Having the last word in the debate (so far), Borins pointed to all those already engaged in the managerial revolution inspired by NPM.

Source: Donald Savoie, "What Is Wrong with the New Public Management?"; Sandford Borins, "The New Public Management Is Here to Stay"; Donald Savoie, "Just Another Voice from the Pulpit"; and Sandford Borins, "A Last Word." All from *Canadian Public Administration* 38(1) (Spring 1995).

greater accountability and efficiency—and to do some political damage. Good explains the dynamics of this problem in the Canadian context:

> It seems that when it comes to program performance information for the purposes of accountability, public servants don't publish for fear of embarrassing their ministers, and Parliamentary Committees don't use what is published because it cannot embarrass ministers. Little wonder progress has been slow and reliable information limited. All this suggests some important limits to new public management.[26]

The focus on citizen input, another key element of the new public management, threatens to reduce members of the population to self-interested seekers of government services. Traditionally, the citizenry in a democracy has responsibilities that contribute to the community as a whole. Unlike the consumer in the marketplace, the democratic citizen must think of things other than the satisfaction of personal preferences. The citizen accepts that some sacrifices may have to be made to ensure equitable access to necessary public services and that some effort has to be made to participate in the political process. Some worry that NPM will make citizens less willing to make these sacrifices and in the end will turn government into a "supermarket state."[27] The plea for greater competitiveness within government and a greater openness to privatizing public services has also produced concerns. For instance, the belief that many public services ought to be shifted to the private sector may give rise to morale problems in the public service, because it suggests that "public service has no intrinsic value."[28] People decide to work in government, not to clean up after the market, but rather to make a contribution to the welfare of the nation.

As with any theory, the new public management has weaknesses that deserve close attention. Ironically, it seems this theory may be fatally flawed, because it takes insufficient notice of government and its highly political environment. Perhaps NPM is trying to take the politics out of public administration, an attempt that has been made before without much success.[29] Nonetheless, the theory has offered another perspective on the operation of organizations, and has contributed to the quest for better administration and management in the public sector.

Managerial Reform in Canada

NPM has affected thinking on public service reform in all of the Anglo-American democracies. However, the degree of acceptance of the tenets of the new public management and overall enthusiasm for this approach has differed across these countries.

Canada's approach has been likened to that of a diner who prefers only to sample a buffet without making a full meal of any one of the offerings.[30] Over the years, the federal government has put forward initiatives clearly inspired by one aspect or another of the new perspective. In the 1980s, it introduced a managerial initiative (known as Increased Ministerial Authority and Accountability) that made available increased autonomy for individual departments in return for agreeing to explicit performance measures and reviews, and a few years later it undertook an effort (Public Service 2000) directed at improving services and reducing the reach of agencies whose job entailed coordinating and controlling line departments. The federal government also privatized some major Crown corporations—CN and Petro-Canada, for example—and created special bodies that would be granted a greater amount of flexibility in order to meet newly-agreed-upon performance targets. It also endeavoured to experiment with new administrative forms that came to be known as "alternative service delivery mechanisms." In the 1990s, the federal government launched two major initiatives (Program Review and La Relève), in a further attempt to institute measures associated with NPM. The former mostly amounted to an attempt to increase efficiency through expenditure reductions, while the latter sought to deal with a growing malaise in the federal public service. At the provincial level, the new public management received basically the same reception, though some provinces (Ontario and Alberta) proved to be more aggressive in pushing public service reform.

These actions revealed a country that preferred a "'pragmatic' and 'experimental'" perspective on public service reform.[31] Some aspects of the new public management could be seen in the aforementioned efforts of the Canadian government at public service reform. The federal government clearly wished to provide for greater managerial autonomy, and there was a concern for increasing the quality of services available to citizens. The privatizations also meant that the federal government agreed with the claim that some public services might safely be transferred to the private sector.

However, the intensity and reach of these efforts paled in comparison with that of other countries involved in such reform. Some countries, for example, required their agencies to engage in competitions for contracts to offer services. In Canada, contracting-out took place, but not to the same extent as in these other places. Similarly, in other nations the majority of public sector entities found themselves in a new organizational arrangement that emphasized autonomy and performance measurement; Canada applied this practice in only a moderate manner. A participant in the Canadian exercises states, correctly, that Canada's approach was "less clearly articulated and less discernable than the new public management models of the United Kingdom, New Zealand, and Australia."[32] In 1998, the head of the federal public service made this clear, listing the aspects of the Canadian model for reform:

1. Unlike some other models of the new public management, the Canadian model rejected NPM's implicit belief that good government was less government. Government and its institutions played an important role in the provision of services and were "essential to a well-performing society."
2. The Canadian model agreed to the need for government to enter into alliances with other actors in society—in other words, to embrace new roles—and to think more closely about the role of government in the future.
3. The Canadian model affirmed that an effective public service needed both an effective policy capacity and a modernized way of delivering services. The latter part of this affirmation acknowledged the claim of the new public management that new organizational forms had to be tried. It also pointed up a weakness in NPM—its failure to address the policy formulation capacities of government—and made it clear that Canada would not make this mistake.

4. The Canadian model acknowledged the significance of a "well-performing, professional nonpartisan public service." With this, the federal government wanted to make obvious the centrality of the public service in any reform efforts and in the delivery of services to Canadians. This was part of the pre-NPM environment and would remain part of any new environment.

5. The Canadian model counted on "leadership from both politicians and bureaucrats." Elected officials were essential to finding the appropriate role for government in a changing world, and appointed officials were "relied upon to put bold and creative ideas before ministers." NPM was sometimes interpreted to mean that managers would be limited to managing, but the Canadian model indicated that the public service would be expected to provide some leadership with respect to policy and as well to work closely with ministers.[33]

The Canadian approach to public service reform indicated a need to change and to adopt aspects of the new public management. It also represented, however, an approach that wanted to maintain qualities and practices that had served Canada well in the past.

The Future

For some, the future of organization theory in relation to government lies in adopting the reform ideas contained in the various scholarly efforts associated with the new public management and comparable ideas or conceptions. As an example, the proponents of the new public organization lay out a process for repositioning an agency away from the bureaucratic form and toward the post-bureaucratic form. Figure 4.1 shows that the process begins with the question of where the organization is at present in terms of its structure and orientation. If the answer is that the agency is too near to the bureaucratic model, the next question asks whether it wants to move toward the post-bureaucratic model. An affirmative answer leads to a third question: How do we get to the new model? A response to this basically comprises the elements that make up the new public organization. Finally, the process addresses the issue of how to make the transition happen, and this revolves largely around the provision of leadership in all parts of the organization and the embrace of certain elements tied to the post-bureaucratic model.

Another perspective on the future is that theory in public administration will move beyond the new public management. It is argued that NPM put forward an intriguing theory or model of organizations in the public sector and helped produce some positive

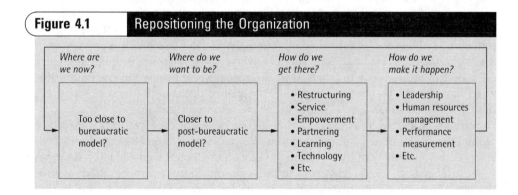

Figure 4.1 Repositioning the Organization

Where are we now?	Where do we want to be?	How do we get there?	How do we make it happen?
Too close to bureaucratic model?	Closer to post-bureaucratic model?	• Restructuring • Service • Empowerment • Partnering • Learning • Technology • Etc.	• Leadership • Human resources management • Performance measurement • Etc.

Source: Kenneth Kernaghan, Brian Marson, and Sandford Borins, *The New Public Organization* (Toronto: Institute of Public Administration of Canada, 2000), 267.

outcomes in government (e.g., better management of public finances). However, it also failed to appreciate the true complexity of public administration, and its prescriptions for action led to shortcomings. Thus, a new "wave" in public management theory and reform must do a better job of appreciating public administration and addressing the limitations and weaknesses of the new public management.[34] One aspect of the new wave is a greater appreciation of the need for a strong policy capacity in government. The public management paradigm of the past two decades concentrated heavily on managing government and slighted the policy-making responsibilities of government. By policy-making, we mean the ability of elected and appointed officials together to address the difficult issues—especially the so-called "wicked" or seemingly unsolvable problems—that face any society.[35] Before we can manage the solutions, we first have to formulate them. Another aspect of the new wave might be an emphasis on the importance of the public service itself so that it can successfully carry out its policy and managerial duties. In the eyes of some proponents of NPM, the public service represented the evils of bureaucracy and had to be severely limited or even dismantled in many areas. The new wave sees the matter differently, and makes the restoration of the public sector as an entity central to its purposes. This requires giving public servants "exciting and meaningful work" in which they possess "the responsibilities and opportunities to make a difference."[36]

A further perspective is that organization theory in relation to government will become less ambitious or grandiose. The new public management represents an attempt to build a model that can be applied to any organizational structure anywhere in the developed world. But this may be impossible for two related reasons. One is that the world of organizations is complex. Grandiose theories such as NPM may be "too crude for the fine-grained distinctions between different sorts and themes of managerialism."[37] What might emerge instead are "middle-range theories" that seek to explain and understand certain types or aspects of organizations—and nothing more.[38] One consequence of this perspective for public management reform would be a greater reluctance to embrace untested recommendations for change. Instead, managers would begin with a listing and acceptance of the *customary requirements of administrative systems.* These include the rules affecting staffing, financial accounting, health and safety standards, record keeping, and other similar matters. Then, they would list the "surreal" or clearly unworkable requirements and endeavour to limit their applicability until such time as they have proven their value through careful examination and review.[39]

The second reason for a more restrained approach to theory is the recognition of the differing cultures and belief systems of nations. Organizations are complex, but so are countries. Theories premised on market-based mechanisms may be more applicable to places where the private sector is held in high regard, but less so in locations that see value in a mixed economy of public and private sector initiatives. This point was revealed in the earlier discussion of the varied reception given to the new public management in the Anglo-American democracies. In countries where government was held in low esteem, NPM initiatives flourished; in others, such as Canada, where people still saw much value in government, the theory fared less well. Fine-grained distinctions are to be found not only in differential managerial arrangements, but also in the nations of the world.

A final perspective to consider is that theorizing about organizations will revolve around the impact of new information technologies. In many minds, NPM already considers IT, because many of its core elements rely on the Internet, email, and other types of technology (e.g., kiosks and email technology contribute to a more citizen-centred delivery of services).[40] But some believe that IT leads away from NPM to a new kind of organizational reality. In this new guise, public organizations become reintegrated (and less decentralized) and better adapted to meet the needs of citizens; and through digitization, they leave behind the world of "paper-based administrative processes."[41]

Though all three of these predicted developments speak to a different aspect of an organization's operation, combined they move toward a situation in which government transforms into a kind of "virtual state."[42] If this kind of theorizing seems appropriate only for readers of science fiction, consider the words of four respected researchers in public administration:

> Instead of electronic channels being seen as supplementary to conventional administrative and business processes, they become genuinely transformative, moving from a situation where the agency "*becomes* its Web site," as a senior official in the Australian Tax Office described this process to us.[43]

The many obstacles facing the implementation of IT—the cost, concerns about privacy, and the natural resistance of bureaucracies to change—mean we are most unlikely to see anything in the near future similar to government organizations existing only electronically.[44] Even the above-mentioned researchers warn against "e-government utopias"[45] and urge us to consider the plausible—and less radical—effects of information technology. Still, it is probably true that not many imagined that one day people would be able to renew car licences at shopping malls or submit their tax returns with the touch of a key. In other words, we would be wise not to underestimate the potential of technology and its impact on public administration.

Conclusion

In this chapter and the preceding two, we have tried to acquire an understanding of the various attempts to develop sound organization theories. The hope might have been that one perspective would clearly emerge as the best, but it is clear that all contribute to our endeavour to accurately describe and explain the operation of organizations. As we move to a consideration of the structures and processes of Canadian public administration in the following chapters, we should keep in mind the insights of Weber, the organizational humanists, and the proponents of the new public management who have tried to present a better theoretical appreciation of organizations.

Notes

1. Peter Aucoin, *The New Public Management: Canada in Comparative Perspective* (Montreal: IRPP, 1995), 31.

2. *Agency Theory* or *Principal-Agent Theory* is another perspective that captures the basic thrust of public choice theory. See Janet V. Denhardt and Robert B. Denhardt, *The New Public Service: Serving, Not Steering* (Armonk, N.Y.: M.E. Sharpe, 2003), 20–21.

3. Aucoin, *The New Public Management*, 8.

4. Donald Savoie, "What Is Wrong with the New Public Management?" *Canadian Public Administration* 38(1) (spring 1995): 113.

5. Thomas J. Peters and Robert H. Waterman, Jr., *In Search of Excellence: Lessons from America's Best-Run Companies* (New York: Harper & Row Publishers, 1982), 31.

6. Ibid., 102, 106–07.

7. Ibid., 238.

8. Drucker quoted in Lisa A. Mainiero and Cheryl L. Tromley, *Developing Managerial Skills in Organizational Behavior: Exercises, Cases and Readings* (Englewood Cliffs, N.J.: Prentice-Hall, 1989), 42.

9. Tom Peters, "Tom Peters's True Confessions," *Fast Company*, 53 (December 2001), 78.

10. Office of the Auditor General of Canada, *Annual Report* (Ottawa: Supply and Services Canada, 1988), ch. 4, "Well-Performing Organizations," section 4.41. Available at www.oag-bvg.gc.ca/domino/reports.nsf/html/8804ce.html. Accessed July 4, 2006.

11. Ibid., section 4.77.

12. Ibid., section 4.85.

13. David Osborne and Ted Gaebler, *Reinventing Government: How the Entrepreneurial Spirit Is Transforming the Public Sector* (London: Penguin, 1993).

14. Ibid., 20, 23. (Emphasis in original.)

15. Michael Barzelay, with the collaboration of Babak J. Armajani, *Breaking Through Bureaucracy: A New Vision for Managing in Government* (Berkeley: University of California Press, 1992), 8.

16. Robert B. Denhardt, *The Pursuit of Significance: Strategies for Managerial Success in Public Organizations* (Belmont, Calif.: Wadsworth Publishing Company, 1993).

17. Ibid., ch. 1.

18. Denhardt and Denhardt, *The New Public Service: Serving, Not Steering*.

19. Kenneth Kernaghan, Brian Marson, and Sandford Borins, *The New Public Organization* (Toronto: Institute of Public Administration of Canada, 2000).

20. Ibid., 4.

21. Andrew Stark, "What Is the New Public Management?" *Journal of Public Administration Research and Theory* 12(1) (January 2002): 1.

22. There have been many attempts to list the elements of NPM. See, for example, Christopher Hood, "A Public Management for All Seasons?" *Public Administration* 69 (spring 1991): 3–19.

23. David A. Good, *The Politics of Public Management: The HRDC Audit of Grants and Contributions* (Toronto: Institute of Public Administration of Canada and the University of Toronto Press, 2003), 198.

24. Barbara Wake Carroll and David I. Dewar, "Performance Management: Panacea or Fools' Gold?" in Christopher Dunn, ed., *The Handbook of Canadian Public Administration* (Toronto: Oxford University Press, 2002), 417.

25. Christopher Pollitt, "How Do We Know How Good Public Services Are?" in B. Guy Peters and Donald J. Savoie, eds., *Governance in the Twenty-First Century: Revitalizing the Public Service* (Montreal & Kingston: McGill-Queen's University Press, 2000).

26. Good, *The Politics of Public Management*, 175.

27. Joel D. Aberbach and Tom Christensen, "Citizens and Consumers: An NPM Dilemma," *Public Management Review* 7(2) (2005): 238.

28. Savoie, "What Is Wrong with the New Public Management?" 118.

29. See Donald Savoie, *Thatcher, Reagan, Mulroney: In Search of a New Bureaucracy*. (Toronto: University of Toronto Press, 1994).

30. Sandford Borins quoted in Peter Aucoin, "Beyond the 'New' in Public Administration Reform in Canada: Catching the Next Wave?" in Dunn, ed., *Handbook of Canadian Public Administration*, 37.

31. Ibid., 38.

32. Good, *The Politics of Public Management*, 154.

33. Jocelyne Bourgon, *Fifth Annual Report to the Prime Minister on the Public Service of Canada* (Ottawa: Privy Council Office, 1998). March 31, 1998. Available at www.pco-bcp.gc.ca/default.asp?Page=Publications&Language=E&doc=5rept97/cover_e.htm. Retrieved July 4, 2006.

34. Aucoin, "Beyond the 'New' in Public Management Reform in Canada."

35. Ibid., 44.

36. Words of a former clerk of the PCO, quoted in ibid., 49.

37. C. Hood, "Public Management, New," in *International Encyclopaedia of Social and Behavioral Science* (Oxford: Elsevier, 2001), 12555.

38. For more on the notion of middle-range theories, see Robert Merton, *Social Theory and Social Structure*, enlarged ed. (New York: The Free Press, 1968), ch. II.

39. Ian D. Clark and Harry Swain, "Distinguishing the Real from the Surreal in Management Reform: Suggestions for Beleaguered Administrators in the Government of Canada," *Canadian Public Administration* 48(4) (winter 2005): 456–57. (Emphasis in original.)

40. Kernaghan, Marson, and Borins, *The New Public Organization*, ch. 10.

41. Patrick Dunleavy, Helen Margetts, Simon Bastow, and Jane Tinkler, "New Public Management Is Dead—Long Live Digital-Era Governance," *Journal of Public Administration Research and Theory* 16: 480, 486.

42. For a discussion of the notion of a virtual state, see Jane E. Fountain, *Building the Virtual State: Information Technology and Institutional Change* (Washington, D.C.: The Brookings Institution, 2001).

43. Dunleavy et al., "New Public Management Is Dead," 480.

44. For more on the obstacles, see Darrell M. West, *Digital Government: Technology and Public Sector Performance* (Princeton, N.J.: Princeton University Press, 2005), ch. 2 and Kenneth Kernaghan and Justin Gunraj, "Integrating Information Technology into Public Administration: Conceptual and Practical Considerations," *Canadian Public Administration* 47(4): 525–46.

45. Dunleavy et al., "New Public Management Is Dead," 486.

Delivering
Government Services

5

Government Departments and Central Agencies

Agriculture and Agri-Food Canada, the Privy Council Office, National Transportation Agency, Department of Public Safety and Emergency Preparedness, and the Millennium Scholarship Foundation represent only a handful of the many administrative bodies at the federal level in Canada. As we shall see, government organizations appear to come in a bewildering array of different names and organizational structures. Some of the bodies are directly controlled by a minister, others are deliberately kept at arm's length so that there is limited ministerial control, and still others almost seem beyond any kind of control. This huge variety of organizations follows from the diverse functions and duties of government. The problems and challenges facing a society require governments to spend money, regulate behaviour, acquire ownership of companies, and exhort people to act in a particular manner. All of these functions and more require differing kinds of government instruments to achieve the most effective delivery of programs and services.

Historically, government services have been delivered through departments, Crown corporations, and independent regulatory agencies, all of which come in many different shapes and forms. But in the last few years there has been an explosion in the number of different delivery mechanisms that governments employ. This innovation in service-delivery mechanisms has been a response to both financial constraints and citizen demands for improved service delivery. In some cases, the innovation has resulted in government's adopting new structures that are variations in the traditional delivery forms. In other cases, governments have employed new means of service delivery, such as partnerships with nongovernmental organizations to share the cost and responsibility for delivering services.

The purpose of this Part is to consider the organizational mechanisms that governments use to deliver public services, and this chapter considers the most traditional instrument for delivering services, the department. It begins with a discussion of the legal foundations of departments, which requires an examination of interactions between departments, the legislature, and the political executive or cabinet. The chapter then discusses various aspects of the functioning of departments and finishes with a consideration of arguably the most powerful departmental forms—the central agencies.

The Legislature, the Executive, and Departments

It is customary to speak of three branches of government—legislative, executive, and judicial. The judicial branch, which consists of the law courts and related institutions, is not discussed in this chapter, but considered in detail later. In Canada, the legislative branch of the federal government consists of the Queen and two houses or chambers—the House of Commons and the Senate. As illustrated in Figure 5.1, the executive branch is technically headed by the Queen, represented in Canada by the **governor general** and the **lieutenant governors** of the provinces. In practice, neither the Queen nor any of her vice-regal representatives ever acts except on the advice of the government of the day as embodied in the prime minister (or provincial premier) and the cabinet. This means that the responsibilities of the executive branch are carried out collectively by cabinet or what is commonly called "the government." All public servants act under the direction and control of the cabinet and are included, therefore, as part of the executive branch. Thus, in this book, the practical, working definition of the executive is the cabinet and the public service.

One sometimes hears that something is done by the **Governor General in Council** or the **Lieutenant Governor in Council**. This means that the governor general or the lieutenant governor has taken some legal action after consultation with the cabinet. It actually means that the cabinet has taken some action; the governor general's or lieutenant governor's signature is a formality.

The congressional system of government in the United States is characterized by a balance of powers between the three branches so that no one branch has authority over any other. In parliamentary systems, such as Canada's, it is an important principle that the executive branch is accountable to the legislative branch (i.e., the branch most directly responsible to the general public). Figure 5.1 shows that the two branches are in fact joined, because cabinet ministers are almost invariably members of the legislative branch. This institutional arrangement helps the legislature to hold the executive accountable for its actions. However, it also offers an opportunity for the executive to control the legislature through the use of party discipline, a possibility that inevitably takes place and which lessens of influence of the legislative branch.

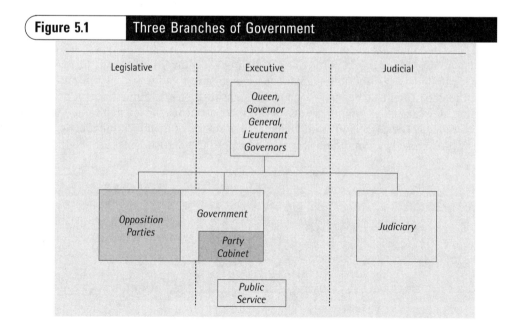

Figure 5.1   Three Branches of Government

Figure 5.2 Basic Structure of Department

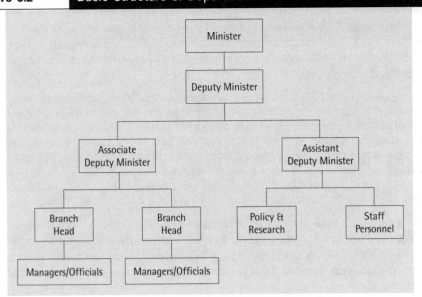

Definition of a Department

It is difficult to establish a precise, working definition of an **operating department**. Legal definitions can be found in pieces of government legislation, but these legislative definitions differ somewhat and they fail to capture the essence of a department, because their purpose is to determine which organizations will be subject to a particular regime of financial or personnel administration. The definition used in this book is that of J.E. Hodgetts, who states that a "department is an administrative unit comprising one or more organizational components over which a minister has direct ministerial management and control."[1] The definition emphasizes—and reminds us—that bureaucratic structures in government are mainly in the business of administering services, and as Figure 5.2 shows it also notes that departments have a number of branches or units that serve to carry out their responsibilities. The definition also highlights a characteristic that distinguishes departments from other delivery forms or mechanisms in government, namely that the minister directly controls and manages operations. The positioning of the minister in Figure 5.2 and the straight line connecting the minister to the department signify this quality of departments. It is a constitutional convention that the minister should very closely supervise the actions of an operating department. This differs from the minister's relationship with regulatory agencies and Crown corporations, in which there are certain understood limits on the minister's direct involvement in the specifics of their day-to-day management.

Classification Systems for Departments

There are so many departments with so many special responsibilities that a number of writers have tried to facilitate understanding of their roles by grouping them in some way. One classification system is based on the general policy fields addressed, or functions carried out by the department, such as "public works, communications, and transportation" and "conservation, development, and promotion of physical resources."[2] Another system adopts a more parsimonious approach and identifies three types of departments by considering the relative power of departments as determined by size, budget, responsibility for coordination, and knowledge or research capability. The three types are horizontal policy coordinative, horizontal administrative coordinative, and vertical constituency.[3] An application of the classification scheme to the present array of departments of the federal government results in the groupings shown in Table 5.1. Of the three types, the "horizontal policy coordinative" departments tend to be the most influential. Doern explains:

> They have inherent high policy influence because of the formal authority they possess and because they afford their occupants the highest number of strategic opportunities to intervene in almost any policy issue if the occupant wishes. They each deal respectively with the traditionally most basic horizontal or crosscutting dimensions of government policy, namely overall political leadership and strategy, foreign policy and the foreign implications of domestic policy fields, aggregate economic and fiscal policy, the basic legal and judicial concepts and values of the state, and the overall management of government spending programmes.[4]

These departments tend to be small in terms of number of employees and size of budget, but very strong in terms of responsibility for coordination and knowledge or research capability. Because of this responsibility for coordination across the activities of other departments, some of them are also called central agencies, as will be discussed later in this chapter.

The "horizontal administrative coordinative" departments are usually felt to be the least influential, in that they are assumed to be the "nuts and bolts" departments that provide the wherewithal for other departments to operate. The Department of Public Works and Government Services, for instance, acts to purchase goods and services for

Table 5.1	Classification of Federal Government Departments	
HORIZONTAL POLICY COORDINATIVE	**VERTICAL CONSTITUENCY**	
Finance	Agriculture and Agri-Food	
Justice	Canadian Heritage	
Privy Council Office	Citizenship and Immigration	
Treasury Board Secretariat	Environment	
	Fisheries and Oceans	
HORIZONTAL ADMINISTRATIVE COORDINATIVE	Foreign Affairs and International Trade	
	Health	
Public Works and Government Services	Human Resources and Social Development	
	Indian Affairs and Northern Development	
	Industry	
	National Defence	
	Natural Resources	
	Public Safety and Emergency Preparedness	
	Transport	
	Veterans Affairs	
	Western Economic Diversification	

other government agencies at the federal level and ensures that public servants have accommodations necessary to carry out their work. However, even these departments have some significance. In the mid-1990s, the Department of Public Works and Government Services had the important responsibility of administrating an initiative called the "sponsorship program," which made available public funds to community groups in an attempt largely to raise the profile of the federal government in Quebec. A commission of inquiry determined among other things that the department badly managed the program and used program funds to reward advertising agencies tied to the Liberal Party of Canada in Quebec (LPCQ) and to help the financially strapped LPCQ itself.[5] The findings of the inquiry contributed to the defeat of the Liberal government of Paul Martin in 2006.

The "vertical constituency" departments are involved in providing services directly to the public. These are high-profile departments, in that they have the largest budgets and deal with a large constituency. In general, they lack the power to intervene in the affairs of other departments, which only comes with the responsibility to coordinate, but their large budget and vocal constituency give these departments significant power. It is difficult for the horizontal coordinative portfolios to intervene too much in the affairs of these departments without raising the ire of the large number of constituents who are dependent on the departments for service.

While it is possible to group departments according to characteristics, it is considerably more difficult to rank these portfolios, or the ministers who hold them, in order of importance. A minister's relative position in cabinet is determined in part by her or his portfolio, but also in large part by such other factors as regional power base, personal diplomatic and judgmental skills, and relationship with the prime minister. In short, no portfolio can be deemed unimportant. All portfolios have significant roles, and they can all lead to substantial embarrassment for the government if the occupant of a portfolio is careless or incompetent.

Organizing Departments

The organization structure of the government is the personal prerogative of the prime minister. While most changes must ultimately be approved by Parliament, the *Public Service Rearrangement and Transfer of Duties Act* gives the prime minister a great deal of power to transfer duties among departments and even create new departments. Paul Martin, on becoming prime minister in 2003, and in the wake of increasing concerns about international security and the threat of terrorism, established the new Department of Public Safety and Emergency Preparedness. He also divided the old Department of Human Resources Development into two new entities—Human Resources *and* Skills Development and Social Development—for the purpose of providing a sharper focus for responsibilities in each of the respective departments. As one of his first duties, Prime Minister Stephen Harper, in 2006, also made changes affecting departmental structures. He focused mostly on combining departments in order to produce a more integrated and synchronized approach to the delivery of programs. For example, he brought together the departments of Foreign Affairs and International Trade "to ensure a coherent approach to foreign affairs and international commerce and to better coordinate the provision of services to Canadians both at home and abroad."[6] Other prime ministers have also found reason to make adjustments to the departmental structure of government. A decade ago, Prime Minister Kim Campbell substantially reduced the number of departments because of the difficulty of coordinating the activities of a large array of administrative units. The desire to have a smaller cabinet also played a role.

Chapter 5 / Government Departments and Central Agencies

It is tempting for each new prime minister to reorganize ministries to suit her or his style of governing, and virtually every prime minister has made certain changes. However, these shifts must be made with care, because major organizational shifts may impose significant tangible and intangible costs on government. The tangible costs arise from the time spent on finding new accommodation, drawing up new organizational structures, preparing new job descriptions, and so forth.[7] Less tangible are the personal costs people feel when their long service in an organization with a particular kind of culture is interrupted by having to integrate into a new department with a vastly different culture.

> Organizing is not a free lunch. Adding new organizations or ministerial portfolios adds complexity, and reorganizing existing ones causes disruption. Neither of these costs should be taken lightly. At a minimum, it can take three years to implement a major organizational change—in many cases five years. Where major adjustments in organizational culture are necessary, even more time may be required. During the time these adjustments are taking place, the time and energy of politicians and officials is occupied with organizational issues, at the expense of the policy and program issues that the organization was meant to address.[8]

One real cost of organizational change is that the resulting departments may be too much for the minister responsible. To address this problem, prime ministers have appointed secretaries or ministers of state in addition to the cabinet ministers who head departments. These secretaries have been assigned specific responsibilities to assist a minister. They are in an intermediate position, in that they are members of the ministry and so are bound by collective responsibility, but they are not necessarily cabinet ministers. These positions will be used to indicate the government's concern about certain issues. For example, Prime Minister Paul Martin created a minister of state for public health to reveal his government's commitment to deal with any future epidemics. However, some prime ministers—such as Prime Minister Harper—may elect to dispense with ministers of state and rely on a core group of ministers to oversee and direct government departments.

The Legislature and Government Departments

Departments are the most closely controlled of all government agencies. Other entities such as regulatory agencies and Crown corporations are deliberately insulated, to some extent, from direct control by the legislature and the executive, but departments have no such insulation. This control begins at the time of the creation of a new department, because a new department can be created only by an Act of Parliament. This enabling legislation sets out the responsibilities of the department and the limits of its authority. The statute establishing the federal Department of Veteran Affairs is typical, being just six pages long and couched in very general terms imposing only broad conditions on the department's operation. The statute provides in part that:

2. (1) There is hereby established a department of the Government of Canada called the Department of Veteran Affairs over which the Minister of Veteran Affairs appointed by commission under the Great Seal shall preside.
   (2) The Minister holds office during pleasure and has the management and direction of the Department. . . .
4. The powers, duties and functions of the Minister extend and apply to
   (a) the administration of such Acts of Parliament, and of such orders of the Governor in Council, as are not by law assigned to any other department of the Government of Canada or any Minister thereof, relating to
      (i) the care, treatment or re-establishment in civil life of any person who served in the Canadian Forces or merchant navy or in the naval, army

or air forces or merchant navies of Her Majesty, of any person who has otherwise engaged in pursuits relating to war, and of any other person designated by the Governor in Council, and

(ii) the care of the dependants or survivors of any person referred to in subparagraph (i); and

(b) all such other matters and such boards and other bodies, subjects, services and properties of the Crown as may be designated, or assigned to the Minister, by the Governor in Council.[9]

For other departments, the conditions and stipulations are more detailed. The federal Department of Health (or Health Canada) is directed to achieve nine goals.[10] However, even here the minister and the department are allowed a great deal of leeway in the pursuit of these departmental aims.

In addition to the initial, enabling legislation, Parliament sometimes passes other legislation affecting departments. This includes both specific legislation, such as setting up a new program and assigning it to a department, and general pieces of legislation that bind all departments in certain matters. Thus, Parliament can specify a department's mandate as loosely or as tightly as it wants, although the usual practice is to provide a broad mandate that allows maximum flexibility to the executive.

Another important element of Parliament's relationship to the executive is the annual budget. Every year the executive must seek parliamentary approval to spend funds in the upcoming year. At a minimum, the members of Parliament, particularly Opposition members, use this opportunity to question ministers and public servants about the operation of their departments and programs. In extreme cases, Parliament might decide to reduce, or even entirely eliminate, an expenditure request or appropriation for a department.

While these methods by which the legislature can affect departmental operations are, legally speaking, correct, reality requires some modification in practice. When the government party holds a majority of seats in the legislature, the government has fairly effective control over the legislation passed. Members of the Opposition can introduce amendments to proposed legislation, including reductions of appropriations, but these are unlikely to be passed. In the case of a minority government, the situation is more complex, but the government usually finds some method of exercising a certain amount of control over activities in the legislature. (But if it cannot exert sufficient control, it will not govern long—as Prime Minister Paul Martin discovered in late 2005.) However, this should not be taken to mean that the government can totally dominate the legislature. Opposition members have certain tools at their disposal to thwart arbitrary government actions. The legislature is a highly public forum, and the government is sensitive to the embarrassment it can suffer when the Opposition rallies public opinion against some unpopular government action. The government, particularly in a majority situation, has a strong position, but not an absolutely commanding one. Opposition parties still have means of holding a government accountable.

This is where the doctrine of individual ministerial responsibility becomes important. This principle, discussed more fully later in this book, holds that a minister is responsible for all actions carried out by her or his department. This means that, even if the minister did not approve an action in advance or had no knowledge of it, he or she must still accept responsibility for the action. This principle is an important element in a system of responsible government, because the minister is the only link between the legislature and the operating department. If the minister could avoid responsibility for the actions of her or his department, the legislature would have no effective way of holding the executive accountable for its actions. Since the minister is accountable for the actions of her or his department, it is important that there be adequate methods available for the minister to control the department.

The Executive and Government Departments

The minister is the political head of the department, and so has line authority over all public servants in the department. Within the provisions of relevant legislation, he or she has full authority to assign duties to departmental employees and supervise their activities. In the preceding chapters, there was some discussion of the difficulties of administrative superiors holding subordinates truly accountable for their actions. The large size and geographical decentralization of most departments, and the incredible demands made on ministers' time in the legislature and in constituency work, make the enforcement of real accountability problematic. However, ministers have a number of tools to assist them.

All ministers have a small personal staff reporting directly to them. The staff members are selected personally by the minister and are not considered to be public servants, but rather the minister's political assistants. They are selected partly for their administrative competence, but unlike public servants they are also selected for their partisan affiliation. Their roles are difficult to define, since every minister uses them differently; however, one role they have in common is assisting the minister to exercise political control over the bureaucracy. Ministers also have more formal, legal means of controlling their departments. The legislation establishing departments and programs seldom specifies in precise detail how all activities are to be carried out, in large part because the legislature is unable to foresee every future possibility. There is usually a clause in this kind of legislation that allows either the minister or the governor in council (that is, the cabinet) to make certain regulations as long as they are consistent with the terms of the enabling legislation. In some cases, this is done in strict legal form through an **order in council**. This is a formal regulation approved by the governor in council and, in the case of the federal government, published in the *Canada Gazette*, a biweekly listing of official announcements prepared by the government. Provincial governments have similar official publications.

These orders in council frequently establish the ground rules governing relationships between public servants and members of the public affected by their actions and decisions. For example, there are lengthy orders in council specifying the rules about access to information and privacy. They describe the sorts of information not available to the public, but they also restrict public servants by specifying those items that must be released. In this sense, regulations are an important means of controlling the actions of public servants.

In a less formal manner, ministers frequently issue internal departmental regulations. These are also binding on all departmental officials, provided that the regulations are within the terms of the enabling legislation. It is these regulations—covering such matters as which form is to be completed in a given case and how a certain situation is to be treated—that are the lifeblood of most large organizations. Over the years, these regulations can accumulate to several volumes.

Organization of a Typical Operating Department

Figure 5.3 shows an organization chart of the federal Department of Transport.[11] At the apex is the minister, who sets the priorities and assumes responsibility for all actions taken within the organization. As explained earlier, the minister may also have a personal staff appointed on a political basis to work directly and personally for him or her, and who are replaced when he or she leaves or the government changes. Their role is to provide the minister with overtly political advice. Most ministers also have a variety of Crown corporations and regulatory agencies reporting to them in addition to their department. As Figure 5.3 shows, two regulatory agencies and ten Crown corporations report to the Minister of Transport.

Figure 5.3

Organizational Structure of Transport Canada

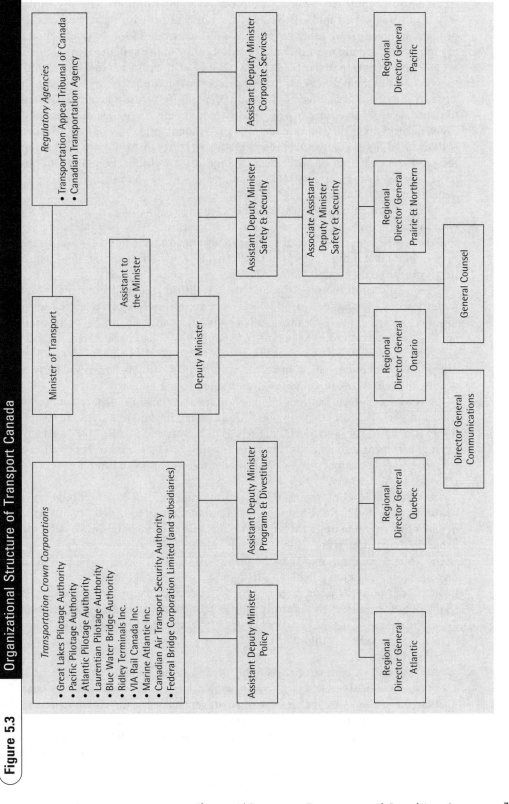

Source: Transport Canada, *2005–2006 Estimates: Report on Plans and Priorities, Treasury Board of Canada*. Reproduced with the Permission of the Minister of Public Works and Government Services, 2006.

Chapter 5 / Government Departments and Central Agencies

The next link in the chain of accountability is the **deputy minister**. Deputy ministers are the administrative (as distinct from political) heads of departments. They are permanent heads of departments in that they do not usually leave when governments change. Unlike ministers, who are politicians, deputy ministers typically work their way up through the ranks of the public service, although in some cases they are brought in directly from other governments or the private sector. In some senses, deputy ministers have the most difficult position in the entire system, because they must act as a connection between the political desires of the minister and the administrative concerns of the public servants in the department. Ministers are not totally insensitive to administrative concerns, any more than public servants are totally insensitive to political ones, but each side brings a different dimension to the issue at hand. Ministers, particularly if they represent a new government, often feel under pressure from colleagues to make changes in programs and activities. It would not be appropriate for public servants to oppose these changes, but public servants are frequently more attuned to the administrative problems posed by change than to its political benefits.

Good deputy ministers must stand between these two concerns, and not be afraid either to impose change on a reluctant department or to advise ministers fully and frankly if their actions will lead to serious administrative problems. And they must keep in mind that if this advice is not delivered in a very sensitive and diplomatic manner, it can be taken for disloyalty.

The relationship between the minister's political staff and the deputy minister requires some explanation. In principle, the system should work very well when the minister is receiving two streams of advice—political advice from her or his staff and administrative advice from the deputy. The minister will then be able to come to a decision after weighing these two types of advice. In practice, the relationship can be rather difficult. Some deputies have complained that political staff function as gatekeepers preventing them from taking important information to the minister.

A word of caution about terminology is necessary. The term "deputy minister" is not used consistently across departments. For example, in the Treasury Board where the minister is called the "president," the senior public servant is called the "secretary." In most government publications, the term "deputy head" is used to cover all of these senior people. In normal discussion around government offices, one frequently hears reference to "the deputy."

Beneath the level of deputy minister, the nomenclature can become even more confusing. Usually, there will be several "assistant deputy ministers" reporting to the deputy minister. Sometimes the superior status of one of these positions will be established by designating it as "associate deputy minister" or "senior assistant deputy minister." This is usually a sign that the position carries a heavier weight of duties or responsibilities than the other assistant deputy minister positions. Also, in the Department of Transport, there is a director general for each of the regions reporting directly to the deputy minister. These positions have almost the same status as the assistant deputy minister in that they report directly to the deputy, but their title indicates that their ranking is slightly lower, usually because they have less weighty responsibilities.

At this point, it is useful to relate this organization chart to some of the material about organizational behaviour covered in earlier chapters. In terms of the line–staff distinction, the line units are the regional directors general, while the staff functions are the assistant deputy ministers in charge of policy and corporate services and the general counsel who is responsible for legal services. A more complete organization chart would also illustrate the functional lines of authority between the line and staff functions.

Central Agencies

The discussion of span of control in one of the earlier chapters drew attention to the fact that as the number of units reporting to the same person increases, that person has more difficulty maintaining control of the units and coordinating their activities. The organization of the government of Canada demonstrates a very broad span of control with numerous departments, agencies, and so forth coming under the direct control of cabinet. This broad organizational structure requires some method of coordinating the activities of the separate departments to prevent overlap and working at cross purposes. One of the methods employed in Canada is the central agency.

There are other ways of dealing with this problem. In Britain, there are many departments headed by ministers who are not members of cabinet. Ministers heading related departments are then grouped under a senior minister who is a member of cabinet. This creates a situation in which the span of control is reasonable both for cabinet, with a relatively small number of senior ministers, and for the senior ministers, each of whom has a reasonable number of non-cabinet ministers reporting to her or him. It provides for both reasonable spans of control and a relatively small cabinet.

It is this latter characteristic that precludes the use of this system in Canada. In Canada, the concept of the representative cabinet is very important. This principle means that many diverse interests must be represented in the federal cabinet. It requires the selection of cabinet members to provide an appropriate balance of geographic, religious, ethnic, linguistic, gender, and other criteria. As a result, the cabinet must be fairly large, to ensure all groups are represented adequately. The principle of a representative cabinet also requires adherence to the concept that all cabinet ministers are equal. If there were a distinction between cabinet and non-cabinet ministers, it would be impossible to achieve the appropriate representative balance with a limited number of senior ministers.

These conventions of representative cabinet and equality of cabinet ministers require the wide span of control discussed above, which in turn requires the presence of some mechanism to coordinate and control the activities of the operating departments. This is the overall role of central agencies.

Definition of a Central Agency

A **central agency** (previously also called a horizontal policy coordinative department) is any organization that has a substantial amount of continuing, legitimate authority to direct and intervene in the activities of departments. The application of any definition, particularly one that contains words such as "substantial" and "continuing," is somewhat arbitrary, but it is widely acknowledged that there are four full-fledged central agencies in the government of Canada—the Prime Minister's Office, the Privy Council Office, the Treasury Board Secretariat, and the Department of Finance.[12]

Central agencies obtain their power either from legislative authority to operate in a particular area or from proximity to someone with legitimate authority, such as the prime minister. They usually do not have a large number of employees, although most of the staff employed are relatively high-level, professional people. Indeed, people working in central agencies have been called "superbureaucrats" in recognition of their skills and influence.[13] Table 5.2 (on page 80) shows the number of people employed in these four agencies, and some of the largest and smallest departments. Even the smallest departments typically have more employees than the central agencies, and the largest departments completely dwarf them.

All four agencies discussed in this section have either been created, or have undergone significant change, as a result of the style of government brought to office by Prime Minister Trudeau in 1968.[14] Trudeau's predecessor, Prime Minister Pearson,

Table 5.2	Number of Full-Time Equivalent Employees in Central Agencies and Selected Departments, 2005–06
CENTRAL AGENCY OR DEPARTMENT	**NUMBER OF EMPLOYEES**
Finance	880
Prime Minister's Office	117
Privy Council Office	846
Treasury Board Secretariat	1,259
National Defence (civilian and military combined)	84,697
Human Resources and Skills Development	12,927
Public Works and Government Services	13,647
Justice	5,035
Public Safety and Emergency Preparedness	727

Source: Treasury Board of Canada Secretariat, *2005–06 Estimates, Part III.* Reproduced with the permission of the Minister of Public Works and Government Services, 2006.

never had a majority government, and so had to be concerned with conciliation and firefighting. However, with a majority government in his first term, Trudeau had the luxury of focusing on specific goals he wanted to accomplish and using such newly fashionable rational tools as cost-effectiveness and systems analysis to attain those goals. His limited experience in working in large organizations could have made him uncomfortable in a bureaucratic environment. As a result, Trudeau wanted competing sources of information so that he did not have to rely solely on the traditional information sources of the operating departments. This was not evidence of distrust of the traditional organizational structures; rather, it was the understandable desire to obtain more than one point of view on an issue before acting. Thus, another major role for central agencies developed in addition to the coordinating role discussed above. Trudeau began to use these agencies as competing sources of information.

It is important to understand that, although every prime minister has left her or his own personal stamp on the government bureaucracy, there has been enough consistency that it is still possible to generalize about the duties of the central agencies. They have two related roles: (1) they are responsible for coordinating both the political and the administrative activities of line departments; (2) they are involved in advising the prime minister and cabinet on policy initiatives and shepherding them through the decision-making and implementation processes.

These roles and responsibilities can be illustrated best by a discussion of the activities of each of these four agencies.

The Prime Minister's Office

The **Prime Minister's Office (PMO)** works directly for the prime minister and has an overtly partisan political role. Its major responsibilities are to serve the prime minister by providing advice on how policy initiatives will be viewed politically in the country, and to assist in other ways that will cast the prime minister in the best political light. Specifically, these responsibilities include planning and coordinating major new policy initiatives, providing liaison with ministers and the party machinery across the country, maintaining good relations with the media, writing speeches, advising on appointments and nominations, and briefing the prime minister concerning issues that

Figure 5.4 | Basic Organization of Prime Minister's Office

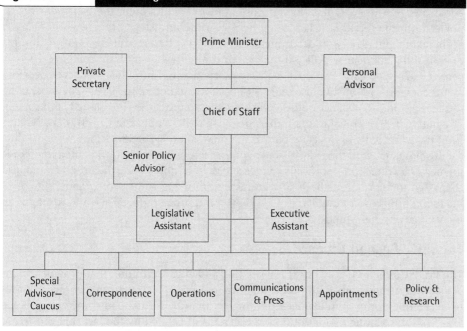

Source: Robert J. Jackson and Doreen Jackson, *Politics in Canada: Culture, Institutions, Behaviour and Public Policy*, 6th ed. (Toronto: Pearson Education Canada, Inc., 2006), 284. Reprinted with permission by Pearson Education Canada Inc.

might come up during daily question period and debate (see Figure 5.4 for the basic setup of the PMO).

Because these functions are all overtly political in nature, the people working in the PMO are partisan appointees. Prime Minister Martin's chief of staff—the senior official in the PMO—had lifelong ties to the Liberal Party in both an appointed and an elected capacity; Prime Minister Harper's chief of staff has been executive director of the Conservative Party and a close advisor of the prime minister when he was the Leader of the Opposition.[15] The partisan nature of appointments to the PMO means that they are there to serve unabashedly the prime minister's political needs and that they hold their positions at the pleasure of the prime minister and always resign when there is a change of government. Sometimes a stay in the PMO can be very short indeed. A few weeks after assuming office, Prime Minister Harper and his newly appointed communications director in the PMO disagreed on the most appropriate manner of handling a delicate situation involving a newly installed cabinet member. The communications officer was relieved of his duties.[16]

A former head of the PMO has argued that the PMO's role should be to establish a "strategic prime ministership."[17] By this, he means that the PMO must assist the prime minister in keeping new policy initiatives on track and avoid being sidetracked. He describes how the prime minister and PMO are continually being confronted with urgent crises. It is imperative, but very difficult, to prevent the urgent from overwhelming the important. He feels that the role of the PMO is to assist the prime minister in identifying the five or six major initiatives he or she wants to accomplish during a term of office, and then making sure the prime minister's energies are expended in this direction rather than on small matters.

The PMO has other important activities of a "housekeeping" nature, such as making travel arrangements and responding to the huge volume of mail sent to the prime minister. The largest number of employees in the PMO is involved in the latter function.

It is difficult to generalize about the relationship between the PMO and operating departments. The PMO has no statutory authority of its own; the office derives its power from the fact that it is headed by the prime minister, through whom it must act in taking initiatives with departments. Its contact with departments is largely limited to consulting about new policy initiatives or dealing with political problems. There is some evidence that the PMO is becoming more involved in policy matters, a development that worries some because of the political orientation of the PMO. The most notable, and notorious, instance of this concern relates to the earlier-mentioned Sponsorship Program, which operated in the Department of Public Works and Government Services from the mid-1990s to the early part of the new century. The PMO took responsibility for this program, with the chief of staff acting as a *de facto* minister, and failed to provide the necessary direction to officials given the task of administering the program and also "bypassed the normal methods of administration of government programs."[18] According to a commission of inquiry, this decision contributed to the misuse and mismanagement of government funds.

The Privy Council Office

The **Privy Council Office (PCO)** is a relatively small organization that provides policy advice and administrative support to the prime minister, cabinet, and cabinet committees. The title of the office comes from the fact that the formal name for cabinet is the Queen's Privy Council. The status of the PCO is illustrated by the fact that the senior public servant in the agency, who is called the clerk (ordinarily pronounced "clark" in the British tradition) of the Privy Council and the secretary to the cabinet, is officially recognized as the head of the public service.

Unlike the PMO, the PCO is staffed by career public servants rather than political appointees. However, the kind of advice provided by the PCO, while not overtly political in the partisan sense, is certainly sensitive to the political pulse of the nation. A former clerk of the Privy Council described the roles of the PMO and the PCO in this manner:

> The Prime Minister's Office is partisan, politically oriented, yet operationally sensitive. The Privy Council Office is nonpartisan, operationally oriented yet politically sensitive.[19]

The Privy Council Office has a number of different roles, including some assigned to it by the prime minister temporarily. However, the major, continuing activities of the PCO fall into the three categories of direct support to the prime minister, assistance to the cabinet and its committees, and advice on machinery of government and operation of the public service. Figure 5.5 provides a simplified version of the organization chart for the Privy Council Office and helps to reveal the three roles of the PCO.

In its first activity, the PCO serves as the prime minister's department, providing advice and assistance on a wide range of matters. The PCO keeps the prime minister abreast of developments in key policy areas and pays particular interest to any issues concerning the constitution. The PCO also briefs the prime minister on relations with the provinces and territories and in this role maintains an active liaison with departments to ensure relationships are operating well and that the position of the federal government is not compromised. A further task is to assist the prime minister in the process of making many appointments to important positions within government, and it also prepares the head of government for meetings with counterparts from other countries. If we look at Figure 5.5 we can pinpoint some of the units responsible for carrying out these activities. Certainly, the clerk of the PCO (pictured at the very top) is actively involved and so are parts of the PCO charged with looking after intergovernmental affairs and senior appointments.

Figure 5.5   Basic Structure of PCO Under Stephen Harper, March 2006

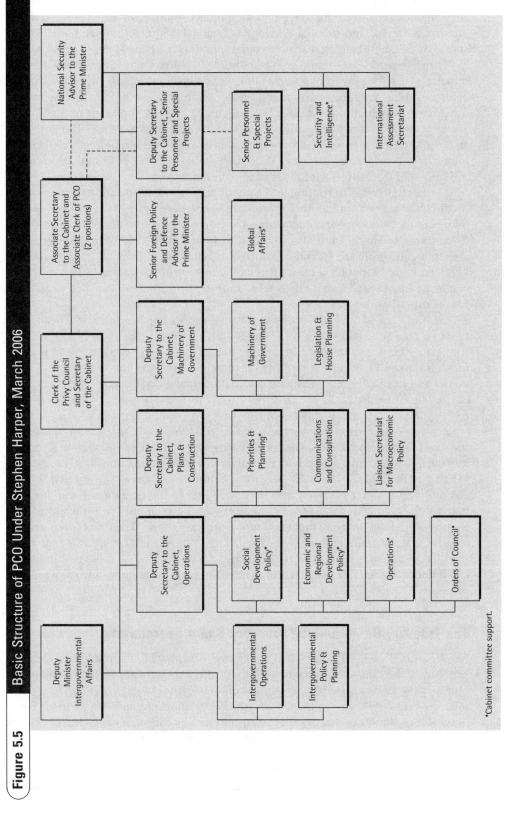

Source: Adapted from the website of the Privy Council Office at www.pco-bcp/gc.ca/docs/Org/OC-March 2006_e.pdf. Reproduced with permission of the Minister of Public Works and Government Services, 2006.

The PCO also provides several different kinds of support for cabinet committees. Organizationally, the office is divided so that there is a small secretariat attached to each cabinet committee, except the Treasury Board, which has its own secretarial arm. As the figure shows, there are secretariats for cabinet committees directed at social development, economic and regional development, global affairs, security and intelligence, and priorities and planning. Each secretariat monitors the general policy environment in the area for which its committee is responsible. The secretariat advises on new policy initiatives or responses to ongoing problems and ensures that all proposals that go before a cabinet committee are in good order. Among other things, this means that the interdepartmental aspects have been discussed and any problems resolved. This aspect of the PCO has prompted some to refer to it as a "gatekeeper." The PCO also assists in the preparation of the agenda of cabinet committee meetings, and in briefing the chairperson of the committee. At the housekeeping level, the PCO arranges for meeting space and maintains the minutes of the meetings.

The last function is in relation to the public service and its operations. In this capacity, the PCO plays a leading role in supporting the government's agenda concerning reform of the public service, and advises the prime minister on the reorganization of departments and agencies. It also advises the prime minister and cabinet about senior appointments within the federal bureaucracy, a reflection of the concern with moving highly competent public servants through senior postings so that they are always employed in a capacity where their talents can be best used and can gain experience for their next position.

The PCO provides a good example of central agency activities and the general position of central agencies in the organizational structure. The duties of the PCO give it the legitimate right to get involved in the activities of every other department of government. It does not have line authority over those departments, but its position as gatekeeper and its proximity to cabinet mean that operating departments always consider advice offered by the PCO very carefully. This helps to explain the complex love–hate relationship operating departments usually have with central agencies.

As with some other major agencies at the federal level, the PCO has been touched by the sponsorship scandal and the consequent investigations. The commission of inquiry looking into the scandal agreed with the opinion of an expert that the PCO "has been or is being politicized."[20] The PCO, according to the commission, is supposed to be a largely nonpartisan agency responsible for tending to the operational and advisory needs of the cabinet decision process; but now it appears that the "political and administrative seem to be merging more and more into each other." The commission recommended that the duties of the PCO be limited to acting as a cabinet secretariat and that the head of the agency be called the Secretary to the Cabinet. The more politically oriented duties of the PCO when acting as the prime minister's direct advisor would be curtailed.[21]

The Treasury Board and the Treasury Board Secretariat

The **Treasury Board (TB)** is a cabinet committee consisting of the president of the Treasury Board, the minister of finance, and four other ministers appointed by the prime minister. The TB differs from other cabinet committees in two respects. It is the only cabinet committee enshrined in legislation—the *Financial Administration Act*—and it is the only cabinet committee that has a large bureaucracy reporting to it—the **Treasury Board Secretariat (TBS)**. In its support to the Treasury Board, the TBS carries out a number of duties relating to the financial, personnel, and management responsibilities of government. The TBS prepares the expenditure budget that the government proposes in the House of Commons each year. It also assesses the performance of government departments, agencies, and Crown corporations and proposes reallocations of expenditures in light of these evaluations. More generally, it seeks to ensure that the TB functions as a kind of general manager of the entire federal government.

The TBS is also responsible for certain aspects of human resources administration. Though it has recently been relieved some its responsibility in this area, it still provides advice to the Treasury Board on issues concerning compensation, pensions, benefits, and the contentious area of labour relations and collective bargaining. It also sets performance expectations for managers and is at the forefront of the effort to develop strategies for the increasingly important area of interdepartmental coordination and horizontal management.

A few years ago, the TBS went through a refocusing of its mandate in an attempt to "ensur[e] value for money and providing oversight of the financial management functions in departments and agencies."[22] This change resulted in the aforementioned divestment of some human resources responsibilities; this left the TBS more time to track the spending activities of departments and other government organizations and conduct exercises necessary for any reallocation of spending from low- to high-priority areas. It may also be that the reports and findings concerning the Quebec sponsorship program have greatly shaken the government and made it more conscious of the need to ensure that the government can be truly accountable to the Canadian people for the expenditure of tax dollars.

From the standpoint of operating departments, the Treasury Board is easily the most active—some might say, intrusive—of the central agencies, simply because there are so many points of contact and so many specific activities for which TB clearance must be obtained. Treasury Board officials are aware that excessive oversight (and accompanying rules and regulations) can stifle department initiatives. Nevertheless, the recent retooling of the TBS suggests that government at this time may be more concerned about control and less about preserving departmental autonomy.

The Department of Finance

The **Department of Finance** is responsible for advising cabinet on matters of economic policy. Thus, the department has an exceedingly broad mandate. It advises on questions of fiscal policy, international trade policy (including tariffs), domestic industrial policy, federal–provincial fiscal relations, taxation policy, and the preparation of the revenue and expenditure budgets (see Figure 5.6 on page 86). Moreover, much of this advice is in relation to policy and programs developed by the department itself and not in relation to the positions and recommendations of individual departments. For instance, the Department of Finance generates proposals for tax reform (such as the GST) and develops suggestions for adjustments to the major arrangements for transferring financial assistance to the provinces. The Department of Finance is just as much a policy-maker as it is a policy advisor, and in this respect might be seen as both a traditional department and a central agency.

With its mandate, the Department of Finance might potentially intervene in the activities of any department involved in policies that touch upon any of the above areas. And, given the breadth of those areas, it is difficult to think of a department that does not. The role of the department does not bring it into the same kind of obtrusive, day-to-day contact with operating departments as that of the TBS, but its concern with economic policy allows it to intervene at strategic points in the policy development process. Its role in the preparation of the expenditure budget helps determine whether the upcoming year will be a lean or a fat one for government agencies. Finance also has a role as the budgetary gatekeeper. Indeed, it has traditionally provided the strongest opposition to new spending programs. This brings the Department of Finance into fairly frequent conflict with operating departments.

Figure 5.6

Organizational Structure of Department of Finance

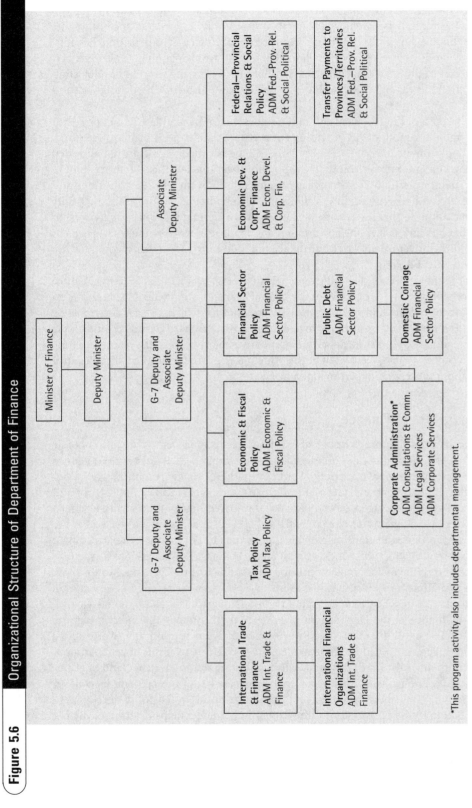

*This program activity also includes departmental management.

Source: *2005–2006 Estimates: Report on Plans and Priorities.* Department of Finance Canada. Reproduced with the permission of the Minister of Public Works and Government Services, 2006.

Central Agencies in the Provinces

It is obvious that the functions performed by central agencies in the federal government will also be necessary in provincial governments. However, the smaller size of the provincial governments usually means that organizational structures are less complex and differentiated. In some provinces, the functions of the PMO, the PCO, and sometimes the TB are all carried out in the premier's office.[23] However, there is a general movement toward the establishment of what is commonly described as an institutionalized cabinet, which is an executive system with a formal committee structure and supporting agencies. Moreover, it was a province—Saskatchewan—that first introduced central agencies as an integral part of the cabinet decision-making process.

Conclusion

This chapter has described the main characteristics of the departmental form of organization, which is usually preferred when the situation calls for strong ministerial control. There are other cases in which it is better for an agency to function at arm's length from the direct control of the minister. The next two chapters will deal with two organizational forms that ensure this distance—the Crown corporation and the regulatory agency.

Notes

1. J.E. Hodgetts, *The Canadian Public Service: A Physiology of Government* (Toronto: University of Toronto Press, 1973), 89.

2. Ibid., ch. 5.

3. There is a fourth type, but it is no longer in use.

4. G. Bruce Doern, "Horizontal and Vertical Portfolios in Government," in G. Bruce Doern and V. Seymour Wilson, eds., *Issues in Canadian Public Policy* (Toronto: Macmillan, 1974), 310–29. This same idea is also developed in G. Bruce Doern and Richard W. Phidd, *Canadian Public Policy: Ideas, Structure and Process*, 2nd ed. (Scarborough: Nelson Canada, 1992), 316–17.

5. See the Commission of Inquiry into the Sponsorship Program and Advertising Activities, *Who Is Responsible? Fact Finding Report* (Ottawa: Her Majesty the Queen in Right of Canada, 2005).

6. Office of the Prime Minister, "Prime Minister Harper Announces New Ministry and Reaffirms Government Priorities," news release, February 6, 2006. Available at http://pm.gc.ca/eng/media.asp?id=684. Accessed July 4, 2006.

7. Gordon F. Osbaldeston, *Organizing to Govern* (Toronto: McGraw-Hill Ryerson, 1992), ch. 7.

8. Ibid., 144.

9. *Department of Veterans Affairs Act*, R.S., 1985, c. V-1. Available at http://laws.justice.gc.ca/en/v-1/264369.html. Retrieved July 4, 2006.

10. *Department of Health Act* (1996, c.6).

11. Treasury Board of Canada, *2005–2006 Estimates: Transport Canada: Part III—Report on Plans and Priorities* (Minister of Public Works and Government Services Canada, 2005), 40.

12. Some argue for the inclusion of additional bodies into the group of central agencies—for example, the Department of Justice. See James B. Kelly, *Governing with the Charter: Legislative and Judicial Activism and Framers' Intent* (Vancouver: UBC Press, 2005), ch. 7.

13. Colin Campbell and George J. Szablowski, *The Superbureaucrats* (Toronto: Macmillan, 1979).

14. Peter Aucoin, "Organizational Change in the Machinery of Canadian Government: From Rational Management to Brokerage Politics," *Canadian Journal of Political Science* 19(1) (March 1986): 3–27.

15. Graham Fraser, "The Man Who Really Saved the Government," *Toronto Star*, May 22, 2005, A4; Jane Taber, "Harper's 'Straight Shooter,'" *Globe and Mail*, February 11, 2006, F2.

16. Don Martin, "PM Can't Keep Blaming Messenger," *National Post*, February 22, 2006, A8.

17. Thomas S. Axworthy, "Of Secretaries to Princes," *Canadian Public Administration* 31(2) (summer 1988): 247–64.

18. Commission of Inquiry into the Sponsorship Program and Advertising Activities, *Who Is Responsible? Fact Finding Report*, 99; Commission of Inquiry into the Sponsorship Program & Advertising Activities, *Who Is Responsible? Summary* (Ottawa: Her Majesty the Queen in Right of Canada, 2005), 74.

19. Gordon Robertson, "The Changing Role of the Privy Council Office," *Canadian Public Administration* 14(4) (winter 1971): 506.

20. Commission of Inquiry into the Sponsorship Program and Advertising Activities, *Restoring Accountability: Recommendations* (Ottawa: Her Majesty in Right of Canada, 2006), 151.

21. Ibid., 143, 152.

22. Office of the Prime Minister, "Stronger Financial Management and Accountability," December 23, 2003. Available at http://pm.gc.ca/eng/accountability.asp. Accessed November 5, 2005.

23. Luc Bernier, Keith Brownsey, and Michael Howlett, *Executive Styles in Canada: Cabinet Structures and Leadership Practices in Canadian Government* (Toronto: University of Toronto Press, 2005).

6

Crown Corporations

Sometimes circumstances appear that cause governments to choose to engage in commercial or business-like activities. The government of Canada, for instance, has over the years operated an airline, provided rail service, and filled up cars with gasoline. Provincial governments have also found themselves offering services normally reserved for the private sector. In deciding how to carry out these business activities, it has been deemed necessary to use an organizational form that offered a fair degree of autonomy, because the traditional departmental form, with its tight ministerial control, was found to be inappropriate. If government was going to run a business, it had to be structured more like a business and be free of any direct political control and excessive rules and procedures. Thus, a different type of organization, the **Crown corporation** or **public enterprise**, has emerged as an significant element in public administration in Canada.

Crown corporations have served important purposes and made available services that Canadians consider essential. However, they have not been without their problems and challenges. Crown corporations are supposed to act as a business and some are expected to make a profit, but at the same time they are expected as a government agency to function in the public interest. At times, these two policy purposes may conflict. Similarly, public enterprises also enjoy some leeway in their operations, but they are also ultimately responsible to a minister and the government. This, too, causes tension. These and other challenges make Crown corporations a controversial matter in the study of public administration in Canada.

This chapter first offers a definition of a Crown corporation and offers a glimpse of the basic structure of these organizational forms. It then discusses trends in the use of this particular kind of government agency and the underlying reasons for the employment of the corporation form. The means of controlling Crown corporations are also considered, and the chapter concludes with some of the criticisms of Crown corporations and related proposals for reform.

Definition of Crown Corporation

A number of different terms are used to denote the organization form under consideration in this chapter. The most common are "Crown corporation," "mixed enterprise," "joint enterprise," and "public enterprise." Sometimes, these terms are used interchangeably, but this section will provide different definitions for each of them.

Separating the corporation form from other forms of government organization is relatively easy. Crown corporations are established either through their own legislation or through incorporation under the federal or provincial companies legislation in exactly the same way as any private sector corporation. Determining what constitutes a corporate form, as distinct from other organizational forms, is not difficult; the difficult part is determining what constitutes a Crown corporation.

One authority defines Crown corporations as "companies in the ordinary sense of the term, whose mandate relates to industrial, commercial or financial activities but which also belong to the state, are owned by the government or the Crown or whose sole shareholder is the government or the Crown."[1] This definition leaves out certain noncommercial entities that are defined as Crown corporations in law at the federal level (e.g., the Canada Employment Insurance Commission and the Canadian Centre for Occupational Health and Safety). While there are valid financial and political reasons for separating these organizations from their related departments, they are excluded from this definition because their method of operation is much more like an operating department than a corporation. But governments may find it appropriate to apply the corporate form to a particular service even though it is without a business-like purpose.

This definition also fails to emphasize that Crown corporations enjoy a greater degree of autonomy than traditional departments. It is important that an organization that carries out government policy be closely controlled by the political executive. However, when an organization has a predominantly commercial mandate, political concerns might interfere with that mandate. The Crown corporation form puts the organization under the control of a board and at arm's length from government control. Another reason for the greater autonomy is that it makes it easier to attract business people to work for Crown corporations. Successful business people frequently have much to offer to government organizations, but they are often uncomfortable coming into an unfamiliar management structure such as an operating department with a political head, central agency controls, and the other trappings of government. They feel more comfortable in the more familiar setting of the corporate form.

Classification

The federal government classifies its corporate holdings in a number of different categories. "Parent corporations" are corporations that are one hundred percent owned by the federal government. Figure 6.1 depicts the present federal Crown corporations according to which department it is accountable. The Canada Post Corporation is, for instance, responsible to the minister of national revenue, while the Canadian Dairy Commission reports to the minister of agriculture and agri-food. These parent corporations can be further classified into two categories, agency corporations and proprietary corporations.[2] The latter type functions much like any business in the private sector; the former also serves a business function, but fails to meet one of the defining qualities usually identified with a commercial operation (e.g., it requires some financial assistance from government). There are also three classes of subsidiaries of a parent corporation—"wholly-owned subsidiaries" and other "subsidiaries" and "associates" held at less than fifty percent.

Figure 6.1   Parent Crown Corporations by Ministerial Portfolio

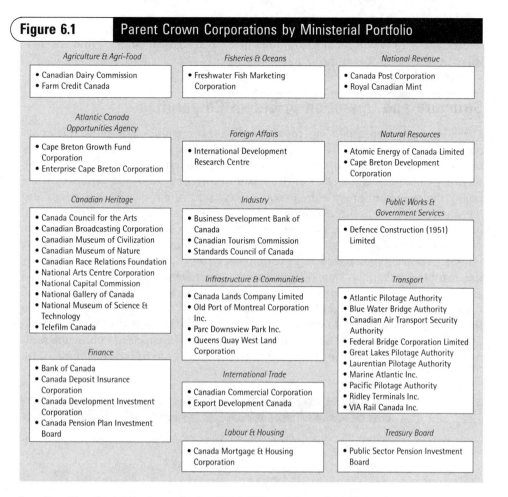

Agriculture & Agri-Food
- Canadian Dairy Commission
- Farm Credit Canada

Fisheries & Oceans
- Freshwater Fish Marketing Corporation

National Revenue
- Canada Post Corporation
- Royal Canadian Mint

Atlantic Canada Opportunities Agency
- Cape Breton Growth Fund Corporation
- Enterprise Cape Breton Corporation

Foreign Affairs
- International Development Research Centre

Natural Resources
- Atomic Energy of Canada Limited
- Cape Breton Development Corporation

Canadian Heritage
- Canada Council for the Arts
- Canadian Broadcasting Corporation
- Canadian Museum of Civilization
- Canadian Museum of Nature
- Canadian Race Relations Foundation
- National Arts Centre Corporation
- National Capital Commission
- National Gallery of Canada
- National Museum of Science & Technology
- Telefilm Canada

Industry
- Business Development Bank of Canada
- Canadian Tourism Commission
- Standards Council of Canada

Public Works & Government Services
- Defence Construction (1951) Limited

Infrastructure & Communities
- Canada Lands Company Limited
- Old Port of Montreal Corporation Inc.
- Parc Downsview Park Inc.
- Queens Quay West Land Corporation

Transport
- Atlantic Pilotage Authority
- Blue Water Bridge Authority
- Canadian Air Transport Security Authority
- Federal Bridge Corporation Limited
- Great Lakes Pilotage Authority
- Laurentian Pilotage Authority
- Marine Atlantic Inc.
- Pacific Pilotage Authority
- Ridley Terminals Inc.
- VIA Rail Canada Inc.

Finance
- Bank of Canada
- Canada Deposit Insurance Corporation
- Canada Development Investment Corporation
- Canada Pension Plan Investment Board

International Trade
- Canadian Commercial Corporation
- Export Development Canada

Labour & Housing
- Canada Mortgage & Housing Corporation

Treasury Board
- Public Sector Pension Investment Board

Source: Crown Corporations and Other Corporate Interests of Canada 2005, page 3, Treasury Board of Canada Secretariat, 2006. Reproduced with the permission of the Minister of Public Works and Government Services Canada, 2006.

There are four other types of corporations that are less directly controlled by the federal government. "Mixed enterprises" are corporations whose shares are owned partly by the Government of Canada and partly by private sector parties. With the recent completion of the privatization of Petro-Canada, there are now no mixed enterprises at the federal level. "Joint enterprises" are similar to mixed enterprises, except that the other shareholder is another level of government. Currently, all of these are in the field of economic development—Lower Churchill Development Corporation Limited, North Portage Development Corporation, and Société du parc industriel et portuaire Québec-sud. The "shared-governance" entity is another type of corporate form. The federal government has no financial interest in these bodies, but can participate in the appointment or nomination of individuals to their governing structures. Examples are the Agricultural and Food Council of Alberta, the Canada Games Council, Wildlife Habitat Canada, and the Canadian Foundation for Innovation. At present, there are 144 shared-governance entities at the federal level. "International enterprises" are "corporate entities created pursuant to international agreements under which Canada holds shares or has a right to appoint or elect some number of members to a governing body."[3] Examples are the International Monetary Fund, the World Anti-Doping Agency, and the International Niagara Committee. There are at present eighteen international enterprises.

"Public enterprise" is the most general term, usually used to encompass all the above terms. This chapter will focus predominantly on parent corporations, although there will be some discussion of the various other types of organizations as well.

Structure and Operation of Crown Corporations

The structure and operation of Crown corporations resemble those of their counterparts in the private sector. To see this more clearly, Figure 6.2 outlines the organizational chart for VIA Rail, a major federal Crown corporation in the business of rail service. At the top sits the chair of the board of directors and other members of the board; their job is to provide the overall direction for the company. The board also has a number of committees responsible for overseeing various aspects of the company's operation. The Audit and Finance Committee, for instance, focuses on the procedures for reporting the financial status of the corporation and on the activities of the internal and external auditors. VIA's committee system, like all such systems, permits the board to break up into smaller groups to examine significant issues in more detail and then to convey the results of their deliberations back to the board. Reporting to the board is the president and chief executive officer (CEO), who is responsible for the management and day-to-day activities of VIA Rail. Unlike Board members, who are typically part-time, the CEO is a full-time official and is expected to have the skills necessary to manage a major Crown corporation. The CEO in turn has underneath

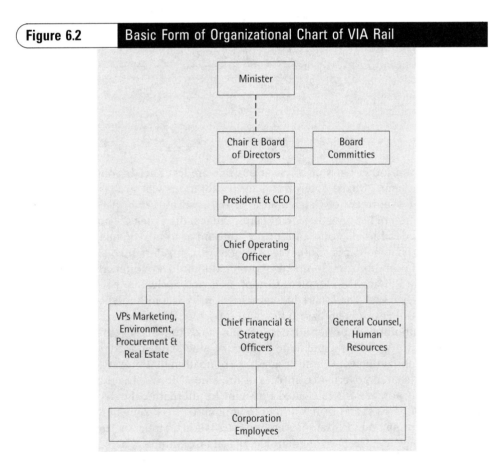

Figure 6.2   **Basic Form of Organizational Chart of VIA Rail**

Source: VIA Rail, *Annual Report 2005.*

him or her a series of company officers responsible for some aspect of the operation of VIA Rail (not all of which are displayed), and below them we find the reminder of the corporation's full-time employees. In looking at the figure, it is important to recall that VIA Rail in general and the company board in particular are accountable to the responsible minister.

Changing Trends in Public Enterprise

Governments grew very rapidly in the 1960s and 1970s, and it is not surprising that public enterprise followed suit. In more recent times, the growth of government has slowed considerably, and the size of the corporate sector has declined as a result of a growing trend toward privatization. However, most recently the sector has stabilized and even realized a little growth.

The Federal Scene

Table 6.1 shows the number of Crown corporations currently held by the federal government and illustrates the trend over the past twenty years. The clear trend is toward a reduction in the number of major corporate entities. In 1984, there were sixty-seven parent Crown corporations, but by 2005 this number had fallen to forty-three. A similar precipitous decline can be seen in the number of most other types of public enterprise. This decline has been caused both by high-profile activities, such as major privatizations, and by simply winding up some inactive corporations and consolidating others. However, we must be careful not to assume that this decline means that no new Crown corporations have been created in the past two decades—twenty-six were added during this time period.[4] Rather, the point is that the net effect has been to reduce the overall presence of most forms of Crown corporations. As well, the table fails to show that the Crown corporation sector at the federal level has enjoyed a small upturn since the turn of the century, though a very modest one.

Table 6.2 (on page 94) provides an idea of the size of the largest federal Crown corporations. Federal Crown corporations are major employers and their assets are impressive. Canada Post Corporation has over 52,000 employees and has assets worth nearly $4.3 billon dollars. Though smaller than the nation's postal service, the Canadian Broadcasting Corporation nevertheless has 7,500 employees and assets of $1.6 billion,

Table 6.1	Federal Crown Corporations by Method of Ownership		
	1984	1994	2005
Parent Crown corporations	67	48	43
Wholly-owned subsidiaries	128	64	25
Other subsidiaries and associates	94	64	25
Mixed enterprises	18	5	0
Joint enterprises	–	3	3
International organizations	–	15	18
Shared governance	29	51	141

Source: Treasury Board of Canada Secretariat, "Crown Corporations and Other Corporate Interests of Canada, " 2005. (Ottawa: Her Majesty the Queen in Right of Canada).

Chapter 6 / Crown Corporations

Table 6.2	Size of Selected Larger Crown Corporations and Total Corporate Sector, 2005	
	EMPLOYEES	ASSETS($1 MILLIONS)
Canada Post Corporation	52,397	$4,314
Canadian Broadcasting Corporation	7,454	1,639
Atomic Energy of Canada	3,221	863
VIA Rail	3,027	911
Canada Mortgage and Housing Corporation	1,814	26,672
Business Development Bank	1,455	9,445
Export Development Corporation	966	20,750
Farm Credit Corporation	1,030	11,405

Source: Crown Corporations and Other Corporate Interests of Canada, 2005; Treasury Board of Canada Secretariat, 2006. Reproduced with the permission of the Minister of Public Works and Government Services Canada, 2006.

and Via Rail, too, employs a significant number of Canadians and has significant financial worth. Despite the presence of these large corporations, the overall number of employees and levels of assets have declined over time, though as noted earlier the number of people working in the Crown corporation sector and the accompanying assets have increased marginally in the past few years.

The activities in which federal Crown corporations have been involved have changed over the years. In the years immediately after Confederation, the federal government was most concerned with nation-building, and so focused on transportation undertakings that would unify the diverse parts of the country. During World War II, the major theme of public policy changed from national unity to national defence, with the creation of many new corporations to supply the war effort.[5] Since the end of the war, federal Crown corporations have become more involved in the areas of finance, insurance, and real estate, and the newest corporations address matters of airport security, economic development, and cultural activities.

It is clear that Crown corporations no longer play such a large role in the economy. For example, with the sale of Air Canada and Canadian National Railways, the federal involvement in transportation is more strategic and regional than predominant. Also, the protracted privatization of Petro-Canada, completed in 2004, ends the federal government's direct financial participation in the oil sector, and there has been almost an ongoing discussion about changing the format of the CBC or even eliminating it altogether.

The Provincial Scene

Provinces have adopted the Crown corporation form in a number of different functional areas. Industrial development, liquor sales, housing, power generation, and research and development have been among the more prominent fields in which Crown corporations have been established at the provincial level. Two provinces in particular have used the corporate form to further their purposes. Saskatchewan has over the years established a number of Crown corporations in an attempt to provide for "a more diversified economy through the creation of secondary industry."[6] The Potash Corporation of Saskatchewan, the Saskatchewan Government Insurance Office, and Saskatchewan Telephones are only a few of the public corporations that have been central the development of Saskatchewan.[7] Quebec is the other province that has relied heavily on Crown corporations for economic development and the training of francophone managers. Hydro-Québec is the most prominent of Quebec's Crown corporations, but others have been set up in the steel, oil and gas, forestry, and asbestos industries.

The major activities in which provincial Crown corporations have been involved have changed over the years. In the early years, one function was dominant—power generation. This gave way to diversification into the trade, finance, insurance, and real estate sectors. More recently, provincial Crown corporations have become involved in industrial and resource development areas, the newest area being insurance. One of the recent trends is the privatization of portions of the electrical corporations in most provinces.

Rationale for Crown Corporations

A recent report on federal Crown corporations nicely captures the causes and overall rationale for their creation: "the federal government has used, and continues to use Crown corporations to deliver public policy when the private sector, other levels of government, or federal departments and agencies cannot satisfy adequately the needs and interests of Canadians."[8] We have already discussed one reason for Crown corporations, namely the desire to create corporate entities in order to escape the tight ministerial control found in departments. This translates into a failure of traditional governmental forms to satisfy the preferences of the citizens of Canada. In this section, the intent is to focus on reasons relating to failures in the marketplace and the limits of the private sector.

Nation-Building, Community Development, and Externalities

Arguably, the most common rationale for the creation of public enterprises in Canada has been the need to make investments necessary for nation-building and community development. Such investments, which have included the establishment of Crown corporations in the areas of telephone services and air and rail travel, amount to an attempt to provide for what are called externalities. Externalities, as Richards writes, "arise when exchanges between two agents inevitably have an impact on non-consenting third parties."[9] Externalities can be both positive and negative. In the case of positive externalities, producers and consumers in the marketplace fail to take into sufficient consideration that their exchange may have beneficial effects on people outside the transaction. The reason for this is that the two parties accrue no direct benefit from these spillover effects even though the larger society gains from their provision. The result is a shortfall in the supply of some good or service. In Canada's history, the private market has been unwilling, for example, to supply rail or air travel in amounts necessary for the building of this country. The response of government has been to create Crown corporations to make up for this deficiency.

Externalities can also be negative in their effect. The two parties engaged in a market transaction may this time cause harm to others, but the transaction continues nevertheless because the market provides no way to force the two parties to pay for this cost. To deal with negative externalities, government may affect market behaviour indirectly by imposing a fine or some other cost on those responsible for the negative effects. However, public authorities may also elect to create a public enterprise to order to deal more directly with the matter. Many provinces, for instance, have set up public corporations responsible for the sale of liquor. As Trebilcock and Pritchard say, "To the extent that the excessive consumption of alcohol is seen to generate externalities in terms of health impairment, public rowdiness, moral degeneration and like effects, a case is made for regulating its distribution."[10] Governments might have chosen to apply rules to private

Chapter 6 / Crown Corporations

retailers of alcohol, but many for one reason or another decided instead to combat the negative externality through the corporate form.

National Goals and Public Goods

Sometimes the external or spillover effects of market transactions represent such a large proportion of the total gains that no private sector actor is willing to supply a particular good or service despite the fact that society benefits from it. We call such goods and services "public goods." To see how public goods emerge, take the example of safer neighbourhoods, a desirable state of affairs for any rational society:

> When you buy a burger, you're the only one to enjoy it, but everyone benefits from safer neighbourhoods. And that's the problem: because everyone can enjoy a public good, there's no incentive for any individual to pay for it, and therefore no business is willing to provide it.[11]

National security, public safety, and effective transportation are only a few of the public goods that emerge in societies. To ensure their provision, governments may elect to create a Crown corporation. The CBC, for instance, was established in part to instil in Canadians a sense of their culture and to help resist the effect of the United States. Because it is difficult to charge for something as ethereal as "Canadian nationalism," markets in Canada have been reluctant to supply it, making government action necessary.

Natural Monopolies

Societies typically frown upon monopolies in the marketplace because they inevitably lead to such undesirable effects as high prices and low-quality products. The preference is usually to have a competitive situation in which many companies vie for the attention of customers. However, in some sectors of economic activity it is not reasonable or efficient to have more than one supplier, a situation we call a "natural monopoly." In Canada, the areas of telephone service, power generation, and some insurance services have traditionally been seen as natural monopolies. In these situations, there is no sense in trying to break up the monopoly, but the necessity of some kind of government is apparent, because natural monopolies, like all types of monopolies, may seek to take actions that produce the unwanted consequences of monopolistic behaviour. As with negative externalities, government may opt for an arrangement in which it regulates a private monopoly, but it may conclude that it should assume responsibility for the supply of the service in question. The many provincial power corporations are the results of government deciding that the best way to deal with natural monopolies is to become the monopoly itself.

Incomplete Information

As Averch writes, "Competitive markets work well when all parties hold just the right amounts of information about the quantity and quality of goods and services offered."[12] But sometimes individuals are without the necessary information and make bad decisions. Again, government can fix this market failure with the regulation of private sector actors; for example, testing and labelling requirements give us a better idea of the quality of such goods as prescription drugs and household foods. But government can also seek to require the required information—to provide a "window" on the private sector—through the setting up of Crown corporations. In the early 1970s, the federal government found itself without the right information to make sound policy for the increasingly important area of oil. Thus, it created a Crown corporation called Petro-Canada in part "to obtain information and advice ... about market conditions and industry performance [in the petroleum industry] without having to rely on private firms to disclose this information."[13]

Fairness

On balance, the private sector works well and provides Canadians with a standard of living that is the envy of many. As shown, the market at times fails to work as well as it might, but government can intervene to end the failures. However, sometimes we are still dissatisfied even after these failures in efficiency are eliminated. Wolf explains:

> ... the distributional results of even well-functioning markets may not accord with socially acceptable standards of equity, or with society's preferences for reducing excessive disparities in the distribution of income and wealth.[14]

Governments can use public enterprise to help address the perception of inequity and unfairness. Crown corporations, for instance, have been established to assist in increasing the chances of gainful employment in areas of the country. Various corporate forms—including the Cape Breton Development Corporation and Enterprise Cape Breton Corporation—have been established in an attempt to provide some stability in the coal mining industry in the Cape Breton area and to investigate future economic opportunities for Cape Breton. This action relates in part to providing a more stable market, but it was motivated by heart-felt worries about the well-being of residents in the community of Cape Breton. The 1969 establishment of the Canadian Saltfish Corporation served a similar purpose, providing greater income stability and other types of assistance to those in the saltfish industry.

This is not a comprehensive list of the reasons for the use of the Crown corporation form. It may also be used, for example, to generate revenue for government and hence act as a kind of tax collector with low visibility. When we purchase items at the local liquor store, we rarely think that the profits arising from these transactions are just another form of taxation, but that is what they are. More interestingly, political reasons may cause governments to turn to Crown corporations. Seeing Crown corporations as responses to concerns in the marketplace assumes that elected officials focus solely on concern with efficiency and equity, but politicians also have an interest in remaining in office.

Political Control of Crown Corporations

One of the reasons for the use of the Crown corporation form of organization is to separate the corporation from direct political control. However, a Crown corporation is a creature of the government, carries out government objectives, and, in many cases, uses government funds. As the federal *Financial Administration Act* says, "Each Crown corporation is ultimately accountable, through the appropriate Minister, to Parliament for the conduct of its affairs."[15] A Crown corporation thus cannot behave in a totally autonomous manner, but the precise method of political control is awkward because of the need for some limited amount of autonomy. This section will examine how the current system of political control of Crown corporations operates.

Establishing the Crown Corporation

The establishment of a Crown corporation offers elected officials an opportunity to exert control over such entities. Crown corporations can be created in various ways, all of which allow for some opportunity for elected officials to establish some kind of accountability framework. The most effective way involves the passage of separate legislation for each new corporation. The Canada Post Corporation Act, for instance, specifies the objects of Canada Post, details the composition and powers of the board, provides for senior officers and administrative staff, authorizes the corporation to make regulations with the approval of cabinet, and sets out arrangements for the financing of Canada Post.[16]

Governments can also incorporate companies under the relevant federal or provincial companies' legislation in the same manner as any private citizen. A minister, or a public servant, prepares the necessary documentation and, in due course, the Crown corporation is in business. These companies have share capital that is legally vested in either the minister or the Crown. At one point, this method was relatively common, but now it requires Cabinet approval and so is used very seldom.

Finally, the government can enter into any sort of contract, which means that it may decide to purchase the shares of a company on the open market or through a private arrangement. The shares so obtained are then vested in either the minister or the Crown. This same heading covers those relatively rare situations in which governments have nationalized companies against the will of the previous shareholders. This requires enabling legislation and usually provokes a court challenge.

The *Financial Administration Act*

The ***Financial Administration Act*** establishes a general framework for the allowable activities and the accountability of Crown corporations. The purposes of the Act are to provide for enhanced accountability and some uniformity in the treatment of Crown corporations, but this uniformity is tempered by the provisions of the various acts that created the corporations.

The specific provisions are discussed at various points in this chapter. The general thrust of the legislation is to stipulate what types of approvals corporations need before they undertake certain activities, and what reports they must file at the end of their year. The *Financial Administration Act* is generally seen as the keystone of formal, legal accountability requirements, but there are a number of other accountability mechanisms based on constitutional conventions.

Ministerial Actions

Though the responsible minister is expected to avoid intruding into the daily operations of Crown corporations, he or she may employ a range of instruments to achieve some control. The minister may rely on the mandate of the corporation, which is typically broad in expression, to give guidance to a Crown corporation. If the minister believes that the corporation is straying from its mission, the minister can cite the objects of the corporation to support his or her case. Nearly all public enterprises are required to present the minister with a corporate plan, and this, too, gives the minister some control. Plans are required to outline, among other things, the corporation's objectives for the year and the expected performance of the corporation in relation to stated objectives. A further vehicle for establishing ministerial control is for the minister to recommend the issuing of "directives," which permit the government "to oblige Crown corporations to deliver on their public policy mandate." What the directive means is that the traditional autonomy of the public enterprise is "set aside" in favour of a government edict requiring the Crown corporation to act in a specific way.[17]

There are also other more informal ways in which the minister may have some say over the activities of a Crown corporation. The minister may communicate directly with the chair of the board of directors and rely on his or her departmental officials through various means to convey the concerns and wishes of the government (e.g., attending board meetings or engaging in exchanges with corporations). But these actions typically have less impact than their formal counterparts.

Parliamentary Control

Control of Crown corporations by Parliament can take the form of approving appropriations or funding. Only the people's representatives can authorize the allocation of financial resources, so Crown corporations must be somewhat attentive to Parliament. Moreover, members of the legislative branch are recipients of overviews of corporate plans, annual reports, and a consolidated report on Crown corporations, and they may also make inquiries of the minister about one aspect or another of their operations. The committees of Parliament also play a role here. Committee hearings are sometimes instituted as a result of information generated by the auditor general or by public concerns about some controversial actions, and more generally "parliamentary committees have the authority to invite chairs and CEOs [of Crown corporations] to appear before them to explain the activities of their organizations."[18] This is an important element of control, but its usefulness is somewhat limited. Elected members have many responsibilities and little assistance in meeting them, which makes it very difficult for them to use the committee system in an effective manner. This situation is exacerbated in the case of Crown corporations, because they see themselves as somewhat removed from detailed political control anyway. Furthermore, unless a corporation needs additional funding or a change in its legislation, there is no automatic mechanism to bring its affairs before a committee and no incentive for the corporation to be totally forthcoming.

Specific Actions

In addition to the general mechanisms of control mentioned already, there are some specific actions that highlight the ability of government to make Crown corporations accountable. Crown corporations must submit detailed annual reports on their operations to ministers, which give senior elected officials an opportunity to compare the actual performance of the corporations with objectives set out in corporate plans released at the beginning of the year. The method of funding also provides opportunities for political control. Self-financing Crown corporations have no need for government funding, so they enjoy a high degree of autonomy. But if the corporation must return to the public treasury on an annual basis and steer its request for funding through the surveillance of an operating department, the Treasury Board, a legislative committee, and ultimately the legislature, it has little more autonomy than an operating department. Ministers and cabinet also play an important role in the appointment of directors and chairs of corporation boards as well as the chief executive officer, which provides government with the opportunity to carefully select the most appropriate individuals to run the corporations. In the case of directors, either the responsible minister or the cabinet makes the final appointment (depending on the legislation), and cabinet has the authority to appoint chairs. As for CEOs, the appointment process can vary, but in most instances cabinet has a direct say in who is picked to manage the day-to-day operations of the corporation. Nearly all directors, chairs, and CEOs serve at the pleasure of cabinet and may be removed without cause.

Criticisms of Crown Corporations

Over the years, Crown corporations have been the object of various criticisms, and recently a series of reports have served to reveal the shortcomings of the public enterprise form.

Proliferation of Corporations and Subsidiaries

One of the most basic—and traditional—criticisms is that there are simply too many Crown corporations and that many of them constitute a questionable use of the corporate form. Some of these entities fail to reflect the qualities of a corporation and hence more properly should assume another organizational form. Others may be deserving of the corporate form, but their usefulness has been brought into question. The privatization push has abated somewhat in recent years, but the continuing relevance of some corporations is not always clear. The CBC originated partly because of the need for a national broadcaster able to reach all Canadians; but now Canada has a number of private television networks that meet this need. Thus, some question the necessity of a public broadcaster in Canada, or at least one that operates in its present form. At the provincial level, there has been similar questioning of some Crown corporations.

Irregular Practices

Recently, the Auditor General of Canada released a damning report on a federal program structured largely to raise the profile of the federal government in Quebec. This initiative, called the sponsorship program, sought to provide funding for community groups and other entities whose activities would make residents of Quebec more aware of Canada and its national government. Part of the report detailed how the Department of Public Works and Government Service, the agency responsible for administering the sponsorship program, and certain Crown corporations seemingly entered into arrangements that violated the public faith in government. In some instances, the department and Crown corporations facilitated the transfer of public monies to private advertising agencies for no apparent reason relating to the program. In others, Crown corporations themselves became recipients of funding available under the program in a way that seemed to be inconsistent with their own internal policies and those applicable to all government agencies. In still other instances, the arrangements, as the report says, involved "using false invoices and contracts or no written contracts at all."[19]

The report of the auditor general revealed that the framework for establishing the accountability of Crown corporations to government requires some attention (more on the framework later). As the federal government admits, officials involved in the sponsorship program "knowingly participated in the mismanagement of public funds," yet this went undetected by authorities outside the corporations.[20] The report also suggested that the governance system and internal operations of Crown corporations must be examined closely. It appears, for instance, that the quality of senior personnel at some corporations leaves something to be desired and that internal audit procedures must be given more weight.

The Commission of Inquiry into the Sponsorship Program and Advertising Activities, set up to investigate further the sponsorship program and related activities, confirmed the allegations of the auditor general in relation to Crown corporations. In one case Via Rail made available to a private company $910,000 to make a TV series on a famous Quebec hockey player. Via had hoped to gain some publicity by its association with the production, but it had also done so with the understanding that the sponsorship program would forward Via Rail $750,000 in the following fiscal year. In the following year, the administrators of the sponsorship program sent a cheque for $862,687.50 to a Quebec advertising firm, which in turn claimed $112,000 for services rendered—none of which were evident—and then forwarded the remaining $750,000 to Via Rail. For its part, Via Rail accepted the three-quarters of a million dollars and adjusted its books to document the difference between the money received and the $910,000 as a marketing expense (see Figure 6.3 for a graphical rendering of these events). The commission provided a withering commentary on this sequence of events:

| PWGSC | $862,500* (March 2000) | Lafleur $112,500 (15%) | $750,000 (March 2000) | VIA Rail $160,000 | $650,000 (Jan 1999) $130,000 (Sept 1999) $130,000 (Sept 1999) | L'information essentielle |

*Figures do not include GST and PST (when applicable).

Source: Adapted from *Report of the Auditor General of Canada,* Chapter 3, "The Sponsorship Program," page 10, Auditor General of Canada, 2003. Reproduced with the permission of the Minister of Public Works and Government Services Canada, 2006.

This was a very irregular and abnormal transaction, especially for a large Crown Corporation. The disbursement of $910,000, unsupported by a contract, relying upon a verbal undertaking by a civil servant, who had no legal right to commit funds from a future fiscal period, that $750,000 would be repaid later, followed by an invoice misrepresenting the transaction, addressed to a communication agency from which Via Rail had no right to claim payment: all of these are improprieties committed by officers of Via Rail, which, it is presumed, wishes never to see repeated. From the point of view of the Canadian taxpayer, the payment...of a commission to Lafleur Communication for simply delivering a cheque to Via Rail is an abuse of public funds which cannot be condoned.[21]

Political Interference

The sponsorship scandal also showed that political interference in the operation of Crown corporations can become a serious issue. Crown corporations can hardly operate efficiently if forced through political forces to take actions inconsistent with their mandate, yet it seems pressure was placed on corporation chairs and CEOs to participate in the sponsorship program even though this contributed little or nothing to their operation. There have been other, similar incidents. In the mid-1990s, then Prime Minister Jean Chrétien spoke personally to the head of the Business Development Bank of Canada (BDC), a Crown corporation established to provide financing to commercial concerns. The purpose of the call was to urge the BDC to look sympathetically upon a request from a business concern located in the prime minister's riding. Though any political official may contact a Crown corporation, it appeared that the prime minister was actually lobbying the BDC with the full force of his office and prestige. For some, including the head of BDC, such action ignores the desire to provide Crown corporations with a degree of freedom that allow for sound business decisions taken in light of the public interest.[22]

Governance System

There are concerns about the governance system of Crown corporations. In the past, the Auditor General of Canada has found in various reports (including the one of the sponsorship program) that directors sometimes lack the skills and capabilities necessary to carry out their duties and that they are insufficiently involved in the hiring of board members and the appointment of chairs and CEOs. A continuing problem, and one that still prevails, is the tardiness in the appointment of senior corporation members. The auditor general is blunt on this point:

It takes too long to appoint board members, chairs, and CEOs. Many board members' terms have expired. Some large Crown corporations are without permanent CEOs.[23]

The federal government itself understands that more attention should be paid to the appointment process. The process, it believes, has to become more transparent or public, and it also "needs to be further refined in order to achieve the correct balance."[24] The latter means that some consideration might be given to enlarging the role of board directors in the appointment process, including the development of selection criteria for chairs and the generation of competency profiles for directors. The directors should also determine the selection process for CEOs.

The governance system of Crown corporations includes an audit committee responsible for reporting to the board on the financial integrity of the corporation and related matters. Here, too, there are concerns. For instance, the quality of information provided to the committee could be higher and the committee itself might better stand up to senior management in the corporation. Clearly the experience of the sponsorship program points up the need to locate weaknesses in the operation of the audit committee.

Oversight

Ministers and cabinet have at their behest various instruments for ensuring political control of Crown corporations. However, the actual strength or effectiveness of these instruments raises some worries. Ministers, for instance, receive corporate plans as part of the accountability process, yet their responses to these plans is limited, partly because the ministers' officials may be without the skills to assess such reports. The minister also expects to have some input into determining the direction of Crown corporations, but the informal communication channels used to realize this expectation are inadequate and the need for a formal process seems evident.

More worrisome are the indications of confusion about the accountability arrangements between government and Crown corporations. A recent report found that CEOs and chairs of such corporations believed "that their accountability was to Parliament rather than to their responsible [M]inister."[25] The participation of a large number of government officials in the review of Crown corporations has also made for some confusion about accountability. The intention is for the Board of Directors is be accountable to the minister who in turn is accountable and answerable to Parliament. But this seemingly simple arrangement has become muddied.

Profits or Public Purpose? Problems of Accountability

One of the most basic problems facing a Crown corporation is whether it ought to function to make a profit or to serve a public purpose. There can easily be conflicts between these two objectives. Crown corporations might cease or limit operations in underpopulated areas in order to reduce costs, but such actions would doubtless clash with their aim of providing services to all Canadians without discrimination.

Determining the amount of control the government should have over the activities of a Crown corporation is not an easy task:

> In the context of responsible government, the most telling questions turn around the problem of establishing a balance between the autonomy that the Crown corporation requires as an organizational form to perform the task it has been given, on the one hand, and the government's need to control and direct the corporation and Parliament's need to oversee or scrutinize it, on the other. This problem of balance runs through every aspect of the complex interrelationships between Parliament, government, and the Crown corporations.[26]

This problem engenders a number of difficulties. It is sometimes suggested that the managers of Crown corporations engage in activities that are contrary to the desires of politicians and that later cause political embarrassment. This situation is frustrating to politicians who must bear criticism, even though they feel that in some cases they have very little control over these corporations. The managers of Crown corporations are also placed in a difficult position because they are frequently ridiculed in the media for their inability to make a profit, or to operate more efficiently, when the problem is sometimes that profit and efficiency have been sacrificed deliberately to political concerns. Of course, when they sacrifice political sensitivity to the profit motive, they suffer for that as well.

Reforms

The problems mentioned above cover a very wide range, but the most serious ones have been identified in the area of accountability. Thus most of the reforms discussed below will be geared to improving accountability.

Privatization

In the context of public enterprises, privatization refers to the sale—wholly or partially—of companies owned by the government. This particular reform has become less prominent in past years, and indeed a recent federal report claims "[t]here is a need to reassert the role of Crown corporations as instruments of public policy."[27] Nevertheless, there remain good reasons for examining privatization as an option when considering the reform of public enterprises. One is that the corporation no longer serves a public policy purpose. Air Canada was at one time an important tool of nation-building and economic development. As the airline industry has matured in Canada, however, it is now clear the country is reasonably well served by a network of airlines, and no one airline serves a more central role than any other. The original market failure has disappeared, making the response to this failure no longer necessary.

A second reason for privatization is that it may improve the efficiency of the privatized company or the services offered by the company. A number of provinces have Crown organizations that have a monopoly over the importation, wholesaling, distribution, and retailing of liquor products. However, one province, Alberta, has privatized the retailing of liquor, and some research shows that Albertans have both better access to liquor stores and a richer selection than those residing in provinces that have maintained their public sector monopolies. Figure 6.4 offers a comparison of the number of alcoholic products available in Alberta and in two provinces in which Crown

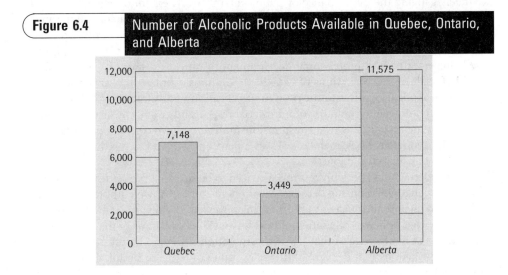

| Figure 6.4 | Number of Alcoholic Products Available in Quebec, Ontario, and Alberta |

Source: Valentin Petkantchin, *Is Government Control of the Liquor Trade Still Justified?* (Montreal: Montreal Economic Institute, 2005), 21. Used with permission.

Box 6.1   A Crown Corporation Strikes Back

The Liquor Control Board of Ontario is the Crown corporation responsible for the retailing of liquor products in Ontario. It rejects the claim that Albertans are better served by the free enterprise approach to selling alcohol. The Board claims that it offers over 16,000 different products to its customers—not the 3,449 cited in Figure 6.4. Prices for alcoholic products also tend to be lower in Ontario than in Alberta. As for the claim that the greater number of stores in Alberta does not lead to more consumption, the LCBO contends that this "contradicts virtually every study done on the impact of increased private sector access."

Source: "LCBO Defends Itself," letter to the editor, *National Post*, October 7, 2005, A21.

corporations control the retailing of liquor. It clearly shows that Albertans have a greater choice of alcoholic products (and without creating an explosion in sales).

At a more practical level, some governments seem to want to sell some of their more profitable Crown corporations, because the inflow of funds will reduce their deficits and outstanding debt. The government of Ontario sold its interest in a major toll highway serving Toronto and the surrounding area; part of the reason was that the sale would generate funds to help bring down the deficit.

Lastly, some governments have an ideological predisposition to favour the private sector at the expense of the public, which drives them to privatize corporations even when there are no other sound reasons to do so. In these cases, elected officials believe that a society in general would be better off if the public sector reduced its size and gave the private sector more responsibility to serves the needs of the citizenry.

External Accountability

Reforms might be made in order to ensure the accountability of Crown corporations to external authorities. The federal government has announced that the responsible minister "will periodically issue a statement of priorities and accountabilities to Crown corporations within his or her portfolio."[28] This is a first step toward making clearer the public policy goals of the government for Crown corporations and providing a basis for more accurately gauging the performance of public enterprises. The auditor general has also reported on deficiencies in corporation reports to ministers and Parliament and the ability of authorities outside the corporations to provide informed comment on corporate plans and the like. One obvious reform, then, is to correct the deficiencies and to provide better training and professional development to officials responsible for briefing elected officials on the operations of Crown corporations. Confusion over the accountability framework also points to the need for clarification of this framework. Key here is the need to reinforce the centrality of ministerial responsibility and the fact that Crown corporations are accountable to the responsible minister. Crown corporations may have to deal with central agencies, members of Parliament, and others, but it is the minister to whom they remain accountable.

In considering these possible reforms, we need to be sure that proper respect is given to the arm's-length relationship between government and its Crown corporations. There is always a danger that ministers and others may overstep the line separating these two entities for either policy or blatantly political reasons. Investigations of the sponsorship program, for example, suggest that "Crown corporations came under pressure to participate in sponsorships that delivered little or no value in terms of building their brand equity."[29] Other instances of political interference reinforce this need to pay constant attention to the balance between autonomy of public enterprises and accountability to government.

Board of Directors

Recent unsettling developments—especially those relating to the sponsorship program—and reports on governance of Crown corporations suggest that boards of directors are central to the successful operation of government's corporate forms. Thus, board members need to be better prepared to take on their duties and to participate as members in training and professional development exercises. A more explicit listing of their role and responsibilities might also impress upon directors the significance of their positions. Directors also have to maintain their independence from management and ensure that the day-to-day demands of corporation officers do not weaken the commitment of directors to the goals and long-term direction of the corporation. To accomplish this end, directors ought to be dissuaded from allowing one individual to function as both chair of the board and CEO; also, the CEO should be the only member of management to sit on the board. A greater role for board members in the appointment of the CEO would also help in this regard. Boards should also give prominence to their audit committees (and establish one if none is present), which are responsible for overseeing financial operations and related matters.[30]

The Government of Canada is contemplating the implementation of many of these suggestions for boards of directors (and has also emphasized the need for transparency in board and corporation operations). Students of public administration are thus afforded an opportunity to watch this particular reform in action and assess its effectiveness.

Conclusion

This chapter has focused on the Crown corporation as an organizational form. Its main value is in carrying on important operations at some distance from the government of the day. The next chapter considers another organizational form that is also at arm's length—the independent regulatory agency.

Notes

1. Patrice Garant, "Crown Corporations: Instruments of Economic Intervention—Legal Aspects," in Ivan Bernier and Andrée Lajoie, eds., *Regulations, Crown Corporations and Administrative Tribunals*, Research Study for the Royal Commission on the Economic Union and Development Prospects for Canada (Toronto: University of Toronto Press, 1985), 4.

2. The "departmental corporation" is a third type of corporate form, but it operates no differently from traditional departmental forms.

3. Treasury Board Secretariat, *Crown Corporations and Other Corporate Interests of Canada, 2005* (Ottawa: Her Majesty the Queen in Right of Canada, 2006), 32.

4. Treasury Board Secretariat, *Review of the Governance Framework for Canada's Crown Corporations* (Ottawa: Her Majesty the Queen in Right of Canada, 2005), 10.

5. Sandford F. Borins, "World War Two Crown Corporations: Their Wartime Role and Peacetime Privatization," *Canadian Public Administration* 25(2) (fall 1982): 380–404.

6. Allan Tupper, "Crown Corporations," *The Canadian Encyclopedia*. Available at www.canadianencyclopedia.ca/index.cfm?PgNm=TCE&Params=A1ARTA0002048. Retrieved July 5, 2006.

7. For more on the history of Crown corporations in Saskatchewan, see John Richards and Larry Pratt, *Prairie Capitalism: Power and Influence in the New West* (Toronto: McClelland and Stewart, 1979).

8. Treasury Board Secretariat, *Review of the Governance Framework for Canada's Crown Corporations*, 10.

9. John Richards, "A Primer on Market and Government Failures," in Thomas M.J. Bateman, Manuel Mertin, and David M. Thomas, eds., *Braving the New World: Readings in Contemporary Politics* (Toronto: Nelson Thomson Learning, 2000), 111.

10. M.J. Trebilcock and J.R.S. Prichard, "Crown Corporations: The Calculus of Instrument Choice," in J. Robert S. Prichard, ed., *Crown Corporations in Canada: The Calculus of Instrument Choice* (Toronto: Butterworths, 1983), 72.

11. Patrick Luciani, *Economic Myths: Making Sense of Canadian Policy Issues*, 4th ed. (Toronto: Pearson Education Canada, Inc., 2004), 121.

12. Harvey Averch, *Private Markets and Public Intervention: A Primer for Policy Designers* (Pittsburgh: University of Pittsburgh Press, 1990), 37.

13. Trebilcock and Pritchard, "Crown Corporations," 70.

14. Charles Wolf, Jr., *Markets or Governments: Choosing Between Imperfect Alternatives*, 2nd ed. (Cambridge: MIT Press, 1993), 28.

15. *Financial Administration Act*, c. F-11, s. 88.

16. *Canada Post Corporation Act*, c. 10.

17. Treasury Board Secretariat, *Review of the Governance Framework for Canada's Crown Corporations*, 18.

18. Ibid., 21.

19. Auditor General of Canada, *Report of the Auditor General of Canada* (Ottawa: Minister of Public Works and Government Services, November 2003), ch. 3, "The Sponsorship Program," 21.

20. Government of Canada, *Review of the Financial Administration Act, Backgrounder*. Available at www.tbs-sct.gc.ca/gr-rg/oag-bvg/media/rfaa-elgfp_e.asp. Accessed October 15, 2005.

21. Commission of Inquiry into the Sponsorship Program & Advertising Activities, *Who Is Responsible? Fact Finding Report* (Ottawa: Her Majesty in Right of Canada, 2005), 225. Emphasis in original removed.

22. See François Beaudoin, "Integrity Has No Price: The Essential Independence of Crown Corporations," *Policy Options*, June 2005: 30–33. Available at www.irpp.org/po/archive/jun05/beaudoin.pdf. Retrieved July 5, 2006.

23. Auditor General of Canada, *Report of the Auditor General of Canada* (Ottawa: Department of Public Works and Government Services, February 2005), ch. 7, "Governance of Crown Corporations," 21.

24. Treasury Board Secretariat of Canada, *Review of the Governance Framework for Canada's Crown Corporations*, 29.

25. Ibid., 14.

26. John Langford. "Crown Corporations as Instruments of Policy," in G. Bruce Doern and Peter Aucoin, eds., *Public Policy in Canada* (Toronto: Macmillan, 1979), 240.

27. Treasury Board Secretariat, *Review of the Governance Framework for Canada's Crown Corporations*, 4. Bolding in original removed.

28. Treasury Board Secretariat of Canada, "President of Treasury Board Releases Review of Crown Corporation Governance—Backgrounder," February 17, 2005. Available at www.tbs-sct.gc.ca/media/nr-cp/2005/0217_e.asp. Retrieved July 5, 2006.

29. Beaudoin, "Integrity Has No Price," 31.

30. For more on these suggestions, see Treasury Board Secretariat of Canada, *Review of the Governance Framework for Canada's Crown Corporations*, chs. 4–5.

Independent Regulatory Agencies

An important aspect of the role of government is to make rules and regulations affecting the operation of both the public and private sectors of any society. These enactments serve to provide a framework to make the economic market function more efficiently and more fairly. They also try to ensure that the workplace is free of any discriminatory practices, and in the case of Canada represent an integral part of the effort to preserve and defend the Canadian culture. It may seem at times that government regulations are too abundant and that the cost of setting rules outweighs any intended benefits. However, a society without regulation is like a game without rules.

This chapter discusses the diverse group of governmental units at the heart of the regulatory activity in Canada. These entities are commonly called **independent regulatory agencies**, and they are probably the most misunderstood bodies of government because few ordinary citizens come into direct contact with them on a regular basis. Compared with the Crown corporations, which deliver the mail, provide transportation, generate electrical power, and employ large numbers of people, regulatory agencies have a much lower profile. But this lack of direct contact between citizens and regulatory agencies masks the very great influence that these agencies have over our everyday lives.

This chapter begins by setting out the definition of a regulatory agency and discussing some of the reasons politicians chose regulatory agencies to accomplish particular objectives. The chapter also considers the basic structure and activities of regulatory agencies, as well as the ways in which these agencies can be controlled and made accountable. The chapter concludes with a discussion of the problems afflicting regulatory agencies and some of the proposed solutions to these difficulties.

While this chapter deals with the general phenomenon of government regulation, it focuses specifically on regulation by regulatory agency rather than by government department. A significant amount of regulation does emanate from government departments, and a lesser amount from other government organizations such as Crown corporations. However, this chapter pays most of its attention to independent regulatory agencies.

Definition of a Regulatory Agency

Defining the phrase "regulatory agency" is a bit like trying to describe the shape of an amoeba. Regulatory agencies come in so many sizes and shapes and with such a variety of duties that it is difficult to generalize about them. The name of the agency is also of little help in identifying it as a regulatory agency. The list of federal regulatory agencies in Canada includes the National Energy Board, the Canadian Dairy Commission, and the Canadian Transportation Agency—none of whose names reveal clear insights into their workings. In attempt to capture the full range of regulatory agencies, a government guidebook on federal organizations simply defines them as "agencies, boards, and commissions."[1] Despite this difficulty, the following definition is an acceptable start:

> A statutory body charged with responsibility to administer, to fix, to establish, to control, or to regulate an economic activity or market by regularized and established means in the public interest and in accordance with government policy.[2]

Two phrases in this definition—"regularized and established means" and "the public interest"—deserve special attention. First, regulatory agencies must set out specific rules of procedure and must follow those rules in working toward a decision. Although regulatory agencies are different from the ordinary law courts in ways that will be discussed later, these agencies do have certain judiciary-like trappings, and the emphasis on "regularized and established means" of acting is one of them. This is a characteristic that separates regulatory agencies from operating departments and Crown corporations. Of course, these latter two types of organization also have restrictions on their actions, but, in general, they are able to make decisions in a manner that is considerably more flexible and sometimes more secretive than that of regulatory agencies.

Second, regulatory agencies are frequently directed to act in "the public interest," but it can be very difficult to define exactly what that means. When an agency is making a decision on rate setting, for instance, it must decide between the interests of consumers, who are members of the public, and shareholders of the company, who are also members of the public. In this situation, the strongest and most principled adherence to the public interest is not a very helpful guide to action. Still, a commitment to the public interest, however defined, is an important influence on the work of regulatory agencies.

Two improvements might be made to the definition given above. First, the emphasis on "economic activity or market" has more to do with traditional forms of regulation than with some of the newer forms of regulation in cultural, environmental, and social areas. A distinction is sometimes made between economic or direct regulation and social regulation:

> Social regulation is aimed at restricting behaviours that directly threaten public health, safety, welfare, or well-being. These include environmental pollution, unsafe working environments, unhealthy living conditions, and social exclusion. By contrast, economic regulation is aimed at ensuring competitive markets for goods and services and at avoiding consumer and other harms when such markets are not feasible. This is accomplished through regulating prices and/or conditions for firms entering specific markets.[3]

At times, the line between these two types of regulation can become fuzzy. An agency responsible for the regulation of firms—economic regulation, in other words—might take actions to further some social goal. For instance, it may set rates or prices in order to assist disadvantaged groups. Also, it is sometimes believed that the two types of regulation are insufficient to capture the nuances of regulatory activity and that the types of regulation should be expanded to include environment and moral regulation. Nevertheless, the twofold distinction supplies a helpful reminder that

Table 7.1	Major Federal Regulatory Agencies

ECONOMIC REGULATION

Canadian International Trade Tribunal

Canadian Transportation Agency

National Energy Board

Standards Council of Canada

Transportation Safety Board of Canada

SOCIAL REGULATION

Canadian Environmental Assessment Agency

Canadian Food Inspection Agency

Canadian Human Rights Commission

Canadian Radio-television and Telecommunications Commission

Indian Claims Commission

regulatory agencies are about more than fixing the market. Table 7.1 lists some of the major federal regulatory agencies by type of regulation.

The second problem with the definition is that it does not mention that a regulatory agency is insulated from direct political intervention when it is making decisions in specific cases, although there is some political control over its general policy direction. As a government publication says of regulatory agencies, "Normally, Ministers are responsible for the policies governing such organizations, but cannot intervene in specific decisions. Thus, the Minister is answerable in general to Parliament for the activities of the organization, but maintains an arm's length relationship with it."[4] The use of the adjective "independent" when referring to regulatory agencies serves to remind us of this quality of autonomy.[5]

The question of the appropriate role of the minister seemingly raises a conundrum or puzzle. He or she is responsible for the policy outcomes of the activities of the agency, but cannot interfere in the making of individual decisions. The purpose of this apparent contradiction is in part "to balance Ministers' accountability for overall policy development and utilization of public resources with the independence needed for these bodies to make specific decisions in a transparent, fair and non-partisan manner."[6] In order to serve a constituency interest, a minister with more direct control over agencies might be tempted to intervene in broadcast licensing decisions or in the setting of energy prices. Neither possibility would be in the public interest.

As with Crown corporations, the arm's-length relationship also serves to make regulatory agencies more attractive to personnel required to carry out the increasingly complex nature of regulation. It is thought that the chances of recruiting experts increase with the prospect of less political intervention and the relative absence of bureaucratic red tape associated with the greater independence of regulatory agencies. Finally, ministers themselves may be reluctant to take on the arduous task of regulation and might welcome in some cases less direct responsibility for this particular activity.

These considerations bring about some changes in the definition presented earlier and suggest an amended version of this definition:

A regulatory agency may be defined as a statutory body charged with responsibility to administer, fix, establish, control, or regulate an economic, cultural, environmental, or social activity by regularized and established means in the public interest and in accordance with general policy guidelines specified by the government. This body is under the general direction of the legislature and a responsible minister with regard to policy matters but possesses relative autonomy of action in making individual decisions within those policy guidelines.

The main advantage of this revised definition is its emphasis on the lack of direct ministerial control over individual decisions made by the regulatory agency. The legislature and the minister set the overall policy of the regulatory agency, but the concept of ministerial responsibility does not have the same meaning with regard to regulatory agencies as it does in the case of operating departments. In fact, it would be inappropriate for a minister to intervene when the agency is making a decision on a specific case.

Functions of Regulatory Agencies

As with the task of defining independent regulatory agencies, it is difficult to generalize about their functions, because the powers and duties assigned to the agencies by their enabling statutes vary widely. One attempt to capture the duties of regulatory agencies states that they "have been established to carry out administrative, quasi-judicial, regulatory and advisory functions within an established policy and legislative framework," and notes that "these functions are by no means mutually exclusive and many agencies carry out multiple roles."[7] Despite the difficulty of sorting out the functions of regulatory agencies, it is possible to identify some tasks common to these bodies.

Adjudicative

This is really the defining function of a regulatory agency, so it is performed by all regulatory agencies. It involves both types of regulation. The federal Competition Bureau makes rulings on matters relating to the operation of private markets; on the other hand, the Canadian Radio-television and Telecommunications Commission (CRTC) adjudicates issues and disputes, addressing among other things Canadian content and the awarding of broadcasting licences. To understand the adjudication function, it is necessary to distinguish a regulatory agency from an ordinary court of law. The law courts are called upon to make a finding of fact and to relate that finding to a relatively precise piece of legislation. If the legislation is not precise in some area, there is usually some precedent set out in a decision on a similar case that can be used to assist in the application of the law. In the case of a regulatory agency, the terms of the law that must be applied are considerably more vague. Statutes containing phrases such as "the public interest" or "public convenience and necessity" are very imprecise guides to action. Therefore, the regulatory agency must act much more on its own initiative in shaping policy than an ordinary court does. A few years ago, the CRTC made two decisions that appeared to some quite contradictory and revealing of the ability of regulatory agencies to follow their own policies. It refused to renew the licence of a Quebec City radio station whose hosts made offensive and insulting comments while on the air; at the same time it agreed to the licensing of a foreign TV station that broadcast graphic images of violence and disseminated reports that some groups found anti-Semitic.[8]

There is a paradox here in that regulatory agencies are required to behave in a judiciary-like manner in considering a case, but they actually make the decision on the basis of policy considerations. This latter point explains why agencies are not bound by precedent. In the many cases in which agencies are allocating scarce resources, they simply could not follow precedent anyway. If all of the available slots on the radio dial have already been assigned, the quality of the next application received is not relevant. The scarcity of slots on the dial precludes approval on the basis of precedent.

Legislative

This function comprises "the ability to make general rules or regulations, in the form of delegated legislation, that have the force of law."[9] Most legislation that establishes regulatory agencies gives them some power to prescribe more specific regulations within the guidelines set out in the legislation. These regulations are referred to as "delegated legislation," because they are made pursuant to powers delegated to the agency in the legislation. They might relate to either policy matters—that is, specify the agency's approach to particular issues—or procedural matters—that is, specify how applications are to be filed and hearings conducted.

Research

Most agencies employ some staff to conduct general research in the policy area that they regulate. The purpose of this research is to allow members to remain conversant with recent trends in the field. For example, it could provide them with an early warning when there is a need for a policy shift. The research staff is also sometimes used to evaluate applications and to provide advice to agency members in making specific decisions.

Advisory

In many ways, the advisory function follows from the research function. As a result of the research conducted and the findings flowing from hearings, the agency members and staff are frequently able to advise the minister and/or the operating department about the need for a fresh consideration of certain policy issues. The regulatory agencies are close to the regulated industry and its clientele. Therefore, they have a good knowledge of emerging problems.

Administrative

Some agencies also have direct administrative responsibility for operating programs. For example, the federal Canadian Food Inspection Agency undertakes inspection and other similar services to ensure food safety, animal health, and plant protection. This administrative responsibility makes the CFIA one of the larger regulatory agencies in terms of number of employees.

This listing of some of the duties of regulatory agencies provides an idea of the rather broad scope and diversity of this organizational form.

Organizational Structure

It is very difficult to generalize about the structure of regulatory agencies, because each agency is different. However, we can make some statements about the general structure of the agencies. Regulatory agencies are virtually always headed by a panel of members. The panel usually consists of five to ten full-time members, but the number can vary quite widely. For example, the Canadian Human Rights Tribunal has fifteen members and the National Parole Board has forty-five. Also, agencies often have part-time members whose numbers are usually somewhat less than those for full-time participants. One member of the panel is designated the chairperson or president, and is considered the administrative head of the agency. He or she usually has the responsibility of assigning fellow panel members to cases, as well as supervising the public servants who work for the agency.

In nearly all cases panel members are appointed by cabinet for specified terms. For instance, members of the National Energy Board are appointed for seven-year terms, while appointees to the CRTC have renewable terms of five years. In selecting people to sit on regulatory panels, cabinet will sometimes look for individuals with knowledge and experience in the area; other times, the capacity of an individual to represent a particular area or interest will be paramount. Some agencies, such as the federal Competition Tribunal, also look for a mix of former justices and laypersons.

The panel members preside over hearings and make decisions, but it is unusual for all members to be present at any one hearing. The agency's legislation will specify the minimum number of members necessary to conduct a hearing. This can be as few as one. Thus, several hearings can be held at the same time, and the work of the agency can be accelerated. Members can be assigned to cases by the chairperson on a random basis, or there can be a committee system that allows members to specialize.

All regulatory agencies have a fairly extensive staff of experts in law, economics, accounting, engineering, or whatever other specialties are required. The main functions of this staff are supporting the work of the members in arranging hearings, conducting both general research and specific investigations concerning individual applications, and advising members on legal and/or technical aspects of their work. With some agencies, the number of staff is rather large, but for many the size of the organization is quite small. The Canadian Food Inspection Agency has a staff of nearly 6,000 people, whereas the Financial Consumer Agency of Canada has only thirty-five.

Figure 7.1 provides the organization chart for one of the larger and more prominent federal regulatory agencies, the National Energy Board. The figure shows the chair, vice-chair, and panel (or board) members at the top, signifying that they are responsible for making the final agency decisions. Immediately below is the chief operating officer, who is in charge of the agency's administrative affairs, and under his or her supervision are the various branches necessary for assisting the panel in making their decisions and monitoring compliance with the rulings of the agency. (The chart contains no reference to the responsible minister, but it is understood that all regulatory agencies must report to a minister.)

Figure 7.1   **Organization Chart of National Energy Board**

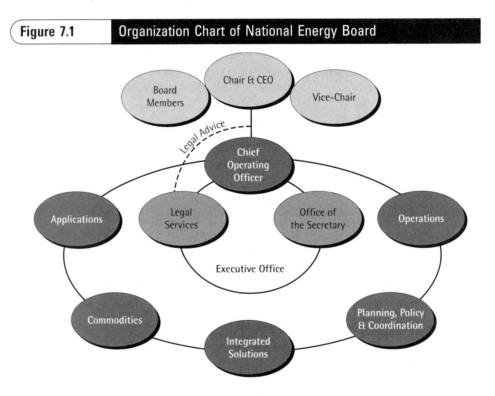

Source: Adapted from National Energy Board, *Annual Report 2005*, page 79. Reproduced with the permission of the Minister of Public Works and Government Services Canada, 2006.

Rationale for Regulatory Agencies

The rationales for independent regulatory agencies follow closely the reasons for using the corporate form to establish Crown corporations. One such reason has already been discussed, which is the need for an organization with a degree of independence from direct political control and the ability to make decisions in an open forum. In this case, the independent regulatory agency represents a response to a failure of government to provide the appropriate organizational form. The traditional departmental structure is simply unsuited to some types of regulation—there is a need to remove some issues from direct ministerial control and the political arena. Another reason for regulatory agencies is to address problems with the operation of various dimensions of the private marketplace. Society relies on the market to allocate its scarce resources in the most appropriate way and also to ensure that distribution of these same resources is fair or equitable. But sometimes the market falls short of expectations because of the presence of what are called "market failures." This attempt to fix market failures is often considered the most important rationale for independent regulatory agencies.

Monopoly

Monopolies constitute one kind of market failure.[10] They occur when one or two private firms dominate a particular sector of industry. For markets to allocate resources wisely—to be efficient—they usually need to be competitive. Markets tend to produce high-quality goods and services at low cost if companies are forced to compete with each other. Alternatively, monopolies typically result in higher prices, a lower quantity of goods, and some insensitivity to the changing interests of the consumer. Regulatory agencies act to maintain competitive conditions in a sector and to break up existing monopolies.

As noted in the preceding chapter, in some instances it *is* in society's interest to have a monopolistic situation, because the lowest cost for a good or service is obtained when there is only one producer. Imagine setting up two or more power lines to service a community or having companies compete to provide hydroelectric power through the building of huge dams. The term "natural monopoly" is used to describe these situations when monopolies are deemed acceptable. Clearly, then, regulatory agencies will not act to end natural monopolies, but they will supervise them to ensure that they do not take advantage of their situation. Like all monopolies, natural monopolies may be tempted to act against the public interest without the discipline of the marketplace.

Control Externalities or "Spillovers"

As also discussed in the chapter on Crown corporations, externalities refer to the spillover effects on a third person or entity created by two agencies engaging in a transaction. The classic example in relation to regulation is pollution. A company produces products for consumers and in so doing creates pollution for the larger society (the third person in this case). Externalities can be both positive and negative in their effect. Pollution clearly has a negative effect, but the inoculation of a child will benefit both the family and all those who might have been infected without the shot. The need for regulating externalities arises because the agents involved in the transaction have no direct interest in taking the spillover effects into consideration. The polluter escapes the cost of addressing the sources of pollution while the family concentrates on its own welfare. Thus, there is a need for a body to set pollution standards that must be followed and one that requires families to have their children inoculated.

Chapter 7 / Independent Regulatory Agencies

Information

For markets to allocate resources efficiently, they need consumers to have the information necessary to make good decisions. A bad decision may, for example, result in the purchase of too much of a product or, worse, the purchase of a product that is physically harmful. An instance of this would be the receipt of health care services of questionable effectiveness or that even threaten the patient's life. Most of the time we have the knowledge required to make sensible decisions in the marketplace but on some occasions we may not. A consumer interested in good eating habits may not know the ingredients of a particular product in the grocery store. When information is missing or imperfect, regulatory agencies can take actions to fill the gap. The practice of health care providers may be monitored or licensed, and companies will be obliged to place the list of ingredients on grocery items.

Smooth Market Instability

Over the years, there has been a tendency toward the use of regulatory agencies for "supply management." The best examples are the marketing boards for such farm products as eggs, milk, and chicken. These agencies work by setting quotas on the overall quantity of the product that can be produced and allocating this quota among specific producers. The effect is to ensure that an excess of supply does not reduce prices paid to producers. Marketing boards have been criticized on the grounds that they increase the price consumers pay. However, they also assure reasonable security of supply by preventing injurious competition that would force some suppliers from the market. In other words, consumers must pay a premium for eggs every time they buy them to ensure that there will always be some eggs available at a reasonable price. Whether the cost is worth the benefit is something every voter must decide for her- or himself.

Equity

The market failures discussed so far represent failures in the efficient allocation of society's resources. With these failures, the market is unable to ensure that we are using resources in the best possible way. A further failure arises when the activities of the private sector distributes income unfairly and makes it difficult for some to secure the basic necessities of life. To deal with this situation, governments may use both income transfers and the tax system in an attempt to redistribute income. For instance, the federal government has a program called the Canada Child Tax Credit that provides additional money to families with low and moderate incomes. But governments may also rely on regulatory activities to achieve greater equity. Minimum wage laws may be instituted to guarantee that people have access to jobs that pay a decent wage, or rates for basic services may be controlled to increase the chances that all have access to gas, water and hydro.[11] In the past, one of the most common regulatory efforts has been the establishment of agencies to administer the regulation of rental accommodation. Housing is an essential service and governments in Canada have seen fit to limit the price of rental units. But in recent years such controls have been phased out, because their cost to society has exceeded their benefits. The fact that regulations and regulatory agencies may introduce new problems when addressing failures in the market will be discussed more fully later.

Low-Cost Option

When a government wants to have an impact on a particular kind of behaviour, it has a number of options, ranging from exhortation, through tax incentives and grants, to coercive legislation. One of the lowest-cost options from the standpoint of the government is simply to say: "Thou shalt not." There is a cost to the government of establishing and operating a regulatory agency, but the impact per dollar spent is usually greater than that of an operating department or Crown corporation because of the regulatory agency's coercive powers.

A classic example of the use of this rationale is the treatment of the Niagara escarpment in southern Ontario. The escarpment is a unique geological formation and prime recreation area. In fact, it is so attractive that private interests would love to develop it for resorts, housing, golf courses, and so forth. In the 1960s, there was considerable pressure on the Ontario government to control development in this area. A number of options were considered, including buying the entire escarpment or strategic portions of it. Not surprisingly, the Ontario government decided to establish a regulatory agency, the Niagara Escarpment Commission, and give it the power to say: "Thou shalt not develop here without prior permission." This was clearly the low-cost option from the standpoint of the government.

Regulation is the low-cost option *only* from the standpoint of the government. As will be discussed in more detail later, regulation can impose significant costs on others. In the Niagara escarpment example, many people saw the value of their land plummet when it became unlikely that it could be used for subdivisions or resorts. It has been suggested that the low cost of regulation makes it particularly attractive to governments facing simultaneous demands for decisive action and for financial restraint.

Apply Specialized Expertise

Many kinds of concerns assigned to regulatory agencies could be handled in ordinary courts. Judges are proficient at sorting through conflicting arguments, separating the important from the trivial, and rendering an impartial decision—all activities associated with the adjudicative function of regulatory agencies. But while judges are learned in the law, they are not expected to have detailed knowledge of the activities of a particular industry or area of activity. Also, we cannot expect judges to apply an integrated, coherent policy in making decisions, for they decide individual cases on the basis of the law. In contrast, members of regulatory agencies develop specialized knowledge over the years, and so are capable of making decisions reflecting consciously conceived policies more quickly than someone who must become familiar with a new issue.

The reasons noted above constitute only a partial listing of the reasons for establishing and preserving regulatory agencies. This diversity of reasons demonstrates why these agencies have such a wide variety of roles.

Political Control of Regulatory Agencies

A central feature of parliamentary control of regulatory agencies is that the legislature, the cabinet, and individual ministers set general policies and guidelines for their activities but are kept at arm's length from their day-to-day operations. This creates a conundrum in that the agency must be accountable to the minister and the legislature, but at the same time it must have autonomy in making individual decisions. The trick, as suggested earlier, is to find the appropriate balance between accountability to elected representatives and autonomy. Weak political control of the agency might allow it to act at cross-purposes with other government agencies, or to make decisions that are not in the public interest. However, excessive political control deflates the morale of the agency and might lead to dominance by powerful interest groups. The conundrum of accountability and autonomy is one of the most difficult problems to handle in discussing regulatory reform. This section will discuss the method of accomplishing this balancing act.

Enabling Statutes and Other Legislation

Regulatory agencies are similar to operating departments and most Crown corporations in that they are formed as a result of enabling legislation, which specifies the structure of the agency, the procedures it must follow in considering cases, the limits of its authority, and the general policies it must apply in making decisions. In some instances, all of these components are specified in one statute; in others, they are divided among a number of pieces of legislation. Legislative committees also check the work of regulatory agencies. They scrutinize the operation of regulatory agencies in the same manner as that of operating departments and Crown corporations. Thus, the committee members can question the minister responsible for an agency and/or the members of the agency about its implementation of policies or its operating procedures.

Standing Joint Committee for the Scrutiny of Regulations

In addition to the policy-oriented legislative committees that oversee the activities of regulatory agencies, there can be specialized committees that review all regulations and delegated legislation. This process was first employed in Saskatchewan in the early 1960s and came to the federal government in 1971 in the form of the Senate and House of Commons Standing Joint Committee on Regulations and Other Statutory Instruments, which has now been renamed the Standing Joint Committee for the Scrutiny of Regulations.

All regulations made under delegated legislation by either operating departments or regulatory agencies are referred to this committee. Its mandate includes reviewing whether the regulation is in line with the authorizing legislation, whether it violates the Charter of Rights and Freedoms, and whether it intrudes into an area that is the prerogative of Parliament. Beyond these specific areas, it does not generally delve into the merits of the regulation. Therefore, the committee has a somewhat legalistic and limited mandate.

Appointment of Members

The decisions of regulatory agencies are made by a panel of members who are appointed by the governor in council, usually after consultation with the minister responsible for the agency. The minister will normally recommend the appointment of persons who share her or his views on the policy area. Johnson has argued that the power of appointment is the most important of all these powers, because it allows the government to establish the "culture" of the agency.[12] In the absence of any direct control over agency decisions, the ability to establish this overall cultural tone is a very important element of accountability. This "cultural" approach is particularly important, since appointees immediately attain a high level of independence after they are appointed. Most appointments are for lengthy fixed terms of office, and members can be removed only "for cause." Therefore, the ability of anyone, including the minister, to interfere in a specific decision is limited.

Policy Statements and Directives

As noted above, it is inappropriate for a minister to intervene in specific cases before an agency. However, a minister, or the cabinet collectively, can issue policy statements or directives to inform the regulatory agency of the government's desires in a particular area. For some agencies it is not clear whether these are binding, but for others the legislation makes it clear that they are binding. These must be general policy statements and not directions concerning specific cases. Thus, it would be inappropriate for a minister to tell an agency: "You must grant this broadcast licence to person A instead of person B." However, it would be quite appropriate for the minister to direct the agency that: "The only applicants who should be considered for this broadcast licence are those who will agree to provide X percent of Canadian content."

These policy statements or directives can be made secretly to the agency, but it is usually considered important that they be made publicly so that all parties appearing before the agency will know what policy statements and directives have been made. It also acts as a constraint on any potential abuse of power by the minister.

Prior Approval of Decisions

In some instances, the decision of a regulatory agency does not become binding until it is approved either by the responsible minister or by the cabinet collectively. The role of the agency in this situation is to provide an impartial hearing to all concerned and to apply its specialized expertise in arriving at a recommendation for a decision. These recommendations are usually given publicly so that the cabinet must consider very carefully both the recommendations and the supporting documentation. If this advice is ignored, allegations of inappropriate political influence can be made.

Appeal

Some legislation dealing with regulation provides the right of appeal to the minister or cabinet. Where this provision exists, the appellant usually has no right to appear personally to argue the case but must state in writing the reasons why the decision should be overturned. The minister or cabinet considers these appeals carefully, but is usually somewhat reluctant to overturn a decision, partly to preserve the morale and integrity of the agency and partly to prevent a flood of similar appeals. This reluctance to overturn decisions probably explains the small number of appeals made to cabinet.

Recently, interested groups appealed a decision of the CRTC to grant satellite radio licences to two Canadian companies with links to large American firms. (Incidentally, our use of CRTC for examples illustrates how some regulatory agencies have a higher profile than others.) The groups complained that the decision required these companies and their partners to include only 10 percent Canadian content in their radio offerings, far below the normal level of 35 percent. There was also a fear that the decision would hurt the chances of solely Canadian concerns to compete in the emerging radio subscription market. Cabinet agonized over the issue—ministers responsible for culture and industry respectively were split badly—but finally it decided against asking the CRTC to reconsider. The promise of the two Canadian companies to add more Canadian content helped sway cabinet to decide against overturning the initial decision of the CRTC.[13]

Cabinet's decision in this case shows that appeal mechanism can be a valuable safety valve even if no action is taken. The availability of an appeal reminds agencies that their decisions can be reviewed, preventing them from behaving in some entirely inappropriate manner. In a less extreme vein, the minister or cabinet can use the selective acceptance of certain appeals to signal changes in policy at the political level. The satellite radio case, for instance, may be foreshadowing the possibility that Canadian-content rules may be less important in the future.

Judicial Control of Regulatory Agencies

Courts can also control the actions of independent regulatory agencies. In so doing, a court rarely changes the decision of an agency, a consequence of the traditional deference of judicial bodies to the decisions of regulatory entities. But the courts may consider the process followed by an agency in the making of a decision and use this as grounds for overturning the decision. Accordingly, the process of making a decision—and not the merit of a decision—is the foundation of judicial review of regulatory actions. When a court decides against a regulatory agency, the latter is free to reconsider the matter, follow the proper procedure, and arrive at exactly the same decision. The court would then be satisfied. A party interested in challenging the quality or merits of a regulation thus must appeal to political authorities.

Creating or Changing a Regulation

The enabling legislation usually gives the agency or department[14] some discretion in establishing specific regulations within the framework set out in its act or acts. This section describes the basic steps in the regulation-making process.[15]

- The process begins when the agency decides that it might need to establish a new regulation or modify an existing one. In so doing, the agency has to ensure that the regulation is indeed warranted. The current federal policy on regulation, for instance, requires that it be demonstrated "that a problem or risk exists, that intervention is justified and that regulation is the best alternative."[16] Once the agency has determined that a regulatory action is required, it will notify all interested parties that it is considering changing regulations using a variety of ways. It may, for instance, place a notice of intent in the *Canada Gazette* (newspaper of government) or develop a website outlining its intentions.
- If the agency decides to go forward with its new or amended regulation, the next step is the preparation of a draft to show what the new regulation will look like. It will also prepare both a Regulatory Impact Analysis Statement (RIAS) and a communications assessment (CA). The RIAS is the agency's formal justification of the regulation it is proposing, showing what the government is going to deliver, how Canadians have been consulted, and what they have said; the CA basically outlines the government's plan for conveying to interested parties and the public what it is attempting to accomplish with the regulatory initiative. At this stage, a public notice of pre-publication, which gives all parties a chance to comment on the draft regulation, and the appropriate papers for cabinet's approval of the regulation will both be drafted.
- The next step is for the Department of Justice and the Privy Council Office (PCO) to review the proposed regulation. The task of the Department of Justice is to ensure that the regulation has a proper legal basis and that it conforms to the Charter of Rights and Freedoms. As for the PCO, it determines whether the regulation meshes with the government's federal regulatory policy and also checks for clarity and a complete presentation of the relevant facts. For various reasons, regulatory agencies may wish to seek an exemption from pre-publication, and the role of the PCO is to ascertain whether the request is valid. Reasons for dispensing with pre-publication include the need to respond quickly to an emergency and the desire to avoid undermining the purpose of the regulation.
- If the proposed regulation withstands these various tests, the minister approves the regulatory proposal and sends it to the Treasury Board for its approval. If the Treasury Board agrees to the regulation, it is then published in the *Canada Gazette* to allow for comment from interested parties.
- After thirty days, the agency submits the proposed regulation to the minister and to the Treasury Board for final approval. The package of materials includes an updated RIAS which reflects discussions and comments arising from submissions of interested parties. At this point, the Treasury Board may approve the regulation, request more consultation with the interested parties, postpone its decision, or reject the regulation.

- If accepted, the regulation is then officially registered with the Privy Council Office and given formal approval by the cabinet and governor general. The regulation is then published in the *Canada Gazette*. After the regulation has been approved, it goes to the Standing Joint Committee for the Scrutiny of Regulations for review. As discussed earlier, the committee has a fairly narrow mandate to review the regulation to ensure that it is within the purview of the enabling legislation and that it does not intrude on a prerogative of the legislature. If the committee is dissatisfied with something, it can only draw this to the attention of the House of Commons. The committee has no authority to delay or overturn the regulation.

Deciding a Case

The adjudication process—the consideration of individual cases—involves a number of elements. The process begins usually with either a complaint or request for action, which is then followed by the agency's notifying all interested parties of the request. The agency will then receive and consider submissions from the parties involved and may at times hold public hearings on the matter. With all the information at hand, the regulatory agency will then make a decision, which in some instances can be appealed to a court of law.

The Canadian Transportation Agency (CTA) is a major independent regulatory agency responsible for the administration of regulations affecting all types of transportation under federal law. Its decision process, as noted above, starts with a complaint or application for a decision.[17] A complaint may involve the charging of air fares or the failure of trains to make accessible their service to disabled persons. On receiving the complaint, the chair of the agency assigns at least two members of the agency's governing panel to address the issue. At the same time, individuals and groups with an interest in the application (called interveners) are also invited to comment. In cases involving direct complaints, the party against whom the complaint is made responds within thirty days of notification and then the complainant has ten days to reply. If members of the panel feel that they require a greater understanding of the issue or the evidence, they may decide to have public hearings at which time the interested parties expand on their written submissions.

The next step is for agency officials who support the work of the CTA panel to analyze the evidence and the relevant regulations and legislation. They then make a report to the panel, which is part of the final consideration of the application by the panel. Lastly, the panel makes a decision, something which must be done within four months of the receipt of the complaint or application unless interests affected by the decision agree that the process be extended. If any party finds fault with the decision, they may appeal to the Federal Court of Appeal if a point of law is at issue within one month of the decision. They may also ask cabinet to consider the decision, and the CTA itself may look at its own decision "if there has been a change in the facts or circumstances pertaining to that decision or order."[18]

The CTA decision process shows that regulatory agencies take very seriously their adjudication duty. The steps in the process are clearly delineated and rules of procedure and appeal are carefully laid out and respected. In recent years, the CTA has set up a second decision process that moves away from formal adjudication and seeks to resolve complaints through informal mediation. The hope is that the informal and cooperative nature of this process will permit "disputing parties to understand other perspectives, identify facts, check assumptions, recognize common ground and test possible solutions"—all of which is difficult to do in the traditional decision process.[19]

Problems with Regulation

The role of regulation and regulatory agencies in society has in the past few years been the subject of a great deal of review. The Organisation of Economic and Co-operative Development (OECD), an international organization interested in government matters, recently completed an examination of regulation in Canada,[20] and the federal government is in the process of responding to the report of an external body on the need for "smart regulation."[21] In this section, some of the main criticisms of regulatory agencies will be considered, and in the next section some of the possible reforms will be discussed.

Cost of Regulation

Although regulation is often seen as the low-cost option from the standpoint of government, it can impose sizable costs on other parties. The most obvious examples are the direct costs incurred by the regulated industry and by other affected parties. The firms in the regulated industry must maintain extensive records in a format specified by the regulatory agency. All parties affected by regulatory agencies incur substantial information costs to keep themselves abreast of initiatives by the agency and by other groups affected by the agency. Then there are legal and other costs involved in preparing a case and actually appearing before the regulatory agency.

However, these direct costs might be only the tip of the iceberg. The major costs of regulation could come from complying with regulations. In the past, the automobile industry was forced to conform to regulations relating to seatbelts, air bags, improved door strength, head restraints, and increased bumper strength. These changes helped increase the safety of vehicles, but they also added substantially to the cost of a car. Similarly, expensive pollution-reduction devices, such as scrubbers, contributed to the battle against environmental degradation, but they also represented a substantial cost to the companies and government agencies at which the new measures were directed. Rent controls, too, fall into this category.

There are also "induced costs" of regulation. Regulations may hinder innovation, because industry research funds and facilities are moved toward meeting regulatory requirements and away from work on "new technology that might improve productivity, reduce costs, and lead to the development of a wider range of new products and services."[22] The length of the regulatory process—for example, in the approval of new pharmaceutical drugs—may also discourage attempts to develop new products that would increase the effectiveness of the health care sector. Productivity gains, too, may be lost as companies expend valuable resources on addressing regulatory concerns, leaving less available for investment in equipment and machinery that may reduce costs and expand capacity. Employment rates, an important indicator of economic health, can also be affected adversely by regulations. Minimum-wage laws can lead to employment loss, because firms are unwilling to pay the stipulated wage for certain jobs.

Regulatory Approval Process

We have already mentioned that the regulatory approval process can negatively affect innovation. There are also other aspects of this process that are worrisome. In its review of regulation in Canada, the OECD applauds the process by which the federal government carries out its examination of regulation proposals, but notes that the process could be made better. It states that the RIAS analyses are "uneven" and that the quantification contained in the examinations might be more rigorous.[23] A more thorough mechanism might also be developed for reviewing the utility of existing regulations—one

| Box 7.1 | Regulation of Genetically Modified Crops and Foods |

As with all countries, Canada is attempting to determine how best to regulate genetically modified (GM) crops and foods. For the most part, it has left this matter up to science experts and representatives from the agri-food industry. Other countries, such as the United Kingdom, have approached this issue differently, providing for more public input and debate concerning the regulation of GM crops and foods. For some scholars, the Canadian approach is unsatisfactory. A more open process is desirable.

Source: Sarah Hartley and Grace Skogstad, "Regulating Genetically Modified Crops and Foods in Canada and the United Kingdom: Democratizing Risk Regulation," *Canadian Public Administration* 48(3) (fall 2005): 305–327.

should never assume that regulations will remain forever effective. Perhaps most disconcerting is that consultation inherent in the approval process has some problems. This is disconcerting because there is a traditional fear that some groups—especially consumer groups with few resources or the interested public—are unable to make their voices heard. In its report, the OECD reveals that interest groups feel that their comments on proposed regulations are insufficiently heeded by government, and that a lack of consistency prevails across departments in the extent and timing of consultations. Interestingly, the OECD uncovers a feeling that too much consultative activity takes place, with the paradoxical effect of reducing its importance. As the report says, "[there is] a sense that the regulatory process is being inundated with consultation, sometimes involving unnecessary duplication," which in turns creates "consultation fatigue" and a subsequent inability to participate in future approval processes.[24] A more recent report corroborates many of these concerns with the approval process, and addresses more directly the concern over consumer groups:

> One objective of public consultations on regulatory issues is to ensure that regulatory authorities are aware of a broad spectrum of perspective and ideas. In this regard, consumer organizations are under-represented in consultative processes and do not have the resources to undertake the research and develop the expertise required to contribute to consultations on regulatory issues.[25]

Regulatory Congestion

The regulatory system, as Doern says, has not been developed "by some all-seeing and all-knowing decision maker"; rather, the various agencies and departments have emerged "'one at a time,' in response to particular pressures." The result is "regulatory congestion" or the existence of a number of uncoordinated regulatory agencies in each of the regulated areas of society.[26] The aforementioned OECD report notes, for example, that federally incorporated financial institutions (banks, etc.) face a "complex web" of over thirty federal and provincial regulatory agencies.[27] To give a concrete understanding of the congestion, Doern lists the agencies, regulations, and requirements confronting a forestry company interested in a new investment:

- A provincial timber management plan
- *Species at Risk Act* requirements
- Permits/requirements under the *Navigable Waters Protection Act*
- *Fisheries Act* requirements
- *Canadian Environmental Assessment Act* requirements
- Provincial permits (of various kinds under several statutes)
- Further *Fisheries Act* and *Canadian Environmental Assessment Act* processes and requirements
- Further requirements downstream or at later stages of the project or investment[28]

As with any kind of congestion, regulatory congestion has unwanted effects. It increases the cost of complying with regulatory initiatives and may act to constrain attempts at developing new and interesting production methods. The congestion and the resulting maze of regulation might also discourage groups from participating in the regulatory process. From a global perspective, the congestion "contributes to a perception of Canada and Canadian regulation as being overly complex, which acts as a disincentive to investment in Canada."[29] At the most basic level, the crowded world of regulations and regulatory agencies produces much frustration and confusion. Regulation is difficult to address and accept without facing a regulatory system that at times defies easy comprehension. Much like a driver caught in traffic jam, companies and firms feel stuck and resigned to going nowhere for the moment.

Ineffective International Regulation

In an increasingly globalized world, it is important that a country's efforts at regulating its interaction with international forces be effective. There is a concern that Canada's actions in this area are "ad hoc and uncoordinated."[30] Too often agencies act to regulate the international sphere without a real sense of overall direction and purpose, and without an awareness of what other Canadian regulatory bodies are doing in this area. We also seem to act even though existing internationally negotiated rules and regulations are workable. As a recent report on regulation on Canada states, "In many cases, international standards are sufficiently developed that Canada can achieve its policy goals without the addition of Canada-specific requirements."[31] The same holds if another country has set a standard that satisfies Canada's interest. Of course, this does not mean Canada should bow to pressures from certain sectors for less international regulation, or refrain from acting when necessary; it only means we should be aware of the fact that country-specific solutions to international problems will become less and less effective in a more and more integrated world.

The charge of ineffectiveness in international regulation includes relations with Canada's largest trading partner, the United States. The two countries often have parallel regulatory bodies and processes, a situation that can lead to higher costs for all concerned. For instance, both countries have bodies that participate together in the regulation of pesticides in North America, but this arrangement is sometimes viewed as "burdensome" and causes some companies to seek approval only in the less-regulated American market.[32] The result is that American farmers may get to use new and more useful pesticides while their Canadian counterparts must be content with older and less effective ones. This problem also reveals a related one: that differences in regulations still exist between the two countries, a condition that "can impede trade and investment." As one report says, "the cross border movement of goods and services is still subject to an array of different regulatory requirements."[33] Some of these differences, to be sure, are the outcome of clear policy differences, but many might be eliminated with little or no detrimental effect to Canadian interests.

Poor Instruments

Traditionally, regulatory agencies have relied on rules and regulation to achieve their purposes. It has been thought that the best way to address pollution, for example, is to establish standards that must be met. Similarly, to achieve certain levels of Canadian content on radio and television, rules are set out with which the stations and networks must comply. But increasingly, it is felt that this "command and control" approach leaves something to be desired, that it is too heavy-handed and suffers from problems of compliance. In place of this approach, some suggest that "economic instruments" be applied to market failures. These are devices that, paradoxically, use market-like incentives to fix the market, and some of these are simple but effective. For example, the use of permits to allow for pollution can produce a situation in which the level of pollution can be controlled. One way this can be accomplished is through issuing the number of permits consistent with an acceptable amount of pollution. Some are uneasy with a system based on allowing something that is supposed to be regulated and minimized, but the use of economic instruments has achieved some success—and acceptance—in the United States.[34]

The Captive Agency Theory

The **captive agency theory** is in many ways complementary to the above arguments about the lack of consumer power in the regulatory process.[35] This theory suggests that, over time, the agency is captured by the industry that it was set up to regulate, and so becomes supportive of that industry. It is a gradual process, in which the agency develops a concern for the orderly development of the industry; this concern gradually comes to mean the protection of the companies currently in the industry from any disruptive forces, such as excessive competition from new entrants.

Proposals for Reform

These perceived problems with regulation have generated many proposals for changes in the regulatory process, some of which are discussed below.

Deregulation and "Smart Regulation"

In Canada, the attractiveness of **deregulation** (and the use of the word itself) has not been as great as in some other Western democracies. Also, Canada has achieved some success in dealing with regulatory inflation of the 1970s and 1980s. Nevertheless, there is evidence that some paring of the existing set of regulations might be warranted. The OECD reports that Canada still suffers from substantial regulatory costs and points to excessive regulation in such areas as telecommunications and trade between provinces.[36] Experience also suggests that deregulation can be a successful policy—the deregulation of the airline industry in Canada, for instance, led to reduced fares and more efficient use of labour.[37] However, the federal government at this time is leaning toward a policy of "smart regulation," in which governments resist the temptation to simply cut away at rules and regulations. Smart regulation amounts to an attempt to make the current regulatory system more effective, and ensuring that that system adapts to the changing economic and social environment. It also seeks to involve all affected parties—governments, industry, and the citizenry—in the creation of regulations.[38] In general, the policy of smart regulation recognizes that well-crafted regulations can contribute to the social and economic well-being of a nation.

Coordination

The problem of regulatory congestion suggests the need for better coordination among regulatory agencies. At the federal level, new mechanisms might be developed to ensure that departments and agencies are able to speak with one another in the process of regulating. Such structures, not surprisingly, already exist, but they seem insufficient to deal with the problem of congestion. Coordination also entails a more clearly articulated government policy on regulation, which can be used to steer regulatory agencies and increase the chances that regulations will be consistent with each other. The problem of congestion also points to the need for a "single point of contact for the entire federal government to liaise with a specific industry sector."[39]

Better coordination of regulatory activities should also be extended to the federal–provincial arena. As within the federal government, new structures could be put in place to reduce the duplication and competition that arises out of the regulatory initiatives of the two orders of government. The External Advisory Committee on Smart Regulation recommends, for instance, the establishment of a cooperative arrangement initiated by the first ministers. Its purpose would be to seek agreement on key regulatory priorities, examine obstacles to cooperation between the two governmental parties, and set out a framework that would shape the regulatory efforts of federal and provincial governments.

Reforming the Process

To deal with problems with the regulatory approval process, a number of actions might be taken. The analysis of the costs and benefits of proposed regulations might be more rigorous, and a framework for measuring the performance of regulations might be developed. The effectiveness of regulations might also be enhanced if the regulatory process made a greater commitment to enforcement and compliance measures; sometimes we forget that regulations are not self-executing and that efforts must be expended to ensure that regulations are properly observed. Regulations might be addressed more quickly if it were recognized that some proposals—the less controversial or less significant ones—required only ministerial approval and did not have to go through the pre-publication process.

Two reforms to the approval process seem especially important. One is to upgrade the quality and expertise of government regulators. The increasing complexity of industrial sectors, especially in the areas of science and technology, challenges regulatory bodies and their officials. Governments can hardly be expected to produce effective regulation if they are unable to understand and appreciate what they are trying to regulate. The other reform is the need to provide financial assistance to outside groups whose participation is vital to the regulatory process but who may be without the necessary resources. Funds are already made available for this purpose, but the evidence indicates that additional assistance is needed.

Conclusion

The most common service delivery mechanisms used by governments are the operating department, the Crown corporation, and the regulatory agency. In this and the previous two chapters, these forms have been discussed, and the reasons for choosing one to accomplish a particular objective have been considered. However, the story is not quite complete. There are a number of other methods of delivering government services, which fall under the very broad heading of "alternative service delivery." These will be discussed in the next chapter.

1. Privy Council Office, "Public Sector Organizations," *A Guide Book for Heads of Agencies* (Ottawa: PCO, August 1999). Available at www.pco-bcp.gc.ca/default.asp?Page=Publications&Language=E&doc=mog/cover_e.htm. Retrieved August 15, 2006.

2. C. Lloyd Brown-John, *Canadian Regulatory Agencies* (Toronto: Butterworths, 1981), 35.

3. Peter J. May, "Social Regulation," in Lester M. Salamon, ed. (with special assistance of Odus V. Elliott), *The Tools of Government: A Guide to the New Governance* (New York: Oxford University Press, 2002), 157–58.

4. Privy Council Office, "Public Sector Organizations."

5. Most texts in public administration simply use the term "regulatory agencies," and even in this text the "independent" is often omitted.

6. Privy Council Office, "Public Sector Organizations."

7. Ibid.

8. CTV News, "CRTC Approves Al-Jazeera for Canadian Viewers," July 16, 2004. Available at www.ctv.ca/servlet/ArticleNews/story/CTVNews/1089894102595_32/?hub=TopSt. Accessed July 5, 2006.

9. Economic Council of Canada, *Reforming Regulation* (Ottawa: Minister of Supply and Services, 1981), 56.

10. For more on this market failure and others, see John C. Strick, "Regulation and Deregulation," in Christopher Dunn, ed., *The Handbook of Canadian Public Administration* (Toronto: Oxford University Press, 2002).

11. Ibid., 266.

12. David Johnson, "Regulatory Agencies and Accountability: An Ontario Perspective," *Canadian Public Administration* 34(3) (autumn 1991): 417–34.

13. Simon Tuck, "Satellite Radio Ruling Upheld," *Globe and Mail*, September 10, 2005, A4.

14. While this chapter deals with regulatory agencies, the regulation-making process is the same for both departments and Crown corporations.

15. For a complete discussion of this process, see Government of Canada, *Regulatory Process Guide: Developing a Regulatory Proposal and Seeking Its Approval.* Available at the Government of Canada Privy Council Office site, www.pco-bcp.gc.ca/raoics-srdc/default.asp?Language=E&Page=Publications&doc=regguide/regguide_e.htm. Retrieved July 5, 2006.

16. Ibid., 15.

17. Canadian Transportation Agency, *Annual Report 2004*, 12–13. Available at www.cta-otc.gc.ca/publications/ann-rpt/2004/cover_e.html. Retrieved July 5, 2006.

18. Canadian Transportation Agency, "The Process for Making Decisions," Available at www.cta-otc.gc.ca/about-nous/decision_process_e.html. Accessed July 5, 2006.

19. Canadian Transportation Agency, *Annual Report 2004*, 12.

20. OECD, *Canada: Maintaining Leadership Through Innovation* (Paris: OECD, 2002).

21. External Advisory Committee on Smart Regulation, *Smart Regulation: A Regulatory Strategy for Canada*, September 2004. The federal government has also set up a website at regulation.gc.ca (accessed July 5, 2006) to deal with regulation and the smart regulation initiative.

22. John C. Strick, *The Economics of Government Regulation: Theory and Canadian Practice*, 2nd ed. (Toronto: Thomson Educational Publishing Inc., 1994), 116.

23. OECD, *Canada: Managing Leadership Through Innovation*, 41.

24. Ibid., 72.

25. External Advisory Committee on Smart Regulation, *Smart Regulation: A Regulatory Strategy for Canada*, 56. September 23, 2004. Available at the Government of Canada Official Web Site, www.pco-bcp.gc.ca/smartreg-regint/en/08/part_1.html. Retrieved July 5, 2006.

26. G. Bruce Doern, "Smart Regulation, Regulatory Congestion and Natural Resources Regulatory Governance," in G. Bruce Doern, ed., *How Ottawa Spends 2004–2005: Mandate Change in the Paul Martin Era* (Montreal & Kingston: McGill-Queen's University Press, 2004), 245, 261.

27. OECD, *Canada: Managing Leadership Through Innovation*, 27

28. Doern, "Smart Regulation, Regulatory Congestion and Natural Resources Regulatory Governance," 247.

29. External Advisory Committee on Smart Regulation, *Smart Regulation*, 30.

30. Ibid., 17.

31. Ibid., 19.

32. Ibid., 20.

33. Ibid., 21.

34. Patrick Luciani, *Economic Myths: Making Sense of Canadian Policy Issues* (Toronto: Pearson Education Canada Inc., 2004), ch. 18.

35. Marver H. Bernstein, *Regulating Business by Independent Commission* (Princeton, N.J.: Princeton University Press, 1955), ch. 3.

36. OECD, *Canada: Maintaining Leadership Through Innovation*, 25, 29, 41.

37. Strick, "Regulation and Deregulation," 271–72.

38. External Advisory Committee on Smart Regulation, *Smart Regulation*, 12–13.

39. Ibid., 33.

8

Alternative Service Delivery

The previous three chapters discussed the traditional types of organizations that governments use for service delivery. Until a few years ago, this was the end of the story about service delivery—virtually all services fit into one of these three molds and were delivered by one of these three entities. But in recent years governments have adopted more flexible mechanisms in the provision of services, and we place these new services into the category called **alternative service delivery (ASD)**. Figure 8.1 reveals the three dimensions along which alternative service delivery may develop.

- Along one dimension, services are moving away from relying on the public sector and toward an acceptance that the private sector is capable of offering public services to citizens. Government may contract with private firms to offer a service or establish a public/private partnership with a non-profit organization for the purpose of operating a program.
- A second dimension measures the extent of federal government control of the delivery mechanism. The newer approaches to service delivery do not require that government control delivery completely. Government may set up special agencies that involve a relaxation of normal ministerial oversight or exploit new technologies that permit services to be offered outside traditional organizational structures.
- A third dimension illustrated in the figure concerns the level of commercialization. This refers to the extent to which the organization makes a profit or generates revenue by selling its goods or services at the point of purchase or service. One of the changes we have seen in recent years is that users now pay directly for more services which government traditionally provided free of charge.

As can be seen, the combination of the three dimensions produces four quadrants in which we can identify various types of services. The lower-left quadrant consists of the traditional kinds of government organizations at the federal level, namely departments controlled and operated by the federal government. The other three quadrants identify methods of service delivery not previously viewed as significant. For example, the bottom-right quadrant includes arrangements, such as contracting out services to private entities, that move away from direct federal government and public sector provision. The figure shows that new organizational entities or services can move along two or more of the three dimensions of alternative service delivery.

This chapter will focus on those items in Figure 8.1 that can be grouped under the very broad heading of alternative service delivery—a phrase with a number of different meanings. The assertion that governments are slow to espouse new ideas might be correct, but when governments seized upon the idea of ASD, they did so with a vengeance. This chapter is not meant to be comprehensive. There are so many examples of ASD being developed every day that there can be no comprehensive catalogue. The purpose of this chapter is to provide a flavour of the concept of ASD and address some of the political and organizational issues it raises.

The chapter will first provide a definition of ASD and discuss some of the reasons why governments have chosen to employ ASD mechanisms. The next section will provide a selective

Figure 8.1 | Opportunities for Alternative Service Delivery Programs

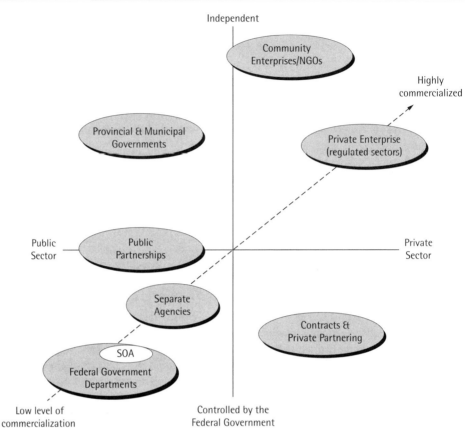

Source: Adapted from *Framework for Alternative Program Delivery*, page 7, Treasury Board of Canada Secretariat, 1995. Reproduced with the permission of the Minister of Public Works and Government Services Canada, 2006.

discussion of some ASD approaches. The chapter ends with a consideration of some of the potential problems in the use of ASD mechanisms.

Definition

There are many definitions of ASD, because it is a relatively new idea and because it covers a broad variety of activities. One definition characterizes ASD as "an organizational option or response to the challenge of improving the capacity of governments to manage change, promote innovation, and meet their infrastructure and service delivery obligation more efficiently and effectively."[1] For its part, the federal government sees ASD as consisting of two related parts, both of which serve to improve the performance of organizations. One part entails the establishment of various structures—whether in or outside conventional department structures—and the other seeks to build a wide variety of partnerships involving governments, the nonprofit sector, and private enterprise.[2] Another definition, one which will be used here, is as follows:

> [Alternative service delivery is] a creative and dynamic process of public sector restructuring that improves the delivery of services to clients by sharing governance functions with individuals, community groups and other government entities.[3]

The same authors go on to say:

> ASD approaches provide a toolbox from which governments can tailor various options to meet their own prevailing needs and demands. ASD is a dynamic spectrum of delivery options that challenge hierarchical public service structures and allow public servants the flexibility to adapt to their future environment.[4]

This definition emphasizes that ASD is "a creative and dynamic process." The traditional approach was that government chose the "one best way" to deliver a service (through an operating department, Crown corporation, or regulatory agency) when a policy was created and stayed with that mechanism for the indefinite future. ASD suggests that there is no "one best way" of delivering a service. The best approach is to consider service delivery as a "toolbox from which governments can tailor various options" to meet the needs of a particular set of circumstances. As those circumstances (e.g., technology of service delivery, characteristics of service users) change, different ASD mechanisms might be employed.

The next part of the definition refers to "public sector restructuring." It is important to understand that ASD is not a minor adjustment in approach, such as a restructuring of field offices. ASD constitutes a form of "sharing governance functions with individuals, community groups and other government entities." Thus, it gives other groups some involvement in the governing process.

One of the common features found in most ASD arrangements is some combination of contractual arrangements, business plans, and performance measures. Basically, this arrangement allows the agency to operate free from onerous day-to-day controls as long as it complies with the terms of its contract, operates according to the business plan prepared in advance, and meets the performance measures agreed to.

Origins of ASD

The intellectual origins of ASD lie in the emergence of the new public management and the belief that "government should concentrate more on developing policy and allow its implementation ... to be taken over by organizations outside government."[5] Important in this thinking was the distinction between "steering" and "rowing" and the assertion that government should centre its efforts on the former.[6] It was felt that government allocated too many of its scarce resources to administration and too little to providing overall direction. What government should do was stick mostly to the crucial task of steering the ship of state and leave the carrying out of public programs to a wide assortment of arrangements which may or may not involve government directly. The steering and rowing analogy was suggesting the separation of policy and advice functions from the operations duties. In making these claims, the proponents of ASD were not saying that government should never "row"—there might be situations in which governments are uniquely situated to implement initiatives. The point was that in the past governments had been too quick to assume that the "steering," and "rowing" functions are always coupled when in fact they might be easily and beneficially separated.

The rise of the new public management supplied the intellectual foundation for the argument in favour of adopting ASD. But other forces provided complementary grounds for supporting a new way of delivering government services.

Citizen-Centred Government

In the past years, people have lost some confidence in their governments and assumed a less deferential stance toward public authorities. At the same time, they have demanded government services that are more directly conscious of the needs of the citizenry and whose implementation may involve those outside of government. In this setting, the provision of services by departments dedicated to the observance of standard rules and procedures are unacceptable. Tussles between government agencies over responsibility for the delivery of services also become unacceptable. What becomes paramount now are organizational forms able to satisfy the varied demands of the people—and not those of bureaucratic structures. As Toby Fyfe says, consumers of public service insist on "timely service, staff knowledge and competence, staff going the extra mile, fair treatment and a satisfactory outcome."[7] The federal government's policy on alternative service delivery says essentially the same thing:

> Citizens … expect the government to improve access to government services and to provide easy, convenient, connected access to a variety of government services and information in one place, or through one interaction. Canadians expect the government to organize service delivery from their perspective as citizens.[8]

The implication of a more citizen-centred government is that the complexity and intensity of citizens' demands must be mirrored in the administrative structures of government, a situation that provides an opportunity for experimentation with new organizational forms and the emergence of ASD.

Reduction in Size and Scope of Government

One of the most frequent arguments heard in favour of ASD is that it will lower government spending and improve the quality of service delivery. Some examples of ASD involve restructuring within government to provide the service better at lower cost. This will occur if governments restructure to rise above the turf wars and focus on the quality of service delivery. ASD also involves giving private sector and nonprofit sector organizations a greater role in service delivery. This will automatically reduce the size of government by hiving off certain responsibilities. Whether this action will result in greater efficiency depends on how efficient the service-delivery organization is.

Flexibility in Service Delivery

Related to the preceding two points is a desire to increase the flexibility in the delivery of services. One of the problems hampering government in service delivery is an excessive emphasis on process control rather than on achievement of results. Because of the large size of most government organizations and the need to maintain ministerial responsibility, there can be excessive amounts of red tape to ensure that rules are honoured. These rules are important to ensure prudence and probity and to prevent mistakes and embarrassment, but they can also sometimes get in the way of good service delivery.[9]

Ideally, governments should be able to adjust their operation and shed the unnecessary red tape, but there are valid reasons why government organizations will always put more emphasis on process control than smaller, more flexible organizations. To get around this emphasis, it might be useful to use other agents for the delivery of certain services. For example, governments have been notoriously slow to respond to new issues because inflexibilities in budgeting systems and staffing rules prevent existing organizations from moving into new areas. In these kinds of situations, it might be better for governments to provide grants to organizations already working in the field than to try to establish a new government organization.

Motivating Employees

One of the major inflexibilities in government administration is the human resources management system. It can be very difficult for governments to move employees around to meet changing demands or to reward or penalize employees on the basis of their performance. These are valuable safeguards for protecting the rights of employees, but they can also introduce rigidities that make it difficult to respond to the needs of citizens.

Private sector and other nongovernmental organizations usually have the flexibility to redeploy employees more quickly and to reward employees more directly for a job well done. For this reason, many people would prefer to work for these types of organizations. They feel a greater sense of accomplishment from being able to get beyond the red tape and meet the needs of citizens directly.

Involvement of Users in Service Delivery

The presence of nongovernmental organizations provides a way of involving users and others who are directly affected by a service in its provision. The traditional governmental approach is based on a concept of ministerial responsibility that emphasizes top-down, hierarchical decision making, with users on the receiving end of decisions made in capital cities. ASD mechanisms can bring users directly into the decision-making process to ensure that services are provided in ways that are more directly responsive to their needs. There are many examples of sport and recreation clubs taking over activities previously run by governments, and providing them in a more responsive manner at a lower cost.

The involvement of users and others can be particularly helpful in dealing with "problems flowing from issues in which goals either are not known or are ambiguous, and in which the means-ends relationships are uncertain and poorly understood."[10] Thus, users will have an idea of what is wrong with the existing situation, but they cannot foresee exactly what needs to be done to change it. Nongovernmental organizations have more flexibility to experiment with different approaches. They can start and stop initiatives fairly quickly without going through a long chain of command.

Alternative Service Delivery Mechanisms

ASD forms and structures can be categorized in many different ways. One way is to classify mechanisms of ASD using the three dimensions outlined at the beginning of the chapter. These three dimensions involve more management flexibility, the movement toward greater involvement of non-government sectors in the delivery of services, and the increasing commercialization of public services. As noted earlier, some services can be seen as moving along more than one dimension and thus can fall into more than one category of service

Management Flexibility

With management flexibility, the aim is to increase the autonomy of officials responsible for the provision of services to the citizenry and to employ new structures or technology within the governmental setting.

- **Special operating agencies.** These are units within departments which are given a greater degree of flexibility than other units in order to carry out their duties more effectively. SOAs must still report to the deputy minister and must also satisfy performance requirements set out in a framework agreement, but they are clearly to be "treated specially" within the department.[11] Department units considered for this status are focused on the provision of services (and not policy) and offer a service that is discrete within the department, and can be easily measured for the purpose of gauging the level of performance. Examples of SOAs in the federal government are Consulting and Audit Canada within the Department of Public Works and Government Services and the Canadian Forces Housing Agency within the Department of National Defence. The former provides consulting and auditing services to agencies in and outside of government and the latter endeavours to satisfy the accommodation needs of men and women in the Canadian armed forces. At present, there are seventeen SOAs at the federal level.

- **Service agencies.** SAs represent a more ambitious attempt than SOAs to provide for greater managerial flexibility. They are established as separate organizations with their own legislation and with a management structure—headed by a chief executive officer—which reports directly to the responsible minister. These institutions are given "special flexibilities" relating to staffing, the establishment of partnerships, and the retention of any generated revenue (which means that SAs are also moving along the commercialization dimension).[12] The Canadian Food Inspection Agency (CFIA) is a separate agency responsible for the delivery of all federal food inspection and quarantine services. With its status, the CFIA is able to engage on its own in a number of activities—such as establishing partnerships with the provinces—that are beyond the reach of traditional departments. The agency also nicely captures the spirit of ASD in general in that it concentrates on the delivery of services and leaves policy matters to others.[13]

- **Public partnerships.** Partnerships both within and between governments may also be seen as a way of achieving greater autonomy in order to offer better service. Within a government, separate departments may realize that entering into informal or formal arrangements with each other may contribute to more effective delivery of services. This is another way of expressing the importance of horizontal management and the need for departments to look across departments within a government. Partnerships with other orders of government may also provide for a more flexible and effective approach to the supply of public programs.

- **New technology.** The development of new technology gives departments more flexibility in the delivery of services. Governments through better technology now allow people to access public services through cheap service delivery points in shopping centres and other public places—renewals of licences represent one example of this at work. Also, website technology facilitates the presentation of information on government services by function rather than by department, a development that pleases citizens eager to acquire services as quickly and easily as possible. Seniors Canada On-Line, for instance, provides information on elderly services available from a variety of federal departments and many provincial governments.[14] The ambition is to employ technology to move right into the homes of citizens. One instance of this already at work is the ability of taxpayers to "e-file" their returns from the comfort of their homes. The Internet, electronic kiosks, toll highway transponders, smart cards (which combine a number of existing cards into one), and computerized databases represent only some of the new technologies being used to deliver services with greater ease and better results.[15]

Private Sector Involvement

Along this dimension we find ASD mechanisms that rely on various types of partnerships between the public and private sector (whether profit or not-for-profit).

- **Public–private partnerships.** This mechanism represents a major way private sector involvement assumes some importance in the provision of public services. These partnerships may be entered into because of the promise of economic gain for all parties, or because governments believe they will result in doing "more or better with less." Partnerships may also facilitate the better use of technology or give historically disadvantaged persons a sense of empowerment through participation in decision-making processes affecting their position. The partnerships themselves can take a number of different forms. For instance, "collaborative partnerships" involve both public and private parties bringing their resources together to meet common purposes arrived at together. An example of such a partnership is that between the federal Department of Employment and Immigration and six prominent aboriginal organizations in order to enrich the quality of the aboriginal labour force. By contrast, "operational partnerships" focus more on the carrying out of responsibilities—for example, environment departments may elicit the help of private sector bodies to help in surveying wildlife.[16] What follows are some prominent—and sometimes controversial—partnerships between government and the for-profit private sector.

- **Build-own-operate-transfer.** This arrangement involves a private sector interest building and operating a service and then turning it over to government after a specified period of time. A good example of this is the Confederation Bridge between New Brunswick and Prince Edward Island. A private sector company built the bridge and was responsible for the full construction cost including any overruns. It was required to complete construction by June 1, 1997, or pay a substantial penalty. The company then operates the bridge for thirty-five years, collecting the tolls (at a regulated rate) and paying all operating expenses. At the end of the thirty-five years, ownership is transferred to the federal government. In this arrangement, the government transfers both the cost of the construction and the risk of cost overruns to the private sector. In return, the private sector organization can make a substantial profit if it operates the structure efficiently. Then the government can profit from the operation of the bridge after thirty-five years. Since the bridge is built to last one hundred years, operating it might yield a substantial amount of money.

- **COGO (company-owned-government-operated).** In this case, a private company builds something for the government, which the government would then operate. For example, Nova Scotia has adopted the P-3 (public–private partnerships) program. Under this program, a private company built a large number of school buildings. The company retains ownership of the buildings and the government pays an annual rent to use them. These kinds of arrangements save the government the large initial construction cost, although it ends up paying the same amount eventually in annual rents. However, this defers the cost over several years, instead of requiring the government to pay a lump sum up front. The government has some flexibility in that it can discontinue use of the buildings if they are no longer needed. Of course, this is limited by the fact that the owner will demand a lease of a certain length of time before it will agree to build the buildings.

- **GOCO (government-owned-company-operated).** This is the inverse of the previous case. In this case, the government owns a facility and allows a private company to operate it. A good example of this is the situation with regard to several large airports. The government has retained ownership of the building but is allowing local airport authorities to operate them in exchange for a fee. This allows government to withdraw from a commercial-type operation for which it is not suited and transfer its operation to a private sector company, which has greater expertise in this area. It also provides for decentralized, local decision making, rather than having all decisions referred to Ottawa.

Commercialization

This category of ASD mechanisms refers to attempts on the part of public agencies to generate revenue and for government to transfer responsibility for the delivery of a service to a nongovernmental entity.

- **User charges.** User charges involve government requiring citizens to pay directly for services that may have been typically available free of charge. This can be as small as charging for copies of government documents or as large or important as entertaining the idea of asking patients to accept charges at the point of receiving health care. User fees serve the purpose of raising revenue to offset the increasing cost of public services. They also seek to change the behaviour of users or at least make them reconsider their behaviour. The increasingly common practice of municipalities charging for garbage collection helps the revenue side of the budget and also makes residents more conscious of the cost of garbage and the need to think more seriously about waste management.

- **Contracting-out.** Contracting-out or outsourcing involves a situation in which government enters into an arrangement with a nongovernmental body to provide a publicly funded service. Instead of supplying the service itself, government elects to buy it from someone else. For some services, such as the building of roads, governments have typically engaged in contracting-out practices; but recently thought has been given to extending the practice to areas historically supplied by government or a nonprofit body—such as hospitals and the operation of schools. "Employee takeovers" is a specific federal initiative designed to achieve the purposes of contracting-out. It involves former employees of a government agency seeking to assume responsibility for the private delivery of a service they offered while employed in government. ETs are done when it is no longer "necessary to continue to perform a function within government, or when the private sector provides the opportunity to perform the work better or at a lower cost."[17] This mode of contracting-out has been applied to such areas as the management of public lands, the formulation of environmental standards, and the provision of painting and campground service. As ETs suggest, the popularity of contracting-out stems in part from the belief that it will provide services more cheaply. This may happen either because private firms are more able to take advantage of economies of scale or because of the competitive bidding process that precedes the awarding of the contract. The popularity of contracting-out also derives from the belief that contracting entities will be able to avoid the rules and regulations that often encumber the efforts of public service agencies—in other words, contracting-out allows government to escape its own failures.

- **Privatization.** The most common form of this type of ASD is the selling of a government entity to profit-oriented concerns. The recent privatization of some high-profile Crown corporations—Air Canada, CN, and Petro-Canada—falls into this category. But it can also involve nonprofit concerns as well, an example of which is NavCanada. This nonprofit corporation was established when the federal government did not want to continue to provide this service, and the airlines were not happy with the way the government was providing it anyway. However, the airlines were also worried about turning this service over to a profit-making private monopoly over which they would have only limited influence. The compromise reached was a nonprofit corporation with a board of directors consisting of five members selected by the users of the system (the airlines); two selected by the employee unions; and three selected by the federal government. These ten would then select four additional members. NavCanada sets its own rates so that it will break even.

Case Study of ASD

In the late 1980s, it became clear that highway congestion in the Metropolitan Toronto area represented a major cost in terms of declining productivity and late delivery of goods.[18] The Government of Ontario decided that the solution to this problem was to build a second highway that ran across the top of Toronto and north of the existing highway, Highway 401, which had come to be so busy that it resembled a parking zone (see Figure 8.2). In

Figure 8.2

Map of Highway 407

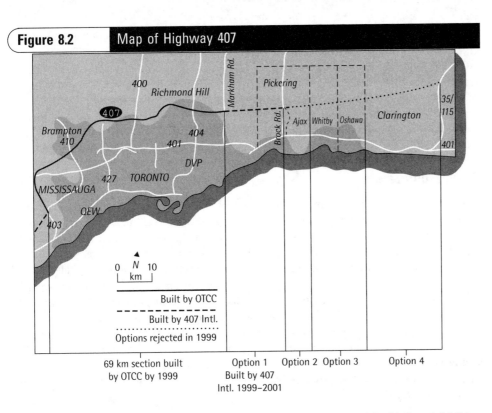

Source: Chandran Mylvaganam and Sandford Borins, *"If you build it . . . ": Business, Government and Ontario's Electronic Toll Highway* (Toronto: University of Toronto Press, 2004), 49.

a remarkably short time, Highway 407 was planned, built, and put into operation. The story of the construction of Highway 407 offers a case study of how ASD can be used in each of its three basic forms. Highway 407 relied on partnerships between the public and the private sector. It also used new government structures to provide for greater flexibility, and commercialized the venture using state-of-the-art electronic tolling technology.

Partnerships

Highway construction in Ontario had always relied on a partnership between government and small private road construction firms. But the desire of the Ontario government to build Highway 407 quickly and using sophisticated technology meant that government now needed a partner whose capabilities far exceeded those of typical road building firms. Through a competitive selection process, the government choose a consortium of consulting engineers, road construction firms, banks, and experts in tolling technology.[19] The Ontario government would provide the financing and specify the construction specifications—the schedule, safety measures, toll operations, and so on— and the consortium would do the actual building. In other words, the public sector steered the project toward completion and private sector did the rowing. A few years after completion of the project, the public–private partnership evolved further when the Government of Ontario sold the new highway to a private interest.

Management Flexibility

With the partnership in place, the Government of Ontario made a decision to provide for more flexibility in overseeing the implementation of the highway construction project. It might have simply assigned the province's Ministry of Transportation this task (a "ministry" is a department in Ontario), which was the standard operating procedure.

Chapter 8 / Alternative Service Delivery

But instead it created what amounted to a service agency in order to avoid "the bureaucracy of the ministry and to create a streamlined, fast-moving body that could deal effectively with a private sector partner."[20] Of particular importance to the new agency was the autonomy to arrange for the financing of the new highway. Central bodies objected to this quality of the agency and wanted approval for financing to go through normal channels. But the premier and cabinet members understood that the ambitious nature of the project meant that unique arrangements were necessary. The agency got its way.

Commercialization

The cost of traffic congestion meant that Highway 407 had to be built. But its construction was audacious in many ways. Here was a plan to build a hugely expensive highway—$1.6 billion—at a time when the Government of Ontario had a large deficit and thus was poorly positioned to undertake such a task.

The answer was to make the highway eventually self-financing through electronic tolling. Though short-term borrowing would be necessary to build the highway, the tolls would soon pay off the loans and perhaps generate a surplus. The introduction of toll highways was politically risky—Ontario highways were without any direct fees—but opinion polls revealed that Ontarians accepted the idea. After some delay due to difficulties in implementation of the technology, on Thanksgiving Day, October 14, 1997, Highway 407 was open for business.[21] (As Figure 8.2 shows, the highway soon after its opening was extended both east and west, but options to allow it to bypass Toronto entirely were rejected.)

Problems with ASD

There is no question but that opening up the issue of service delivery rather than always assuming there is a "one best way" is beneficial. But certain caveats must be raised, because problems may arise with the adoption of ASD.

Steering and Rowing

At the heart of ASD is the belief that a separation of policy and operations results in better performance. Allow the minister to do the steering and develop new innovative ways of carrying out the rowing function. But this may produce coordination problems as the public service morphs from a relatively small number of large departments into a "flotilla" of ASD mechanisms.[22] It may be simply too difficult to move the ship of state in a desired direction with the widespread adoption of ASD. Policy might also suffer, because the separation makes it hard for operations people to provide feedback on the workability of policies. More unsettling, the greater use of ASD may produce "policy lock-in," an outcome that emerges when new agencies generate new supporters unwilling to countenance any changes in the operation of ASD. Good and Carin explain:

> Are autonomous agencies undermining policy objectives by creating constituencies that will compel governments to maintain existing policies? Agencies are created but rarely closed or merged. Policy can become what agencies do, not what government proposes.[23]

The separation of steering and rowing duties is meant to make government leaders more able to develop plans and strategies for government. But, ironically, it might do the exact opposite, and the consequence is a weakening of democratic practice. Appointed officials, not elected ones, begin to run government.

Where Is the Public Interest?

Increasing responsiveness to users and more emphasis on the bottom line—two aspects of ASD—sound like two very positive values, but is it possible to be too responsive to users or too profit-driven so that the broader public interest is ignored? Take, for example, the question of what a national parks agency should do when it has the opportunity to make huge sums of money from tour operators.[24] If there is excessive emphasis on the profit motive, the agency will be forced to behave in a way that many Canadians would not see as beneficial in the long run. The emphasis on the bottom line and being user-friendly is important, but governments are elected to further the public interest.

Loss of Accountability

A major intent of ASD is to offer services at arm's length from government so that they can be delivered in a more flexible manner with greater responsiveness to users. The danger is that accountability linkages may be weakened at the same time. In some cases, the traditional governmental accountability linkages will be supplanted by other types of accountability mechanisms. In the case of NavCanada, the users now have direct representation on the board of directors. But in other instances the accountability challenge is not so easily surmounted. Let us assume a federal ASD agency has authority to enter into partnerships with either another order of government or an entity in the private sector. Also assume that something goes wrong. Who is accountable? Is it the head of the ASD agency, his or her counterpart at the provincial level, the federal minister formally responsible for the agency, or perhaps the provincial minister to whom the provincial official reports? The lesson here is that governments need to choose very carefully the types of services that are given this arm's-length treatment. In some cases, other mechanisms work very well in ensuring accountability, but not always.

Labour Relations

Many forms of ASD involve moving government employees into a different regime within government or even into a private sector organization. On the positive side, this will frequently loosen the constraints of government human resources management systems and allow employees greater flexibility in working conditions, including the opportunity to earn merit pay. However, many employees fear that they will lose the protection that comes with the government human resources management regime. The right to provide merit pay for a job well done is also the right to withhold merit pay for possibly venal reasons. Some employees do not like moving out of the protective situation of the government system. Some make even stronger claims that ASD initiatives are aimed at breaking strong unions or preventing the establishment of a union. These issues all must be considered by the government spinning off the service and the organization taking over the service.

ASD is also changing the nature of the workforce. Long-serving, full-time employees are being replaced by limited-term contract employees. This is beneficial to governments to the extent that it increases their flexibility and reduces labour costs. However, this temporary workforce will have very little loyalty to their present employer. It is also very difficult to develop an organizational culture or an organizational memory with so many employees passing through the revolving door.

Savings and Performance

The apparent cost savings and other benefits associated with ASD arrangements involving public–private partnerships can go unrealized. Using these arrangements, the government

Box 8.1	ASD and the Walkerton Tragedy

In the spring of 2000, the water supply of Walkerton, a town in southwestern Ontario, became contaminated. Seven residents lost their lives and many more got very sick. Some claim that this was a direct consequence of the provincial government introducing an ASD-like measure. The government had taken away responsibility for water testing from the provincial environment department and given it to private laboratories, and only required the labs to report their results to municipal authorities and not to departmental officials. In the case of Walkerton, the labs determined the water was contaminated and sent the results to the Walkerton Public Utilities Commission, but the commission did not act on these results immediately. An inquiry set up to examine the Walkerton crisis observed that the slow response to the results probably caused many more to become sick than would have been the case with a more rigorous reporting system. A challenge for students of public administration is to take a close look at the case and determine whether the performance of ASD was wanting.

Source: Judith I. McKenzie, "Walkerton: Requiem for the New Public Management in Ontario?", *International Journal of Environment and Pollution* 21(4) (2004): 309–24.

hopes to transfer part of the financial risk to a private partner, but this often fails to happen and the public partner ends up assuming most of the risk. Another expectation is also often dashed, namely that the inclusion of the private sector will result in lower costs and greater efficiencies because of economies of scale, greater experience, and better innovation skills. One reason for the unmet expectations is that the price of bargaining, monitoring, and possibly renegotiating partnerships are often high, especially when some of the participants engage in various forms of "opportunism" (threats of bankruptcy). Governments sometimes also believe—mistakenly—that the use of private partners will make hard policy choices more palpable to the public. Then there is the occasional contract failure—a euphemism for a situation in which the arrangement collapses for one reason or another and government is left with the task for cleaning up the mess. At first, ASD appears to offer government substantial benefits—in effect, a "free lunch." But a closer look suggests that the lunch can turn out to be unappetizing and quite expensive.[25]

A related question is whether the overall performance of ASD is worth the effort. Studies suggest that ASD mechanisms can produce good results, but it may be that the same level of performance might have been achieved with existing institutions. Australia, for example, has achieved positive outcomes by making adjustments to traditional bureaucratic structures rather than by introducing new ones.[26] The adjustments include more accountability, greater flexibility, and the introduction of some competitive forces. This sounds a lot like ASD, except that the gains are generated without constructing totally new arrangements.

Rebalancing the System

There is no doubt that the advent of alternative service delivery has had a very beneficial impact on service delivery. It has prompted governments to review virtually every service they deliver. Even when this review has not resulted in new organizational arrangements, it has frequently caused governments to revise and improve their own way of delivering services. However, as frequently happens with innovations, ASD may have been somewhat oversold. It is beneficial; it is not a cure-all.

1. Toby Fyfe, "Alternative Service Delivery—Responding to Global Pressures," *International Review of Administrative Sciences* 70(1): 639.

2. Treasury Board Secretariat, "Alternative Service Delivery." Available at www.Tbs-sct.gc.ca/asd-dmps/index_e.asp. Accessed July 6, 2006.

3. Robin Ford and David Zussman, "Alternative Service Delivery: Transcending Boundaries," in Robin Ford and David Zussman, eds., *Alternative Service Delivery: Sharing Governance in Canada* (Toronto: KPMG Centre for Government Foundation and Institute of Public Administration of Canada, 1997), 6.

4. Ibid., 7.

5. David Zussman, "Alternative Service Delivery," in Christopher Dunn, ed., *The Handbook of Canadian Public Administration* (Toronto: Oxford University Press, 2002), 53.

6. David Osborne and Ted Gaebler, *Reinventing Government: How the Entrepreneurial Spirit is Transforming the Public Sector* (New York: Penguin, 1993), ch. 1.

7. Fyfe, "Alternative Service Delivery," 639.

8. Treasury Board Secretariat, "Policy on Alternative Service Delivery," April 1, 2002, 15. Available at www.tbs-sct.gc.ca/pubs_pol/opepubs/TB_B4/asd-dmps_e.asp. Accessed July 6, 2006.

9. Barbara Wake Carroll and David Siegel, *Service in the Field* (Montreal & Kingston: McGill-Queen's University Press, 1998).

10. Gilles Paquet, "Alternative Service Delivery: Transforming the Practices of Governance," in Ford and Zussman, eds., *Alternative Service Delivery*, 33.

11. Treasury Board Secretariat, "Becoming a Special Operating Agency," 1. Available at www.tbs-sct.gc.ca/pubs_pol/opepubs/TB_B4/bsoa-doss_e.asp. Accessed July 6, 2006.

12. Zussman, "Alternative Service Delivery," in Dunn, 59.

13. Kenneth Kernaghan, Brian Marson, and Sandford Borins, *The New Public Organization* (Toronto: Institute of Public Administration of Canada, 2000), 104.

14. Kenneth Kernaghan, "Moving Towards the Virtual State: Integrating Services and Service Channels for Citizen-Centred Delivery," *International Review of Administrative Sciences* 71(1): 124–25.

15. Sandford Borins, "On the Frontiers of Electronic Governance: A Report on the United States and Canada," *International Review of Administrative Sciences* 68 (2002): 199–211.

16. Kernaghan, Marson, and Borins, *The New Public Organization*, 186–95.

17. Treasury Board Secretariat, "Scope of ASD," 5. Available at www.tbs-sct.gc.ca/asd-dmps/soa_e.asp. Accessed July 6, 2006.

18. The case study is based on Chandran Mylvaganam and Sandford Borins, *"If You Build It . . . ": Business, Government and Ontario's Electronic Toll Highway* (Toronto: University of Toronto Press, 2004).

19. The arrangement was a little more complicated than this, in that the losing consortium in the bidding process was given responsibility to handle the toll technology.

20. Mylvaganam and Sandford Borins, *"If You Build It . . . "*, 55.

21. Some assessments of Highway 407 are less positive than the one presented here. See Aidan R. Vining, Anthony E. Boardman, and Finn Poschmann, "Public–Private Partnerships in the US and Canada: 'There Are No Free Lunches,'" *Journal of Comparative Policy Analysis* 7(3) (September 2005): 199–220.

22. Guy Peters quoted in Kernaghan, Marson, and Borins, *The New Public Organization*, 119.

23. David A. Good and Barry Carin, draft of "Alternative Service Delivery," August 2003. Prepared by the Canadian Team as part of the CEPRA project on "Sector and Regional Specifics of Reformation of Budgetary Institutions," 23–24.

24. David Zussman, "Government's New Style," *Management* 8(2): 21–23.

25. See Vining, Boardman, and Poschmann, "Public–Private Partnerships in the US and Canada: 'There Are No Free Lunches.'"

26. Kernaghan, Marson, and Borins, *The New Public Organization*, 119.

Politics, Values,
and Public Administration

9

Frameworks, Values, and Bureaucratic Power

Public administration is in part the study of organizational structures that deliver government services and accompanying theories about the behaviour of these organizations. Departments are thus given close consideration, because they play a prominent role in the formulation and administration of government policies and programs. Crown corporations and independent regulatory agencies (and the new alternative service delivery mechanisms) also receive a great deal of attention, as they too are central to the basic operations and purposes of government. And to better appreciate these entities, we undertake a review of theories and models relating to the structure and actions of organizations. But public administration is more than just the examination of organizational theories and structures. It also seeks to uncover the interactions of bureaucratic entities both within themselves and with other entities in the political process. A failure to undertake this kind of investigation of the machinery of the government would be akin to visiting a factory in the dead of night. You would see the machinery and be told how it is supposed to operate, but you could not understand how it really works until you saw it humming, whirring, clanking, and occasionally breaking down. It is thus important to see how appointed officials relate to one another and with political and judicial officials in the three branches of government. Our interest also extends to the interactions of public servants with interest groups, parties, the media, and other governments.

The intent of this chapter, and the next one, is to provide a framework for understanding the interactions of public servants with others in the political process. This framework is necessary because relations between appointed officials and nonbureaucratic actors are complex. In later chapters, we examine the details and intricacies of these relationships, but first we need some guidance on how to approach this topic in public administration. The chapter begins with a discussion of power and the type of interactions in which public servants participate. From here, it moves to consider the values that motivate or steer bureaucrats in their interactions. The chapter closes with an examination of the nature or character of interactions that involve appointed officials. The next chapter offers a closer look at two values central to public administration: integrity and accountability.

Institutional Framework

Public servants interact with a number of entities in the political process. These interactions can be reduced to three basic types, each of which is shaped by the exercise of power. One type involves relations within an organization, be it a department, Crown corporation, regulatory agency, or alternative service delivery structure. A second type of interaction addresses relations between an organization and other entities within government, and a final type sees appointed officials dealing with bodies existing outside government. These three types of interactions, as will be shown, form the basis of the framework for the examination of bureaucratic relationships in the political system.

The Concept of Power

The key concept underlying the basic institutional framework is one that is central to scholarly writings in political science, organization theory, and public administration—namely, **power**. Social science literature contains various definitions and usages of power and the closely related concepts of influence, control, and authority. It is generally agreed that power is a relational concept. It is, therefore, useful for describing and explaining relations between and among organizations, groups, and individuals—and indeed, as we shall see, between and among governments. Power is defined here as "the capacity to secure the dominance of one's values or goals."[1] A similar definition explains power as "the capacity of an individual, or group of individuals, to modify the conduct of other individuals or groups in the manner in which he desires, and to prevent his own being modified in a manner which he does not."[2]

Control and Influence

There are two forms of power: control and influence. **Control** refers to that form of power in which A has authority to direct or command B. For example, a deputy minister wields control over a subordinate when he or she exercises statutory or other authority to order the subordinate to act in a certain way. **Influence** is a more general and pervasive form of power than control. When B conforms to A's desires, values, or goals by suggestion, persuasion, emulation, or anticipation, then A exercises influence over B. For instance, a deputy minister may influence another deputy minister by persuading him or her to take a particular action. Influence can sometimes cause power to flow upward when administrative subordinates who possess special expertise in some field exercise influence over hierarchical superiors in the form of "authority of expertise" or "expert power." Bachrach and Lawler assert that influence "is the mode of power that both gives subordinates the capability of manipulating superiors and gives superiors the capability of getting more from their subordinates than is specified in the formal role obligations."[3]

To exercise control, A must have authority in the sense of having access to the inducements, rewards, and sanctions necessary to back up commands. This is "authority of position" or "position power." A may also exercise influence over B through "authority of leadership" or "personal power," which involves the use of such means as persuasion, suggestion, and intimation rather than direction, supervision, and command. Moreover, authority of position allows A to exercise influence as a result of "the rule of anticipated reactions."[4] Application of this rule is evident in the innumerable instances in which administrative officials "anticipate the reactions" of those who have the power to reward or constrain them. Officials tend to act in a fashion that would be applauded—or at least approved—by those whose favour they seek. Thus, those actors ordinarily perceived as exercising control, such as hierarchical superiors, can also exercise influence by affecting another actor's decisions in an informal, unofficial—even unintentional—way.

What distinguishes actors with the capacity to exercise both control and influence from those possessing only influence is that the former have at their disposal sanctions and inducements formalized by law and the organization chart. Influence over public organizations and public servants within these organizations can be exercised by those who do not have legally or formally sanctioned power to command or supervise. For example, pressure groups may seek favours from public servants by offering inducements or imposing penalties, but they have no legal or formal capacity to compel compliance to their wishes. This does not mean, however, that such influence cannot be as effective as control or, in some instances, even more effective. A public servant may well grant special favours to pressure groups despite formal directions to the contrary from an administrative superior. Thus, influence can be exercised by those without either authority of position or authority of leadership through a variety of means, including persuasion, friendship, knowledge, and experience.

Internal and External Interactions

The preceding analysis provides the basis for the development of a framework showing the patterns of interaction both within public organizations and between these organizations and other participants in the political process. These interactions involve in large part the reciprocal exercise of power in the form of control, influence, or both types of power. From the perspective of any one organization, these interactions can be classified into the three types mentioned earlier and which are given the following labels: internal, external within government, and external outside government. As Table 9.1 shows, the first type of interaction involves activities within a department or "intradepartmental relations." These relations can involve staff and line officials combining their efforts to produce policy options or assistants to the minister interacting with appointed officials. This type of interaction also includes the deputy minister carrying out his or her roles, the most important of which is providing advice to the minister. The role of the minister in relation to the department also falls within this type of interaction. As with all forms of interaction, both control and influence fashion relations within a department.

Table 9.1	Institutional Framework	
TYPE OF INTERACTION	**ACTIVITIES**	**PARTICIPANTS**
Internal	Intradepartmental	Line and staff Field officials
External within government	Interdepartmental Executive-bureaucratic Legislative-bureaucratic Judicial-bureaucratic	Other departments and agencies PM, cabinet, central agencies Parliament and agents Federal and provincial courts
External outside government	Intergovernmental Governmental- nongovernmental	Provincial/territorial/local governments Pressure groups, media, public, parties

The second type covers relations between individual organizations and other bodies within government. An increasingly important duty of public servants is coordinating their activities with their counterparts in other organizations found in government. These "interdepartmental" or horizontal relations arise from the growing complexity of problems facing government and the recognition that a single department is often unable to address challenging policy issues. Appointed officials must also interact with the prime minister and cabinet located in the executive branch as well as with the central agencies which serve the most senior political players in government. The other two branches of government, the legislature and the judiciary, also require the attention of appointed officials. The courts may come into contact with public servants through questioning the legality of bureaucratic actions, and the people's representatives in the House of Commons undoubtedly will indirectly—or even directly—query public servants about their actions. The final type of interaction involves public servants going outside their government and interacting with nongovernmental actors. The latter include pressure groups, the media, interested members of the public, and the extraparliamentary wing of the political parties. In these relations, public servants exercise some control in acting on behalf of the minister, but more often than not the successful use of influence will determine whether public servants achieve their aims. The final type of interaction also encompasses relations with other governments. The centrality of federal-provincial-territorial relations to Canadian politics reveals the importance of this particular interaction. Public servants recognize that almost any activity of government requires some kind of consultation with the other orders of government.

In these various interactions between appointed officials and others in the political process, power can flow in two directions. Public servants are not defenceless against pressures put on them by these other actors. An examination of the real or potential impact of controls and influences over the public service must account for the potent resources public servants can use to resist pressure and to exert power over others, such as expertise, experience, budgetary allocations, confidential information, and discretionary powers to develop and implement policies and programs. These resources may be used in various ways. Public servants may prevail over political superiors by virtue of special knowledge of a policy area, or they may feed selected bits of information to journalists to enhance support for a certain program.

Public Service Values

Underlying the various types of relations between public servants and others in the political process is the exercise of power by participants in order to secure or realize their **values**. An understanding of the dynamics of these relations depends on an appreciation of the prevailing values or "enduring beliefs that influence our attitudes and actions."[5] As with all players in the political process, public servants have a value system in which social, political, administrative, and personal values are ranked in terms of importance. The focus here is on the administrative or public service values. An awareness of these values facilitates an understanding of the actions and behaviour of public servants in their various types of interactions.

A review of Canadian administrative history shows that among the most important public service values are neutrality, accountability, efficiency, effectiveness, responsiveness, representativeness, and integrity. These are often described as "traditional" values. In the past decade, "new" values have emerged alongside the older ones, and these include service, innovation, teamwork, and quality.

Neutrality

It is essential to distinguish between political neutrality, in the sense of nonpartisanship, and value-neutrality. Most public servants preserve their neutrality in terms of partisan politics; they cannot, however, reasonably be expected to be value-neutral, because they are actively involved in politics in the broad sense of the authoritative allocation of values for society. The value system of individual public servants is crucial to an analysis of bureaucratic behaviour and bureaucratic power, because they cannot be completely value-neutral in making and recommending decisions. Indeed, public servants have never been value-neutral, and they have become less so as their discretionary powers have increased. Many of the decisions they make oblige them, or give them the opportunity, to inject their own views as to which values should take priority. The difficulty of ensuring the responsible exercise of power under these circumstances helps to explain the importance of accountability.

Accountability

The quest for **administrative accountability** arises largely from the reality that public servants are not value-neutral. Accountability involves concern for the legal, institutional, and procedural means by which public servants can be obliged to answer for their actions. The questions commonly asked about the accountability of public servants are: Who is accountable? To whom is accountability owed? For what is accountability owed? By what means can accountability be achieved? Accountability is a pervasive theme in this book, both because it has been one of the major values in the evolution of Canadian public administration and because of its current importance. Since the early 1990s, there has been a major shift in emphasis from accountability for process—for the way things are done—to accountability for results—for what is achieved.

Efficiency and Effectiveness

Despite the current concern with accountability, the dominant value in Canadian public administration over the past century has been efficiency. Moreover, much of the emphasis on accountability has really been directed to holding public servants accountable for the economic, efficient, and effective use of public funds. The values of economy, efficiency, and effectiveness are interdependent but distinct in meaning. **Economy** refers to the acquisition of the appropriate goods and services at the best possible price. **Effectiveness** is a measure of the extent to which an activity achieves the organization's objectives. **Efficiency** is a measure of performance that may be expressed as a ratio between input and output, and it can be used as a general indicator of the ability of any individual, organization, or government to expend scarce resources in the most profitable or sensible manner.

Responsiveness

Responsiveness refers to the inclination and the capacity of public servants to respond to the needs and demands of both political institutions and the public. Thus, public servants are expected to be responsive to two major groups of participants in the political system. The first includes political executives and legislators; the second includes the general public as well as various public groups and individuals affected by the decisions and recommendations of public servants.

Representativeness

A representative public service is one in which employees are drawn proportionately from the major ethnic, religious, and socioeconomic groups in society.

Representativeness in the public service is closely tied to several other public service values. For example, the argument is frequently made that a more representative public service is a more responsive public service. In the belief that the attitudes of representatives of a group will be similar to the attitudes of the whole group, a representative public service is deemed to be more responsive to the needs of the public and more effective in giving policy advice. However, it is also argued that if efforts to achieve a representative public service mean that the most qualified persons are not hired, the efficiency and effectiveness of the service will be adversely affected.

Fairness and Equity

For most practical purposes, the terms fairness and equity can be used interchangeably. Equity is one of the major values to be balanced in determining the merit of persons seeking appointment to the public service, and the courts and governments are now putting greater emphasis on procedural fairness. Considerations of procedural fairness have gradually expanded beyond the boundaries of administrative law to the administrative processes of the public service. Public servants are increasingly expected—or required—to consider whether their decisions and recommendations are fair both in substance and in procedure. This heightened emphasis on fairness and equity is based largely on the recognition of the significant power that public servants exercise over the rights and livelihood of individual citizens.

There is a complementary relationship between the values of fairness and responsiveness in that procedural fairness might be said to require that public servants be responsive to the public through various mechanisms for public participation. It is also obvious that fairness can clash with such values as efficiency and effectiveness.

Integrity

Integrity refers here to ethics in public administration. The integrity of public servants is extremely important to the preservation of public trust and confidence in government. Recent experience in Canada and elsewhere indicates that increased vigilance is required to ensure that public servants adhere to high ethical standards.

New Values

As a result of the extensive public service reforms that have taken place since the mid-1980s, a number of so-called new public service values have emerged. Several of these new values are closely associated with the new public management approach to public administration. Among the most prominent of these new values are service, innovation, teamwork, and quality. Other values of increasing importance are openness, communication, trust, and leadership. Some of these new values (e.g., service) complement certain traditional values (e.g., responsiveness), but other new values (e.g., innovation) may clash with some of the traditional values (e.g., accountability).

Sources of the Bureaucrat's Values

A focus on the bureaucrat's values is especially important because bureaucratic behaviour may be explained or interpreted in terms of the interplay among the individual bureaucrat's values, and between the bureaucrat's values and the values of those with whom he or she interacts. Before an individual joins the public service, his or her general value system, as well as particular attitudes and orientations toward the public service, are molded by powerful and enduring forces. This is accomplished through the process of socialization in which various agencies—the family, peer groups, schools, and others—construct our values. Thus, an individual enters government service with values that will significantly affect his or her decisions. Moreover, in varying degrees, the socializing agencies continue to affect the bureaucrat's values during his or her public service career.

However, the organization that employs the individual is itself a powerful socializing agent. The individual's personal values and perceptions of the public service are altered by a process of organizational socialization that begins the very day he or she is recruited for a public service position. **Organizational socialization** refers to the process through which the individual learns the expectations attached to the position he or she occupies in the organization, and selectively internalizes as values some of the expectations of those with whom he or she interacts.

Nature of Interactions

Our institutional framework outlines the various types of interaction in the world of public administration, but it fails to reveal the nature or character of relations involving appointed officials and others in the political process. One way to gain an initial insight into these relationships is to consider the workings of the convention of **political neutrality**. The convention in its essence depicts appointed officials loyally and anonymously serving the wishes of elected representatives in the making and administration of government initiatives. The important implication of this depiction is that the actions of public servants reflect in large part the values of others in the political process. The reality, however, is that bureaucratic actors are able to inject their own values into the governing system and in so doing exercise considerable power. The convention of political neutrality can be seen as consisting of six elements, each of which is considered below.[6]

1. The Politics–Administration Dichotomy

The political neutrality of public servants has traditionally rested on the possibility of the separation of politics and administration, and on a related distinction between policy and administration. According to the **politics–administration dichotomy**, political executives and legislators are concerned with the formation of policy, and public servants are concerned with its implementation. Policy decisions are political; administrative decisions are nonpolitical. However, abundant evidence points to the important political and policy advisory roles of public servants.

The distinction between politics and policy on the one hand and administration on the other has been central to the evolution of both the study and the practice of public administration. From 1887 to the end of World War II, most prominent writers on public administration wrote within a framework of a dichotomy between politics and administration. Woodrow Wilson's celebrated essay of 1887, "The Study of Administration," is usually taken as the point of departure for academic and theoretical writing on public administration in North America. Wilson contended that

> the field of administration is a field of business. It is removed from the hurry and strife of politics. ... [A]dministrative questions are not political questions. ... "Policy does nothing without the aid of administration," but administration is not therefore politics.[7]

Wilson's distinction between politics and administration was accepted and perpetuated by such other pioneers as Frank Goodnow (1914), L.D. White (1926), and W.F. Willoughby (1927). In their writings, "the politics–administration dichotomy was assumed both as a self-evident truth and a desirable goal; administration was perceived as a self-contained world of its own, with its own separate values, rules and methods."[8]

Set in proper historical perspective, these questionable views are more comprehensible. During the late 19th and early 20th centuries, administrative reform efforts in both the United States and Canada were devoted to eradicating patronage from the public service, with a view to promoting efficient administration. A separate but overlapping development that had its origins in industrial organization in the United States was the scientific management movement. This movement, which pursued efficiency in large-scale organizations by seeking the most rational means—the "one best way"—of performing any organizational task, had an enormous impact on the public service reform movement throughout the developed world. In both the United States and Canada, the two elements of the reform movement—efficiency through the elimination of patronage and efficiency through scientific management—reinforced one another and became integral components of the merit system.

Concurrent with this pursuit of impartial and efficient administration was a steady growth in the discretionary powers of public servants. While efficient staffing of the service required the separation of politics and administration, the need for effective development and execution of public policy drew administrative officials into the political maelstrom—not in the sense of partisan activity but in the sense of involvement in the authoritative allocation of values for society. Public servants formulated rules and regulations to put flesh on the skeletons of vaguely worded statutes, enforced these rules and regulations, and adjudicated disputes arising from this enforcement. Moreover, the complicated and technical nature of public policy issues meant that political executives had to rely increasingly on public servants for policy advice and for the management of large-scale public organizations.

During the 1930s, writers on public administration who recognized the significant and growing political role of the bureaucracy lived uncomfortably with the textbook dichotomy between politics and administration. The dichotomy came under increasing attack during the war years as many scholars gained practical administrative experience in government. Shortly after the war, a number of political scientists launched an assault on the notion that politics and administration were, or could be, separated. Among this group of postwar authors, Paul Appleby stands out for his defence of the proposition that "public administration is policy making. ... Public administration is one of a number of basic political processes."[9] In less celebrated and more broadly focused works than those written by Americans, British and Canadian writers during this period demonstrated a growing recognition of the blurring of the traditional constitutional line between politicians and public servants in the parliamentary–cabinet system of government.

By 1960, the interdependence of politics and administration had been enshrined in the theoretical literature on public administration and accepted by the major actors in the political system. By this time, however, recognition of the reality of bureaucratic power in the political process led to suggestions that public servants should become "agents of social change." Public servants were encouraged to promote new and creative ideas and solutions in social policy by aggregating and articulating the needs of unorganized and disadvantaged groups (e.g., consumers, the poor), and by stimulating groups and individuals to make demands on government for remedies to their social and economic ills. It was clear that public servants who undertook such activities were likely to clash on occasion with political and administrative superiors who did not perceive the proper role of public servants to be active initiators of social change. The basic question was the extent to which appointed public officials could, or should, share with elected representatives the responsibility for stimulating and responding to social change. Discussion of public servants as social change agents was intermingled with the movement for increased **citizen participation** in governmental decision making. This movement, which was centred in the United States, brought both politicians and public servants into more direct contact and confrontation with the general citizenry.

The relevance of these developments for the relationship between politics and administration was that some of its supporters called for a reformulation of the traditional roles of politicians and public servants.[10] It was argued that public servants, because of their expertise and experience and their close contacts with members of the public, are better qualified than political executives or legislators to determine the public interest. Public servants must, however, establish a value system with a focus on human dignity or administrative humanism; they should not simply reflect the values of their political masters. Implicit also was a resistance to political control over public administration. This new movement in public administration drew attention to the actual and potential power of public servants and to the importance of their value system for decision making in government; however, it did not resolve—indeed, it complicated—the issue of finding an appropriate balance between the power of public servants and that of elected representatives.

Some aspects of the new movement in public administration in the United States had little spillover effect on the study and practice of public administration in Canada. However, scholars and practitioners in Canada were acutely aware that the line between politics and administration had become increasingly indistinct as both politicians and public servants participated actively in policy development. Senior public servants, for instance, made (and continue to make) significant discretionary decisions as to the policy options to be set before their political masters. In the development and presentation of these policy options, public servants were expected to be attuned to the political, as well as the administrative, financial, and technical, implications of their recommendations. Despite the variety of available sources of policy advice outside government, the very technical, complex, and time-consuming nature of certain policy issues obliged ministers to continue to rely heavily on the advice of their officials.

In the sphere of the administration or implementation of government initiatives, public servants also exercised substantial power. In the course of interpreting, clarifying, and applying policy, public servants significantly influenced the success of policy decisions made by ministers and legislators. The care and enthusiasm with which public servants administered policy greatly affected the success of public programs. A series of individual, relatively minor decisions in a particular policy area could have a significant cumulative impact on the extent to which the original intent of cabinet and Parliament was realized. More generally, many government policies and programs made available to public servants a great deal of discretion in how they were to be implemented. The discretionary powers of public servants in policy implementation were especially evident in the making and enforcement of regulations under authority delegated to them by Parliament, or sub-delegated to them by a minister or by cabinet. The statutory provisions authorizing the making of regulations were often phrased in general or imprecise language that permitted public servants to exercise significant discretion both in the wording of the regulations and in the application of their provisions to particular cases.

In recent years, in Canada and elsewhere, the politics–administration dichotomy has made a comeback—but with a twist. Thinking associated with the theory of new public management has emphasized the importance of separating policy and administration in order that public servants can direct most of their attention to finding innovative ways of managing public programs. But as the preceding sentence suggests, this thinking has emphasized that the task of public servants is not to administer or follow rules and regulations, but rather to manage and discover creative measures by which to deliver services. What has thus emerged is a new dichotomy, namely the "politics–management dichotomy."[11] Political developments have also worked in the same direction. Political leaders have emerged who believe that appointed officials wield too much power and that the participation of the bureaucracy in the formulation of policy should be severely limited. Appointed officials, they argue, should be like their counterparts in the private sector and concern themselves solely with management—and leave policy matters to the people's representatives:

> The challenge was to refocus the role of the civil service so as to stress management rather than policy-making... the new political leadership felt that the policy advisory role of the civil service was "deeply illegitimate." Nonelected officials had become too powerful in shaping policy, and it was important to send them back to a more legitimate role. Their job was to implement policy decisions and to manage government resources more efficiently.[12]

In looking at this history of the politics–dichotomy, it can be seen that politics and policy cannot be easily separated from administration. Nonetheless, the distinctions commonly made between politics and administration, policy and administration, and policy formation and implementation serve a useful analytical and practical purpose. They enable political theorists to distinguish—not in an absolute sense but as a matter of degree and emphasis—between the constitutional and legal functions of political executives and public servants. While the policy role of public servants has led some writers to refer to them as "permanent politicians" and "ruling servants," they remain, in fact and in democratic theory, subject to the overriding authority of elected representatives and the courts. It is useful, then, to refer to the predominance of ministers in policy formation and the predominance of public servants in policy implementation, while acknowledging that both ministers and public servants are involved in both policy formation and implementation.

2. Appointments

A second component of the ideal model of political neutrality is the practice whereby "public servants are appointed and promoted on the basis of merit rather than of party affiliation or contributions." Political patronage involves the appointment of people to government service on the grounds of contributions, financial or otherwise, to the governing party; it is a blatant violation of the doctrine of political neutrality. Indeed, the appointment is made on the basis that the appointee is, politically, not neutral but partisan. Such appointments clash with the merit principle, according to which Canadians have an opportunity to be taken into account for a position in the public service, and that selections reflect ability to carry out the requirements of the job.[13]

Over the years, various legislative efforts have been made to put in a staffing system that reflects the tenets of the merit principle, and for the most part these efforts have been successful. But patronage appointments have certainly not disappeared. A review of debates in the House of Commons in recent decades reveals numerous allegations and denials regarding the use of patronage in staffing the public service. Many of the alleged patronage appointments have been to lower-level or part-time positions in which the appointees are so far removed from policy development that their appointment has a negligible effect on the status of political neutrality. Opposition parties, the news media, and the general public have shown greater interest in senior positions that are filled by patronage appointees rather than on a competitive basis by persons from within or outside the public service. The prime minister and the cabinet have the authority to appoint deputy ministers; heads and members of agencies, boards, and commissions; ambassadors; high commissioners; consuls general and certain other diplomatic representatives; and federal judges. Moreover, officials in the Prime Minister's Office are selected by the prime minister, and cabinet ministers' assistants are also chosen in an overtly partisan manner. All these appointments are exempt from the appointing power of the **Public Service Commission**, the agency responsible for overseeing appointments to the federal public service.

Among the persons who may be, and frequently are, appointed to exempt positions are retired legislators, defeated candidates of the governing party, and party supporters who have made significant financial or other contributions to the party's fortunes. Defeated or retired cabinet ministers have also enjoyed particular success in finding a comfortable niche in government service. Finally, the expansion of the personal staff of cabinet ministers has increased the importance of this group as a source of patronage appointments.

Such appointments are often denounced on the grounds that they are made more on the basis of partisanship than merit. Nevertheless, the government has the authority to make these appointments on whatever basis it deems appropriate. A measure of merit is achieved with respect to the most senior posts, because the government is usually unwilling to bear the embarrassment that the appointment of an incompetent partisan may bring. Moreover, party supporters are more likely to find their reward in appointments to Crown agencies, boards, and commissions than to the regular departments of government. There have been few partisan appointments to deputy ministerial posts, at least in the federal sphere.

The number of patronage appointments in each of the categories examined above is relatively small, but, taking all the categories together, the number of senior positions filled by patronage appointees is substantial. The impact of these appointments on bureaucratic power is difficult to measure with any precision. However, such appointments limit the influence of career public servants by blocking access to some of the highest positions in government. Moreover, long-serving officials are obliged to share their influence in the policy process with newcomers who may have fresh ideas and unorthodox approaches and who may not share the administrative values to which most public servants have become socialized.

3. Political Partisanship

The ideal model of political neutrality requires that public servants not "engage in partisan political activities."[14] However, the relevant history shows that this has not always been observed.

During the first fifty years of Canada's political history, the issues of political partisanship and political patronage were intimately linked. Patronage appointments were rewards for service to the governing party. Many of the appointees sought to enhance their progress within the public service by continuing their partisan support of the governing party after their appointment. Thus, when a new party came to power, it replaced these persons with its own supporters.

In an effort to eliminate this practice, legislators provided in the 1918 *Civil Service Act* that no public servant could "engage in partisan work in connection with any ... election, or contribute, receive or in any way deal with any money for any party funds."[15] Violations were punishable by dismissal. The penalty was so severe and so clearly stated that, with the exception of the right to vote, the impact of the act was the political sterilization of Canada's federal public servants. Despite this effective weakening of the link between patronage and political activity, the rigid restraints imposed in 1918 remained virtually unchanged until 1967. The primary explanation was the desire to ensure the political impartiality of public servants in the performance of their advisory and discretionary powers.

The *Public Service Employment Act* of 1967 liberalized the longstanding restrictions on political activity. Section 33 of the Act provided that public servants, unless they were deputy heads, could stand for election to public office if the Public Service Commission believed that their usefulness would not be impaired by their candidacy. Employees were not permitted to work for or against a candidate for election to a federal or provincial office, or for or against a political party; they were permitted, however, to attend political meetings and to make contributions to the funds of a political candidate or party. In 1991, the Supreme Court of Canada struck down Section 33 with the result that, except for deputy ministers, there are virtually no statutory restrictions on the political rights of federal public servants.

In provincial governments, a common pattern has emerged with respect to public servants who wish to become candidates for public office. Although the number of senior and other officials who are prohibited from such activity varies from province to province, most public servants seeking candidacy and election may receive a leave of absence for a period preceding the date of the election. Employees who are elected must resign their public service position. In several provinces, however, an employee who is elected but who ceases to be a representative within five years will be reinstated to government service. In regard to other forms of political activity (e.g., membership in political parties; attendance at political meetings, rallies, and conventions; making and soliciting financial contributions; canvassing for a political candidate), the rules vary considerably across provinces. In virtually every province, the right of public servants to support the party of their choice or no party at all is specifically protected by statute.

The fact that most public servants may now stand for election and engage in a broader spectrum of political activities has heightened the general level of partisan activity and consciousness in Canada's public services, especially among younger employees. However, officials in senior and sensitive posts are usually required to refrain from partisan activity; thus, those officials most actively involved in policy formation and in the discretionary application of policy retain their impartiality. Also, officials with many years of government experience have difficulty overcoming their ingrained avoidance of political activity. Some public servants may justifiably perceive overt partisanship as an obstacle to promotion to the senior ranks of what is, substantially, a politically neutral public service.

Restrictions on the political partisanship of public servants, in both the federal and provincial spheres of government, have been challenged in the courts under the Canadian Charter of Rights and Freedoms. The issue is, for the most part, framed in terms of the need to strike the most appropriate balance between the political rights of public servants and the political neutrality of the public service. Section 2 of the Charter guarantees the fundamental freedoms of expression, peaceful assembly, and association, and Section 1 provides that the guarantees to rights and freedoms under the Charter are subject to "such reasonable limits prescribed by law as can be demonstrably justified in a free and democratic society." The issue before the courts, then, is whether the limits on the political partisanship of public servants can be demonstrably justified to be reasonable in contemporary Canadian society. Recent court decisions indicate that there is a clear trend in the direction of extending the political rights of public servants. As noted, the Supreme Court struck down Section 33 of the federal *Public Service Employment Act*, largely on the grounds that the wording of the section was so vague as to be unduly restrictive and, therefore, unreasonable.[16]

4. Public Comment

The admonition that public servants "not express publicly their personal views on government policies or administration" is an integral component of the ideal model of political neutrality. The prime reason given by contemporary governments for restrictions on public comment is the need to preserve the confidence of the public and of political superiors in the impartiality of public servants.

Strict interpretation of this rule of official reticence requires that public servants not express personal opinions on government policies, whether they are attacking or supporting those policies. As explained below, this convention has been supplemented by statutory prohibitions relating to political partisanship and to the use of confidential information, by decisions of administrative tribunals, and by written guidelines.

Public servants on leave of absence to seek election are of course obliged to express personal and partisan views on campaign issues. Those who wish to return to government service if they are defeated may find it prudent to show discretion in their public statements, especially with respect to the policies and programs of the department to which they may wish to return. Public servants, whether seeking election or not, are normally prohibited by an oath of office and secrecy, and by the *Official Secrets Act*, from disclosing or using for personal gain confidential information acquired by virtue of their government position. It is a serious offence to criticize government policy or administration; the use of confidential information for this purpose would greatly compound the offence.

Formal written guidelines on public comment are so sparse that considerable uncertainty exists as to the rights of public servants in this area. It is well established in the public service legislation of modern democratic states that the role of public servants in policy development and implementation requires that they enjoy fewer political rights than other citizens. In the area of public comment, the difficulty is to strike an appropriate balance between freedom of expression and political neutrality.

As a result of the intimate links among politics, policy, and administration described earlier, public servants often enhance understanding of the political and policy process through their speeches and writings on the machinery of government and the administrative process. However, the major burden of explaining the political system to the public is likely to remain with politicians and scholars.

Public advocacy of administrative reform and constructive criticism of government activities may complement the public servants' information and conciliation functions. However, the participation of public servants in these forms of public comment is restricted by their political superiors, who bear public responsibility for the operations of government. Denunciations and overtly partisan assessments of government policy or administration tend to be clearer than other forms of public comment in their manifestation, and in the certainty of their punishment. Both the traditional admonition against public comment and recent decisions by administrative tribunals prohibit such activity unless public servants are on leave of absence to seek election.

The unwritten rule against public comment is subject to varying interpretations and applications in contemporary society. Public servants are now involved in forms of public comment not explicitly covered by the conventional rule, and the nature of this involvement constitutes a significant departure from a position of political neutrality. It appears that public servants will increasingly be required to attend public meetings to provide information about government policies and programs, and they are more and more asked to arrange and operate the many consultative processes with the interested public. As a result, the public will become more aware of the influence that public servants bring to deliberations on public policy matters. It is often difficult for public servants to discuss government policy without indicating, inadvertently or otherwise, some measure of the influence they have—or might have—over the content of policy.

5. Anonymity and Ministerial Responsibility

As noted early in this chapter, the ideal model of political neutrality requires that "public servants provide forthright and objective advice to their political masters in private and in confidence; political executives protect the anonymity of public servants by publicly accepting responsibility for departmental decisions." The anonymity of public servants depends, in large measure, on the vitality of the doctrine of individual ministerial responsibility, according to which ministers are personally responsible to the legislature both for their own actions and for those of their administrative subordinates. Thus, public servants are not directly answerable to the legislature and their minister protects their anonymity. But over the years events have revealed that ministers will not invariably protect the anonymity of their officials by refusing to name or blame them publicly.

Public service anonymity also depends significantly on factors other than the operation of ministerial responsibility. Departures from political neutrality in the areas of patronage and political activity also diminish official anonymity, but the greatest threat is probably the expansion of public comment described earlier. The increased interaction of public servants with both individual citizens and specific "publics," or clientele groups, reveals the nature of official involvement in policy development. The cumulative impact of the growing information and conciliation functions performed by public servants is a gradual, but significant, decline in official anonymity.

The anonymity of public servants has also been diminished by their more frequent appearances before legislative committees. Their diplomatic skills are often severely taxed as they strive to describe and explain their department's programs fully and frankly, while preserving their loyalty to their minister and their reputation for impartiality. On occasion, however, legislators, pressure groups, journalists, and others concerned with the committees' deliberations can discern the actual or potential power of public servants in the policy process.

The pervasive role of the news media in contemporary society has been reflected in increased media coverage of the activities and identities of public servants. The media and public servants share a desire to inform the public about government programs. Public servants utilize the media for public relations and publicity—to tell their department's story and to sell their department's programs. The media serve as excellent channels of communication to the public for officials engaged in public comment that requires the description and explanation of government programs. The media, in turn, analyze the purposes and, whenever possible, identify the personalities involved in the development and administration of programs. This media coverage helps to limit bureaucratic power by exposing the activities of public servants to public questioning and criticism.

The extent to which public servants are exposed to the public's gaze through the news media depends largely on the position they occupy, on current interest in their department's activities, and on their personal views and those of their minister on anonymity. Certain public servants (e.g., a deputy minister of finance) are better known because of the enduring importance of their position; others receive publicity during periods of public controversy in their sphere of responsibilities.

Since the early 1990s, there has been greatly increased emphasis on improving government service to the public by pushing decision-making power down the administrative hierarchy and out to field offices. This means public servants will be in more direct and more frequent contact with their clients and other stakeholders, thereby becoming more visible to the public generally.

Although the tradition of anonymity remains strong among public servants, their visibility has been heightened by changes in political institutions and practices, and by the media's response to demands for more public information. This gradual decline in official anonymity is likely to continue, revealing the significant role of public servants in the political process.

6. Permanence in Office

The preservation of political neutrality requires that "public servants carry out policy decisions loyally regardless of the position of the party in power. As a result, public servants have security of tenure during good behaviour and satisfactory performance." Thus, in the event of a change of government, official neutrality helps to ensure continuity of administration by competent and experienced public servants, as well as the provision of impartial advice on policy options and the loyal implementation of policy decisions. Security of tenure enables a career public servant not only to establish and wield influence in the policy process but also to continue to exercise such influence even if there is a change in the governing party. Long tenure enables public servants to acquire knowledge and experience, both in specific policy fields and in the political–administrative system within which policy decisions are made. Permanence in office for public servants increases their power vis-à-vis politicians. Ministers cannot match the expertise of their senior officials, and the frequent rotation of ministers among departments prevents them from accumulating much experience in particular policy areas.

As public servants, especially at the senior levels, become more overtly or apparently political, the argument for political appointments to senior posts is strengthened. Thus, permanence in office depends largely on adherence to the elements of political neutrality already described. The merit system is designed to bring about a more permanent public service by minimizing the number of patronage appointments and avoiding a turnover of personnel following a change of government. Senior public servants are not permitted to engage in partisan political activity or public criticism of government. Finally, the preservation of ministerial responsibility and public service anonymity helps to protect officials from public identification as supporters or opponents of particular policies.

Despite these efforts to achieve the fact and the appearance of administrative impartiality, Opposition party leaders have frequently promised, if elected, to turf out senior officials because of their assumed contribution to government policies to which these leaders are opposed. Therefore, public servants must be able to demonstrate the capacity to adapt quickly and effectively to the requirements of a new governing party.

When permanence in office for public servants has been combined with longevity in office by a particular political party, a change of government presents an especially difficult challenge to the capacity of public servants to serve different political masters impartially. It is understandable that senior officials who have worked closely with ministers in the development of existing policies should be apprehensive about the arrival of a new governing party. In the past, there have been instances in which incoming governments have experienced some tension with the senior public service. New ministers complained that their officials presented them with few options and used "entrapment devices" to ensure that the wishes of the public service—and not those of the government—won the day.[17] But many new ministers found few difficulties and determined that "the higher civil service was as effective at advising the new government as it had been the old."[18] These differing views suggest that the extent of bureaucratic power varies according to such factors as the policy or program under consideration, the department or agency involved, and the style and competence of ministers and their officials.

There is some support in Canada for a system of political appointments similar to that in the United States. Supporters of a politicized public service usually cite the various benefits from political appointments to senior public service posts. These include a strong commitment to implementing the policies of the new government, an injection of new ideas and approaches toward government policies and processes, advice on policy issues that is more sensitive to their partisan political implications, and greater trust by ministers in their policy advisors. Under this system, the incumbents of the most senior public service positions would be replaced whenever a change in government occurred. Some senior appointments would thus be held on a temporary rather than a permanent basis. The power of career public servants would be reduced, because they would not normally be appointed to the highest administrative posts. However, assuming regular changes in the governing party, the tenure of senior political appointees would be too brief to enable them to exercise as much power based on experience and expertise as do career public servants.

At present, a shift to a system of political appointments either in the federal government or in most provincial governments is unlikely. Career public servants in Canada can normally expect security of tenure during good conduct, adequate performance, and political neutrality.

Political Neutrality and Bureaucratic Interactions

The preceding discussion of the six elements of political neutrality shows that the operations of Canada's public services are not in accord with a strict interpretation of the traditional doctrine of political neutrality. In so doing, it has also shown the character of some of the more important interactions between appointed officials and others in the political process. The discussion has also offered a glimpse of the underlying bases and relations of power. The following summarizes the main points arising from this consideration of political neutrality and its implications for an understanding of the dynamics of public administration in Canada:

- Politics, policy, and administration are closely intertwined. Politicians and public servants are involved in both the making and the implementation of policy decisions. Elected officials, notably cabinet ministers, make final decisions on major policy matters, but public servants influence these decisions and make decisions of their own under authority delegated by cabinet and the legislature.
- The vast majority of public servants are appointed on the basis of merit or fitness to do the job. One implication of this is that appointed officials bring a great deal of expertise to their positions. Some public servants are appointed on the grounds of contributions to the governing political party, but, at a senior level, most of these political appointments are made to agencies, boards, or commissions rather than to regular government departments. Patronage appointments continue to be made at relatively low levels of the public service in several Canadian jurisdictions.
- Public servants are permitted to engage in certain partisan political activities. The extent of permissible participation varies across governments but it is gradually increasing. Public servants who wish to stand for public office are required in most governments to seek permission for a leave of absence. They are also forbidden to engage in partisan political activity while at work, and their political and administrative superiors are forbidden to coerce them into performing partisan work.
- Public servants in most governments are prohibited from expressing publicly their personal views on government policies or administration, especially if these views are critical of the government or partisan in nature. Moreover, they are forbidden by law and tradition to engage in any forms of public comment in which they make use of confidential information to which they are privy by virtue of their official position. However, many public servants are required to engage in public comment as part of their official duties, and this particular duty is becoming a greater part of the responsibilities of appointed officials.
- Public servants provide forthright and objective advice to their political masters in private and in confidence; political executives normally protect the anonymity of public servants by publicly accepting responsibility for departmental decisions. Public service anonymity has been diminished to some extent by the role public servants are required to play in explaining policies and programs to the public and to legislators. In this role, public servants must be careful not to infringe on their

minister's sphere of responsibility by justifying or speculating on government policy.

- Public servants usually execute policy decisions loyally, irrespective of the philosophy and programs of the party in power and regardless of their personal opinions; as a result, public servants usually enjoy security of tenure, except in the event of staff cutbacks, unsatisfactory performance, or bad behaviour.

Conclusion

This chapter has sought to develop a framework for examining the interactions between public servants and other actors in the political process. It has also endeavoured to reveal the values that shape the behaviour of bureaucrats in their interactions and to provide some sense of the nature of these relationships.

1. John F. Pfiffner and Frank P. Sherwood, *Administrative Organization* (Englewood Cliffs, N.J.: Prentice-Hall, 1960), 77.

2. R. H. Tawney, *Equality* (London: G. Allen and Unwin, 1931), 229.

3. Samuel B. Bachrach and Edward J. Lawler, *Power and Politics in Organizations* (San Francisco: Jossey-Bass Publishers, 1980), 41.

4. See Carl J. Friedrich, *Man and His Government* (New York: McGraw-Hill, 1963), ch. 11.

5. Kenneth Kernaghan, Brian Marson, and Sandford Borins, *The New Public Organization* (Toronto: Institute of Public Administration of Canada, 2000), 45.

6. The six elements were first set out in Kenneth Kernaghan, "Politics, Policy and Public Servants: Political Neutrality Revisited," *Canadian Public Administration* 21(3) (fall 1976), 433. Unattributed quotations specifying the elements are from this source.

7. Woodrow Wilson, "The Study of Administration," reprinted in Peter Woll, ed., *Public Administration and Policy* (New York: Harper and Row, 1966), 28–29.

8. Wallace S. Sayre, "Premises of Public Administration: Past and Emerging," *Public Administration Review* 18(2) (1958): 103.

9. Paul Appleby, *Policy and Administration* (University, Ala.: University of Alabama Press, 1949), 170.

10. Eugene P. Dvorin and Robert H. Simmons, *From Amoral to Humane Bureaucracy* (San Francisco: Canfield Press, 1972).

11. Donald J. Savoie, *Thatcher, Reagan, Mulroney: In Search of a New Bureaucracy* (Toronto: University of Toronto, 1994), 282.

12. Ibid., 173–74.

13. R.H. Dowdell, "Public Personnel Administration," in Kenneth Kernaghan, ed., *Public Administration in Canada*, 4th ed. (Toronto: Methuen, 1982), 196.

14. For a definition of political activity and an account of the arguments usually raised for and against the political activity of government employees, see Kenneth Kernaghan, "Political Rights and Political Neutrality: Finding the Balance Point," *Canadian Public Administration* 29(4) (winter 1986): 639–52.

15. *Canada Statutes*, 8–9 Geo. v, c. 12.

16. *Osborne v. Canada* (Treasury Board) (1991), 82 D.L.R. (4th) 321 (S.C.C.).

17. Flora MacDonald, "The Ministers and Mandarins," *Policy Options* 1 (September/October 1980): 29–31.

18. J.R. Mallory, *The Structure of Canadian Government* (Toronto: Macmillan, 1971), 116.

Responsibility, Accountability, and Ethics

In the preceding chapter, we discussed the importance of appreciating that public servants engage in a series of interactions. In these interactions, a number of values shape and structure the actions of appointed officials, two of the most significant of which are accountability and integrity. Accountability is important because there is a desire for public servants to act with the understanding that they are in one way or another responsible for the consequences of their actions. The significance of integrity lies in the fact that we wish appointed officials to adhere to principles of proper or ethical conduct in their relations with others and in the carrying out of their duties and responsibilities. Together, the two help produce what might be called the responsible public servant. There is, however, a problem with this emphasis on accountability and integrity, and that is ensuring that these two values do in fact inform the behaviour of public servants. Events both recent and past indicate that the process of inculcating the values of accountability and integrity in the actions of bureaucratic officials in Canada is incomplete. More attention apparently needs to be given to ensuring that these two most important values are central in the minds of bureaucratic actors.

The purpose of this chapter is to provide a discussion of the values of accountability and integrity so we can better grasp their importance to public administration. The chapter begins with an acknowledgment that there is concern about responsible behaviour on the part of both political and administrative officials, and then moves to a discussion of theories of administrative responsibility and accountability. The chapter also discusses the value of integrity and its association with rules of ethical behaviour. In approaching this chapter, the reader should be aware of scholarly efforts to distinguish accountability from responsibility. Typically, these efforts conclude that responsibility refers to the field or area of activity over which an official has been empowered to act. As for accountability, it refers to explaining or defending the carrying out of responsibilities and possibly accepting sanctions for unsatisfactory performance. But as the chapter will show, it is difficult to maintain this distinction—the terms are often used interchangeably.[1]

The Responsible Public Servant

During the past thirty years in particular, public concern about accountability in government has been stimulated in Western democratic states, including Canada, by events involving illegal, unethical, or questionable activities by both politicians and public servants. Discussion of incidents of political espionage, conflicts of interest, disclosures of confidential information, and alleged wasteful spending have revealed that both the general public and students of government disagree among themselves as to what constitutes irresponsible conduct, who should assume blame in particular cases, and what the penalty should be.

The scope and complexity of government activities have become so great that it is often difficult to determine the actual—as opposed to the legal or constitutional—locus of responsibility for specific decisions. Political officials in the executive branch are held responsible for personal wrongdoing. They are not, however, expected to be accountable by way of resignation or demotion for acts of administrative subordinates about which they could not reasonably be expected to have knowledge. Yet it is frequently impossible to assign individual responsibility to public servants for administrative transgressions either, because so many public servants have contributed to the decision-making process or because public servants place the blame back on the elected officials.

While the involvement of political executives in unlawful or questionable activities has drawn much public attention to the issue of *political* responsibility, the status of *administrative* responsibility or accountability has also become a matter of increasing anxiety. Elected officials make the final decisions on major public policy issues, but public servants have significant influence on these decisions and have authority to make decisions on their own that affect the individual and collective rights of the citizenry.

Concern about the preservation of administrative responsibility is shared in varying degrees by all major actors in the political system—whether they be political executives, legislators, judges, interest group and mass media representatives, members of the general public, or public servants. As a result of efforts by these various actors to promote responsible administrative conduct, the decisions of public servants are subject to an almost bewildering assortment of controls and influences.

Theories of Administrative Responsibility

The Conventional Theories

The traditional concepts of administrative responsibility may be explained by reference to the celebrated debate between Carl Friedrich and Herman Finer during the period 1935–41.[2] Both Friedrich and Finer correctly identified the source of burgeoning bureaucratic power as the rapid expansion of government's service and regulatory functions. However, they disagreed vehemently on the most effective means of guarding against abuse of administrative discretion so as to maintain and promote responsible administrative conduct. Their disagreement was, in large part, an outgrowth of their differing conceptions of the capacity of political systems to adapt to change and of the proper role of public servants. To achieve administrative responsibility, Finer put primary faith in controls and sanctions exercised over public servants by the legislature, the judiciary, and the administrative hierarchy. In his insistence on the predominant importance of political responsibility (i.e., responsibility to elected officials), he claimed that "the political and administrative history of all ages" had shown that "sooner or later there is an abuse of power when external punitive controls are lacking."[3]

Friedrich relied more heavily on the propensity of public servants to be self-directing and self-regulating, the measure of which was their responsiveness to the dual standard of technical knowledge and popular sentiment. While he admitted the continuing need for political responsibility, he argued that a policy was irresponsible if it was adopted

> without proper regard to the existing sum of human knowledge concerning the technical issues involved . . . [or] without proper regard for existing preferences in the community, and more particularly its prevailing majority. Consequently, the responsible administrator is one who is responsive to these two dominant factors: technical knowledge and popular sentiment.[4]

Friedrich asserted also that "parliamentary responsibility is largely inoperative and certainly ineffectual" and that "the task of clear and consistent policy formation has passed . . . into the hands of administrators and is bound to continue to do so."[5]

Finer admitted this problem but stressed the necessity of remedying the several deficiencies of political control over administrative officials. He believed that the means of legislative control should be improved. He argued further that public servants should not determine their own course of action. Rather, the elected representatives of the people should "determine the course of action of public servants to the most minute degree that is technically feasible."[6] Finer presented an excellent summary of both his position and his critique of Friedrich's stand in his explanation of "the two definitions" of administrative responsibility:

> First, responsibility may mean that X is accountable for Y to Z. Second, responsibility may mean an inward personal sense of moral obligation. In the first definition the essence is the externality of the agency or persons to whom an account is to be rendered, and it can mean very little without that agency having authority over X, determining the lines of X's obligation and the terms of its continuance or revocation. The second definition puts the emphasis on the conscience of the agent, and . . . if he commits an error it is an error only when recognized by his own conscience, and . . . the punishment of the agent will be merely the twinges thereof. The one implies public execution; the other hara-kiri.[7]

Finer described the sum of Friedrich's arguments as "moral" responsibility, as opposed to his own emphasis on "political" responsibility.

Friedrich's contention that administrative responsibility can be more effectively elicited than enforced raises a critical issue for contemporary discussion of the subject. He believed that responsible conduct depended to a large extent on "sound work rules and effective morale."[8] To this end, he suggested that the environment of government employment be changed. Public servants were to be granted the right to organize into staff associations and to bargain collectively with the government. Furthermore, responsibility to technical knowledge could not be assured unless public servants were permitted to discuss policy issues publicly, a position that Finer rejected in favour of the anonymity of the public servant.

An understanding of the Friedrich–Finer debate is an essential foundation on which to construct subsequent discussion. It raises several of the major issues of administrative responsibility still being debated by contemporary scholars, albeit in a vastly different social and political environment. The strength of Finer's approach lay in his recognition of the continuing need for political controls over the bureaucracy. Its primary weakness lay in his failure to anticipate the inadequacy of these controls to ensure administrative responsibility in a period of ever-accelerating political and social change. The strength of Friedrich's argument rested on his awareness of the deficiency of solely applying political controls. Its major weakness lay in the difficulty of reconciling conflicts between the two criteria of technical knowledge and popular sentiment.

Objective and Subjective Responsibility

Frederick Mosher provides a broader, more inclusive classification than the Friedrich–Finer categories by making a distinction between objective responsibility (or accountability) and psychological or subjective responsibility. According to his widely accepted definition, **objective responsibility** "connotes the responsibility of a person or an organization to someone else, outside of self, for some thing or some kind of performance. It is closely akin to *accountability* or *answerability*. If one fails to carry out legitimate directives, he is judged irresponsible, and may be subjected to penalties."[9] Psychological or **subjective responsibility**, by way of contrast, focuses

> not upon to whom and for what one is responsible (according to law and the organization chart) but to whom and for what one *feels* responsible and *behaves* responsibly. This meaning, which is sometimes described as *personal* responsibility, is more nearly synonymous with identification, loyalty and conscience than it is with accountability and answerability.[10]

Thus, Mosher views administrative responsibility as a broad concept that includes administrative accountability as one of its two major components. However, the presence of subjective or psychological responsibility is more difficult to discern than that of objective responsibility, but there is some evidence of its existence and its influence. Past surveys of deputy ministers have revealed that the most senior public servants believe they are personally responsible for controlling the finances of their departments and that the person they felt more responsible to was themselves.[11] Despite the importance of this notion of subjective responsibility, it is accountability (objective responsibility) that has received by far the most public and scholarly attention.

Administrative Accountability

The questions commonly asked about the accountability of public servants are: *Who* is accountable? *To whom* is accountability owed? *For what* is accountability owed? *By what means* can accountability be achieved?

The current emphasis on accountability is a result of both the need to strengthen accountability in government generally and the very broad interpretations that the word accountability has gradually acquired. For example, a federal royal commission looking into government management saw accountability as "the activating, but fragile, element permeating a complex network connecting the government upward to Parliament and downward and outward to a geographically dispersed bureaucracy grouped in a bewildering array of departments, corporations, boards and commissions."[12] This definition portrays well the breadth of meaning currently given to the notion of accountability in government. It is, however, too sweeping a definition to be very useful in operational terms; moreover, it covers the accountability of both politicians and public servants, whereas our primary concern is with public service accountability. A narrower and, for our purposes, a more useful definition of **administrative accountability** is:

> the obligation of public servants to be answerable for fulfilling responsibilities that flow from the authority given them. . . . Internal accountability holds public servants answerable to their line superiors for their own actions and the actions of their subordinates. . . . External accountability holds public servants answerable to the public as well. The normal channel through which this requirement is satisfied is the minister.[13]

This definition is good, for it captures two of the three components commonly associated with **"accountability"**, namely designation of responsibilities and the need to answer for the carrying out of these responsibilities. What has to be added (and which may be implicit in the answerability component) is taking action to correct any perceived deficiencies and to accept sanctions for failures in performance (or benefits for good work).[14] This definition also works because it draws attention to the fact that public servants are only directly accountable to a limited number of political actors, and that to hold public servants accountable, one must be able to exercise authority over them. Indeed, a more useful distinction than that between internal and external accountability is that between direct and indirect accountability. Public servants are directly accountable only to political and administrative superiors, to the courts, and to any internal governmental authorities (e.g., central agencies) to which accountability is required by law or the administrative hierarchy. They are not directly accountable to the legislature, to pressure groups, to the news media, or to the general public. However, they are generally required to explain their decisions and actions to these entities, and they may feel a sense of psychological or personal responsibility toward them.

Enforcing accountability for the exercise of bureaucratic power has become more difficult, as our public services have grown in size and their responsibilities have grown in complexity. The decision-making process in government is often so lengthy and complicated that it is difficult to single out those public servants who should be held responsible for specific recommendations and decisions. Moreover, as will be explained, the present application of the doctrine of ministerial responsibility does not ensure that ministers will be held responsible for misadministration in their departments.

Another obstacle on the road to accountability is the wide range of authorities to which public servants are deemed accountable. While, in general, it is agreed that public servants are accountable first of all to their minister, in practice public servants receive directions, rewards, and penalties from a variety of sources. This is one of the major differences between public and private sector administration.

Administrative Ethics

Integrity is a central public service value. It can be interpreted to cover a broad range of bureaucratic behaviour, but it is used here in a limited sense to refer to administrative or **public service ethics,** or principles and standards of right conduct for public servants. Certain principles and standards of ethical behaviour (e.g., honesty, promise-keeping) are of such enduring importance in all walks of life that they can be described as ethical values. These ethical values can be used to resolve conflicts between such public service values as responsiveness and efficiency; they can also be applied to clashes between public service values on the one hand, and social values such as liberty and equality, or personal values such as success and wealth, on the other. Consider, for example, public servants whose political superiors direct them to conceal information about a threat to the public's health. The conflict between accountability to their superiors and their sense of responsiveness to the public might be resolved according to the ethical value of honesty. Integrity in the sense of ethical behaviour can in some instances override all other values.

Opportunities for public servants to become involved in unethical conduct arise from the power they exercise in the development and administration of public policy. Senior public servants with discretionary authority and confidential information have the greatest opportunities to benefit from unethical conduct. But temptations to engage in unethical behaviour exist at all levels of the administrative hierarchy and at all levels of government (e.g., a senior official with contracting authority in a federal department or a secretary in a municipal government with access to confidential development plans).

Historically, the public's interest in the ethical conduct of government officials, whether politicians or public servants, has waxed and waned as instances of wrongdoing have been exposed, publicized, debated, punished, and then forgotten. But since the early 1970s, there has been continuing anxiety among the public and within governments about the ethical standards of public officials. There is increasing recognition that the ethical dimension of public administration has been unduly neglected in the past.

Much of the public and media concern about public service ethics has centred on conflicts of interest and, to a lesser extent, on issues of political partisanship, public comment, and confidentiality. Among the many questions of current concern in these problem areas are the following: What kinds of gifts or entertainment should public servants accept from someone with whom they do business? Under what circumstance is moonlighting acceptable? Is an apparent conflict of interest as serious as an actual conflict? To what extent should public servants participate in partisan political activity? To what extent should public servants criticize government policies and programs in public? Under what circumstances, if any, are public servants justified in leaking government information?

The effective management of these issues is generally considered to be essential to public trust and confidence in government. Over the past years, governments have responded to heightened public concern about these issues by drafting statutes, regulations, guidelines, and codes dealing with ethical conduct. However, these high-profile issues constitute only a small proportion of the total field of ethical problems. Many other ethical issues of considerable importance receive comparatively little public attention. These are issues that relate less to the use of public office for private, personal, or partisan gain and more to ethical and value conflicts and dilemmas that arise in the performance of administrative duties. Among these issues are the following: Under what circumstances, if any, should public servants lie to the public? Should public servants zealously implement a policy that they think is misguided? Do public servants owe their ultimate loyalty to their political superiors? To the public? To their perception of the public interest? To their conscience? Is it appropriate to bend the rules to assist a member of the public who is especially needy or especially deserving? Is the public interest the same thing as the interest of the government in power? What level of risk should a public servant take with the public? Where ought the balance be struck between a representative public service and an efficient and effective public service?

Compared to issues like conflict of interest and confidentiality, the several questions raised above have not only received less public attention but are also less amenable to management by written ethics rules. Thus, the effective management of these issues requires that ethics rules in general and ethics codes in particular be supplemented by other means of promoting ethical behaviour. Indeed, an ethics framework for a government department might include a wide range of components.[15] For example, governments might make the assessment of ethical behaviour a part of the basis for appointments and promotions in the public service and set out a statement of values and a corresponding code of ethics. The framework might also provide for an ethics counsellor responsible for providing guidance on the ethical rules and an education program for public servants on ethical action and its importance. A procedure for auditing the policies and procedures for promoting ethical behaviour and a confidential hotline for public servants to discuss moral dilemmas might also be considered for inclusion in the framework.

Despite the several components of this kind of framework, the most common approach to promoting ethical conduct is the use of a code of ethics, especially for dealing with conflict-of-interest problems. The remainder of this section examines, in turn, the costs and benefits of codes of ethics; the form, content, and administration of these codes; and their implications for administrative responsibility.

Costs and Benefits of Codes of Ethics

Disclosures of unethical conduct by government officials during the early 1970s prompted several governments to assess the desirability of providing or improving ethics rules. By the end of the decade, the federal government and most provincial governments had adopted written rules, often in the form of codes of ethics, to regulate the ethical behaviour of public servants. Developments in the municipal sphere of government were slower.

A code of public service ethics is a statement of principles and standards about the right conduct of public servants. It usually contains only a portion of a government's rules on public service ethics, and is therefore a more narrow term than ethics rules, which refer to statutes, regulations, and guidelines. The form, content, and administration of ethics codes differ significantly from one government to another. Indeed, much of the dispute over the usefulness of codes of ethics arises from the fact that such a wide variety of instruments are described as codes. The situation is further complicated by the fact that public servants may be subject not only to their government's code of ethics but also to codes developed for their own profession (e.g., law, engineering).

Even the most vigorous advocates of codes of ethics for public servants acknowledge that they are not a panacea for preventing unethical behaviour. There is, however, much disagreement over how useful codes actually are. Perhaps the most common criticism of codes is that the broad ethical principles contained in many codes are often difficult to apply to specific situations. A second, related concern is that codes of ethics, even if they contain detailed provisions, are difficult to enforce; indeed, many contain no provision for their enforcement. Third, the large scale and complexity of government make it difficult to draft a code that can be applied fairly and consistently across a large number of departments. Fourth, codes can adversely affect the individual rights and private lives of public servants whose ethical behaviour is beyond reproach. Consider the effect on individual privacy of the requirement in some governments that public servants disclose not only their own financial interests but also those of their spouses and dependent children. Finally, certain ethical and value issues, such as determining what measure of risk to the public is acceptable, are not easily amenable to management by ethics rules in general or ethics codes in particular.

However, codes can reduce uncertainty among public servants about what constitutes ethical and unethical behaviour. First, unwritten rules in the form of understandings and practices leave much room for argument about the content of rules and what the penalties must be for violating them. Second, codes can promote public trust and confidence in the ethical behaviour of public servants. Taxpayers can be better assured, for example, that they will be treated fairly and impartially, and that public servants are less likely to use their positions for personal gain. Third, codes can reduce unethical practices by discouraging and punishing them. They provide one of several means by which political leaders and senior managers can hold public servants accountable for their activities. Fourth, codes can sensitize public servants to the reality that the ethical and value dimensions of their decisions and recommendations are as important as, and often more important than, the technical, legal, and political dimensions. Finally, the development of a code of ethics may prompt governments to reassess their existing written or unwritten rules so that the rights and participation of public servants in regard to certain activities (e.g., political partisanship, outside employment) may be enhanced.

The Style and Substance of Ethics Rules

Although Canadian governments have taken varying approaches to the form, content, and administration of their ethics rules, it is widely acknowledged that the best approach is a code of ethics that contains comprehensive coverage of the major ethical problem areas and effective means for the code's administration. It is useful to codify existing rules by bringing them together in a single document, or at least incorporating in that document reference to service-wide rules already existing in statutes and regulations.

Form. Safeguards against unethical conduct can take the form of statutes providing for prosecution and punishment by the regular courts (e.g., Criminal Code provisions on bribery and corruption) or of regulations or guidelines administered within the government itself. Prosecution by the courts (e.g., under the Criminal Code) is too blunt an instrument to apply to most unethical practices. Many instances of unethical conduct fall into a "grey zone": they are unacceptable but cannot be effectively handled by the courts. In other cases, it is debatable whether an offence has actually been committed, since many ethical issues are complex and the offence may be more apparent than real. In such circumstances, governments are required to exercise judgment as to what penalty, if any, is appropriate. Penalties can range from a reprimand to dismissal.

Content. The content of codes of ethics has focused so heavily on conflicts of interest that it is useful to elaborate on this problem area. A **conflict of interest** may be defined as a situation in which a public employee has a private or personal interest sufficient to influence, or to appear to influence, the objective exercise of his or her official duties. Conflicts of interest receive a great deal of public attention, because of the prospect of financial gain from such activities and because of the many varieties of the offence. Among the varieties of conflict of interest are accepting benefits, outside employment, and post-employment. *Accepting benefits* of significant value from individuals, groups, or firms with whom the employee has official dealings sometimes borders on bribery and corruption, which is punishable under the Criminal Code. Recently, a senior official with the federal Department of Health was given a one-year jail sentence for receiving personal benefits amounting to more than $200,000 in return for illegally transferring public funds to an aboriginal treatment centre.[16]

However, the propriety of accepting gifts or hospitality is usually judged on the basis of whether the benefit to the employee is of sufficient value to be likely to influence—or *appear* to influence—the objective discharge of that person's responsibilities. The federal *Values and Ethics Code for the Public Service* warns about the risk of accepting gifts, hospitality, and other benefits, but says as well that the acceptance of such benefits is fine under certain conditions (e.g., infrequently given, emerge from activities relating to responsibilities of officials).[17]

Outside employment, or "moonlighting," constitutes a conflict of interest when that employment reduces significantly the time and effort public servants devote to their official duties, or when that employment is incompatible with their duties. Thus, a public servant who slept all day on the job after driving a taxi all night would be in a conflict-of-interest situation; so would a public servant responsible for regulating marine safety who also worked for, or owned, a company selling marine safety equipment. A similar example would be a government plumbing inspector with a part-time plumbing business who offers to come back after hours to fix, for a price, some plumbing he or she had just inspected.

The *post-employment* problem arises when a public servant resigns or retires from government to join a firm with which he or she has had official dealings, or that could benefit unduly from information that the public servant acquired while in government. There is often concern that this person may have conferred benefits on the firm in the hope of future employment, or that the firm might gain a competitive advantage by gaining access to confidential information, including trade secrets. To protect against these possibilities, the above-mentioned federal *Values and Ethics Code* states that former public servants within a year of resigning or retiring are unable to accept a job with an entity with which they had relations in the period one year before their end of employ-ment in the federal public service.[18]

Administration. The effective administration of ethics rules in these several problem areas is critical to success in promoting high ethical standards. Provisions for administration of the rules ideally should include publicity, enforcement, and grievance procedures. In governments with a large number of employees and administrative units, it is usually necessary to delegate to individual departments and agencies responsibility for elaborat-ing on service-wide rules and for administering the rules for their own employees.

Most varieties of conflict of interest are covered in the federal government's *Values and Ethics Code for the Public Service.* Both new and current employees are required to cer-tify that they have read and understood the code, and that they will observe it as a con-dition of appointment and employment.

Ethics Rules, Education, and Leadership

Written rules can be useful in promoting the high ethical standards required of public servants. However, as noted earlier, not all ethical problems can be handled by ethics rules. Such rules are of limited use in helping public servants to develop skills in the analysis of ethical and value issues and in the resolution of these issues. It is desirable to complement formal rules with formal education, training programs, and exemplary role models.

An increasingly important means of promoting ethical behaviour is to sensitize pub-lic servants to the ethical and value dimensions of public service during their pre-employment education and in-service training. Recognition of the importance of this approach can be seen in the growing number of courses on public service ethics in uni-versities and government departments.

The influence of administrative superiors is also an extremely important means of promoting ethical behaviour. The *Values and Ethics Code*, for instance, states that deputy heads of departments are obligated to "encourage and maintain an ongoing dialogue on public service values and ethics within their organizations, in a manner that is relevant to the specific issues and challenges encountered by their organizations."[19] However, some contemporary governments, and many individual departments, are so large that even senior officials have personal contact with a relatively small percentage of their employees. Therefore, there is now less assurance than there used to be that the influ-ence of public service leaders on ethical matters will flow down the administrative pyr-amid. This explains in part why many senior public servants support the codification of ethical standards as a means of nurturing responsible administrative behaviour.

The Public Interest

The concept of the public interest is very closely related to the issues of administrative responsibility and administrative ethics. Indeed, responsible administrative behaviour is frequently assessed in terms of the public servant's ability to resolve conflicts among administrative and other values according to the criterion of the public interest. Moreover, the public interest has been proposed as the dominant ethical principle or standard for bureaucratic behaviour. One author describes the public interest as "the highest ethical standard applicable to political affairs,"[20] and the federal *Values and Eth-ics Code* states right up front that the "democratic mission of the Public Service is to assist Ministers, under law, to serve the public interest."[21]

The concept of the public interest, like that of administrative responsibility, has been interpreted in various ways. It has been defined as "the general will," "the wisest and most foresighted interest," a moral imperative "resting on natural law foundations," and "compromise...as the optimum reconciliation of the competing claims of special and private interests."[22] Each of these definitions is, to some extent, partial or deficient. In the context of administrative decision making, for example, the first three definitions are too nebulous to provide sufficient guidance to the public servant. However, the interpretation of the public interest as the best possible accommodation of conflicting interests provides an essential element of specificity.

The accommodation of the claims of various interests connotes a power struggle among competing groups, each possessing approximately equal access to the decision maker and devoting roughly equivalent resources to the struggle. In reality, both access and resources of money, organization, supporters, and research capacity vary among different groups. Moreover, the interests of some segments of the population may not be represented because these segments are underprivileged, uneducated, uninformed, inarticulate, unorganized, underfunded, or simply uninterested. Even if the whole range of relevant interests is taken into account, the definition is still incomplete. Public interest theorists commonly assert that the public interest is not the mere sum of particular interests, no matter how evenly and equitably these interests are represented. Frequently, these interests are too shortsighted or are unable, on their own, to reach an accommodation of their various claims. In these cases, the critical contribution to the determination of the public interest comes from the decision maker—often a public servant.

However, the avenue to some decisions runs through myriad conflicting and complementary values. Among the obstacles along the road is the temptation to succumb to personal or narrow interests when a decision in the broader interest of the general public or of substantial segments of the general public is required. The extent to which public servants are likely to suppress self-interest in a quest for the public interest is a matter for debate. Should the ultimate aim be the development of officials who have a broad, altruistic, and idealistic devotion to government policies and programs? Or is the inculcation of loyalty to specific programs or administrative units a sufficient and more realistic goal? Do those who envisage the eventual predominance of self-directing public servants actively pursuing human dignity in every decision have an unduly optimistic view of human nature?

Determining the Public Interest[23]

The resolution of value conflicts in the light of the public interest is sometimes a difficult challenge for public servants. Except in situations where public servants have been given complete discretionary authority, they may be able to shift the burden of choice among contending values to their hierarchical superior. Hierarchy in administration is a prime safeguard of administrative responsibility: it forces "important decisions to higher levels of determination or at least higher levels of review where perspectives are necessarily broader, less technical and expert, more political."[24] At the highest policy-making levels of government, it may be argued that, in the final analysis, the determination of the public interest is the task of the elected representatives. Public servants cannot, however, escape the responsibility of providing their political masters with the best possible advice. Moreover, if only in the cause of personal survival, public servants cannot evade the responsibility of pointing out the political, economic, and social costs and benefits of selecting one course of action over another.

Scholarly writings on the public interest demonstrate the difficulty of establishing specific and immutable criteria for how the public interest is determined in any given situation. The public interest may fruitfully be viewed as a dynamic concept. Its content changes from one situation to another and depends, in large part, on the values of both the decision maker and the interests whose claims are considered. Nevertheless, public servants can be provided with some guidelines for acting in the public interest. They need to recognize their biases to ensure that they do not ignore important considerations and interests, and to ask the right questions of themselves and others before making a decision. Among the questions to be asked are: Am I certain that my personal values—and my self-interest—are not overwhelming all other values? Have I identified and consulted "all stakeholders likely to be affected" by my decision? Have I ensured that "the procedures followed in obtaining information and consulting those affected are fair and open"? Have I done "the most comprehensive analysis of the costs and benefits that is possible in the circumstances"?[25]

An important distinction may be made between a passive and an active pursuit of the public interest. The public servant who considers the claims only of organized special interests, and whose range of values is narrow and inflexible, is passive in the search for the public interest. By way of contrast, the public servant who seeks the views of all relevant interests, and whose value framework is comparatively broad and flexible, is in active pursuit of the public interest. Both orientations have their virtues and drawbacks, depending on the issue at hand and the level of the organizational pyramid at which the decision is being made.

Administrative Responsibility and the Public Interest

The passive and active orientations toward the public interest may be linked with our earlier distinction between objective and subjective (psychological) responsibility. In a brief and admittedly oversimplified fashion, the main characteristics of two hypothetically extreme types of public servant—the objectively responsible and the subjectively responsible official—are suggested here.

Objectively responsible public servants feel responsible primarily to the legal or formal locus of authority and take a passive approach to the determination of the public interest. Their most prominent characteristic and value is accountability to those who have the power to promote, displace, or replace them. The controls and influences that they internalize in the form of public service values are those expressed by their hierarchical superiors. In making and recommending decisions, they anticipate and reflect the desires of their superiors, who have legitimate authority and who may easily threaten or impose penalties to ensure compliance. Public servants of this type do not actively seek the views of policy actors other than their superiors unless they are required to do so. For example, they consult parties with an interest in impending regulations only if such consultation is required by law or is expected by their superiors. Their foremost public service values include accountability and efficiency. They do not take initiatives or risks that may get them or their superiors into trouble. They are, for example, likely to err on the side of caution in their communications with the media. They also prefer, if possible, that their political and administrative superiors resolve any value dilemmas and determine the content of the public interest for them.

Objectively responsible public servants perceive themselves as ultimately responsible to the general public through the administrative hierarchy, the political executive, and the legislature. Their behaviour is based on the possibility and the desirability of separating policy and administration—even at the senior levels of the public service. In Finer's terminology, they are, therefore, "politically" responsible.

Subjectively responsible public servants are a striking contrast. They feel responsible to a broad range of policy participants and are active in the pursuit of the public interest. Their most outstanding characteristic and value is commitment to what they perceive to be the goals of their department or program. Since they view the expectations of a variety of policy actors as legitimate, the sources of their public service values are numerous and diverse. Subjectively responsible public servants are frequently in conflict with their superiors, but they are not influenced much by the threat of negative sanctions. They seek the views of interests affected by their decisions and recommendations in the absence of, and even in violation of, any legal or formal obligation to do so. Their primary public service values include responsiveness and effectiveness. They are innovative, take risks, and bend the rules to achieve their objectives. They urge their superiors to follow certain courses of action and are prepared to resolve for themselves the value dilemmas they encounter in their search for the public interest. Subjectively responsible public servants are, for example, more likely than others to engage in "**whistle-blowing**"—that is, exposing actions of political and administrative superiors that are illegal, unethical, or unduly wasteful of public funds.

The subjectively responsible public servant rejects the possibility and desirability of separating policy and administration—especially at the senior echelons of the bureaucracy. To use Finer's language again, officials of this type are "morally" responsible in the sense that they look to their own consciences rather than to "external punitive controls" for guidance.

Neither the purely objective nor the purely subjective type is appropriate as a model of the responsible public servant. Some characteristics of both types produce conduct that scholars and public officials generally view as undesirable. Undue emphasis on certain elements of objective responsibility may lead to behaviour that is unresponsive or ineffective. At the other extreme, too great an emphasis on particular aspects of subjective responsibility may bring equally undesirable results in the form of unaccountable or inefficient behaviour.

If the public service was composed predominantly of either objectively or subjectively responsible public servants, it would tend to manifest the same objectionable features. The "ideal" situation, then, is a public service in which each public servant strikes that balance between the objective and subjective elements of responsibility that is appropriate to his or her responsibilities and level in the hierarchy.

Conclusion

This chapter has tried to convey the importance of the values of accountability and integrity in the actions of public servants. Without a commitment to these values, the quality of the interactions between appointed officials and others in the political process will be less than it might be. It will also be difficult to secure the achievement of the public interest, the intent of any rational government. Clearly, accountability and integrity are high on the list of public service values.

In this part of the text, we have constructed a framework for better assessing an essential element of public administration, namely the relations between public servants and others who participate in the activities of the public sector. Part 3 has made it clear that values are important in understanding the motivation of actors in the political process. In Part 4, we commence a detailed examination of various types of interactions entered into by public servants.

1. For a recent effort to establish a distinction between responsibility and accountability, see James Ross Hurley, "Responsibility, Accountability and the Role of Deputy Ministers in the Government of Canada," in *Commission of Inquiry into the Sponsorship Program & Advertising Activities, Restoring Accountability: Research Studies Volume 3: Linkages: Responsibilities and Accountabilities* (Ottawa: Her Majesty the Queen in Right of Canada, 2006), 124–28. Aucoin and Jarvis are two who note that the terms are often employed synonymously. See Peter Aucoin and Mark D. Jarvis, *Modernizing Government Accountability: A Framework for Reform* (Ottawa: Canada School of Public Service, 2005), 104.

2. Carl J. Friedrich, "Responsible Government Service Under the American Constitution," in Carl J. Friedrich, William Carl Beyer, Sterling Denhard Spero, John Francis Miller, and George A. Graham, *Problems of the American Public Service* (New York: McGraw-Hill, 1935), 3–74, and "Public Policy and the Nature of Administrative Responsibility," in Carl J. Friedrich and Edward S. Mason, eds., *Public Policy* (Cambridge: Harvard University Press, 1940), 3–24. Herman Finer, "Better Government Personnel," *Political Science Quarterly* 51(4) (December 1936): 569–99., and "Administrative Responsibility in Democratic Government," *Public Administration Review* 1(4) (1941): 335–50. The most comprehensive statements of the opposing positions are found in the 1940–41 exchange of articles.

3. Finer, "Administrative Responsibility," 337.

4. Friedrich, "Public Policy," 12.

5. Ibid., 10, 5.

6. Finer, "Administrative Responsibility," 336.

7. Ibid.

8. Friedrich, "Public Policy," 19.

9. Frederick C. Mosher, *Democracy and the Public Service* (New York: Oxford University Press, 1968), 7–10.

10. Ibid., 7. (Emphasis added.)

11. Royal Commission on Financial Management and Accountability, *Final Report* (Ottawa: Supply and Services, 1979), 458, 471.

12. Ibid., 9.

13. Government of Ontario, Management Board of Cabinet, "Accountability," OPS Management Series (Toronto: Queen's Printer, 1982).

14. Paul G. Thomas, "The Changing Nature of Accountability," in B. Guy Peters and Donald J. Savoie, eds., *Taking Stock: Assessing Public Sector Reforms* (Montreal & Kingston: McGill-Queen's University Press, 1998), 352. Thomas actually has four components, but the fourth one—monitoring to guarantee compliance with assigned duties—seems implicit in the others. In another article, Thomas seems to pare down his definition of accountability to three components. See Paul G. Thomas, "Introduction," in B. Guy Peters and Jon Pierre, eds., *Handbook of Public Administration* (London: Sage Publications, 2003), 549.

15. For a listing of the factors that might make up such a framework, see Kenneth Kernaghan, *The Ethics Era in Canadian Public Administration* (Ottawa: Canadian Centre for Management Development, 1996).

16. Gloria Galloway, "Health Canada Official Jailed for Taking Gifts," *Globe and Mail*, March 12, 2005, A8.

17. Treasury Board of Canada Secretariat, *Values and Ethics Code for the Public Service* (Ottawa: Her Majesty the Queen in Right of Canada, 2003), 25–26.

18. Ibid., 31.

19. Ibid., 15.

20. C.W. Cassinelli, "The Public Interest in Political Ethics," in Carl J. Friedrich, ed., *Nomos V: The Public Interest* (New York: Atherton Press, 1962), 46.

21. Treasury Board of Canada Secretariat, *Values and Ethics Code for the Public Service*, 6.

22. Rowland Egger, "Responsibility and Administration: An Exploratory Essay," in Roscoe Martin, ed., *Public Administration and Democracy: Essays in Honor of Paul H. Appleby* (Syracuse: Syracuse University Press, 1965), 311–13.

23. For an examination of four major approaches to operationalizing the public interest, see Kenneth Kernaghan and John Langford, *The Responsible Public Servant* (Halifax: Institute of Research on Public Policy, 1990), ch. 2.

24. Mosher, *Democracy and the Public Service*, 212.

25. Kernaghan and Langford, *The Responsible Public Servant*, 49–50.

The Bureaucracy in the Political Process

11

The Executive and the Bureaucracy

Part 3 constructed a framework for investigating the types and character of relations between appointed officials and other actors in the political process. In Part 4, we investigate these interactions in detail. The purpose here is to reveal the dynamic quality of public administration, to demonstrate that the study of bureaucracy goes beyond the consideration of organizational forms. Part 4 also seeks to show that the life of appointed officials can be exciting—and tension-filled—as they interact with powerful public figures and institutions.

There is probably little argument with the claim that the most significant set of interactions involving public servants and other actors takes place in the executive branch of government. The high level of significance associated with these relations arises from the fact that the executive is the powerhouse of parliamentary government. It is responsible for setting the direction of government, formulating important policy initiatives, and implementing the programs and services that form the basis of the public sector. The executive sphere of government includes the governor general and provincial lieutenant governors, but the focus is on the other elements of the executive, namely the political executive—the prime minister, cabinet, and individual ministers—and the public service or permanent executive. These latter two components of the executive relate in a way that produces various kinds of interactions outlined in the institutional framework, and the most prominent of these is the direct relationship between public servants and the political executive. Central to the governing process—and the world of public administration—is how appointed and elected officials team up to carry out the crucial functions and duties of the executive branch.

In this chapter, we first examine the key principles of interactions between bureaucrats and their political superiors. The chapter then moves to a consideration of the key actors in the executive branch and their relations with each other. The chapter concludes by outlining the interaction that brings together all the major participants within the executive branch, which is the cabinet approval process.

Key Principles of Executive–Bureaucratic Interaction

Coordination and ministerial responsibility are centrally important in explaining relations between and among political executives and public servants. In this chapter, we will see that the cabinet and the public service are the primary instruments for coordinating the development and implementation of public services. Moreover, coordination is closely related to two fundamental principles of government and public administration: collective ministerial responsibility (or cabinet responsibility) and individual ministerial responsibility.

Ministerial Responsibility

According to the principle of **collective ministerial responsibility**, ministers are responsible as a group (i.e., as members of the cabinet) for the policies and management of the government as a whole. The cabinet must resign if it loses the confidence of the legislature, which means losing the support of the majority of the members of the House of Commons (or of a provincial legislature). Individual ministers must, in public, support the decisions of the cabinet, acting as a collectivity in order to maintain at least the appearance of cabinet solidarity. More specifically, ministers are required, in private, to work out a consensus on the content of public policies and on the allocation of resources for developing and implementing these policies. Ministers who cannot support a cabinet decision in public are expected to resign from the cabinet.

The principle of **individual ministerial responsibility** is subject to varying interpretations. In general, however, it refers to the responsibility of the minister, as the political head of a department, to answer to the legislature and, through the legislature, to the public both for his or her personal acts and for the acts of departmental subordinates. The minister is also legally responsible for the policies, programs, and administration of his or her department.

Coordination and Hierarchy

The principles of collective and individual ministerial responsibility significantly determine the nature of power relations both between politicians and public servants and among public servants themselves. The principles have an especially important effect on the organizational design of the executive sphere of government. Organization charts of the government of Canada typically depict this sphere as a hierarchical arrangement of offices. Aside from the governor general, the prime minister and the cabinet stand at the pinnacle of the hierarchy from which lines of authority flow down to departments headed by cabinet ministers and to Crown or non-departmental agencies reporting to cabinet ministers. Those central agencies that have departmental form and that report to a ministry (e.g., Department of Finance, Treasury Board Secretariat) are normally portrayed as equal in status to the regular operating departments strung horizontally across the chart. Other central agencies (e.g., the Prime Minister's Office and the Privy Council Office) are shown in a staff (advisory) relationship to the prime minister and the cabinet.

However, the organization chart discloses little about the complex pattern of power relations in the executive realm, especially insofar as these relations involve the exercise of influence rather than control. It exposes only the bare bones of political–bureaucratic interaction. This organizational skeleton reveals simply the formal lines of authority through which control moves down the governmental pyramid and accountability moves up; the "informal organization" is hidden from view. Similarly, an organization chart of a single department or agency that purports to describe the reality of administrative life as simply a hierarchy of superior–subordinate relationships or as a chain of command is misleading.

The deficiencies or "pathologies" of bureaucracy in general, and of its hierarchical feature in particular, have been discussed at length elsewhere.[1] Hierarchy does, however, serve several important purposes. One of these is particularly relevant to a discussion of ministerial responsibility: hierarchy provides for unity of command and of direction both at the top of the government (by the prime minister or premier and the cabinet) and at the top of government departments (by ministers). In other words, it promotes accountability. Hierarchy also facilitates **coordination**. Beginning with the cabinet as the central coordinating mechanism of government, various means of pursuing policy and administrative coordination permeate the executive–bureaucratic arena. We shall see that ministers, in fulfilling both their collective responsibility for coordinating government as a whole and their individual responsibility for coordinating their departments, are obliged to rely heavily on senior public servants in central agencies and departments. We explain in the next chapter the increasing emphasis in recent years on horizontal relations between government departments.

Aside from hierarchical control, power in the executive sphere is exercised in the form of influence. This is demonstrated well by the literature on the **bureaucratic politics** approach to policy-making. This approach focuses "primarily on the individuals within a government, and the interaction among them, as determinants of the actions of a government."[2] The interaction of these individuals, either within or between administrative units, may involve conflict, bargaining, compromise, and persuasion rather than hierarchical control.

Key Role of the Deputy Minister

While ministers play the leading roles in the political system as a whole, they share centre stage with their deputies in the executive–bureaucratic theatre of government. "Any defence of ministerial responsibility that did not take into account the real and independent role of the deputy in the administration of government would ultimately prove destructive to the doctrine itself."[3] Easily the dominant bureaucratic actors in executive–bureaucratic relations are the deputy ministers of government departments and their central agency equivalents (e.g., the clerk of the Privy Council, who is also secretary to the cabinet; the secretary of the Treasury Board). Deputy ministers play such a pivotal role in the decision-making process that an effective means of understanding the place of the public service in the Canadian political system is to view the system from their perspective.

Deputies yield the spotlight to ministers on policy decisions, but as supporting actors they perform onerous advisory and administrative roles. In carrying out these responsibilities, deputies must be sensitive not only to administrative, technical, and financial considerations but also to the partisan political implications of their advice and actions. They are, in addition, entangled in the net of bureaucratic politics within their departments, and between their departments and other administrative units. In short, deputies are challenged to perform the difficult feats of keeping their noses to the grindstone, their ears to the ground, and their backs to the wall. Moreover, deputies are required to look in three directions to find the audience for their performance. As Figure 11.1 on page 180 shows, they must look upward to their political superiors, laterally to their administrative peers (e.g., other deputy ministers), and downward to their departmental subordinates. In the performance of these roles, deputy ministers appear to be responding more and more to the prime minister and his close set of advisors for advice on priorities and other matters. The belief has been that the deputy minister is first and foremost the senior departmental official, but developments suggest that interactions between deputy ministers and the prime minister's most senior advisors in the central agencies (and the prime minister him- or herself) are assuming greater significance.

Figure 11.1 | **Relations of Deputy Ministers**

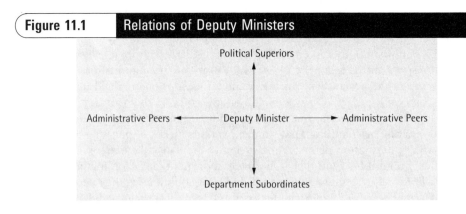

As Savoie says, "Deputy ministers are now as much a part of the centre of government as they are the administrative heads of their departments."[4]

The pervasive role of deputy ministers will be evident in this chapter's discussion of relations among public servants, the prime minister, and the cabinet. This chapter covers the deputies' role of supporting their ministers' collective responsibility to cabinet; the next chapter examines their central role as the administrative heads of government departments.

The Prime Minister and Cabinet

The Prime Minister

In the Canadian political system, the prime minister (or a provincial premier) and his or her cabinet colleagues possess the foremost power and responsibility for making and implementing public policy. In very large part, they determine the political and policy parameters within which the many participants in the political system interact. In the executive realm of government, the cabinet, acting in part through cabinet committees, provides the general framework of policies for which public servants must devise programs and for which resources must be allocated to the many departments and agencies. Given the individual and collective responsibility of ministers for the performance of the public service, they must strive to control and influence bureaucratic behaviour. They evaluate and coordinate policy and program proposals emanating from departments and bring partisan political considerations to bear on these proposals. They also initiate policy proposals of their own. In their capacity as cabinet members, federal ministers receive a great deal of political, policy, and administrative support, primarily from the central agencies (the Prime Minister's Office, the Privy Council Office, the Treasury Board Secretariat, and the Department of Finance). This central agency support is generally channelled to ministers in their capacity as members of cabinet and cabinet committees. In their capacity as political heads of government departments, ministers receive this assistance primarily from their deputy ministers and, to a lesser extent, from the political staff in their ministerial offices.

The federal cabinet is located at the centre of a complicated network of political–bureaucratic relations, and the prime minister is the central figure in that network. It is generally acknowledged that the prime minister is much more than "first among equals" in relation to cabinet colleagues. In fact, it is sometimes suggested that the prime minister's power has been aggrandized to the point where Canada has "prime ministerial government" or "court government" rather than cabinet government.[5] Under this new type of governing system, the prime minister makes the final decisions

Box 11.1   The Prime Minister and Power

Notwithstanding the limits on his or her power, the prime minister is a very influential player in Canadian politics. In the early part of the 1990s, Canada, Mexico, and the United States were putting the finishing touches on an important trade deal. The Americans were worried that the new Canadian trade minister in the incoming government of Jean Chrétien might be against the deal. "What happens if we work all this out and then your new trade minister doesn't agree?" asked an American representative. Prime Minister–elect Chrétien responded, "Then I will have a new trade minister the following morning." Such is the power of the prime minister.

Source: Donald J. Savoie, *Governing from the Centre: The Concentration of Power in Canadian Politics* (Toronto: University of Toronto Press, 1999), 108.

on the most important matters with the assistance of only a few trusted advisors. The role of cabinet is reduced to dealing with routine issues and acting as a "kind of focus group for the prime minister" when he or she needs to acquire a better understanding of an issue.[6] The notion of the political executive acting collectively disappears and is replaced by one that depicts a high concentration of influence in the hands of one individual. With his impressive set of "levers of power", the prime minister has an "unassailable advantage" over other members of cabinet.[7] As the term "court government" suggests, the prime minister is akin to a monarch who rules absolutely in his or her court with a small group of selected courtiers.

Certainly, the prime minister is a dominant figure by virtue of having responsibility for leading the governing political party, chairing the cabinet, acting as a chief spokesperson for the government, and appointing and removing both ministers and deputy ministers. Moreover, the prime minister can control and influence government departments (and individual public servants) both directly and indirectly. But there are constraints on the ability of the prime minister (and provincial premiers) to exercise this power fully. The prime minister's time is so precious that he or she can afford to become actively involved only in those few policy areas or issues in which he or she has a personal interest or that command attention on the grounds of urgency or partisan politics. As chairperson of cabinet, the prime minister is the key actor in the central policy-making and coordinating institution of government, but he or she alone cannot direct or coordinate the activities of the vast number of bureaucratic actors in government. The prime minister must rely on the assistance of cabinet colleagues and central agencies. Moreover, ministers can through various actions resist the wishes of the first minister and in so doing reveal the limits of prime ministerial power. Even backbenchers, aligned with cabinet members, can on occasion not only frustrate the will of the prime minister but help precipitate his or her early departure.[8]

Cabinet Committees

Taken together, cabinet committees are responsible for helping to coordinate policies and programs, to allocate human and financial resources, and to control the public service. Except for the Treasury Board, which is a cabinet committee provided for in the Financial Administration Act, the existence and responsibilities of cabinet committees are determined by the prime minister. The number, duties, and importance of cabinet committees and the cabinet committee system as a whole have evolved over time, largely in an attempt to strengthen political control over the making and coordination of public policy:

- The significance and sophistication of the cabinet committee system in the federal government have increased greatly since the late 1930s, and especially since the mid-1960s. Before World War II, there were only three cabinet committees. In 1939, ten new committees were created to facilitate and coordinate Canada's war operations; the most important of these was the War Committee chaired by the prime minister. Between 1945 and 1964, cabinet committees were largely ad hoc; they were usually created to consider specific issues referred to them by cabinet, and they were abolished when their job was done.[9]

- In 1968, then–prime minister Lester Pearson modified the cabinet committee system by replacing the ad hoc committees with nine standing committees so as "to obtain, under the Prime Minister's leadership, thorough consideration of policies, co-ordination of government action, and timely decisions in a manner consistent with ministerial and Cabinet responsibility."[10] In 1968, Pearson created the Priorities and Planning Committee, which he chaired, to set overall government priorities as a framework for expenditure decisions. The practice of requiring that matters be considered by cabinet committees before coming to the full cabinet was initiated, and public servants were permitted to attend cabinet committee meetings on a more regular and frequent basis.

- The general configuration of the cabinet system that existed until mid-1993 dates from the election of Pierre Elliott Trudeau as prime minister in 1968. He reorganized the cabinet committee system "to permit a greater centralization of functions and the delegation of certain powers of decision to the committees."[11] The reduction of the number of standing committees to eight and the setting of regular times for the weekly meeting(s) of each committee improved the attendance of ministers. An extremely important innovation was expanding the powers of the committees from making recommendations to cabinet to allowing them to take certain "decisions" on their own. These decisions, called "committee recommendations," were annexed to the agenda for cabinet meetings and were routinely ratified unless a minister specifically requested that they be discussed in full cabinet. As a result of these changes, the number of cabinet meetings declined considerably while the number of cabinet committee meetings increased dramatically.

- Prime Minister Joe Clark reformed the cabinet committee system in 1979. The Priorities and Planning Committee was replaced by an Inner Cabinet of twelve ministers that had final decision-making authority; the full cabinet, which met less frequently than under Trudeau, confined its deliberations primarily to coordination and to politically sensitive or controversial questions. The most important organizational initiative of the Clark government was the introduction of the Policy and Expenditure Management System (PEMS), also called the "envelope" system. Though this system was quite complicated, the overall aim of PEMS was to give cabinet greater control over the management of both policies and expenditures. This objective was pursued by integrating the processes of policy making and fiscal and expenditure planning within the cabinet committee system. More specifically, PEMS was designed to ensure that the government's decisions on priorities and policies were closely integrated with the allocation of resources. Policy decisions and related expenditure decisions were made by the same cabinet committee and at the same time.

- When Trudeau returned to office in 1980 he abolished the Inner Cabinet, restored the Priorities and Planning Committee, and strengthened PEMS. Then, in 1984, Prime Minister John Turner simplified the cabinet system by reducing the number of cabinet committees and dismantling two so-called new central agencies—the Ministries of State for Economic and Regional Development and for Social Development—that had been created under Trudeau and Clark. He also eliminated what were called "mirror committees," which were committees composed of deputy ministers that served as public service counterparts to the policy committees of cabinet.

- Brian Mulroney, elected in 1984, made several changes in the cabinet system designed, in large part, to centralize and strengthen control over expenditure decisions. PEMS was abolished, but the already central role of the Priorities and Planning Committee was enhanced. It had authority to review the decisions of the other cabinet committees and became the sole cabinet committee with authority to approve expenditures on new "big ticket" items. Treasury Board had responsibility for approving expenditures on smaller items. Thus, the policy committees of cabinet no longer determined the allocation of funds from the resource envelopes; rather, they were expected to focus their attention on policy. To this end, the committee system was further restructured. The former broad sectoral committees (e.g., Social Development, Economic and Regional Development) were abolished, but the number of committees increased from ten to fourteen because four new policy committees were created. Membership in each committee was reduced from twenty-two to twenty-three ministers to eight to twelve ministers.

  The Priorities and Planning Committee was also reformed. During the period from 1968 to 1993, this was the leading cabinet committee. Until early 1989, it was composed of the prime minister as chairperson, the chairpersons of the other cabinet committees, the minister of finance, and a few additional ministers chosen either because of the prime minister's respect for their views or to achieve regional representation. The committee was responsible for deciding upon the fiscal framework, for establishing overall government priorities, for detailed consideration of major policy issues, for federal–provincial matters of general import and problems of a cross-cutting nature that involved more than one cabinet committee, and for managing the expenditure of public funds in several policy sectors. In 1989, the size of the committee was expanded and its membership made more representative of the various regions of the country. This was appropriate, because the committee had effectively replaced the cabinet as the executive decision-making body of the government. Cabinet became largely a forum for partisan political discussion.

  Since the Priorities and Planning Committee was now about the same size as the full cabinet had been thirty years earlier, the Operations Committee, which had emerged as an informal committee early in 1988, became extremely influential. It had formal authority to review the agendas of the policy committees and to examine any policy proposals that might create expenditure problems before these proposals were considered by the policy committees. In effect, it acted as a gatekeeper to the Priorities and Planning Committee and set the cabinet agenda. The final Mulroney reform was the creation of the Expenditure Review Committee, chaired by the prime minister. It was responsible for ensuring that expenditures were directed to the government's top priorities and that expenditure control contributed to deficit reduction. This committee was abolished in late 1992.
- In 1993, Prime Minister Kim Campbell effected a major reorganization of the federal government. She reduced the number of departments from thirty-two to twenty-five and eliminated six cabinet committees, including the Priorities and Planning Committee. The five remaining cabinet committees were the Operations, Treasury Board/ Special Committee of Council, Economic and Environmental Policy, Social Policy, and House Leader's committees. The full cabinet was restored as the central decision-making body for the most important issues facing the government. Prime Minister Jean Chrétien, who succeeded Campbell in 1993, retained most of the changes made by Campbell and made some of his own. He appointed twenty-four ministers, who were members of cabinet, and eight secretaries of state, who were part of the ministry but not cabinet members. Upon reelection in 1997, Chrétien increased the number of ministers to twenty-seven. During his two terms, there were only four cabinet committees and full cabinet remained as the central decision-making body.

- One of the first acts of Prime Minister Martin, in 2003, was to make some important changes to the cabinet committee system. He resurrected the Priorities and Planning Committee, suggesting a group smaller than cabinet was necessary to set the direction for government. The prime minister also brought back the Expenditure Review Committee, an indication that fiscal prudence was key to the Martin government. The Prime Minister set up five policy committees (Domestic Affairs, Global Affairs, Canada–U.S. Security, Public Health & Emergencies, Aboriginal Affairs) as well as an Operations Committee to orchestrate the flow of policy papers through the new committee system (and the Treasury Board remained). All together, it appeared that the Martin cabinet was much more active than its predecessor, though some of the new committees were mainly strategic in orientation and met only infrequently (all of Chrétien's cabinet committees gathered weekly). The prime minister himself was quite busy, for he chaired four of the committees and, of course, the full cabinet. In looking at the new Martin cabinet, some rightly said that it "ha[d] some remarkable similarities to that of the Mulroney government."[12] Given that the Mulroney cabinet system had appeared somewhat cumbersome at times, the Martin government might have found itself engaged—if had lasted longer—in some cabinet-remaking exercises.
- The government of Stephen Harper has maintained some aspects of the Martin cabinet system. Both Priorities and Planning and Operations remain intact—the former to "provide strategic direction on priorities for Canadians" and the latter "to ensure effective day-to-day governing."[13] The Treasury Board is also part of the Harper cabinet system, and three new policy committees—Social Affairs, Economic Affairs, and Foreign Affairs and National Security—have been established (see Figure 11.2). As for the role of the prime minister, early reports suggest that Harper subscribes to a "hub and spoke" management style,[14] which portends a first minister reluctant to delegate responsibility to cabinet committees and more at home with making decisions individually with the relevant minister. Such an arrangement has the potential to amplify the power of the prime minister, and it heightens the possibility that the Harper government may reflect qualities associated with prime-ministerial government.

As can be seen, the evolution of the cabinet committee system is long and detailed, but it should be clear that an essential purpose of the system was to ensure that cabinet and its committees—and not individual departments with their ministers and senior

| Figure 11.2 | Cabinet Committee System of Harper Government |

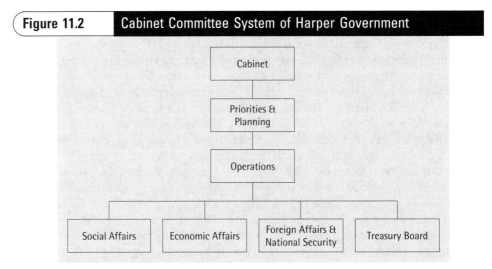

public servants—made the important decisions of government and established the public priorities of the day. The cabinet committees constituted one of the mechanisms to control the extent of bureaucratic influence.

Central Agencies

As noted earlier, there is some debate about which administrative units should be described as central agencies. In this chapter, the focus is on the Prime Minister's Office (PMO) and the so-called traditional central agencies, namely the Department of Finance, the Privy Council Office (PCO), and the Treasury Board Secretariat (TBS). The senior officials of these agencies have been, as mentioned in earlier chapter, called the "superbureaucrats," because they "are among the most powerful public servants in government" and because "in performing their duties they often cross the line between bureaucrat and policy maker."[15] The detailed description of the functions of these agencies provided earlier will not be repeated here. This chapter is concerned with the interaction between these central agencies and other actors in the executive–bureaucratic sphere of government.

The role of central agencies in assisting political executives to control and coordinate government policies and programs began to expand in the late 1960s. In serving both the prime minister and the cabinet, central agency officials control and influence departmental officials by affecting the allocation of human and financial resources, the organization of governmental and departmental machinery, and the coordination of intergovernmental relations. Central agencies thereby help to promote such administrative values as efficiency, effectiveness, and accountability.

During the early years of the first Trudeau government, elected in 1968, the PMO and the PCO were reorganized and expanded so as to improve their advisory and coordinating functions. The growth in the staff and expenditure of these offices led some commentators to compare them to the White House staff and the Executive Office of the President in the United States, and to suggest that the expansion of these offices was part of the prime minister's objective of "presidentializing" the Canadian political system and enhancing prime-ministerial power. This suggestion, as noted earlier, may exaggerate matters. Moreover, there is wide recognition that "political executives require elaborate machinery and large staffs devoted to coordination and control just to get on with the job of governing."[16] The relative importance of the PMO and the traditional central agencies has shifted since 1968, but all have continued to play a prominent role in supporting the prime minister and the cabinet.

It is notable that the PMO is a central agency unlike the others, being primarily a partisan instrument of the prime minister. The overriding concerns of PMO officials, who are political appointees rather than career public servants, are the political fortunes of the prime minister and the governing party. While they owe their first loyalty to the prime minister, these officials also serve the political interests of the cabinet as a whole. The PMO helps to ensure that the prime minister is knowledgeable about major policy issues, especially their political implications, and that he or she has an alternative source of information to that provided by departmental ministers and officials. The sheer power of the PMO can be seen in the fact that it may—if necessary—"undercut a [departmental] proposal when briefing the prime minister" and certainly will "not hesitate to offer policy advice or to challenge a cabinet minister."[17] Participants in the executive branch must take heed of the PMO.

In contrast to the PMO, officials in the PCO are generally career public servants who are nonpartisan; they are, however, highly sensitive to political considerations. The Department of Finance and TBS are also composed of career public servants. The prime minister and cabinet rely heavily on the central agencies to control and influence the behaviour of departmental public servants. This is especially evident in the sphere of

Box 11.2   **Profile of a Clerk of the PCO**

Kevin Lynch, 55, is the Clerk of the PCO in the new government of Stephen Harper. He is a focused individual who likes to examine things closely. He also knows just about all the major players in the government—partly because of his time as deputy minister of the Department of Finance. He is also driven and unafraid of working hard. While at Finance, he told his staff at a meeting that it is important to find a good balance between work and home life. The get-together was held on a Sunday.

Source: Brian Laghi, "New Clerk of the Privy Council Known as a Strategic Thinker," *The Globe and Mail*, February 22, 2006, A4.

financial management, where the Department of Finance and the TBS are critical forces in influencing and facilitating cabinet decisions on the management of financial resources.

The prime minister and, to a lesser extent, cabinet ministers, with the assistance of central agencies, exercise important functions in the sphere of human resources management, particularly in the staffing area. The prime minister and the cabinet make what are called governor in council appointments to the senior levels of the public service. The choice of deputy ministers is, by convention, the prerogative of the prime minister, who receives advice from the secretary to the cabinet and normally discusses possible candidates with the minister of the department in question. With respect to senior positions in agencies, boards, and commissions, the prime minister usually consults with those ministers whose portfolio or region of the country is affected by an appointment. These appointments are made by the governor in council—that is, by the governor general, upon the recommendation of the prime minister and his or her colleagues.

The prime minister wields substantial power both in expenditure and human resources management and in the organization of the machinery of government. He or she is advised in performing this function by the Clerk of the Privy Council and Secretary to the Cabinet, who is supported by a secretariat in the PCO. As mentioned earlier, the relationship between the prime minister and the head of the PCO has recently become even closer. Traditionally, the clerk has tried to find a balance between serving as secretary to the cabinet and as the chief advisor to the prime minister. But events and research suggest that the clerk now spends much more time and effort looking to the needs of the prime minister, having become effectively the prime minister's deputy minister, and as a result spends less time on the operation and needs of cabinet.[18]

Cabinet Approval and Cabinet Documents

Figure 11.3 shows the process by which departmental proposals for new public policies or programs are approved, amended, or rejected by cabinet committees and by cabinet, and how cabinet's decision, in the form of a record of decision, serves as authority for the allocation of resources for the implementation of those policies. It also illustrates the formal and informal interaction among the major players in the executive–bureaucratic arena. Cabinet committees and central agencies clearly play an important role, but policy proposals are formally prepared by government departments and are presented by a minister to the appropriate cabinet committee, usually in the form of a document called a **Memorandum to Cabinet**. A minister's policy proposals can, of course, be influenced by a variety of sources, including political parties, interest groups, and individual citizens, and central agencies may also intervene to offer some direction. Moreover, proposals are

Figure 11.3 Process of Cabinet Approval

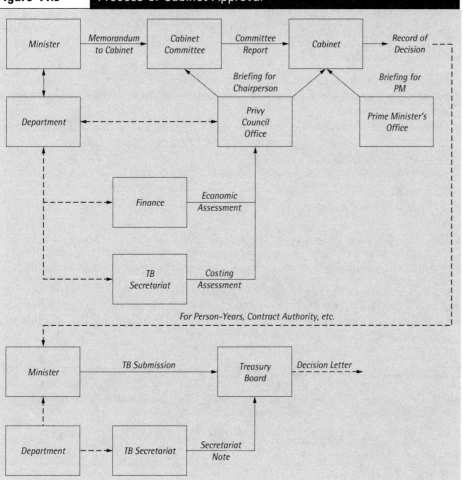

increasingly a product not of individual departments, but rather of departments working together.[19] The dotted lines in Figure 11.3 between the department and central agencies show that the two entities may meet before submission of the memorandum in order to work out any policy difficulties in the proposal. Once in cabinet, the proposal goes to the appropriate cabinet committee, which is assisted in its deliberations by briefings from the central agencies. Following its examination of the Memorandum, the committee makes a recommendation to cabinet in the form of a committee report. Here, too, the briefings of the PCO and the PMO are part of the process. Approval by cabinet take the form of a record of decision that is circulated to all ministers for any necessary followup; it also serves as basis for seeking approval from Treasury Board for any necessary financial and human resources necessary to carry out the approved policies (the process for which is outlined in the lower part of Figure 11.3). Though the cabinet approval process has many aspects, it rests on two basic principles. One is that ministers may bring to cabinet proposals emanating from their area of responsibility; the other is that all ministers may offer informed comment (and not casual remarks) on matters coming before cabinet and for which they are collectively responsible.[20]

The Memorandum to Cabinet is the mechanism by which policy proposals are brought forward by ministers for consideration and approval by their cabinet colleagues.

It is also the formal means by which deputy ministers provide confidential policy advice to their ministers. The Memorandum usually has two parts—a three-to-five page Ministerial Recommendations (MR) section and a slightly longer Background/Analysis section (maximum of six pages).[21] The MR, the more significant of the two sections, has the following basic structure:

- Issue statement outlining the matter to be discussed at cabinet
- Set of recommendations for which the sponsoring minister is seeking support and supporting rationale
- List of considerations associated with the recommended course of action; these might include the legal difficulties, any adverse consequences, gender implications, and the views of provinces and territories
- Details on consultation with and reaction of the party caucus and members of Parliament
- Statement of risks accompanying the proposed action and strategies for addressing these risks
- Expected results of the new program or policy and how the results may be measured
- Cost implications of the ministerial recommendations
- A communications plan for managing the release of the new government initiative

The Background/Analysis section provides additional on matters considered in the MR and lays out the options that formed the basis of the analysis of the issue under review. Cabinet members are free to peruse the background and analysis documents, but almost all are far too busy to do so.

As can be seen, cabinet memoranda are based on extensive research and consultations both inside and outside government. They also require a good amount of insight into the existing political and policy environment. The sponsoring minister is putting his or her government's reputation and political future on the line, so the demands of a Memorandum to Cabinet are severe. Moreover, the document requires a deft hand at writing, someone who can successfully persuade in a few short pages.

Ad Hoc Relations

It is typically thought the cabinet approval process represents the most important interaction between public servants and political executives. But increasingly it appears that significant relations are developing outside this process. Prime ministers are often impatient with the deliberative quality of the cabinet process and seek a quicker resolution of a matter, or they may believe that an issue—especially major ones—would be better handled differently. Pierre Elliott Trudeau addressed his most important concerns outside of the cabinet system, and Brian Mulroney committed Canada to major constitutional change and the Canada–U.S. Free Trade Agreement without any cabinet consultation. In truth, it is easy to find evidence that all prime ministers since the advent of the modern cabinet system have seen fit to bypass or sidestep their own creation. In the late 1990s, former prime minister Jean Chrétien wanted a special program for student scholarships to be accepted without any kind of change, so he ignored the cabinet system. One of Chrétien's advisors elaborates on this decision:

> If we had respected the process, the idea would never have come out at the other end the way we wanted it. Intergovernmental affairs would have argued that the matter was provincial, not federal. Human Resources Development would have said that the idea was in its jurisdiction, while Heritage Canada would have made a similar claim. The prime minister asked one of us to call Paul (Martin, minister of finance) and his deputy minister to let them know what we were doing. In that way he got what he wanted.[22]

When the decision is made to engage in ad hoc decision making, the prime minister inevitably reaches for his key central agency officials who provide the necessary advice and counsel. The heads of the PMO and PCO will be included in this group, and so might senior officials in the Department of Finance and the Treasury Board Secretariat, especially if the issue involves money or the budget. The prime minister may also want assistance from individual departmental officials who have been targeted for their skills and ability to get governments out of trouble or help them exploit an opportunity. Some are uneasy with such dipping into the public service, for it ignores accepted procedures and hierarchical arrangements and evinces little respect for the public service as an important body. But this is the nature of ad hoc relations between political officials and their appointed counterparts. The prime minister wants an issue addressed quickly and smartly, so the focus is on finding the right individuals and slighting institutional arrangements.

Conclusion

The emphasis in this chapter has been on interaction between the prime minister and the cabinet on the one hand, and central agencies and departments on the other. We now turn to an examination of interaction between government departments, between departments and central agencies, and among the central agencies themselves.

Notes

1. See, for example, J. March and H. Simon, *Organizations* (New York: John Wiley & Sons, 1958), and Robert K. Merton, ed., *Reader in Bureaucracy* (New York: The Free Press, 1952).

2. Graham T. Allison and Morton H. Halperin, "Bureaucratic Politics: A Paradigm and Some Policy Implications," *World Politics* 24 (Supplement, 1972): 43.

3. Royal Commission on Financial Management and Accountability, *Final Report* (Ottawa: Supply and Services, 1979), 42.

4. Donald J. Savoie, "The Federal Government: Revisiting Court Government in Canada," in Luc Bernier, Keith Brownsey, and Michael Howlett, eds., *Executive Styles in Canada: Cabinet Structures and Leadership Practices in Canadian Government* (Toronto: University of Toronto Press, 2005), 41.

5. See Savoie, "The Federal Government."

6. From a minister in the Chrétien government quoted in ibid., 31.

7. Ibid., 33.

8. For more on this point, see Susan Delacourt, *Juggernaut: Paul Martin's Campaign for Chrétien's Crown* (Toronto: McClelland & Stewart, 2003).

9. See W.A. Matheson, *The Prime Minister and the Cabinet* (Toronto: Methuen, 1976), 83–91.

10. Lester B. Pearson, press release, January 20, 1968, Office of the Prime Minister.

11. Pierre Elliott Trudeau, "Statement by the Prime Minister on Cabinet Committee Structure," press release, April 30, 1968, Office of the Prime Minister.

12. Evert Lindquist, Ian Clark, and James Mitchell, "Reshaping Ottawa's Centre of Government: Martin's Reform in Historical Perspective," in G. Bruce Doern, ed., *How Ottawa Spends 2004–2005: Mandate Change in the Paul Martin Era* (Montreal & Kingston: McGill-Queen's University Press, 2004), 339.

13. Stephen Harper, "Prime Minister Harper Announces New Ministry and Reaffirms Government Priorities," news release, February 6, 2006, Office of the Prime Minister.

14. Brian Laghi, "Discipline, Control Mark PM's Management Style," *Globe and Mail*, April 8, 2006, A1.

15. Colin Campbell and George J. Szablowski, *The Superbureaucrats: Structure and Behaviour in Central Agencies* (Toronto: Macmillan, 1979), 1.

16. Colin Campbell, "Central Agencies in Canada," in Kenneth Kernaghan, ed., *Public Administration in Canada: Selected Readings* (Toronto: Methuen, 1985), 13.

17. Savoie, "The Federal Government," 24.

18. Ibid., 37.

19. Donald J. Savoie, *Breaking the Bargain: Public Servants, Ministers and Parliament* (Toronto: University of Toronto Press, 2003), 201.

20. Ian Clark, "Recent Changes in the Cabinet Decision-Making System in Ottawa," *Canadian Public Administration* 20 (summer 1985): 198. For a more up-to-date discussion of the rules and principles of cabinet decision making, see Machinery of Government Secretariat, Privy Council Office, "Annex B: Cabinet Decision Making," *Accountable Government: A Guide for Ministers* (Ottawa: Her Majesty the Queen in Right of Canada, 2006). Available at the Privy Council Office site, www. pco-bcp.gc.ca/default.asp?Language=E&Page=Publications&doc=guidemin/ accountable-guide_ e.htm#b. Retrieved July 10, 2006.

21. This is the format use by the government of Prime Minister Paul Martin.

22. Savoie, *Breaking the Bargain*, 201.

Interdepartmental and Intradepartmental Relations

The interactions between and within government agencies and departments constitute an important part of activities within the executive sphere of government. Relations between public servants and their political superiors in cabinet usually receive the most attention when we look at this branch of government. But we need to recognize that the relations in departments, which involve the responsible minister, the deputy minister, and other departmental officials, also deserve our attention. Some notice must also be given to the interactions between and among departments, especially in a time when the demands of policy making pay little attention to departmental boundaries and require that departments work with each other. Then there are the interactions between officials in line departments and the central agencies. The desire of governments to coordinate their actions alone ensures that bureaucrats within the Privy Council or the Department of Finance will deal with senior appointed officials in departments responsible for the formulation and administration of government programs.

This chapter begins with an examination of interdepartmental relations and the importance of addressing the fact that most policy matters now cut across departments. The chapter emphasizes the need to recognize that the challenge of horizontal management is at the heart of interdepartmental relations, and that this challenge is sometimes not met successfully. The evolution of relations between central agencies and line agencies is also addressed with a view to gauging the true impact of central agencies. Some believe that in their relations with departments central agencies direct and dominate most matters, but others insist that the demands of governing make it difficult for any agency to do more than just keep up with the almost daily demands and crises of government. The chapter also looks at relations within departments, with the focus being on the minister, the deputy minister, and ministerial assistants.

Interdepartmental Relations

Governments are sensitive to the fact that virtually all policy issues cut across departmental boundaries and that many of them also cut across governmental and even national boundaries. In recent years governments in Canada have become even more aware of the importance of interdepartmental relations. A greater and greater number of issues are now handled through horizontal arrangements, and these issues are often central to the mandates of government. Senior officials meet regularly to consider interdepartmental matters and are explicitly evaluated on how well they manage their interactions with other departments and agencies. Health departments wishing to introduce new initiatives need to check with social service and treasury departments to ensure that the full implications of their action are appreciated. The same holds for taxation initiatives, where the views of finance, revenue, and justice departments are typically required. Moreover, vigorous attempts are made to include all the relevant interests—including those outside of government—to increase the chances that issues are handled effectively. This last development has become so evident that the equating of horizontal management with interdepartmental relations no longer really holds. Other levels of government, citizen groups, and nongovernmental organizations must also be counted among the players in horizontal relations.

The cross-cutting feature of policy issues is the most obvious reason for the significance of horizontal relations. A basic truth in Canadian public administration is that "[h]orizontal management is often the only or the best way to get results."[1] The idea that the societal demands upon government can be met satisfactorily through vertical relations in which individual departments handle matters internally is without foundation. Globalization and its demand that governments act in compliance with new global rules and regulations has also made it necessary for government to better coordinate their actions, and this too leads to greater horizontality in government. The competitiveness inherent in globalization as well requires that governments act as a team in order to succeed. A further reason for the importance of horizontal relations is the heightened expectations of a citizenry who insist that government be able to deliver services and programs that require the participation of more than one department; citizens resist any attempt to force them to go from one department to another to get what they want from government. These same citizens also "demand equal and fair treatment from their governments," an outcome that also requires public agencies to better harmonize and coordinate their efforts.[2] Finally, the inefficiencies inherent in overlap and redundancy can be more easily discovered and eliminated through attempts at managing horizontally. Only by going beyond the perspective of individual departments and agencies can we see the unnecessary duplication in government.

Horizontal Management

Interdepartmental relations and the more general concept of **horizontal management** can be seen as consisting of four dimensions (see Figure 12.1).[3] One is the initial "mobilization of teams and networks" necessary for addressing the policy challenge. This requires that all parties involved share in the leadership of the initiative and participate in creating the team. A joint effort of the federal Departments of Industry, Foreign Affairs, and Agriculture to push Canadian interests in international markets has benefited from leaders from each agency participating actively in the effort, and paying attention to teamwork has enabled various agencies to work together for over thirteen years on restoring the St. Lawrence River. This first dimension also demands a committed effort to construct a common culture among the team members. Departments initially approach horizontal arrangements with various perspectives and beliefs rooted in their

Figure 12.1 | Dimensions of Horizontal Management

Mobilization of teams and networks ⟶ Shared framework ⟶ Building supportive structures ⟶ Maintaining momentum

Source: Canadian Centre for Management, *Moving from the Heroic to the Everyday: Lessons Learned from Leading Horizontal Projects* (Ottawa: Canadian Centre for Management Development, 2001), 6.

own experiences, and attempts must be made to bridge these differences with the construction of a new language common to all involved. Health Canada and Human Resources and Development Canada, two federal agencies, were assigned to work together on developing programs for addressing the needs of children and their families, and the first challenge was to "develop a subsidiary vocabulary that worked for both groups."[4] Before departments can work together successfully, they have to be able to communicate with each other.

The second dimension of interdepartmental relations is the development of a "shared framework." The task here is to articulate the goals of the initiative and to do so in a manner that respects the view of all parties. This second dimension also addresses arguably the most important issue in horizontal relations, namely accountability. Accountability traditionally entails reporting upward to a more senior official or politician, but collective efforts across and outside departments fit uneasily into the typical accountability arrangements. Actions have to be taken to ensure accountability, at the same time taking into consideration that there is usually more than one superior in horizontal relations. A public servant working with other departments is responsible to his or her departmental supervisor, but this same public servant may feel answerable or obligated to others engaged in the interdepartmental exercise:

> Traditional accountability frameworks within the Public Service of Canada are vertical. They are based on the principle of ministerial responsibility. They establish a clear hierarchical structure of authority and, in turn, accountability within departments. Horizontal initiatives also create accountabilities between partners and may also include mechanisms to provide accountability more directly to citizens.[5]

The third dimension is "building supportive structures" to underpin the effort at horizontal management. In the past, interdepartmental committees have been seen as the prime instrument for effecting relations between departments and interests, and they are still evident. However, with the increasing importance of horizontal relations has come a rich series of supporting structures. At one end of the continuum of structures, we can find informal structures that are used to facilitate discussion among various departments and interests outside government. Ad hoc or exploratory committees are structures set up quickly to examine an emerging issue without necessarily making a commitment to any further activity. Moving along the continuum we discover support structures which revolve around agreements set out in various types of memoranda protocols and whose purpose is to obligate various parties to a particular action. Formal structures form the other end of the continuum of horizontal structures, and here too we find great diversity. There are co-chaired advisory committees, joint decision-making committees, joint-coordination centres, regional councils, and the creation of new agencies or secretariats. The last type is especially interesting for it amounts to an attempt to institutionalize the process of horizontal management. An example of this at the federal level is the creation of the Leadership Network, which was established to consider the recommendations of an exercise looking into addressing difficulties in the public service.

The fourth and last dimension is "maintaining momentum." In some instances, the initiative will be short-term, but in many others it will be a long-term effort. In fact, some instances require a continual departmental commitment to consulting with other departments and interested parties. As a result, attention will have to be paid to maintaining momentum for exercises in horizontal management. This means finding a leader—a "champion"—who will give energy to the project and inspire others to continue with the effort. Often the champion will be a senior official, perhaps even the minister, because he or she has the authority and the presence to motivate others. Maintaining momentum also means building on small victories. Members of the interdepartmental effort of the federal government to better manage the oceans created momentum and progress by targeting smaller areas of concern and doing so through the use of pilot projects. The same group might have attempted implementing right off a national strategy for oceans, but this most likely would have resulted in frustration and possible failure. "Start small and work up from there" was the advice followed.[6] Others things to keep in mind to ensure momentum are carefully arranging the transition from one part of the project to another, learning from any mistakes, and ensuring sound communication among members engaged in the initiative.

Effectiveness of Horizontal Management

The sheer abundance of horizontal relations in government indicates that we expect such relations to lead to more effective government actions. The causes of horizontality in government suggest that no public authority can be satisfied with departments and agencies acting on their own. And the evidence in fact points to successes in horizontal relations—the four dimensions of horizontal management can be seen as a recipe for success in these kinds of endeavours. However, interdepartmental relations and those that include interests outside government can also have their problems and costs. The cost most identified is the amount of time required to operate in a horizontal manner. Interdepartmental relations translate into more meetings, more planning, more drafting, and generally more talking. Further, the cost in time is sometimes not worth the effort at horizontal management, as suggested by a reluctant practitioner of this type of management:

> I think there is too much emphasis on horizontality. Often, it is just a "talkfest." At the end of the day you haven't accomplished much. Too many departments that have little bearing on the bottom line get to be invited to the table.[7]

A second problem is the differences that may arise between departments and other interests over the appropriate action: "Horizontal coordination often means departments intruding on each other's policy space, which can then lead to resentment and more competition."[8] In the late 1990s two federal departments, Environment Canada and Natural Resources Canada, combined their efforts to produce a new climate policy, but "significant tensions" between the two agencies soon surfaced over the appropriate course of action.[9] A problem related to this is the possibility that the best policy response may not be chosen. Instead, a compromise will be put forward in order to resolve differences. As one participant in interdepartmental relations testifies, "your position gets diluted because you have to compromise with the other guys."[10] Recently, Immigration Canada and Human Resources Development Canada worked together to produce an immigration policy that would make Canada more economically creative and productive. The two differed on the best action, and in the end one department (Human Resources and Skills Development Canada) consented to wishes of the other in order for the process to continue. If this happens too often, the effectiveness of interdepartmental relations declines and the purpose of horizontal management becomes, not good public policy, but the resolution of differences. Another concern is that one of the dimensions of horizontal management requires all involved to think across and sometimes outside government, but most officials have not been trained to think this way; they tend to think in terms of individual departments and being accountable only to their departmental superiors. Horizontal management is equivalent to "pulling against gravity"—we conceptualize government as up and down, but we are now being asked to think across.[11] A report on horizontal management makes the same point:

> Horizontal management forces us to give up our interventions guided by the sole limited interests of the source organization. We are therefore confronted with the fragilization of participants who can be led to take positions that are more beneficial to the project than to their organization.[12]

These problems do not mean that interdepartmental relations should be rejected, because such relations are here to stay. But they do mean that architects of horizontal management need to anticipate and to take into consideration the challenges of getting people in different departments to work together. It is also important to grasp the sheer magnitude of the task facing those who engage in horizontal relations. Figure 12.2 (on page 196) depicts the many federal departments and programs (and other actors) that seek to address the homeless problem in Toronto, many of which must eventually be coordinated through horizontal relations if this social issue is to be addressed successfully.

Relations between Departments and Central Agencies

It is widely held that the expansion in the size and power of central agencies that occurred in the late 1960s and early 1970s reduced the power of both the ministers and senior officials of operating departments. The control and influence exercised by central agencies in the coordination of policy development, and in the allocation of human and financial resources for departmental programs, led to considerable tension in the relations between the agencies and line departments. The filtering of departmental policy and program proposals through cabinet committees and central agencies helped ensure that ministers and their senior officials understood the implications of their proposals for other departments and for the government as a whole. However, ministers and their officials spent a great deal of time and effort lobbying and bargaining with their counterparts in other departments and in the central agencies. It was an extremely time-consuming process for ministers, and it tended to reduce their individual authority and influence in the cabinet decision-making system.

In the mid-1980s, the Turner and Mulroney governments decided that the number and influence of central agencies helped make the decision-making system too complicated. Too much emphasis was being put on the process of policy formulation as compared to policy content. Several reforms were introduced to bring about a simpler, more hierarchical model of cabinet government. One of the reforms included the abolition of two central agencies, and another sought through various means and arrangements to bring about a greater measure of delegation to departments and to reduce the reporting requirements to various central agencies. The trend toward greater departmental autonomy accelerated as the argument became widely accepted that departments could be more flexible and responsive if they were subject to fewer central agency controls. In her short period as prime minister, Kim Campbell reduced substantially the number of cabinet committees and rolled two central agencies into existing ones. The intent in part was again to give individual ministers and their departments more leeway and to limit the reach of central agencies. Jean Chrétien appeared ready to follow in the footsteps of his predecessor. Though he had substantial experience with the Trudeau cabinet system and its central agencies, he elected to keep Campbell's changes and committed his government to a process in which ministers and their senior officials managed their departments without much interference from central agencies. However, the Chrétien years also revealed at times a prime minister who wished to concentrate

Figure 12.2 The Challenge of Horizontal Relations

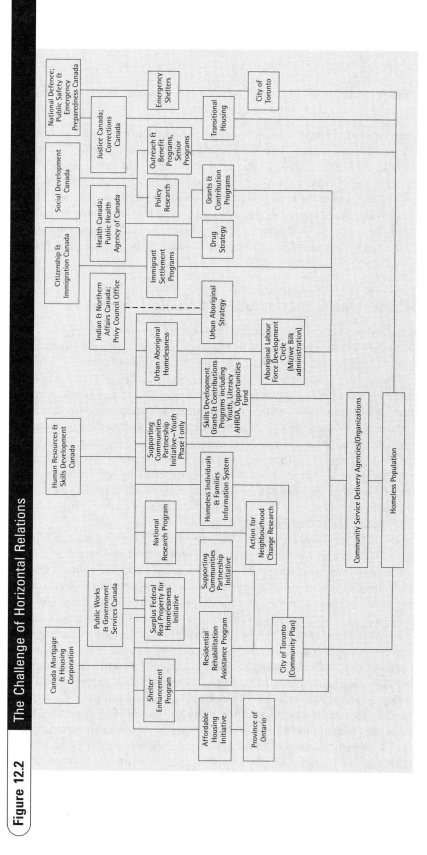

Source: *Report of the Auditor General of Canada*, Chapter 4, "Managing Horizontal Initiatives," page 35, Auditor General of Canada, November 2005. Reproduced with the permission of the Minister of Public Works and Government Services Canada, 2006.

Box 12.1	The Power of Central Agencies

As mentioned earlier, the sponsorship program entailed the federal government providing financial support to community groups who might help raise the profile of Canada and its national government in Quebec. A key part of the administration of the program involved a senior manager in the Department of Public Works and Government Services (PWGSC) working directly with the PMO. At one point, a newly appointed assistant deputy minister in PWGSC attempted to exercise his oversight authority over the aforementioned PWGSC manager by making inquiries about the sponsorship program. Shortly thereafter, a PCO official called the deputy minister of PWGSC and told him that the assistant deputy minister was "asking too many questions" and that he was not to interfere in the administration of the program. The message was understood.

Source: Commission of Inquiry into the Sponsorship Program & Advertising Activities, *Who Is Responsible? Fact Finding Report* (Ottawa: Her Majesty in Right of Canada, 2005), 156–57.

power into his own hands and those of a small number of trusted people in cabinet and the Prime Minister's Office. Thus, for some, the role of the central agencies under Chrétien was as strong as ever. Their job was to help the prime minister decide upon the important issues while making sure that ministers and departments did not draw the prime minister away from addressing the high-priority issues. The power of the central agencies in the Chrétien years could also be seen in their ability to control ministers "who may create problems for the prime minister or the government" and to become "involved in whatever issue they and the prime minister think they should."[13] Under Prime Minister Martin, a similar feeling persisted that central agencies, especially the PMO, had a great deal of influence and orchestrated matters basic to the survival of a minority government.[14]

In some minds this seeming resurgence of central agencies, as with the allegation of prime ministerial government, distorts the true state of affairs. The small size of central agencies alone limits the capabilities of central agencies—the PMO, for instance, has barely a hundred members, which pales in comparison with most line departments. As Thomas says, "a sense of proportion requires some recognition that central agencies are relatively small in terms of staff members and they cannot possibly arrange to be present where all significant policy events are taking place."[15] The frenzied nature of government and its propensity to roll from one crisis to another also argues against a set of central agencies coolly managing the affairs of governments while keeping departments in line:

> [I]n the instantaneous world of contemporary politics, driven by the headlines and the deadlines of the media, daily life in the central agencies seems to an outsider to be chaotic, frantic, intense and short-term.[16]

A possible resolution of these differences about the influence of central agencies over departments may lie in a look at the recent role of central agencies in horizontal relations. Here, the expectation of departments is for central agencies to initiate attempts at coordinating the activities of two or more departments. With their formal authority and closeness to the prime minister and cabinet, central agencies are seen as necessary for jump-starting efforts in horizontal management. Central agencies seem willing and able to perform this task, but no more than this, and it is up to departments to provide the necessary staying power and substantive knowledge for any effort in horizontal management. Because of the demands of government and the multiplicity of policy centres, central agencies are unable to attend to the daily operation of coordinating bodies. As a participant in some efforts in horizontal management says, "The Privy Council Office or the Treasury Board Secretariat often don't want to get their hands dirty or simply do not have the capacity to do so."[17] The exception to this is crisis situations, in which central agencies have the necessary capability and motivation. What emerges from this examination is a relationship in which central agencies do assume the lead with the understanding that departments will have the autonomy—sometimes forced upon them—to carry out the exercise. Perhaps this is a fair way to see, in general, the nature of relations or interactions between central agencies and departments.

Intradepartmental Relations

The internal structure of government organizations varies from one category of organization to another, but in general departments and those central agencies with a departmental form are organized in a broadly uniform manner. They are structured in a pyramidal fashion, with a minister as the political head and a deputy minister as the lead administrative official of a formal organization with layers of interlocking superior–subordinate relationships descending to the base of the pyramid.

The Minister

At the top of all departments sits the minister, who is usually an *elected* member of the party in power and who is appointed by the prime minister. In this position, the minister is responsible for all actions of the department, a reality confirmed by the convention of individual ministerial responsibility. Individual statutes also seek to specify the duties of the minister in relation to the department, and the prime minister may supplement these directives with missives of his or her own. Within this framework, ministers undertake certain actions necessary to their position within the department. They will need, first of all, to define departmental priorities in order to give some direction to the department. In this exercise, the ministers are aided by the deputy minister, political advisors, and central agency officials (the last of whom may provide ministers with "mandate letters" outlining issues for the department). In some cases, the minister rests content with serving the interests of their departmental clients and staying away from the larger policy issues. In others, he or she articulates a set of policy priorities or even formulates a mission-like project for the department.[18] But in all cases the minister realizes that there is a certain "sink or swim" quality to being a minister, which requires that the head of the department take some kind of initiative.[19] If not, the department flounders and eventually someone else assumes effective control.

Facing all ministers is the challenge of ensuring that departmental personnel work diligently to serve the government and the country. Given the significance of this challenge, the temptation on the part of the minister is to manage the department, but this would be a mistake. A minister actively engaged in department management soon "becomes so swamped with work that he or she cannot spend the time required to set the agenda and define the major policy or management thrusts for the department."[20] Most ministers appreciate this problem, and limit themselves to setting out their broad expectations about the management of the department, and then leave the actual managing to the appointed officials. Ministers also seek to establish good relations with their senior administrative staff and ensure that the latter are able work with any political appointees in the minister's office. In addition, they make efforts to get to know not only the senior personnel, but also the department as a whole and what is key to its operation. A minister must also effectively represent the department in various political arenas. The minister defends the department in Parliament, pursues its priorities in cabinet, and puts the department's best face forward when dealing with interest groups and the media.

The individual responsibility of ministers as political heads of departments links the cabinet to the bureaucracy, and it establishes the minister as the locus of formal authority in the departmental hierarchy for both policy formulation and policy execution. Ministers not only make the final decisions on policy questions; they also bear constitutional, legal, and political responsibility for the proper administration of their departments. In practice, ministers look for assistance to their senior departmental officials, especially to the deputy minister, who is the administrative head of the department. As noted in the previous chapter, the deputy minister occupies a pivotal position. He or she has to have an understanding of the minister's world—elections, public opinion, Parliament—and what are the core concerns of the departmental head. At the same time the deputy minister appreciates that he or she also works in the field of administration and its concerns for procedures, horizontal management, and rules and regulations. As Savoie says, "They are half in the political world and half in the public service, sandwiched between the neutral civil service and the partisan political ministers."[21] This location places great pressure on deputy ministers, but also gives them a bird's-eye view of the political and bureaucratic spheres of government and makes them well positioned "to determine what is possible and what is not." Ministers recognize this fact about deputy ministers and fully "expect their deputies to help them get their proposals through the system...."[22] But both the deputy minister and the minister know that ultimately it is the minister who makes the final decision. The relationship between the two has been described as "something akin to a marriage, where both partners should work toward developing a trusting relationship with open communication."[23] However, it is also a marriage in which the dominant partner is evident—the minister.

Relations between the deputy and the minister are complicated by the fact that the prime minister appoints all deputies. This arrangement, among other things, reminds the deputy ministers that they must take into consideration the collective concerns of the entire government as well the wishes and goals of the first minister. It also means that deputies are expected to answer to both the minister and the prime minister.

The Deputy Minister

The authority of the deputy minister is based on both statutes and conventions. These authorities can be translated in a set of basic roles for the deputy minister (see Figure 12.3). The role most apparent is the provision of advice and assistance to the minister. This advice, which is to be timely, frank, and "presented fearlessly," includes the offering of the "best possible policy options based on impartial review of the public good and the declared objectives of the Minister and the government."[24] This advice is to enable the minister to meet the mandate of the govern-

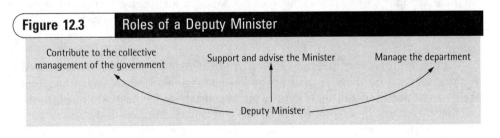

Figure 12.3   Roles of a Deputy Minister

Contribute to the collective management of the government

Support and advise the Minister

Manage the department

Deputy Minister

Source: Gorden Osbaldeston, "Job Description for DMs," *Policy Options* (January 1988).

ment and in turn serve the interests of all Canadians. Aside from policy advice, the deputy minister can put forward to the minister his or her views on legal, administrative, or technical issues that concern the department and the minister. As suggested earlier, the deputy minister also provides political advice, which is not guidance on how the minister and the government can best remain in government but rather views on how program initiatives will fare in light of the existing pressures both in and outside government. The deputy may, for instance, suggest to the minister that a particular proposal will be received poorly because of the opposition of powerful interest groups or because of the strong objections of other departments or influential central agencies. In all cases, the minister has the authority to ignore the advice of the deputy and act against it. Nevertheless, the deputy minister has the duty and responsibility to make known his or her opinions—both policy and political—to the minister.

The provision of advice is the dominant role of the deputy and one most valued and exercised. It is closest to the interests of the minister and the government, and this fact will influence the behaviour of deputies eager to please their superiors and to secure advancement in the public service. Many deputies also find this role to be the most interesting and one that best challenges their skills and talents. But another role, the contribution to the collective management of government, is becoming more significant, and in fact some suggest it has assumed the top spot in the list of deputy-ministerial duties. This particular role refers to a number of activities. It includes making sure the department respects government-wide practices and standards set by such bodies as the Treasury Board and the Public Service Commission. Responding to the demands of the Privy Council Office and other central agencies also falls into this category of responsibilities. Then there are the demands of horizontal management with other departments and interests lying just outside the walls of government. Indeed, this particular duty has become so large that it has fundamentally changed the work of deputy ministers. Deputies traditionally focused on their individual department, but now they concentrate more and more on the collective interests of government and their varied processes.[25]

Deputy ministers are also expected to carry out a third role, which is to spend some of their precious time on the internal management of their departments. The average line department has thousands of employees, often located in a maze of regional and local offices and all attempting to respond to a multitude of demands. So the deputy has to pay attention to what goes on in his or her department. Much of this work is delegated to associate and assistant deputies and middle-level managers, but the deputies nevertheless have to concern themselves with such issues as the hiring of senior people, the articulation of preferred management approaches, the formulation of workable, policies the administration of financial resources, and the provision of overall leadership. Many of these departmental responsibilities are prescribed in law. The *Financial Administration Act* makes the deputy minister directly responsible "for the prudent management of allocated resources" and the *Public Service Employment Act* places many duties affecting human resources management in the hands of the deputy.[26] To perform this third role, it has been suggested that deputy has to have a good understanding of the substance of the department and an appreciation of "how to manage in a government environment."[27]

Deputy ministers can, and do, become overloaded and sometimes overwhelmed by the combined burdens of their policy and management duties. What has long been said of ministers can be said of deputy ministers—they have too much to do and they do too much. A recent survey reveals that deputy ministers in the federal government work on average nearly 70 hours weekly, some putting in many more hours than this. A typical day of a deputy minister begins around seven or eight o'clock and

Figure 12.4   Accountability Network of a Deputy Minister

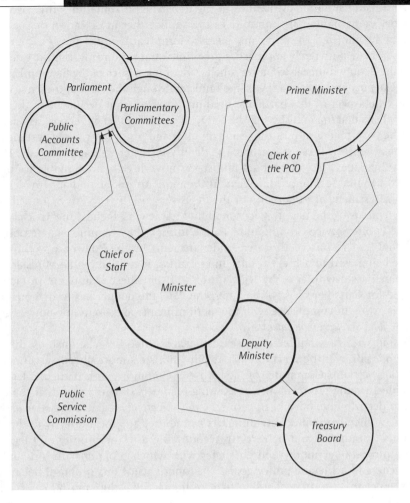

Source: Gordon Osbaldeston, *Keeping Deputy Ministers Accountable* (Toronto: McGraw-Hill Ryerson, 1989), 8.

ends about twelve or thirteen hours later, and on two or three nights of the week the responsibilities of a deputy require attendance at formal events or meetings of one kind or another.[28]

Accountability of the Deputy Minister

"Deputy ministers are required to manage a complex set of multiple accountabilities which arise out of the various powers, authorities and responsibilities attached to the position."[29] This rather prosaic or colourless formulation nevertheless captures an important truth, namely that the accountability of the bureaucratic sphere relies heavily on the deputy remaining responsible and answerable to a great number of bodies (see Figure 12.4). Though deputies are directly accountable only to political and administrative superiors and to the courts, and are not accountable to the legislature or entities outside government, they must indeed attend to a web of accountabilities stretching far and wide. The roles of the deputy minister convey one of the most important accountability relationships, which is that between the deputy minister and the minister. The minister needs to be assured that the deputy is acting in a way that respects and promotes ministerial and governmental priorities. The deputy minister is also accountable to the minister in the sense of explaining and fixing administrative errors and addressing systemic difficulties in the department; sometimes this also means going before parliamentary committees to supply either information or answers on behalf of the minister. The prime minister also forms part of the deputy's accountability network. The deputy rarely approaches the prime minister directly, but the expectation is that the deputy minister will always be aware of the wishes of the first minister. Usually, the deputy will speak to the prime minister through the clerk of the Privy Council Office. One aspect of this particular accountability relation occurs when the deputy minister fears that the minister may be acting in a manner that either goes against a policy of the government or puts the prime minister and his or her cabinet at some risk of embarrassment. In these situations, the deputy minister will approach the clerk to explain the issue. Also, the deputy minister is now directly accountable to the clerk by way of the Performance Management Program, an initiative that provides for an annual assessment of the quality of the deputy's work by the Privy Council Office. Other elements of the deputy's accountability framework include the Treasury Board and the Public Service Commission. To the former, deputy ministers are obliged to show that the "resources allocated to departments by the Board are well managed and are being used to achieve results and priorities identified by the Minister, by the government as a whole, or by legislation, and that these results are in fact being achieved for Canadians."[30] To the latter, the PSC, the deputy has to demonstrate he or she is acting in compliance with the merit principle and exercising powers granted by the *Public Service Employment Act*.

Despite the heavy burden of these existing accountability relationships, there have been proposals over the years to make deputy ministers more directly accountable to the Public Accounts Committee of the House of Commons. This particular legislature committee has the responsibility of assuring members of Parliament that funds allocated to departments have been properly and effectively spent. In past years, it has been recommended that deputy ministers be required to report directly to the Public Accounts Committee and be directly accountable for "the probity and legality of expenditures, the economy and efficiency with which programs are run, and their effectiveness in achieving policy goals."[31] Proponents of this proposal believed this arrangement to be more realistic in light of the fact that the minister can hardly be aware of administrative activities in a large government department. Due largely to the investigations into the sponsorship program, this proposal to make the deputy minister more responsible to the Public Accounts Committee has experienced a resurgence and support for it appears to be growing. It thus seems possible that the accountability framework facing the deputy minister is to become even more complicated and demanding.

Ministerial Staff

Relationships between ministers and deputy ministers are complicated further by the role of the minister's office staff. Ministerial assistants, often referred to as political aides or political staff, are appointed by the minister and are usually described as "exempt staff" because they are not subject to the provisions of the *Public Service Employment Act*. Since the tenure of ministerial assistants is tied directly to that of the minister, they are subject to the vicissitudes of partisan politics. A measure of employment protection has traditionally been assured, however, by the *Public Service Employment Act*, which provides that a person who has served at least three years as an executive assistant, a special assistant, or a private secretary to a minister is entitled to a position in the public service for which he or she is qualified at a level at least equivalent to that of private secretary to a deputy minister. Ministerial assistants frequently take advantage of this opportunity.[32] However, the government of Stephen Harper has introduced legislation that ends this practice. The proposed law merely allows ministerial staff to enter into internal job competitions within the federal public service for up to one year after leaving their position.[33]

Since the early 1960s, the size of the minister's office staff has gradually increased; however, the influence of ministerial staff has not only waxed and waned over that period but has also varied among ministers and departments. Until the Progressive Conservative government of 1984, ministers were usually authorized under Treasury Board guidelines to hire an executive assistant, a policy advisor, as many special assistants as funds permitted, one private secretary, and support staff. Some ministers supplemented this staff by seconding departmental public servants and/or using departmental funds to hire employees on a contract basis. Upon its election in 1984, the Progressive Conservative government upgraded the quality of ministerial staff by authorizing each minister to hire a chief of staff at a substantial salary. The chiefs of staff were intended to function, not as senior policy advisors to the minister, but as the minister's chief political advisors and as the managers of the minister's office. They did, however, play a more significant policy role than their predecessors. Following its election in 1993, the Chrétien government abolished the chief of staff role and reduced the resources devoted to ministerial assistants, but this did not stop them from continuing to contest the counsel of senior appointed officials. On coming into office, Prime Minister Martin reinstated the position of chief of staff with a substantial increase in remuneration over the salary paid to senior ministerial assistants in earlier years.[34]

The Functions of Ministerial Assistants

The overall purpose of a minister's office is to "provide Ministers with advisors and assistants who are not departmental public servants, who share their political commitment, and who can complement the professional, expert and non-partisan advice and support of the Public Service."[35] This statement, drafted by the PCO, clearly shows that the main function of ministerial assistants is to offer political advice on all matters coming into the minister's office, including proposals emanating from the department and its public servants. In offering this advice, the primary motivation of the assistants is to "protect their Minister and government from any action or issue that might adversely affect their chances of re-election."[36] The major players in the minister's office—the Chief of Staff, the Senior Policy Advisor, the Director of Communications, and the Director of Parliamentary Affairs—are all focused on this particular function. A related function concerns liaising with senior departmental officials, the Prime Minister's Office, other ministerial chiefs of staff, and any other bodies crucial to the political survival of the minister. A third function is managing the minister's office, which means handling the office budget, correspondence, work flow, and staff, and a further still function relates to managing a most important commodity in political life, namely the minister's time. This last, the role of time manager, involves juggling the minister's extremely onerous schedule.[37] See Figure 12.5 (on page 204) for the basic personnel and structure of a minister's office.

Ministerial Staff and Departmental Officials

Clearly, any government hopes that there will be harmonious and productive relations between ministerial staff and departmental officials, and that this can be achieved through a clear understanding of the respective duties. The aforementioned PCO document emphasizes the complementary relationship between the two—one is nonpartisan, the other clearly partisan—and the need to respect these differing roles. A Treasury Board publication stresses the same, saying that ministerial staff and departmental members will collaborate in "overseeing policy development on behalf of the minister."[38] Sometimes the hope of harmonious relations is achieved, but other times difficulties arise between the two parties. The precipitating factor usually seems to be

Figure 12.5   Basic Structure of a Minister's Office

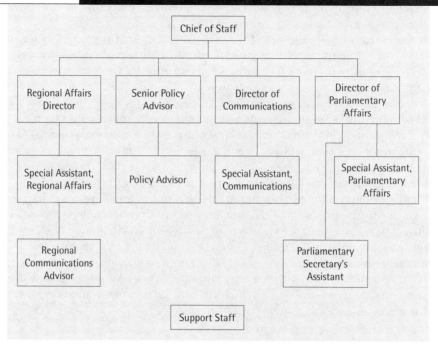

Source: Treasury Board of Canada Secretariat, *Guidelines for Ministers' Offices* (Ottawa: Her Majesty the Queen in Right of Canada, February 2006).

the belief of departmental officials that the minister's staff has intruded too much into the process of policy development. One former deputy minister conveys the exasperation of some departmental officials:

> The role of the ministerial assistant should centre around the relationship with the caucus, the constituency and the Minister's personal schedule; when they stick to that kind of knitting there is no problem. The difficulties arise when they start to act like Leo the 10th, "God has given us the papacy, now let us enjoy it." They want to be policy hounds and think they know all about it, and usually the intellectual apparatus is an ideological disposition—Christian, free market, union—and on that basis, they try to influence departmental policy.[39]

As the quotation suggests, departmental members feel that ministerial staff are without the technical skills to contribute to the formulation of policy and programs, and instead merely trumpet one belief system or another—none of which are helpful. Ministerial staff, of course, can also add to the discomfort by voicing beliefs that the bureaucracy is bereft of innovative policy ideas and lacking in its appreciation of the minister's political needs. As noted, relations between the two parties can be good, usually when each side respects the other and especially when departments understand that political staff can make important contributions to the development of policy. However, it does appear that any appreciation of this relationship must begin with the understanding that, in the words of a former deputy minister, "[t]here is always an inherent tension between a Minister's office and the department."[40] Like oil and water, the two are difficult to mix.

Conclusion

The story of interaction among the major players in the executive–bureaucratic arena is clearly a complicated one, but in essence it is one of swings in the pendulum of power between political executives and public servants, and between departments and central agencies. Public servants exercise a great deal of control and influence in the policy process, and political executives are not always successful in holding public servants accountable for the exercise of this power. No matter what changes are made in the decision-making system, public servants continue to play a pervasive and significant role. Control over the bureaucracy by the prime minister (or premier) and the cabinet is, however, only one means of holding public servants accountable and responsible for their actions and decisions. The bureaucracy is far from a monolithic entity. We have seen in this chapter that public servants compete with, and are constrained by, other public servants. Subsequent chapters will show that additional actors in the political system—namely, legislators, judges, pressure groups, and the public—also check bureaucratic power.

1. Canadian Centre for Management Development, CCMD Roundtable on the Management of Horizontal Initiatives, *Moving from the Heroic to the Everyday: Lessons Learned from Leading Horizontal Projects*, 2001, 3. Available at Canada School of Public Service site, www.myschool-monecole.gc.ca/Research/publications/html/horinz_rt/horinz_rt_1_e.html. Retrieved July 10, 2006.

2. Task Force on Horizontal Issues, *Managing Horizontal Policy Issues*, December 1996, 4. Available at Canada School of Public Service site, www.myschool-monecole.gc.ca/Research/publications/pdfs/horize.pdf. Retrieved July 10, 2006.

3. Canadian Centre for Management Development, loc. cit.

4. Ibid., 11.

5. Ibid., 20.

6. Ibid., 35.

7. Herman Bakvis and Luc Juillet, *The Horizontal Challenge: Line Departments, Central Agencies and Leadership* (Ottawa: Canada School of Public Service, 2004), 48–49. Available at Canada School of Public Service site, www.monecole-myschool.gc.ca/Research/publications/pdfs/hc_e.pdf. Retrieved July 10, 2006.

8. Ibid., 46.

9. Ibid., 35.

10. Ibid., 48.

11. Ibid., 24.

12. Jacques Bourgault and Rene Lapierre, *Horizontality and Public Management, Final Report to the Canadian Centre for Management Development, the Leadership Network, the Federal Regional Council—Quebec and the École nationale d'administration publique* (Ottawa: Canadian Centre for Management Development, 2000), 10.

13. Donald J. Savoie, *Governing from the Centre: The Concentration of Power in Canadian Politics* (Toronto: University of Toronto Press, 1999), 102–03.

14. Graham Fraser, "The Man Who (Really) Saved the Government," *Toronto Star*, May 22, 2005, A4.

15. Paul G. Thomas, "The Role of Central Agencies: Making a Mesh of Things," in James Bickerton and Alain-G. Gagnon, eds., *Canadian Politics*, 3rd ed. (Peterborough: Broadview Press, 1999), 139.

16. Paul G. Thomas, "Governing from the Centre: Reconceptualizing the Role of the PM and Cabinet," *Policy Options* 25 (December 2003/January 2004): 85.

17. Bakvis and Juillet, *The Horizontal Challenge*, 54.

18. Savoie, *Governing from the Centre*, 244–45.

19. Gordon Osbaldeston, "Dear Minister," *Policy Options* 9 (June/July 1988): 5.

20. Ibid., 10.

21. Donald J. Savoie, *Breaking the Bargain: Public Servants, Ministers and Parliament* (Toronto: University of Toronto Press, 2003), 136.

22. Ibid., 138.

23. Gordon Osbaldeston, "Job Description for DMs," *Policy Options* 9 (January 1988): 33.

24. Government of Canada, Privy Council Office, *Guidance for Deputy Ministers*, June 20, 2003. Available at the Privy Council Office site, www.pco-bcp.gc.ca/default.asp?Page=Publications&Language=E&doc=gdm-gsm/gdm-gsm_doc_e.htm (go down about 5 screens). Retrieved July 10, 2006.

25. Savoie, *Breaking the Bargain*, 166.

26. James Ross Hurley, "Responsibility, Accountability and the Role of Deputy Ministers in the Government of Canada," in Commission of Inquiry into the Sponsorship Program & Related Activities, *Restoring Accountability: Research Studies*, vol. 3: *Linkages: Responsibilities and Accountabilities* (Ottawa: Her Majesty the Queen in Right of Canada, 2006), 132–33.

27. Osbaldeston, "Job Description for DMs." 34.

28. Jacques Bourgault, *The Contemporary Role and Challenges of Deputy Ministers in the Federal Government of Canada* (Ottawa: Canadian Centre for Management Development, January 2003), 19–20.

29. Government of Canada Privy Council Office, Guidance for Deputy Ministers (about 12 screens down).

30. Ibid. (about 15 screens down).

31. Royal Commission on Financial Management and Accountability, *Final Report* (Ottawa: Ministry of Supply and Services, 1979), 374–75.

32. For more on ministerial assistants, see Treasury Board of Canada Secretariat, *Guidelines for Ministers' Offices*, February 2006. Available at the Treasury Board of Canada Secretariat site, www.tbs-sct.gc.ca/pubs_pol/hrpubs/mg-ldm/gfmo_e.asp. Retrieved July 10, 2006.

33. *The Federal Accountability Act, C-2, s. 101*. At this point, the legislation is awaiting approval of the Senate.

34. Liane E. Benoit, "Ministerial Staff: The Life and Times of Parliament's Statutory Orphans," in Commission of Inquiry into the Sponsorship Program & Related Activities, *Restoring Accountability: Research Studies, Volume 1: Parliament, Ministers and Deputy Ministers* (Ottawa: Her Majesty the Queen in Right of Canada, 2006), 163–64.

35. Government of Canada, *Accountable Government: A Guide for Ministers 2006* (Ottawa: Her Majesty in Right of Canada, 2006), 29.

36. Benoit, "Ministerial Staff," 178.

37. For more on the duties of ministerial assistants, see Jeanne Flemming, "The Role of the Executive Assistant to a Federal Minister," *Optimum: The Journal of Public Sector Management* 27(2) (1997), 63–68.

38. Treasury Board Secretariat, *Guidelines for Ministers' Offices* (Ottawa: Her Majesty the Queen in Right of Canada, 2006), Appendix A.

39. Benoit, "Ministerial Staff," 185.

40. Arthur Kroeger quoted in ibid., 183.

13

The Legislature and the Bureaucracy

The interactions between public servants and the legislative branch are in a way unlike any other relationship involving appointed officials and other actors in the political process. When public servants deal with senior politicians in the cabinet decision process or with appointed officials in other departments, the relationship is usually a direct one. The public servant helps to draft a memorandum for cabinet's consideration or engages in exercises of horizontal management with counterparts in other agencies. However, a large part of the public servant's relationship with legislative members is conducted *indirectly* through individual ministers. Constitutional conventions require that elected officials in the executive assume responsibility for the actions of government and that appointed officials remain invisible or effectively nonexistent. If members of the House of Commons wish to better understand some development in a department or get to the bottom of an apparent mistake in the administration of a program, they are unable for the most part to interact with the official literally responsible for the action. Rather, they must to go to the minister in charge of the department in question and hope that the appropriate remedies will be applied.

It is probably no surprise to learn that the legislature is not always satisfied with this arrangement and has worked to assemble other, more direct, relations with appointed officials. Though always acting on behalf of the minister, public servants may sometimes be called to appear before parliamentary committees, at which time they come face to face with members of the legislature and their queries. There have also emerged a number of officers or agents of Parliament who report to the legislature on various aspects of the administrative operations of government and seek to help individual constituents deal with the frustrations of bureaucratic practices. But even with these relations, the most important way in which the legislature interacts and attempts to control and shape the actions of public servants is to do so indirectly through their questioning and investigation of the responsible ministers.

The foregoing paragraphs indicate that a main concern of this chapter is the examination of the doctrine of individual ministerial responsibility. This is the convention that structures the indirect relations between legislators and public servants. The chapter defines the convention and assesses its ability to provide for government that is both answerable and accountable to the people and their representatives. The chapter also looks at how a series of offices assist Parliament to deal with the public service in relation to such matters as information, privacy, and the finances of the nation. Lastly, the chapter considers various reform proposals for making the convention of individual ministerial responsibility work better. As will be seen, the most prominent proposal is to allow for a more direct link between the legislature and senior public servants.

Ministerial Responsibility and Political Neutrality

The conventions of collective and individual ministerial responsibility are separate but interrelated unwritten rules of behaviour in the operation of parliamentary government. *Collective responsibility*, in its application to the government as a whole, prescribes that the prime minister and the cabinet must resign or ask the governor general for dissolution of Parliament if the House of Commons passes a vote of non-confidence in the government. In its application to individual ministers, collective responsibility prescribes that a minister must support government decisions in public, or at least suppress any public criticism of them. If ministers find a particular decision unacceptable, they must either stifle their objections or submit their resignation.

This chapter centres on individual rather than collective responsibility. In the academic literature, several meanings and implications are given to **individual ministerial responsibility**, but there is agreement that it means in a nutshell that the "minister is responsible for everything done in the department."[1] Two components flow from this pithy formulation of one of the most important conventions of British governmental tradition. The first is that the minister is accountable to Parliament for all the administrative errors of his or her departmental subordinates, in the sense that he or she must resign in the event of a serious error by these subordinates. This component of ministerial responsibility is often described as a myth, but it will be shown that this criticism follows from a misunderstanding of the operation of individual ministerial responsibility. The second component of the convention is that the minister is answerable to Parliament in that he or she must explain and defend the actions of his or her department before Parliament. The importance of this component is ignored or minimized by some commentators on ministerial responsibility in Canada.

Though separate from the doctrine of individual ministerial responsibility, the conventions of **political neutrality** and anonymity deserve attention, because they also shape relations between the legislature and the public service. Seen together, these two conventions imply a number of things, and elsewhere in this text we explore the full ramifications of political neutrality and anonymity.[2] But for now it is sufficient to observe that the conventions can—as with the doctrine of individual ministerial responsibility—be boiled down to two propositions. One is that all activities of public servants are carried out "in the name of the minister" and that appointed officials are for all intents and purposes invisible in the public sphere. Deputy ministers, for instance, may appear in person before a parliamentary committee to answer queries and provide information, but this is to be seen only as that the deputies are acting "on behalf of the minister". If the minister is to be the locus of responsibility, public servants must remain anonymous and not divert interest away from the person responsible for the actions of the department. The second proposition is that public servants neither "promote" nor "defend" the policies and decisions of government. Their job begins and ends with the supply of facts and information; public servants "should not act or be seen to act as the 'agents' of Ministers by publicly defending their Minister."[3] Also, public servants ought to refrain from engaging in any overt political activity that may detract from their ability to serve the minister. The convention of political neutrality implies a certain loyalty to the minister and the government. For convenience, public service anonymity will be included under the broad heading of political neutrality. Accordingly, when we speak of the operation of individual ministerial responsibility, the reference is to the related conventions of individual ministerial responsibility and political neutrality.

Box 13.1   "The Bargain"

Another way to think of the doctrines of individual ministerial responsibility and political neutrality is that together they amount to a "bargain" between the minister and appointed officials. Public servants give the minister their professionalism, nonpartisanship, and loyalty in exchange for security of tenure and anonymity or protection from political attacks. Both parties benefit form this arrangement, and hopefully so do the purposes of good government.

Source: Donold J. Savoie, *Breaking the Bargain: Public Servants, Ministers, and Parliament* (Toronto: University of Toronto, 2003).

The Resignation of Ministers

The first component of ministerial responsibility requires that a minister resign if a serious administrative error committed by her or his department is exposed. Despite frequent calls by opposition parties for ministerial resignations on the grounds of actual or alleged departmental mismanagement, in practice ministers do not resign as penance for administrative bungling in their department. It is now almost universally accepted that it is unreasonable to hold ministers personally responsible, in the form of resignation, for the administrative failings of their subordinates. Ministers cannot hope to have personal knowledge of more than a small percentage of the administrative actions taken by their officials. A report of a parliamentary committee makes the point:

> The notion that a minister could still enjoy the intimate knowledge of the daily workings of his or her department and thus could be held account for operational and administrative actions may have been valid in the 19th century but is no longer so under contemporary circumstances.[4]

It might even be said that at no time was it realistic, as demonstrated in the fact that not a single federal minister has resigned because of administrative misdoings. Moreover, it is not clear whether it would ever be in the public interest for ministers of government to become too concerned with departmental operations, for they have more important matters to address.

A seemingly more sensible and acceptable approach to this first component of individual ministerial responsibility is articulated in a government document written for federal ministers:

> In practice, when errors or wrongdoing is committed by officials under their direction, Ministers are responsible for promptly taking the necessary remedial steps and for providing assurances to Parliament that appropriate corrective action has been taken to prevent reoccurrence.[5]

Authorities on the doctrine of individual ministerial responsibility agree with this interpretation, saying that in cases of "administrative shortcomings" the minister "is expected to take corrective action and is personally responsible for that action."[6] The corrective action inevitably involves an internal investigation of the matter and an attempt to make changes that minimize the chances of the mistake occurring again. Corrective action may also involve disciplinary action of one kind or another against one or more appointed officials.

All this is not to say there is no obligation for ministers to resign or to accept personal responsibility under any circumstances. Cases do arise in which personal culpability of a minister is evident—for example, the personal conduct of the minister violates societal norms—or in which the magnitude of the error causes the government considerable embarrassment. A failed policy initiative intimately connected to the minister may also offer grounds for resignation or at least consideration of it. But even if the minister accepts full responsibility in such situations, the practical effects on his or her career depend largely on personal, partisan, and situational factors. Parliament itself has no authority to unseat the minister; only the head of the government has that power. However, if the minister under attack is an unpopular member of cabinet, if the electorate is unusually enraged, or if the government is in a minority position in Parliament, the prime minister might be tempted to seek or accept the minister's resignation. In the past ten years, only a handful of federal ministers have resigned their positions because of allegations relating to their behaviour. One resignation followed from a minister's attempt to help a constituent gain a positive decision from the Immigration and Refugee Board—a violation of his own government's code of ethics; another took place was heard on a plane talkimg about confidential matters; still another arose from the minister giving a former girlfriend a government contract without going through the normal tendering process. Another minister resigned when it came to light that he had authorized funding to an educational institution managed by his brother. The most recent resignation, in early 2005, stemmed from allegations that the federal immigration minister gave help to individuals with their immigration problems in exchange for offering some assistance to her election campaign in 2004.[7]

These cases show clearly that ministers do not resign to atone for either serious mismanagement by their officials or personal administrative mistakes. They all relate instead to personal misconduct and a failure to heed their own government's guidelines for ministerial behaviour. Thus, the demand for ministerial resignations on the grounds of misadministration may appear to be a feeble weapon in the parliamentary arsenal of opposition parties. Yet this component of ministerial responsibility has important consequences for both ministers and public servants. Parliamentary and public calls for one's resignation, like the probability of being hanged the next morning, effectively concentrate one's attention. A minister's efforts to refute or defuse the allegations are vigorously supported by his or her senior officials, whose duty it is to keep their minister out of trouble. The reputation and career prospects of public servants tend to prosper or suffer along with those of their minister.

The Answerability of Ministers

The second component of ministerial responsibility corresponds closely to its current practice. Ministers do explain and defend their department's policies and administration before Parliament, especially during Question Period. Opposition members and, on occasion, government backbenchers use a variety of other opportunities (e.g., motions, Opposition days) to seek information and explanations from ministers. But an inordinate amount of parliamentary, media, and public attention centres on the daily oral Question Period. It is notable that ministers almost always respond to questions in their sphere of responsibility, although they can be obliged neither to answer nor to give reasons for refusing to answer. A strong impetus to answer to Parliament is that a minister may suffer adverse political consequences for declining to do so. The Speaker of the House of Commons has observed that he "is not in a position to compel an answer—it is public opinion which compels an answer."[8] Certainly, a minister who refuses to answer questions on an important issue, especially if he or she does not provide a reasonable explanation for his or her position, receives severe criticism from Opposition members and the media. There is, therefore, both constitutional and political pressure on ministers to justify their department's actions to Parliament.

The willingness of ministers to answer questions in the legislature does not ensure that all their replies are informative, plausible, or even comprehensible. Experienced ministers tend to be artful dodgers who often bob and weave to avoid direct hits from Opposition inquiries and allegations. Brian Chapman admits that ministerial responsibility "may be a useful tag for harrying ministers in Parliament," but he notes that "even then it smacks rather of a verbal game of cowboys and Indians."[9] Nevertheless, on the premise that ministerial evasion and circumlocution on a serious matter may be motivated by a desire to conceal politically embarrassing information, both Opposition members and journalists may be prompted to investigate the matter more vigorously.

The fact that a single, identifiable minister is answerable for the activities of a specific department assists backbench members of the legislature in their handling of constituents' inquiries or complaints about government administration. A question in the legislature is sometimes the last recourse of a member who has been unable to obtain a satisfactory answer through private correspondence with a minister.

Although, as noted earlier, ministers are not expected to resign for departmental errors made during their predecessors' term of office, they must answer to Parliament for those errors. This rule ensures a focus of continuing responsibility for government administration, despite changes in the political heads of departments or in the governing party itself. Parliament's capacity to control and influence public servants is enhanced because one minister is required to answer for administrative actions, no matter when these actions took place. Incumbent ministers will usually be obliged to rely heavily on their departmental officials for knowledge of what occurred during the tenure of their predecessors. In such situations, the ability of ministers to answer to Parliament for their department rests largely on the continuity of administration provided by their permanent public servants. Thus, the operation of ministerial responsibility is closely tied to the permanency in office of public servants. Permanency, in turn, depends on the preservation of several of the other elements of political neutrality described earlier.

Political Neutrality

The convention of political neutrality entails an attempt to ensure that public servants remain both anonymous and nonpartisan or neutral in their actions. Some of the prescriptions associated with their two aims, such as maintaining a strict separation between policy and administration or prohibiting public servants from engaging in some political activities, are either clearly unrealistic or ones whose violation is not fatal to the operation of responsible government. But the increasing failure to observe one of the prescriptions, that public servants remain anonymous, may have serious implications for the convention of ministerial responsibility. In the past few decades, developments have chipped away the anonymity of public servants. One has been the refusal of some ministers to accept responsibility for a certain action and instead either literally name the public servant responsible or place blame on the departmental bureaucracy as a whole. As experts on ministerial responsibility write, "Over the past two decades, there have been notable occasions on which Ministers have allowed public servants to be held to account publicly."[10] One fairly recent instance of this occurred when a federal minister said her department's accounting procedures were from the "Dark Ages" in an attempt to explain some alleged instances of mismanagement of job creation programs.[11] A couple of years earlier, a minister named a public servant (and a chief of staff) whom they thought was personally responsible for admitting into Canada a former senior official in the government of Iraq.

The other developments, though less sensational, may be even more important, because they involve institutional changes and not the wishes of a few ministers to escape responsibility:

• Public servants now routinely appear before legislative committees to provide factual answers to queries of elected representatives. Though every effort is made to ensure that these appearances refrain from an attempt to defend or justify the actions of the minister, the fact is that public servants are becoming well known to people within the legislative branch.

- Access to information legislation allows any interested party an opportunity to gain access to documents that may reveal the role of administrative officials. It is possible now to follow the decision-making trail associated with a decision whose controversial nature may concern those outside the department.
- There exist now a number of officers or agents of Parliament whose task is to help elected representatives to examine the actions of public servants. Arguably the most powerful of these agencies—and the most intimidating for public service—is the Office of the Auditor General. This particular agency not only conducts audits, but increasingly strives to determine the performance of departments and their officials.
- The media have become much more pervasive and aggressive in their efforts to tell their readers and listeners about the activities of government. As a result, public servants find themselves increasingly a part of the media's stories. Also, the desire of government to consult more with interest groups and the public has brought public servants more into personal contact with a greater and greater number of people.[12]

The declining anonymity of public servants may have serious implications for the doctrine of individual ministerial responsibility. One of the attractions of ministerial responsibility is that it clearly establishes a locus of responsibility for any wrong-doings of one kind or another in a department. If a problem emerges, members of legislature know where to go for answers. There is no need to go looking for the actual culprits—one only has to determine who is the responsible minister. But the loss of anonymity blurs this locus of responsibility, and tempts some to pursue civil servants in the hope of locating the individual truly responsible for some disturbing development. With this blurring comes the fear that determining responsibility amounts to finding a needle in a haystack—that no one may be found responsible. A related implication is that there may arise a wish to formally divide responsibility for a department more clearly between the minister and the deputy minister, and thereby effectively end the anonymity of public servants. Already, deputy ministers have direct responsibility for certain administrative departmental matters. It has always been understood that these are carried out within the ambit of individual ministerial responsibility, but the proposal for clearer division of responsibility poses questions about the survivability of this understanding. We will explore this matter further at end of this chapter.

Legislative Control and Influence

The convention of individual ministerial responsibility, which is the basis for the major relationship between the legislature and public servants, constitutes the major means by which elected representatives in the legislative branch hold appointed officials accountable. When an administrative error occurs, the minister in theory accepts responsibility and promises to take the necessary remedial actions. But these latter actions are handled internally, and the public rarely finds out what penalties, if any, are imposed. And if a minister refuses to accept responsibility, the doctrine of political neutrality makes it difficult to affix the blame on the public servant actually responsible. Clearly, there is a need for further ways or mechanisms by which the legislature can control appointed officials and their actions. Put differently, interactions between Parliament and public servants go beyond the doctrine of individual ministerial responsibility.

Agents of Parliament

A second way of ensuring responsibility in government involves agents or officers of Parliament who report directly or indirectly to Parliament. These agents serve two related purposes. One is "to assist Parliament in holding ministers and the bureaucracy accountable."[13] As was shown earlier, it is difficult for Parliament by itself to ensure responsible action in the executive and the bureaucracy, so it has been thought necessary to set up bodies that "supplement the principles of ministerial responsibility as a basis for accountability."[14] The second purpose is to handle concerns and complaints of citizens about the actions of government. In these two capacities—and especially the first—the agencies act as watchdogs, helping members of the legislature to ensure that officials in the executive are acting responsibly.

At the federal level there exists no authoritative statement on which government bodies qualify as officers of Parliament. However, most agree that any list of such agents would include at least the Office of the Auditor General, the Chief Electoral Officer, the Commissioner of Official Languages, and the Information and Privacy Commissioners. The newly established Office of the Ethics Commissioner would mostly likely be put on the list. There is some question of whether the Canadian Human Rights Commission and the Public Service Commission deserve to be called agents of Parliament, but for our purposes they shall be. This rather long list of watchdog agencies provides an interesting contrast to their provincial counterparts, who tend to be fewer and often consolidated in the office of the **Ombudsman**. The focus of the Ombudsman is on the second role of watchdog agencies, namely the investigation of individual citizen complaints of government. At one time or another, there have been recommendations for the establishment of federal Ombudsmen, but the preference at the federal level has been to set up what amount to mini-Ombudsmen.

- *The Office of the Auditor General (OAG)* is one of the watchdog agencies that report directly to Parliament rather than through a minister. This status symbolizes the importance of this office, easily the most prominent and arguably the most influential of all the agents of Parliament. The auditor general, the lead official in the office, reports annually to Parliament on whether departments have kept proper financial records and whether public funds have been spent as appropriated by Parliament. The auditor general also carries out audits of select government programs whose regard for economy and efficiency are in question and that have failed to put in place measures to determine their effectiveness. These particular audits, which attract much public attention, inevitably lead to recommendations for fixing the problems. Though the auditor general's office has always had a certain visibility, its prominence in recent years has increased with the investigation of such government initiatives as the sponsorship program. Ministers and public servants are even more fearful now that the annual reports and select audits will single out their department or program for examination—and criticism. Clearly, then, the auditor general has been quite successful in serving Parliament in its attempt to ensure responsible government. However, its very success has caused some to question the power and influence of this office.

- *The Office of the Information Commissioner (OIC)*, set up in 1983, administers the *Access to Information Act* by investigating complaints about denial of public access to government information. The office has no authority to force government to provide access, but instead acts as a mediator between the complainant and government. However, the Information Commissioner may ask for a review of a complaint by the Federal Court of Canada if it believes that "an individual has been improperly denied access and a negotiated solution has proved impossible."[15] As with many of the agents of Parliament, the OIC has gained greater visibility in recent years. In the case of the

OIC, the cause of this development has been more and more attempts to use the *Access to Information Act* and growing frustration with the government's failure to be more forthcoming.

- *The Office of the Privacy Commissioner*, also established in 1983, implements the *Privacy Act* and inquires into complaints from persons who believe that their privacy rights have not been properly respected. This involves either violation of privacy rights or a failure to recognize persons a right of access to their own personal information which may be under the control of private companies or the federal government. Reporting directly to Parliament, the Privacy Commissioner seeks to resolve complaints through mediation and conciliation, but has the authority to force people to give evidence in an attempt to resolve cases.

- *The Office of the Commissioner of Official Languages*, created in 1970, administers the *Official Languages Act* by, among other things, protecting the right of any citizen to deal with and be a recipient of services from the federal government in either French or English and to ensure the right of any person at the federal level to work in either of the two official languages. As part of his or her duty, the Commissioner of Official Languages addresses any complaints in relation to the *Official Languages Act* and may appeal to the Federal Court of Canada for the purpose of seeking an appropriate resolution of a matter.

- *Elections Canada* is an independent body reporting directly to Parliament and whose responsibilities include ensuring compliance with federal electoral legislation, making Canadians aware of elections in Canada, and reviewing the amount of spending by candidates, parties, and other during elections. The Chief Electoral Officer heads the agency.

- *The Office of the Ethics Commissioner*, set up in 2004, has the task of administering the Conflict of Interest Code for members of the House of Commons and the Conflict of Interest and Post-employment Code for Public Office Holders. The first refers to all members of the House of Commons when they are carrying their parliamentary duties, and the second refers to elected, and some appointed, officials in the executive branch (ministers, ministers of state, parliamentary secretaries, ministerial staff, and others). Almost immediately on being set up, the office found itself faced with some difficult cases relating to the ethical behaviour of both politicians and appointed officials. Disappointed with the actions of the office in these cases, some have called for the resignation of the Ethics Commissioners while others lamented the seeming appearance of another "toothless watchdog" of Parliament.[16]

Two other bodies are sometimes included in the list of agents of Parliament. One is the Public Service Commission, which serves Parliament in a number of ways but should be seen in general as the guardian of the merit principle in human resources management. The promotion of merit through the elimination of patronage has been a dominant concern of the Commission. The second body is the Canadian Human Rights Commission, set up in 1978. The purpose of this agency is to make certain "that the principles of equal opportunity and non-discrimination are followed in all areas of federal jurisdiction."[17] In fulfilling this aim, the CHRC looks into claims of discrimination, audits employers to ensure compliance with the rules and laws of employment equity, and develops information packages to provide people with a better appreciation of a discrimination-free workplace and the role of the CHRC in achieving this end.

In assessing the value of watchdog agencies, one expert on public administration in Canada claims that "Parliament has benefited greatly from the availability of parliamentary agencies as an alternative source of information about the performance of the executive."[18] Watchdog agencies are without the power to require any action on the basis of their reports, but the sheer publicity they generate and the arming of Parliament with more information make them "influential agents of accountability."[19] The overall intent of the agencies is to help the legislature to make government more responsive, and it can be said that this aim has been met. However, this is not to say that the agents are without their problems. The difficulty of defining what constitutes an agent of Parliament suggests some uncertainty about the structure and purpose of watchdog agencies. Public servants also feel some resentment toward these agencies. From their perspective, agents of Parliament make excessive demands on the public service, and these watchdogs focus only on the negative and make little or no mention of successes. Sometimes they are also too eager to pin the blame for some error on the public servant and not the responsible minister.

Parliamentary Committees

Parliamentary committees are another means by which the legislature can exercise control or influence over the public service. The functions of parliamentary committees may be divided into policy development (primarily involving evaluation of the purpose and content of proposed legislation), review of existing policies, and scrutiny of departmental administration (especially through examination of the estimates). In practice, these functions often overlap, and committee members put varying emphasis on each function.

The House of Commons has three basic types of committees: standing committees, special committees, and legislative committees (and subcommittees may also emerge).[20] Most of the standing committees (e.g., Agriculture and Agri-Food, Canadian Heritage, Environment and Sustainable Development) focus on a substantive sphere of government policy. Each committee covers one or more departments and agencies and in some cases the list of organizations can appear almost overwhelming. For example, the Committee on Agriculture and Agri-Food deals with the Department of Agriculture, the Canadian Grains Commission, the Canadian Food Inspection Agency, the Canadian Dairy Commission, the Farm Credit Corporation, the National Farm Products Council, the Canadian Wheat Board, and the Pest Management Regulatory Agency. The other standing committees are called specialist standing committees; they include such committees as the Public Accounts Committee. There are at present twenty-five standing committees in all, but the number can change from time to time. There are also a few joint standing committees of the Senate and the House of Commons (at present, the Joint Committee on Scrutiny of Regulations and the Joint Committee on the Library of Parliament).

Special committees represent a second type of committee, and they are set up as required to examine such specific issues as acid rain, child care, or same-sex marriage; once the committee presents its final report, it ceases to exist. Legislative committees, another type of committee, are established to examine specific government bills. A legislative committee has been set up to deal with the first major piece of legislation of the Harper government (the *Federal Accountability Act*). One advantage of legislative committees has been that the expertise, experience, and interests of the legislators can be matched to the subject matter of the legislation.

The Public Accounts Committee, the Access to Information, Privacy and Ethics Committee, the Government Operations and Estimates Committee, and the Standing Joint Committee on Scrutiny of Regulations all deserve special attention. They enjoy a greater measure of independence from cabinet control, because, unlike other committees, they are chaired by a member of the Opposition. The Public Accounts Committee examines both the public accounts (i.e., the government's year-end financial statements) and the auditor general's report as a basis for making recommendations to the House of Commons. With the assistance of the auditor general, the committee has uncovered, investigated, and reported on several scandals involving the expenditure of public funds, and has recommended corrective action in many other instances in which public money has been improperly spent. The primary function of the Standing Joint Committee on the Scrutiny of Regulations is to scrutinize the use of delegated legislative authority by cabinet, ministers, and public servants. The committee reviews statutory instruments—that is, the rules, regulations, orders, etc. made by the executive under delegated legislative authority. The other two committees, which are relatively new, deal with issues relating to information and ethics (Access to Information, Privacy and Ethics) and the examination of central agencies and the process of financial management (Government Operations and Estimates).

Figure 13.1 shows the floor plan of a typical committee room. As can be seen, the setup resembles the House of Commons in some respects, with government members on one side of the room and Opposition members on the other (with the chair at the head of the table). Committees often invite individuals (experts, representatives of organizations, public servants) to appear in order to give the committees a better insight into some matter, so provision is made for witnesses. Journalists and members of the general public may attend committee meetings, and staff resources are available for committee members.

At first glance, it might be concluded that the parliamentary committee system is well equipped to monitor the activities of the executive branch and the public service. The reality, however, is otherwise. A poll of public servants revealed that parliamentary committees and members of Parliament are considered very unimportant when it comes to influencing policy development—appointed officials considered them a "*minor process obstacle.*"[21] The well-known prominence of the executive branch in parliamentary government also increases the chances that the impact of legislative committees on the public

Figure 13.1 — Setup of House of Commons Committee Room

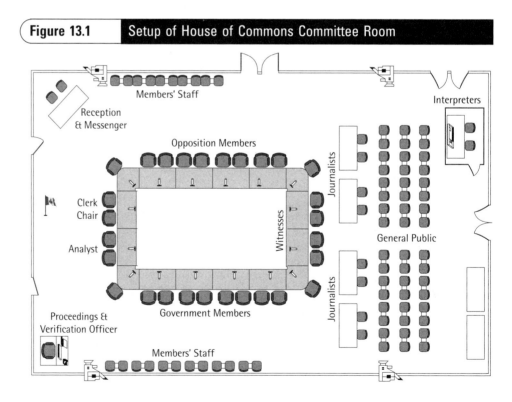

Source: *Committees, Practical Guide*, 8th Edition, page 7, Procedural Services, House of Commons, 2006. Reproduced with the permission of the Minister of Public Works and government Services Canada, 2006.

service will be only minimal. In recent years, attempts have been to strengthen the Canadian parliament and its committees. On becoming prime minister, Paul Martin introduced a plan to place greater resources with legislative committees and to give them a better opportunity to review the legislation and appointments of the government.[22] Some changes have been introduced following this committee, but it is unclear whether they have had any real effect.

Reform

A number of proposals have been put forward over the years to change relations between the legislature and the public service. The preceding section mentioned one set of changes: adjustments to the operation and mandate of legislative committees. This suggested change points to arguably the most important discussion of reform, namely a rethinking of the convention of individual ministerial responsibility. As will be seen, such thinking leads even to a consideration of the reconceptualization of the place of the public service in government.

The convention of individual ministerial responsibility is on balance workable and serves an important function. In fact, it is essential to the operation of responsible government in Canada and helps to ensure that public authorities remain accountable to the citizenry. However, some have indicated that the traditional understanding of the convention of individual ministerial responsibility might be adjusted to provide for more accountable government. The major adjustment suggested in relation to public administration is that deputy ministers be made more directly accountable to Parliament for the administration of department affairs. Already, legislation assigns certain statutory responsibilities to the deputy minister relating to financial management, personnel management, and the use of the two official languages, but these responsibilities are undertaken in the understanding that they are exceptions to the rule that deputies are accountable only to the minister for their duties. In 1979, the Royal Commission on Financial Management and Accountability noted that "deputy heads are not regularly held accountable in a systematic or coherent way for program management and departmental administration" and recommended that deputy ministers "be liable to be held to account directly for their assigned and delegated responsibilities before the parliamentary committee most directly concerned with administrative performance, the Public Accounts Committee."[23] The commission believed that the recommendation strengthened the convention because it established "a more precise alignment between accountability and responsibility."[24] In 1985, a special House of Commons committee looking into parliamentary reform observed that the operation of individual ministerial responsibility "undermines the potential for genuine accountability on the part of the person that ought to be accountable—the senior officer of the department."[25]

The thoughts and recommendations of the two bodies went unheeded, but recent cases of alleged misadministration have given new life to the issue. In 2002, former prime minister Jean Chrétien said that "new measures will be introduced to provide for more explicit accounting by deputies for the affairs of their department" and mentioned the British tradition of designating their senior officials (equivalent to deputies) as "accounting officers" responsible for answering directly to Parliament "for the financial administration of departmental funds voted by Parliament."[26] The result of the prime minister's announcement was a statement outlining the duties and accountabilities of a deputy minister in which the deputy is obligated to go before parliamentary committees to offer a clear picture of the administration of their department. In other words, little change was made to the doctrine of ministerial responsibility.

Chapter 13 / The Legislature and the Bureaucracy

A more recent development has been the release, in 2005, of a report of the House of Commons Standing Committee on Public Accounts dealing with individual ministerial responsibility and the federal sponsorship program. The report noted that a number of administrative wrongdoings had been committed in the administration of this program, but it had been difficult to determine responsibility for these wrongdoings because of the workings of the convention of ministerial responsibility. Ministers who headed the department that housed the sponsorship program refused to take responsibility on the grounds that they relied on their officials to carry out the implementation of the initiative. As for the deputy, his duty was to serve the minister and to recognize that political officials determined departmental actions, even if he believed that such actions might be inconsistent with acceptable practices and rules. Implicit in these statements was the belief that senior officials had no accountability relationship with Parliament. The report included testimony from one expert witness who said that the work of the committee had shown that "something is seriously wrong with the way the principle of responsibility is construed and practiced in Canada."[27] The committee saw a solution to this problem in adopting the above-mentioned British practice of designating senior public servants as "accounting officers." With this change, the deputy minister could be questioned more directly by Parliament and with the understanding that he or she would be held personally responsible for the "financial accounts of their departments and held to account for the performance of their duties before the Public Accounts Committee."[28] The committee made it clear that such a proposal would be consistent with the convention of ministerial responsibility, because the minister would have the opportunity to overrule a deputy in instances when the two disagree on a course of action relating to the administration of the department. In cases where the minister sought to ignore advice of the deputy, the latter would make this clear in writing to the minister and forward copies of the correspondence to the auditor general and the comptroller general (located in the Treasury Board Secretariat). If the minister still wanted to continue, he or she would inform the deputy in writing of this decision. As with the earlier correspondence, this letter from the minister would be forwarded to the auditor general and the comptroller general. This arrangement, the committee felt, would provide the deputy with an incentive to come forward and be frank and open about administrative irregularities, something that allegedly failed to take place in the sponsorship program. All in all, the committee believed that, with its proposal, it had accomplished the difficult task of maintaining the convention of ministerial responsibility while enhancing public service accountability to Parliament:

> These measures clarify the doctrine of ministerial accountability by making a distinction between a minister's policy role and a deputy minister's ... administrative role while preserving the minister's ultimate responsibility and accountability for the actions of his or her department.[29]

To make this point even clearer, the committee relied on the formulation that senior officials are accountable *to* the minister, while they are accountable *before* the committees of Parliament. The distinction reminds all that the minister is ultimately responsible for all that takes place within the department.

The commission of inquiry set up to examine the sponsorship program came to similar conclusions as the PAC about the operation of the doctrine of ministerial responsibility. It agreed with the need to make clearer the responsibility of the deputy for the administration of the department and recommended procedures akin to those associated with the position of accounting officer in the United Kingdom. The proposal for identifying deputies as accounting officers has also captured the attention of the new government of Stephen Harper, which has included the proposal (with some adjustments) in legislation seeking to make government more accountable through a set of reforms.[30]

The various proposals for adjusting the convention of ministerial responsibility to make deputy ministers more directly accountable are well-intentioned and respond to disappointments with the operation of the convention. Nevertheless, these proposals may not be without their own problems. Some critics of such proposals suggest that the deputies, like ministers, can hardly "be expected, in this day and age, to meet impossible standards of knowledge of internal departmental doings."[31] Another concern is that the proposal relies on being able to make clear distinctions between policy and administrative matters—the former belong to the minister, the latter to the deputy—yet this kind of distinction is difficult to make. In fact, in light of the competitive situation in Canadian politics, one might expect any administrative wrongdoing to elevate quite quickly into a political issue. Still another concern is that the proposal weakens the major attraction of the convention of ministerial responsibility, which is its ability to place the locus of responsibility clearly on the shoulders of one individual. With the proposal, we now have two people who are responsible, an arrangement that opens up the possibility of each shifting responsibility—and blame—to the other. As well, there is the possible effect on the public service. "With direct public service accountability to Parliament, public servants could be chastised by parliamentary committees, with all proceedings captured in an official transcript that is publicly available.... There is obviously the potential for public servants, and the public service in general, to suffer harm in this process."[32] The proposal also assumes that the solution to greater accountability lies in tweaking the "bargain" between minister and public servant. But for some the world of public administration has become a much more crowded place, in which both minister and public servant have had to make room for a host of other relations involving media, public opinion, other ministers, and the prime minister.[33] In other words, the achievement of truly accountable government relies on the successful interactions between the minister and the growing multitude of actors in the political process.

Another proposal for reform is more a plea to look more closely at the doctrine of individual ministerial responsibility in order to see that the minister is accountable for some administrative actions. This follows from the belief that we too easily allow ministers to escape any responsibility for administrative foul-ups or wrongdoing. After an examination of various attempts to define individual ministerial responsibility, Justice Gomery of the Commission of Inquiry into the Sponsorship Program and Advertising Activities argued that all ministers have the duty to "give attention to policy and program implementation and, in concert with the Deputy Minister, to be assured that adequate means to deliver government policies are in place."[34] This means that mistakes in administration may arise from the failure of the minister to carry out his or her duties in relation to the implementation of programs. If it is accepted that ministerial acceptance of blame arises from instances in which the minister has some personal involvement, it might be accepted that errors in administration require the resignation of the minister. At a minimum, it demands an examination of whether the mismanagement does indeed flow from the shortcomings of the minister in setting up the appropriate administrative framework for the implementation of departmental policies and programs.

This line of thinking brings us back to past beliefs that the minister is responsible for virtually everything that takes place within the department. We have shown that many believe this understanding to be unreasonable and inconsistent with the true meaning of individual ministerial responsibility. But the belief that ministers should assume more responsibility for administrative wrongdoings has taken on new life because of the sponsorship scandal. It seemed much too easy for ministers who headed the department that administered the sponsorship program to escape any serious consequences by simply promising to take the appropriate corrective action. What this suggests is that we should make sure the grounds for ministerial resignation—which are the direct personal involvement of the minister—are not present in cases of mismanagement and misadministration. It is also a healthy reminder that ministers are indeed responsible for all that takes place within their department, and that ministers cannot evade this responsibility by delegating or transferring it to appointed officials. Testimony given by the former head of the Privy Council Office at the Commission of Inquiry into the Sponsorship Program and Advertising Activities is telling on this point:

> **Mr. Himmelfarb:** Now, it is true…that in a large department, a complex department, a minister cannot possibly be expected to know all the details, nor is anyone implying that they would, but they can't expect to know all the details or all the aspects of a program, and the style of ministers and their relationship with deputies varies extraordinarily. There is a lot of flexibility. There are some active ministers that one might describe as micromanagers, positively or negatively, depending on one's view, who are much more actively on top of the details and others who trust much more the public service to do that. In a sense, that is a shared accountability and the public service has to—that, by the way, does not in any way diminish the accountability of the elected official. It is non-delegatable.
> **The Commissioner:** If he chooses not to micromanage, he nevertheless remains responsible?
> **Mr. Himmelfarb:** Exactly so. Exactly so, Commissioner.[35]

An Independent Civil Service

The discussion of relations between appointed officials and the legislature leads to an interesting and controversial issue: whether the public service should be seen in some instances as an independent branch of government. The prevailing belief is that public servants have only one commitment, and that is to serve the minister and the interests of government in power. But the proposal for turning the deputy minister into an accounting officer, for example, suggests that public servant may have a commitment that goes beyond the minister. The operation of the sponsorship program proves instructive on this point. An official with the Department of Public Works and Government Services, the agency responsible for the sponsorship program, felt that the administration of the program amounted to an illegal activity, and looked for an opportunity to report this matter to someone outside the department and the executive branch. This last occurrence and similar ones have led the federal government to pass legislation that supports public servants in the reporting of administrative wrongdoings ("blowing the whistle") to an independent agency. All of these developments appear to point to the conclusion that the bureaucracy has in some circumstances an obligation that competes with its loyalty to the minister and the government in power. When the law is broken or when the actions of government put in peril the health or safety of persons (including public servants), appointed officials are obliged to act in the public interest and divulge these unwelcome events. The fact that such divulgences may harm the government is unimportant. Sossin discusses the important implication of this line of reasoning:

> The conventional view is that the civil service has no constitutional identity apart from the government it is serving at the time. … I suggest an alternative view, one that sees the constitutional identity of the Crown as constituted by both a political executive and the civil service as *independent* and interdependent components.[36]

The quote suggests that the interdependent nature of the relationship between the civil service and government remains intact. But added to this relationship is the notion that the bureaucracy is also independent from the political executive. For constitutional support of this claim, it might be argued that inherent in the convention of political neutrality is the contention that appointed officials in some instances must have the ability to act in a way that may be contrary to the wishes—the political wishes—of the government in power.

Conclusion

This chapter has examined the relations between the legislative branch and appointed officials, and how the attempt of parliamentarians to keep the public service accountable is largely shaped by conventions and understandings. We have seen that the doctrine of individual ministerial responsibility has been central to the successful operation of parliamentary government, but that changes to this convention may be necessary to keep up with the demands for greater accountability in government. However, we have seen that this is a delicate exercise, and it may result in a loss of the traditional benefits of individual ministerial responsibility without any consequential gains. The attempt to make this convention more workable represents one of the biggest challenges for those interested in sound public administration in Canada.

Notes

1. Donald J. Savoie, *Breaking the Bargain: Public Servants, Ministers and Parliament* (Toronto: University of Toronto Press, 2003), 3.

2. Interpreted broadly and including the convention of public service anonymity, political neutrality entails the separation of administration from politics and policy; the selection and promotion of public servants on the basis of merit rather than partisanship; the avoidance by public servants of partisan political activity and the public expression of personal views on government actions; the provision by public servants of confidential advice to their ministers; ministerial protection of public service anonymity; and the loyal implementation of government decisions by public servants, regardless of their personal views.

3. Peter Aucoin, Jennifer Smith, and Geoff Dinsdale, *Responsible Government: Clarifying Essentials, Dispelling Myths and Exploring Change* (Ottawa: Canadian Centre for Management, 2004), 37.

4. Standing Committee on Public Accounts, House of Commons, *Governance in the Public Service of Canada: Ministerial and Deputy Ministerial Accountability*, May 2005, [about 19 screens down]. Available at the Parliament of Canada site www.parl.gc.ca/infocomdoc/38/1/parlbus/commbus/house/PACP/report/RP1812721/PACP_Rpt10/PACP_Rpt10-e.pdf. Retrieved July 10, 2006.

5. Government of Canada, *Accountable Government: A Guide for Ministers* (Ottawa: Her Majesty in Right of Canada, 2006), 5–6. Available at the Government of Canada site, http://pm.gc.ca/grfx/docs/guide_e.pdf. Retrieved July 10, 2006.

6. Aucoin, Smith, and Dinsdale, *Responsible Government*, 32.

7. The following provides a brief summary of these resignations: "Scandalography," *National Post*, June 20, 2005, AL8.

8. House of Commons, *Debates*, February 6, 1978, 567.

9. Brian Chapman, *British Government Observed* (London: George Allen and Unwin, 1963), 38.

10. Aucoin, Smith, and Dinsdale, *Responsible Government*, 39.

11. Bruce Wallace, "Money to the Wind," *Maclean's*, February 7, 2000. Available at www.macleans.ca/topstories/canada/article.jsp?content=30065. Retrieved July 10, 2006.

12. Aucoin, Smith and Dinsdale, Responsible government, 38–39.

13. Paul G. Thomas, "The Past, Present and Future of Officers of Parliament," *Canadian Public Administration* 46(3) (fall): 288.

14. Ibid., 293.

15. Home page, October 4, 2003, Office of the Information Commissioner site, www.infocom.gc.ca/menu-e.asp. Accessed July 10, 2006.

16. Editorial, "Another Toothless Watchdog," *National Post*, June 18, 2005, A16.

17. "Our Mandate," Canadian Human Rights Commission site, www.chrc-ccdp.ca/about/mandate-en.asp. Accessed July 10, 2006.

18. Thomas, "The Past, Present and Future of Officers of Parliament," 295.

19. Ibid.

20. Other types of committees are the joint committees with both Senate and House of Commons membership, the Liaison Committee (committee of all the chairs of standing committees), and the Committee of the Whole (the House of Commons sitting as a committee). For more information on parliamentary committees, see "Types of Committees," the Parliament of Canada site, May 12, 2006, www.parl.gc.ca/compendium/web-content/c_g_committees-e.htm#2. Retrieved July 10, 2006.

21. Parliamentary Centre, *Backgrounder*, October 2004, 5. (emphasis in original.)

22. Government of Canada, *Ethics, Responsibility and Accountability: An Action Plan for Democratic Reform* (Ottawa: Her Majesty the Queen in Right of Canada, 2004).

23. Quoted in Standing Committee on Public Accounts, House of Commons, *Governance in the Public Service of Canada: Ministerial and Deputy Ministerial Accountability*, May 2005, [17].

24. These are in fact the words of a parliamentary committee paraphrasing the intent of the commission. See ibid., [18].

25. Quoted in ibid., [19].

26. Aucoin, Smith, and Dinsdale, *Responsible Government*, 41–42.

27. Ibid., [3]. Also see C.E.S. Franks, "Putting Responsibility and Accountability Back into the System of Government," *Policy Options*, October 2004, 64.

28. Ibid., [20].

29. Ibid., [21].

30. Government of Canada, *Federal Accountability Action Plan: Turning a New Leaf* (Ottawa: Her Majesty the Queen in Right of Canada, 2006), 30–31. Available at Government of Canada site, www.faa-lfi.gc.ca/docs/ap-pa/ap-pa_e.pdf. Retrieved July 10, 2006.

31. Aucoin, Smith, and Dinsdale, *Responsible Government*, 40.

32. Ibid., 78.

33. David E. Smith, "Clarifying the Doctrine of Ministerial Responsibility As It Applies to the Government and Parliament of Canada," in Commission of Inquiry into the Sponsorship Program & Advertising Activities, *Restoring Accountability: Research Studies, Volume 1: Parliament, Ministers and Deputy Ministers* (Ottawa: Her Majesty in Right of Canada, 2006), 117.

34. Commission of Inquiry into the Sponsorship Program and Advertising Activities, *Who Is Responsible? Fact Finding Report* (Ottawa: Her Majesty the Queen in Right of Canada, 2005), 39.

35. Ibid., 36.

36. Lorne Sossin, "Speaking Truth to Power? The Search for Bureaucratic Independence in Canada," *University of Toronto Law Journal* 55(1) (winter 2005): 15–16. Emphasis added.

14

The Judiciary and the Bureaucracy

The interactions of public servants with the political process extend beyond the legislative and executive branches of government, for they also include relations with the third branch of government, the judiciary. These relations revolve around an attempt by the judiciary or the courts to make sure that appointed officials are functioning within the confines of the law. In carrying out their duties, public servants have to observe legal rules governing procedure, jurisdiction, and respect for individual rights and freedoms. When this fails to happen, courts may be asked to intervene in order to address an administrative wrong. An aggrieved citizen may apply to the courts for relief because a government agency denied her an opportunity to make her case for a particular public benefit. A corporation might also seek to quash a government search of its premises on grounds that the search violates a provision of the Canadian Charter of Rights and Freedoms. A multitude of situations dealing with the administration of government programs and policies can precipitate relations between the courts and the permanent executive.

The intent of this chapter is to investigate that part of the political process which deals with public servants and the courts. The chapter outlines the structure of the Canadian judiciary and discusses how a body of law—administrative law—has arisen to shape judicial review of bureaucratic actions. The chapter also makes clear the grounds for court action in relation to the administration of public servants and the various remedies to violations of administrative law.

The Canadian Judiciary

Unlike the executive and legislative branches of government, which are integrally linked, the judiciary is independent from the others. The independence of judges is considered crucial to the impartial or unbiased administration of justice. Without this separation, the courts would be vulnerable to political pressures emanating from the other branches and find themselves unable to carry out the unbiased adjudication of disputes about the law. Various measures, including tenure in office for judges during good behaviour, are used to guarantee that judges remain independent.

The structure of the judicial system in Canada is shown in Figure 14.1. This structure is determined by the *Constitution Act of 1867*, which provides for federal and provincial courts, but permits cases to be appealed from provincial to federal courts. Section 101 of the act authorizes the Parliament of Canada to establish a court of appeal for the entire country and any other courts required for the "better administration of Canadian laws." This is the legal foundation for the federal courts. As for the provincial courts, Section 92 (14) grants the provinces exclusive authority over the administration of justice in the provinces, "including the Constitution, Maintenance, and Operation of Provincial Courts, both of Civil and Criminal Jurisdiction, and including procedure in Civil Matters in those Courts." But 91 (27) of the Act confers on the federal Parliament exclusive jurisdiction over criminal procedures, and Sections 96, 99, and 100 give the federal government power over the appointment, salaries, and removal of all judges found in the upper tier of provincial courts. Clearly, the drafters of the Constitution wished the two levels of government to act together in the administration of justice.

The names of the courts in the provinces vary, but the structure is basically the same. In the upper tier of the provincial court system in each province is a superior court that, depending on the province, bears the name of Supreme Court, Superior Court, or High

Figure 14.1 — Structure of the Canadian Court System

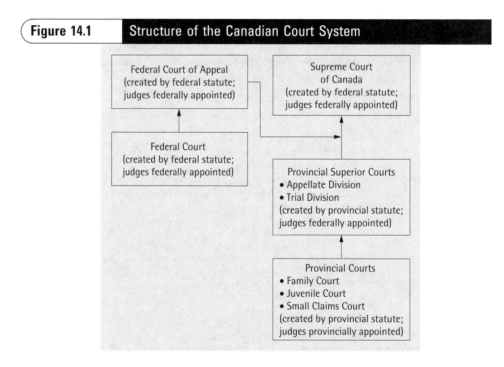

Source: *An Introduction to Government and Politics: A Conceptual Approach,* 7th Edition by DICKERSON/FLANAGAN. © 2006. Reprinted with permission of Nelson, a division of Thomson Learning: www.thomsonrights.com.

Court. As the figure shows, the court has both trial and appellate divisions that consider cases arising out of federal, provincial, or constitutional laws (and in some provinces the divisions are two separate courts). They also hear appeals from the lower provincial courts. The lower tier of the system encompasses courts usually referred to as the "provincial courts." These courts handle such matters as minor criminal acts, juvenile offences, family problems, and small claims. The provinces have the authority to appoint justices to these courts.

The major federal courts are the Federal Court, the Federal Court of Appeal, and the Supreme Court of Canada. The Supreme Court, the highest court in the land, hears appeals from the other federal courts and the superior provincial courts. It also considers questions of law referred to it by the federal cabinet when there is some doubt about the legality of a legislative enactment. This expansive jurisdiction of the Supreme Court makes it really a "national" court and not a federal one.[1]

The two other prominent federal courts are central to the study of administration and law, and figure prominently in the study and practice of administrative law. (A less prominent federal court is the Tax Court of Canada, whose jurisdiction largely concerns considering income tax appears.) The Federal Court has jurisdiction to first hear cases involving claims made against the federal government and decisions of most federal boards, commissions, and other regulatory bodies. In other words, it is set up primarily to adjudicate disputes about how appointed officials at the federal level carry out and implement laws and regulations. The Federal Court of Appeal considers appeals from the decisions of the Federal Court and has exclusive jurisdiction to review the decisions of select federal tribunals. These two courts are unique in the sense that they are established to hear matters relating only to federal law.

Judicial Review of Administrative Action: The Focus on Agencies

The role of courts in relation to public administration is to review the actions and decisions of appointed officials. Judicial decisions in this area have led to a body of **administrative law**, which "deals with the legal limitations on the actions of government officials, and on the remedies which are available to anyone affected by a transgression of these limits."[2] This definition of administrative law tells us that judicial review can lead to concrete actions that can reverse or nullify the behaviour of public officials. A court may nullify the decision of a regulatory agency to deny a licence to a radio station or rule against a government body responsible for the administration of pension benefits.

Historically, judicial review of administrative action and the accompanying body of administrative law have received relatively little attention from students of public administration. But interest in this area has increased substantially in the past three decades. This development was partly due to the recognition of the extensive regulatory and adjudicative powers now exercised by administrative officials. As Gall writes, "there has been a proliferation of legislation at both the federal and provincial levels of government delegating authority to ... tribunals composed of persons possessing expertise in particular areas to set policy and render decisions accordingly."[3] These tribunals—as will be shown—represented the major concerns of courts when it came to administrative law. A further stimulus for increased interest in administrative law was the creation in 1970 of the Federal Court of Canada (now divided into two courts) and the court's review of administrative behaviour. The establishment of this court meant that there was now a judicial body set up specifically to deal with administrative law.

Judicial review of administrative action can apply to any government form that is perceived to be in violation of principles of administrative law. Appointed officials located in departments, Crown corporations, independent regulatory agencies, and any other agency are vulnerable to court action. But typically the focus of administrative

Chapter 14 / The Judiciary and the Bureaucracy

law is on nondepartmental structures that are given a degree of independence unavailable to most departments and that address regulatory matters. In other words, judicial review concentrates on independent regulatory agencies or what administrative law often refers to as "tribunals." The presence of this heightened degree of independence from direct ministerial control makes judicial review especially important with respect to regulatory agencies; the fact that regulatory agencies are often obliged to follow a due process of rules and procedures also makes them worthy of consideration by the courts. Included among these tribunals are those that perform centrally important and politically sensitive regulatory functions, such as the National Energy Board, and those that play a specialized adjudicative role bearing on individual rights, such as the Immigration and Refugee Board.

Discretionary Powers

The importance of judicial review and other means of control over administrative action arise largely from the exercise of discretionary powers by public officials. Discretionary powers "are those which involve an element of judgement of choice by persons exercising them and comprise all government functions from fact finding to setting standards."[4] Public servants exercise a striking number and variety of discretionary powers under delegated legislative authority. Most of these powers are delegated to cabinet, but they are also conferred on ministers and individual officials and on various departments and tribunals. With the prominence of discretionary powers comes the greater possibility of actions that contravene laws of administration. A regulatory agency may make a decision that violates rules of procedural fairness, or act without the necessary legislative authority. Yet there are good reasons for discretion. A minister could hardly find time to decide upon every application for a licence or to ensure that environmental standards are being properly observed. The desire to put more decision-making authority in the hands of experts also explains the acceptance of giving officials choice in the administration of government affairs; elected officials understand that the complexities of government require that knowledgeable appointed officials be given the opportunity to grapple with the challenges of governance. The same desire for discretion also reflects the need to shape the actions of government to serve the differing demands of individual citizens.

Review and Appeal

The authority of the court to undertake a review of administrative behaviour and decisions follows from their inherent capacity to rule upon the legality of government actions. Societies based on the rule of law recognize the need for bodies that can address claims of improper behaviour on the part of appointed officials:

> Judicial review deals with the right of an individual to apply to a court to review the actions and decisions of administrative tribunals. This right originates from the basic legal principle known as the "Rule of Law." It recognizes the right of every individual to apply to the courts to ensure that an administrative tribunal's authority to act is set out in legislation and that the administrative tribunal stays within the limits of authority that are granted to it by the legislation.[5]

The review authority of the courts can also be found in laws and statutes that specifically state that the action of a certain tribunal or agency may be reviewed by the courts. Statutory enactments may in addition allow for an "appeal" of a decision to a judicial body. By appeal, we mean expanding the scope of judicial review to a consideration of the merits of the decision or whether the action in question was reasonable. Federal legislation, for instance, might provide individual Canadians with the right to appeal an assessment of their tax returns to a tax court. This is different from judicial review, which relates largely to procedural matters, errors in law, and absence of appropriate jurisdiction—and not an examination of the merits or correctness of the decisions. What is important here is that the inherent right of judicial review does not extend to an appeal to the courts. Without the appropriate statutory or legislative provision for an appeal, the courts will remain reluctant to consider claims about the reasonableness of an administrative action: "Unlike judicial review of administrative action, the general rule is that no appeal exists unless specifically provided for by statute."[6]

Classification of Function

A central issue with respect to judicial review of administrative discretion has traditionally been the *classification* of the function being performed by the tribunal or other type of government organization. The functions are "judicial," "quasi-judicial," and "administrative." The nature of the function being exercised is important in deciding whether and on what grounds the courts will grant relief. Though there is a distinction between judicial and quasi-judicial—the latter involves some discretion and the former none—historically the courts have used the terms interchangeably, because the rules of natural justice apply to both and because each directly affects the rights of a person. The more important distinction is between the administrative and the quasi-judicial or judicial functions. If the function affects individual rights and is based on law, it is considered quasi-judicial or judicial; if the function is without effect on rights and emerges out of a policy decision, it is thought to be administrative in nature.

Until recently, the courts usually reviewed the exercise of a judicial or quasi-judicial function, but not of an administrative function. In other words, there are limits to the application of administrative law. However, this distinction has become significantly less important. The courts now see themselves as capable of considering all three functions. This development might seem to mean at first glance that the reach of administrative law extends to all actions of government, in light of the fact that all government decision-making includes an element of administration. However, this perception exaggerates the implication of applying administrative law to administrative functions. Policy and legislative decisions whose purpose carries right across the country or province and are without application to individual persons, groups, or corporate entities are usually considered beyond the reach of administrative law and the courts. Thus, administrative law and its grounds for judicial review could not be used against government decision making that led to new federal–provincial fiscal arrangements or international trade agreements. Alternatively, a decision to deny a radio licence or refuse compensation for an alleged workplace injury would be fair game for court action.

Grounds for Review

A key aspect of the role of the courts in public administration is the set of reasons or grounds for pursuing judicial review of the actions of appointed officials. Statutes or written laws may provide citizens with an opportunity for courts to consider their concerns. In the absence of such legislation, a person may rely upon common law or judge-made grounds for challenging administrative action. The advent of the Canadian Charter of Rights and Freedoms has supplied a further basis—violation of a protected right or freedom—for gaining access to the courts. Accordingly, then, outside of ordinary statutory law, there are four grounds which can be used to review the legality of an administrative action:

- Breach of rules of natural justice
- Acting outside the jurisdiction conferred by the law by exceeding its powers, abusing its powers, or committing errors of procedure

- Making errors of law
- Violating provisions contained in the Canadian Charter of Rights and Freedoms

Natural Justice

The two fundamental principles of natural justice are, as expressed in Latin, *Audi alteram partem* (Hear the other side) and *Nemo judex in sua causa debet esse* (No one should be a judge in his or her own cause). The *audi alteram partem* principle encompasses the notions that a party whose rights might be affected should have the following:

- Adequate notice of the allegations against him or her and of the tribunal's intention to make a decision and knowledge of the case to be made against him or her
- The right to be heard, specifically to present proofs and arguments
- The right to cross-examine witnesses and sometimes the right to legal representation
- The right to an adjournment for a reasonable period of time to allow for preparation of his or her case

In the case of *Suresh v. Canada (Minister of Citizenship & Immigration)*, the Minister of Citizenship and Immigration refused, among other things, to disclose information used to support the deportation of Mr. Suresh.[7] The Supreme Court ruled that the minister had to make available to Suresh all information that she had about his case. The decision accorded with an element of natural justice, which states that "a fair hearing can only be had if the parties affected by the tribunal's decision know the case to be made against them."[8] Interestingly, in a companion case, the Supreme Court decided that full disclosure was unnecessary because the individual had failed—unlike Suresh—to show that he would suffer torture upon being sent home.[9] The two cases reveal an important point about judicial review and natural justice, namely that the *audi alteram partem* principle depends on the circumstances of the case.

According to the *nemo judex in sua causa* principle, all forms of bias should be excluded from the proceedings and decisions of tribunals. The courts may intervene if there is evident a "reasonable apprehension" of bias, and this may arise from such factors as kinship, friendship, or business relations with a party to the proceedings, hearing appeals from one's own decisions, or manifesting undue hostility toward one of the parties. In the leading case on bias, parties expressed concern that the Chair of the National Energy Board might be unable to act in a disinterested fashion during hearings that included a consortium with which the chair had been formerly involved.[10] In a split decision, the Supreme Court of Canada found against the National Energy Board; but, interestingly, it was a dissenting judge who articulated the "reasonable apprehension" test that would guide the courts when dealing with bias. The test itself simply asks what an informed person would decide after having considered thoroughly the claim of bias. Recently, in the midst of the proceedings of the commission of inquiry looking into the sponsorship program, lawyers for former prime minister Jean Chrétien sought through the courts the removal of the inquiry's commissioner on grounds of bias. The commissioner had stated, during inquiry proceedings, that the evidence suggested "a conspiracy of silence" in the Chrétien government over the events surrounding the investigation of the sponsorship program.[11] Counsel for Mr. Chrétien believed that this comment (and earlier ones as well) indicated that the commissioner was biased against their client and could not objectively assess the facts. The former prime minister eventually withdrew his claim against the commissioner, but then launched a new suit after the release of the first report of the commission of inquiry in November of 2005.

The two principles of natural justice explained above have traditionally applied only to tribunals exercising judicial or quasi-judicial functions, not to those exercising administrative functions. However, in several decisions over the past few decades, the Supreme Court of Canada has developed a new doctrine of "fairness" that effectively allows for the extension of the rules of natural justice to tribunals whose functions are classified as administrative. The key case in this development was *Nicholson v. Haldimand-Norfolk Regional Board of Commissioners of Police*, in which a probationary constable was dismissed without reasons given or an opportunity to respond to those reasons. Even though the Board of Commissioners was exercising an administrative function, the Supreme Court decided that a duty of fairness required that reasons be given and that Nicholson be offered a chance to defend his position.[12]

Ultra Vires

The Latin phrase *ultra vires*, which means "beyond the power," represents a second ground for legal challenges of administrative actions. The courts will generally intervene and grant relief where a tribunal has acted outside the scope of authority bestowed on it by its governing statute. Where there has been an excess of powers, the courts have found all types of decisions ultra vires, whether judicial, quasi-judicial, or administrative. Indeed, excess of powers is the primary ground for judicial review. To take a hypothetical and extreme example, the action of a pension tribunal in granting a driver's licence would be declared ultra vires. The determination of whether there has been an excess of powers obliges the courts to examine the enabling statute very carefully to see if Parliament has empowered the tribunal to act in a certain situation. In *Bell v. Ontario*, the Ontario Human Rights Commission had acted upon a complaint concerning discrimination in a rental housing unit.[13] The Supreme Court ruled that the authority of the Commission authorized it to deal only with a certain kind of housing unit—but the unit in this case failed to fit into this category. Accordingly, the court stopped any action against the alleged discrimination.

Another aspect of this second ground, that of *errors of procedure*, also requires that the courts look to the enabling statute. Parliament may specify that a tribunal exercise its powers according to specific procedures. We have already seen that on grounds of natural justice the courts may require tribunals performing judicial or quasi-judicial functions to follow certain rules of procedure. Regardless of natural justice principles, the courts will insist that tribunals follow the procedural rules set out in the statute; otherwise, the decision stemming from errors of procedure will be declared ultra vires.

An *abuse of power* occurs when a tribunal uses its power for a purpose not authorized by Parliament under the enabling statute. Thus, in considering whether there has been an abuse of power, and consequently whether a decision is ultra vires, the courts tend to look beyond the enabling statute to examine Parliament's intent. Abuse of power is usually expressed in terms of discretion exercised by a tribunal for ulterior purposes, in bad faith, or on irrelevant grounds. In the celebrated case *Roncarelli v. Duplessis*, the Supreme Court of Canada found abuse of power when the attorney general (who was also the premier) of Quebec directed a licensing commission to cancel a tavern owner's liquor permit because he had acted as bondsperson for persons accused of distributing allegedly seditious literature. The commission's decision was declared to be beyond its powers, and Justice Rand stated:

> In public regulation of this sort there is no such thing as untrammelled "discretion," that is, that action can be taken on any ground or for any reason that can be suggested to the mind of the administrator; no legislative act can, without express language, be taken to contemplate an unlimited arbitrary power exercisable for any person, however capricious or irrelevant, regardless of the nature or purpose of the statute. ... "Discretion" necessarily implies good faith in discharging public duty; there is always a perspective within which a statute is intended to

operate; any clear departure from its line or objects is just as objectionable as fraud or corruption.[14]

Errors of Law

The courts may also review the decisions of tribunals for errors of law on the face of the record. The "record" for this purpose includes not only the formal decision but also the reasons for the decision, documents initiating the proceedings, documents on which the decision is based, and documents cited in the reasons for the decision. The words "on the face of the record" indicate that the courts will not review a decision unless the error is apparent.

Forms of Relief

We turn now to a consideration of the common-law or ancillary remedies that the courts may use after the grounds for judicial review have been established. Statutory or direct remedies, namely appeal and review procedures provided by statute, are sometimes available, but the common-law remedies are employed when no other form of relief is available, convenient, or effective:

- The most frequently used writs in Canada are certiorari and prohibition. *Certiorari* is a writ issued by a superior court to quash a decision already taken by an inferior tribunal, whereas *prohibition* is a writ to restrain a tribunal from taking a certain action.
- *Mandamus* is a writ used to compel an inferior tribunal to exercise the authority conferred on it by statute. Unlike certiorari and prohibition, this writ is not restricted to tribunals exercising a judicial or quasi-judicial function. To obtain the writ of mandamus, an affected party must show that the tribunal is authorized or required to perform a certain duty, that it has been asked to perform that duty, and that it has refused to perform the duty.
- *Habeas corpus* is used to require that a person who has been detained be brought before a court for the purpose of determining whether the detention is legal. This writ is not used much in the sphere of administrative law. It is normally restricted to immigration cases, where it is often used to challenge orders for custody or deportation.
- *Quo warranto* is a writ used to inquire into whether an appointment to a public office established by statute is legal. Its use has in large measure been made unnecessary by statutory provisions relating to appointments to public office.
- An *injunction* is a remedy that requires an inferior tribunal to take a particular action or, more commonly, to refrain from taking some specified action beyond its powers. An injunction is generally available only if an equally effective alternative remedy is not available. It can be used against tribunals exercising administrative, as well as judicial or quasi-judicial, functions.
- An *action for declaration* (or *declaratory judgment*) asks the court to declare and define whether some act taken or proposed by a tribunal is beyond its powers. Like an injunction, a declaration is available for administrative as well as judicial or quasi-judicial decisions. Actions for declaration are infrequent. Moreover, they are normally combined with requests for other forms of relief, notably injunctions.
- *Damages* is a remedy that requires that a certain amount of money be paid to compensate for an injury or wrong done to an individual. Tribunals, like ordinary citizens, are liable to an action for damages. Obviously, the remedy of damages is most useful in situations where the tribunal has already taken some action or decision. A remedy like certiorari that simply quashes the original decision would be of little help once the harm has been done. The remedy of damages is available for administrative as well as judicial and quasi-judicial functions. Damages were awarded

against the attorney general (and premier) of Quebec in the case of *Roncarelli v. Duplessis* mentioned earlier.

Privative Clauses

The courts clearly have the authority and grounds to review administrative action and to apply the appropriate remedies. But equally clear is the power of the legislative authority through the doctrine of parliamentary sovereignty to restrict the actions of judicial bodies. With a view to allowing administrative tribunals to operate efficiently and quickly, Parliament and the provincial legislatures have used this power to enact **privative clauses** to deprive courts of the power to undertake reviews of administrative action. Sometimes the clauses take the form of straightforward provisions that specifically state that no judicial review shall take place. Other times the effect is achieved through such a wide grant of power that the grounds for any kind of judicial review fall away. Here is how a private clause might be worded that seeks to explicitly deny the possibility of judicial review of an administrative action:

> No decision, order, direction, declaration, or ruling of the tribunal shall be questioned or reviewed in any court, and no order shall be made or proceedings taken in any court, whether by way of injunction, declaratory judgment, certiorari, mandamus, prohibition, or quo warranto, or otherwise to question, review, prohibit, or restrain the tribunal or any of its proceedings.

Until the late 1970s, Canadian courts generally gave little effect to privative clauses because of the belief that the courts should exercise their inherent supervisory jurisdiction over inferior tribunals if these made unreasonable decisions. Since that time, however, the courts have paid more heed to privative clauses as part of a growing confidence in the role of tribunals:

> Traditionally, the courts often intervened and substituted their opinion for the opinion of the administrative tribunal. In contrast, the more recent trend is for the courts to "defer" or respect the decision of the administrative tribunal especially dealing with matters where the courts recognize that the administrative tribunal has more expertise.[15]

The increasing deference of the courts, however, fails to extend to a complete acceptance of privative clauses. Judicial bodies may ignore them if a tribunal "is obviously in excess of its jurisdiction" or when its actions are 'patently unreasonable'...[16]

Canadian Charter of Rights and Freedoms

The Canadian Charter of Rights and Freedoms, which came into force in 1982, has had a significant effect on the role of the courts in public administration. Prior to the Charter, judicial review of administrative relied on rules limited to issues of procedural fairness, appropriate jurisdiction, and errors of law. Also important, these were rules legislative authorities could seek to nullify through privative clauses and other statutory enactments. The Charter enlarged the reach of administrative law to include the rights and freedoms contained within it and gave a constitutional basis to important aspects of administrative law; no longer, for example, could elected officials deny rules of natural justice, because they were now entrenched in a constitutional document. Judicial review of administrative action had lived in the shadow of parliamentary supremacy and the authority of the legislature to make or remake any laws it wished. Now the Charter has ushered in a new era that gives the courts a final say.

The Charter has already had a considerable effect on the working lives of public servants at all levels of government. Many decisions, especially in the lower courts, have greatly affected public servants' day-to-day work, particularly those in the area of criminal justice. Police officers, for example, must be aware of a person's right to be informed of his or her right to counsel, and they have to be careful about how they conduct their searches and detain individuals suspected of illegal action. The Charter has also forced governments in Canada to engage in "Charter-proofing" exercises in order to protect both existing and proposed legislation from constitutional challenges. The federal Department of Justice, for instance, has examined statutes "to forestall litigation by identifying and removing provisions that might violate the Charter." It has also supported new legal units within departments that seek to defend new policies and programs against a Charter challenge.[17] The efforts of the justice department have been quite successful in limiting Charter challenges in recent years, but this, too, reveals the influence of the Charter, for now the formulation and implementation of government policy is heavily shaped by the Charter and its interpreters in the courts. In some respects, this last effect on relations between the judiciary and government officials in the executive sphere is unsettling, because the courts may be without the expertise to have such a significant impact on public policy. The more important point for students of public administration, however, is the increasing significance of interactions—both direct and indirect—between public servants and the courts.

Many sections of the Charter are pertinent for administrative law, but Sections 7, 8, and 15 have an especially important effect on the conduct of public administration. Section 7, on legal rights, provides in part that "[e]veryone has the right to life, liberty and security of the person and the right not to be deprived thereof except in accordance with the principles of fundamental justice." In the *Singh* case, the Supreme Court held that it was a breach of "the principles of fundamental justice" not to provide an oral hearing to refugee claimants.[18] Legal scholars have observed that the wording of Section 7 constitutionalizes the procedural aspects of natural justice (or the duty to be fair). The aforementioned case *Suresh* also revolved around a violation of Section 7 and the principles of fundamental justice.

Section 8 provides that "[e]veryone has the right to be secure against unreasonable search and seizure." The enormous potential for the courts to use this section to protect individual rights against government action is demonstrated in the case of Mario Duarte.[19] The issue in the case was whether, under the Charter, the police could legally have an informer record, surreptitiously and without a judicial warrant, his conversation with a suspected drug dealer. The Supreme Court had asserted in previous cases that the primary value served by Section 8 of the Charter is privacy, and in the Duarte case the court came to the defence of personal privacy in the face of increasingly sophisticated surveillance technology. Justice La Forest stated:

> The very efficacy of electronic surveillance is such that it has the potential, if left unregulated, to annihilate any expectation that our communications will remain private. A society which exposed us, at the whim of the state, to the risk of having a permanent electronic recording made every time we opened our mouths might be superbly equipped to fight crime, but it would be one in which privacy no longer had any meaning.[20]

Other important cases have emerged out of Section 8. In *Southam*, the Supreme Court invalidated a government search of the premises of the *Edmonton Journal* because in part the body that issued the search warrant was not a disinterested or unbiased party.[21] In making this decision, the court provided a test for a reasonable search and seizure, which would help guide the courts in future cases dealing with this section of the Charter.

Section 15 provides that "[e]very individual is equal before the law and has the right to the equal protection of the law without discrimination and, in particular, without discrimination based on race, national or ethnic origin, colour, religion, sex, age, or mental or physical disability." There have been a number of legal cases involving this provision of the Charter and the daily work activities of public servants. In the *Little Sisters* case, the Supreme Court addressed the actions of customs officers charged with the duty of determining whether books entering Canada from the United States were obscene. The court held that the officers violated the equality provision by targeting or giving special attention to shipments to a Vancouver bookseller that focused on books for gay and lesbians.[22] In *Eldridge*, the Supreme Court ruled that hospitals which refused to provide sign-language interpreters to patients offended Section 15.[23] In *Halperin v. the Attorney General of Canada et al.*, a City of Toronto clerk declined to issue a civil marriage licence to gay and lesbian couples until she received further direction.[24] This action helped precipitate a challenge of the common-law definition of marriage (union of two people of the opposite sex) and a decision of the Ontario Court of Appeal that found the definition inconsistent with Section 15. This and similar decisions in other provincial courts led to the introduction of a new federal law that defined marriage in a way that provided for same-sex marriages.

Utility of Judicial Review

Even though the importance of judicial review of administrative action has increased substantially as a result of the Charter, judicial review has several deficiencies as a means of preventing and remedying abuses of bureaucratic power. The courts review only a miniscule number of the millions of decisions made annually by administrative authorities; the success rate of litigants is not high; neither the amount of money nor the issue involved is usually significant enough to justify the high cost of the proceedings; and judicial review tends to focus on certain areas of public administration (labour relations, tax assessment, and licensing) so that many other areas are relatively untouched. However, the evidence also suggests that public servants believe that the courts over the past two or three decades have changed the way they function. A quarter of a century ago, appointed officials "rarely thought about the courts as they went about their work," but now federal officials claim the "courts are never far from people's minds when planning departmental activities."[25] As with many other players in the political process, the courts have seemingly made life more complicated for appointed officials and their superiors.

Conclusion

This chapter has shown that relations between the courts and administrative officials represent an important part of Canadian public administration and that it appears this importance is increasing. Public servants must be aware that the political process has become more sympathetic to demands for greater judicial review of administrative actions.

Notes

1. Peter Hogg, *Constitutional Law of Canada*, loose-leaf edition (Toronto: Carswell, current), 7.1(a) or 7.3.

2. David P. Jones and Anne de Villars, *Principles of Administrative Law*, 4th ed. (Toronto: Thomson Carswell, 2004), 3.

3. Gerald Gall, *The Canadian Legal System*, 5th ed. (Toronto: Thomson Carswell, 2004), 540.

4. Law Reform Commission of Canada, *A Catalogue of Discretionary Powers in the Revised Statutes of Canada* (Ottawa: Information Canada, 1975), 2.

5. Lisa Braverman, *Administrative Tribunals: A Legal Handbook* (Aurora: Canada Law Book, Inc., 2001), 89.

6. Jones and de Villars, *Principles of Administrative Law*, 545.

7. 2002 S.C.C. 1, 37, 37 Admin. L. R. (3d) 159 (S.C.C.).

8. Jones and de Villars, *Principles of Administrative Law*, 258–59.

9. Ibid., 260–61. 2002 SCC 2 (S.C.C.).

10. Ibid., 368–71. (1976), [1978] 1 S.C.R. 369 (S.C.C.).

11. Daniel LeBlanc and Tu Thanh Ha, "Chrétien Wants Court to Oust Gomery," *The Globe and Mail*, March 4, 2005, A1, A4.

12. *Nicholson v. Haldimand-Norfolk Police Commrs. Bd.* (1979), 1 S.C.R., 311.

13. Jones and de Villars, *Principles of Administrative Law*, 137.

14. *Roncarelli v. Duplessis* (1959) S.C.R. 121 at 140.

15. Braverman, *Administrative Tribunals*, 92.

16. Robert W. Macaulay and James L.H. Sprague, *Practice and Procedures Before Administrative Tribunals*, loose-leaf edition (Toronto: Thomson Carswell, current), 1–9.

17. Heather MacIvor, *Canadian Politics and Government in the Charter Era* (Toronto: Nelson Thomson, 2006), 185. See also James B. Kelly, *Governing with the Charter: Legislative and Judicial Activism and Framers' Intent* (Vancouver: UBC Press, 2005), ch. 7.

18. *Singh v. Minister of Employment and Immigration* (1985) 17 D.L.R. (4th) 422.

19. *Mario Duarte v. Her Majesty the Queen* (1990) 1 S.C.R. 30.

20. Ibid., 44.

21. [1984] 2 S.C.R. 145 (S.C.C.).

22. *Little Sisters and Art Emporium v. Canada (Minister of Justice)*, [2000] 2 S.C.R. 1120. For more on this case, see MacIvor, *Canadian Politics and Government in the Charter Era*, 192–93.

23. *Eldridge v. British Columbia (Attorney General)*, [1997], 3 S.C.R. 624.

24. *Halperin v. AG Canada et al.* (2003), 225 D.L.R. (4th.) 529.

25. Donald J. Savoie, *Breaking the Bargain: Public Servants, Ministers, and Parliament* (Toronto: University of Toronto Press, 2003), 249.

Intergovernmental Administrative Relations

Relations and interactions between governments in Canada represent an important aspect of the Canadian political system. A few decades ago, an expert on Canadian federalism said with some humorous intent that national security, garbage collection, and the post office appeared to be the only matters that existed outside the boundaries of intergovernmental relations.[1] He was probably closer to the truth than he believed, and now it might be the case that no public issue truly escapes the attention of those engaged in affairs between governments in Canada. The prime minister meets with provincial and territorial counterparts in settings resembling get-togethers of heads of state in order to revolve issues of national importance, and ministers from all kinds of departments at both levels are given responsibility for seemingly everything else. One consequence of this situation is that public servants are necessary to assist elected officials in the management of the Canadian federation. Public administration thus concerns itself with relations not only *within* government, but also *between* governments. Appointed officials are often close by when prime ministers and premiers negotiate the major issues of the day, and ministers depend on their advisors when seeking to formulate policy which concern both federal and provincial governments. Public servants, particularly those who specialize in intergovernmental relations, are also expected to take the lead in sorting out the administrative details of federal–provincial agreements and to address matters whose significance requires the attention of only appointed officials at both levels of government.

This chapter seeks to provide a comprehensive view of intergovernmental administrative relations. It discusses the meaning and evolution of federalism in Canada, and examines some of the key areas of federal–provincial relations. It also provides a close-up view of the machinery that facilitates relations between elected and appointed officials of the different orders of government. An attempt is made as well to reveal the nature of relations between intergovernmental officials and the power they wield in carrying out their responsibilities.

Federalism and Intergovernmental Relations

Federalism may be defined as a political system in which the powers of the state are formally divided between central and regional governments by a written constitution, but in which these governments are linked in an interdependent political relationship.[2] In the Canadian context, this definition captures the enduring legal and constitutional rudiments of Canadian federalism, the politics that pervade the federal system, and the necessity for intergovernmental interaction. Though federalism entails an element of independence in the sense that each level of government is sovereign in its area of responsibility, the fact is that in modern federal states the orders of government tend to be highly interdependent and interactive. Uncertainty over the interpretation of areas of responsibility, the tendency of most policy areas to spill from one area of jurisdiction into another, and the sheer competitive nature of the federal relationship ensure that the two orders of government will interact with each other. There have been attempts to disentangle the two orders of government, but the reality of "shared rule" nearly always prevails.[3]

Broadly interpreted, the term **intergovernmental relations** embraces not only federal–provincial relations but also interprovincial, federal–provincial–territorial, federal–municipal, and provincial–municipal relations. The main emphasis in this chapter is on federal–provincial (and territorial) liaison, but specific reference is made also to the activities of officials involved in interprovincial relations.[4]

Evolution of Federalism

Figure 15.1 depicts the various periods in the evolution of federalism in Canada, differentiated by the distribution of power and influence between the two orders of government. The term **quasi-federalism** characterized the early decades of the Canadian federation during which the federal government dominated the provincial governments, in part by making frequent use of the federal constitutional powers to disallow and

| Figure 15.1 | Evolution of Canadian Federalism |

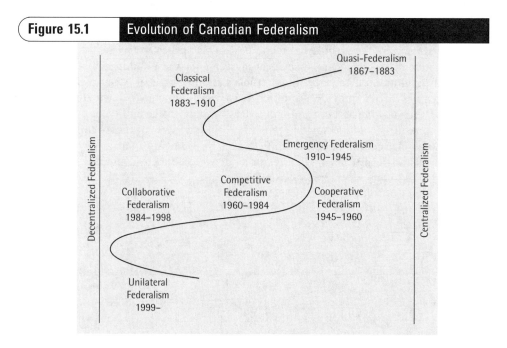

Source: Robert J. Jackson and Doreen Jackson, *Politics in Canada: Culture, Institutions, Behaviour and Public Policy*, 6th ed. (Pearson Education Canada, Inc., 2006), 194. Reprinted with permission by Pearson Education Canada Inc.

reserve provincial legislation. The degree of subordination of provinces to the federal government has led some to call this period "colonial federalism." The next stage was **classical federalism**, which approached K.C. Wheare's celebrated "federal principle," which held that the powers of government are divided "so that the general and regional governments are each, within a sphere, co-ordinate and independent."[5] Between the late 1800s and 1930, with the exception of World War I, provincial powers gradually increased as a result of strong political leadership in certain provinces and judicial decisions favouring the provinces in constitutional disputes with the federal government. Both the federal and provincial governments enjoyed exclusive jurisdiction in certain policy fields, and jurisdictional conflicts were resolved by the courts. Increased federal–provincial consultation was formally recognized by the first federal–provincial conference of first ministers (the prime minister of Canada and the provincial premiers) held in 1906, and federal assistance for the financing of provincial responsibilities began in such areas as transportation and agriculture. The growing importance and expense of the provinces' responsibilities for health, education, and welfare required not only federal subsidies but also a provincial search for new revenues through the use of such forms of taxation as personal and corporate income taxes.

The period of World War I was one of **emergency federalism**. The courts supported the federal government's exercise of broad powers, enshrined in the Constitution, over the economy and over matters of property and civil rights, which, in peacetime, were clearly within provincial jurisdiction. After the war, including the Depression years, the courts resisted the exercise of this emergency power. During World War II, and for a short time afterward, the federal government again used the emergency power to control many matters that were normally within provincial jurisdiction. "There can be little quarrel with Professor Wilfred Eggleston's observation that 'in 1914–19 and again in 1939–45 . . . the emergency provisions of the constitution turned Canada for the time being into a unitary state.'"[6]

It is difficult to pinpoint the precise date when **cooperative federalism** emerged, but Donald Smiley noted in the early 1960s that the development of Canadian federalism since 1945 had been "a process of continuous and piecemeal adjustment between the two levels of government," and that these adjustments had overwhelmingly been made through "interaction between federal and provincial executives" rather than through formal constitutional amendment or judicial interpretation.[7] Under cooperative federalism, the constitutional division of powers was preserved, but federal and provincial ministers and public servants engaged in consultation and coordination to reach joint decisions on policies and programs of mutual concern. However, it was clear during this period of cooperation that the federal government was the senior partner and that intergovernmental relations relied on direction from national authorities.

In the 1960s provincial governments gradually acquired the expertise and influence to deal with the federal government from a stronger position. The Quiet Revolution, which "unleashed a progressive nationalism that transformed Quebec,"[8] helped precipitate this movement toward what came aptly to be known as "competitive federalism."[9] Regional loyalties, especially in western Canada, contributed as well to the increasing combativeness of federal–provincial relations. For the next three decades or so, the two orders of government wrangled over the likes of fiscal transfers to the provinces, the pricing of oil, and amendment of the Constitution. In the early 1990s, the character of federalism in Canada began to change again, partly because of fiscal difficulties at the federal level and partly because of the recognition that some challenging policy issues required the participation and agreement of both orders of government. "Collaborative federalism" led to important agreements between federal and provincial governments in areas such as trade, environment, social policy, and income support for families.[10] What underlay this period was a belief that "national goals are achieved . . . by some or all of the 11 governments and territories acting collectively."[11] Some believe that federalism has most recently assumed a new form, unilateral federalism or "federal unilateralism."[12] With its fiscal problems fixed, the federal government is now better positioned financially to impose new arrangements on the provinces and to even act independently in areas largely provincial. It may be that federalism has turned full circle and returned to its initial stage in which the national government guided and controlled federal–provincial relations.[13]

There is one last development to mention in the evolution of intergovernmental affairs, and that is the efforts of new entities to acquire literally and figuratively a seat at meetings involving the two orders of government. Aboriginal peoples constitute one such entity striving to open up the intergovernmental process. According to Abele and Prince, the inclusion of aboriginal representatives is already taking place: "Participation by Aboriginal organizations in intergovernmental relations is occurring at the federal, provincial/territorial, and federal–provincial–territorial levels; and with political executives and senior public servants."[14] However, it is argued that more needs to be done, that both orders of government should make clear their responsibilities for aboriginal affairs and include aboriginal representatives in the processes and structures integral to intergovernmental relations. Cities represent another entity wishing to break into the intergovernmental process. They "face the challenges of rapid population growth, geographic sprawl, immigrant settlement, and cultural integration," all of which demand a multilevel governance approach in which federal, provincial and urban governments get together to exploit their respective "comparative advantage" to address problems in large metropolitan areas.[15] Moreover, multilevel governance is also better adapted to dealing with the opportunities made possible by the fact that cities are somewhat paradoxically becoming key sites in the newly globalizing world.

Intergovernmental Relations

Intergovernmental relations can be broken down into a series of specific relations shaping areas important to the governing of Canada. Three of the most important areas are those which affect fiscal matters, the Constitution, and policies addressing major public concerns.

Federal–Provincial Fiscal Relations

While federal financial assistance to provincial governments dates to Confederation and was especially important during the Depression, federal–provincial fiscal relations (and now territorial) have been an especially prominent theme in Canadian federalism since World War II. At present, the federal–provincial financial relationship includes four major elements: tax collection agreements, the Canada Health Transfer, the Canada Social Transfer, and Equalization.

The tax collection agreements are an arrangement between the federal government and provinces that allows the federal government to collect both federal and provincial personal taxes (except for Quebec) and corporate taxes (except for Alberta, Ontario, and Quebec), and to remit the provincial portion of the taxes to the provinces. The purpose of this agreement is to provide an administrative convenience to provincial governments, and to limit tax competition between provinces by establishing some uniformity in the method of calculation. In recent years, many provinces have sought to vary the method of calculation in their respective jurisdictions by introducing new tax measures for personal incomes. As Leslie and his colleagues say, the collection agreements "have become increasingly more permissive in terms of accommodating differences among the provinces in how they choose to tax their residents."[16] The result has been to reduce the degree of uniformity in the taxation of personal incomes but also to give the provinces more opportunity to act in a manner more consistent with their individual needs.

| Figure 15.2 | Estimated Federal Transfers to Provinces and Territories, 2005–06 (total $62.7 billion) |

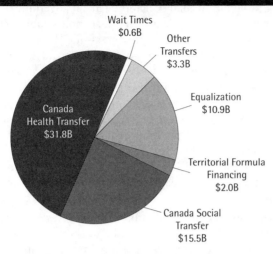

*Both cash and tax transfer components are included. Equalization associated with the tax transfers under CHT/CST is included in both CHT/CST and Equalization. Total has been reduced by $1.3 billion to avoid double-counting.

Source: Finance Canada website at www. fin.gc.ca/Fedprov/ftpte.html. Reproduced with the permission of the Minister of Public Works and Government Services Canada. 2006.

The other three elements of the federal–provincial financial relationship involve transfer payments from the federal government to the provinces and territories. Figure 15.2 depicts the large amounts of federal funding made available under these arrangements.

- The Canada Health Transfer helps establish the foundation for Canada's health care system, called medicare. Under this arrangement, the federal government provides financial assistance to help provinces and territories pay for their health care plans. The assistance takes the form of cash grants and tax points. Cash grants, as the name suggests, are simply transfers of money; tax points are made available by the federal government reducing its tax rates and allowing the provinces to increase their rates by a percentage equal to the federal decrease. The CHT represents a huge transfer of money—estimated at $32 billion in 2005–06—so it is not surprising that the federal government attaches conditions to its health transfers. To be eligible for the transfers, the provincial and territorial health plans must respect the five principles of medicare: universally available to all, comprehensive in its coverage of health care, administered on a nonprofit basis, reasonably accessible to all Canadians and no direct patient fees for insured services, and portable in the sense that citizens remain covered when outside their home province. Failure to observe these principles may result in a withdrawal of federal funding, a possibility that makes the provinces unhappy with the attachment of strings to federal assistance.

- The Canada Social Transfer (CST), which amounted to $15.5 billion in 2005–06, is directed at postsecondary education and social services and assistance. As with the Canada Health Transfer, the CST includes both cash grants and tax points; but unlike the health transfer, very few conditions are attached to this transfer. Indeed, there is only one stipulated condition: that provinces cannot impose residency requirements on persons seeking social assistance or social services. The absence of conditions is explained in part by provincial sensitivity to any federal attempt to influence educational programs in the provinces and the recognition that the administration of social services programs requires much flexibility. The fact that few conditions accompany the CST should not be interpreted to mean that the provinces may do anything they want with the money (including spending it on other areas). Political pressure will often force them to allocate most or even all of the money on services designated by the CST agreement.

- Equalization is a program through which the federal government makes grants to provinces that have a weak tax base and are as a result unable to generate sufficient revenues. Over the years, the recipient provinces—the "have-not" provinces—have been the four Maritime provinces, Quebec, Manitoba, and Saskatchewan; traditionally, only Ontario and the two most westerly provinces have been ineligible for equalization payments. Recently, British Columbia has become a recipient due to a weakening economy, while burgeoning resource revenues have made Saskatchewan ineligible for payments in one of the recent years. The purpose of the program is to allow the have-not provinces to provide adequate public services to their citizens without imposing excessively high taxes (a similar transfer called Territorial Formula Funding is directed at the territories). Given that the program aims to assist provinces in building up all their services means, there is no need for accompanying conditions targeted at any particular program.

This summary may imply a fair amount of stability in fiscal relations between the two levels of government, but this could not be further from the truth. At one time, the tax collection arrangements involved the provinces agreeing not to levy personal and corporate income tax in return for payment from the federal government; now the provinces are on the brink of almost revolutionizing these arrangements. Initially, health arrangements relied on the federal government matching provincial spending on medical and hospital services; health care was then combined with postsecondary education to create a new arrangement, then with postsecondary education and social services, and at present it is by itself in the Canada Health Transfer. As the experience of health care shows, arrangements for postsecondary education and social services have also been quite fluid. And Equalization has as well experienced changes over time, and has most recently experienced a major adjustment in the calculation of annual increases in payments under the program.[17]

Federal–Provincial Constitutional Relations

The impact of federal–provincial relations on the evolution of Canada's constitution is a long and intricate story in which many of the constitutional issues have had an important financial aspect as well. There have, however, been a number of constitutional developments with special relevance for contemporary federal–provincial relations and consequently, for the officials involved in these relations. A series of federal–provincial conferences that began in the 1960s sought agreement on various matters relating to constitutional reform. These efforts were given enormous impetus by the election of the separatist Parti Québécois government in Quebec in 1976 and the 1980 referendum campaign on "sovereignty-association," at which time the federal government promised constitutional change. Also, during the 1970s and early 1980s, intergovernmental tensions were severely exacerbated by sharp disagreements over the ownership of natural resources, especially petroleum, and over the allocation of the revenues flowing from the exploitation of these resources. The dispute raged not only between the federal government and the energy-producing provinces (especially Alberta) but also between these provinces and the energy-consuming provinces (especially Ontario).

For the 1980–81 constitutional meetings, the first ministers agreed upon an agenda containing many contentious items. However, following the failure of the September 1980 meeting of first ministers, and after lengthy debate in the federal Parliament, the provinces were presented in November 1981 with a federal proposal for constitutional change, which all provinces, except Quebec, finally accepted. Agreements were reached on only a few of the agenda items, and these agreements were enshrined in the *Constitution Act of 1982*, which was approved formally by the British parliament. This act provided an amending formula ensuring that all changes to the Constitution would henceforth be made in Canada; a charter of rights and freedoms; a commitment to the principle of equalization; confirmation of provincial ownership of natural resources; and affirmation of the existing rights of aboriginal peoples. Federal action during this period supported former prime minister Trudeau's assertion that cooperative federalism was dead. Moreover, there was little evidence of negotiations at work: federal–provincial conference diplomacy was replaced by unilateral federal decision making.

During the late 1980s and the early 1990s, the major focus of attention in intergovernmental relations was on the Meech Lake Accord and the Charlottetown Agreement. The Meech Lake Accord, formally referred to as the Constitution Amendment, 1987, was negotiated by the first ministers, with the assistance of their public service advisors, and was signed on June of 1987. The Accord consisted of a number of proposals for constitutional amendment that would serve "to bring Quebec back into the constitutional family" after Quebec's refusal to accept the *Constitution Act of 1982*. The Accord was to come into effect when it was ratified by the legislatures of all eleven governments. Under the terms of the *Constitution Act*, that ratification had to occur within three years—that is, by June 23, 1990. During the three-year period, federal and provincial public servants played a significant advisory role in the protracted negotiations over the ratification of the Accord; these negotiations culminated in a highly publicized and acrimonious First Ministers' Conference in mid-June 1990. The conference appeared to have reached agreement on ratification of the Accord, but two provinces (Newfoundland and Manitoba) failed to obtain ratification before the June 23 deadline. Among the major objections to the Accord were its recognition of Quebec as a distinct society, its decentralization of power from the federal government to the provinces, its requirement of unanimous consent for Senate reform, and its lack of recognition of the rights of aboriginal peoples. Intergovernmental tensions were greatly exacerbated by the unwillingness of some provinces to ratify the Accord, and by the unwillingness of the federal and Quebec governments to agree to major modifications. Following the death of the Meech Lake Accord, the province of Quebec announced its unwillingness to participate in any constitutional conferences for the foreseeable future and began formal consideration of its future association with the rest of Canada.

Beginning in 1991, a renewed effort to reach agreement on constitutional reform began. Widespread consultations involving participants from all parts of the country and many meetings of the First Ministers and senior public servants led to the August 28, 1992 Consensus Report on the Constitution. This report was known generally as the Charlottetown Agreement and was agreed to by first ministers (including the premier of Quebec), territorial leaders, and aboriginal leaders. The agreement's comprehensive proposals for constitutional change included, among other things, provisions for a social and economic union, the recognition of Quebec as a distinct society, the protection of minority language rights, the reform of the Senate and the Supreme Court, a reduction of overlap and duplication among governments, and the recognition of the inherent right of self-government for aboriginal peoples. These proposals, which had extremely significant implications for intergovernmental relations, were submitted for approval in a national referendum held on October 26, 1992. The agreement was rejected by a majority of almost 55 percent of voters.

The period since the rejection of the Charlottetown Agreement has been called a return to "constitutional normalcy."[18] There have been no major constitutional proposals, and the emphasis has been on meeting the challenges of Canadian federalism through non-constitutional means. Some regret this trend and argue for a return to constitutional reform, but most Canadians and their governments seem more than content to leave the Constitution alone. Intergovernmental officials now find themselves

Chapter 15 / Intergovernmental Administrative Relations

spending less and less time on the Constitution, a development that appears conducive to establishing cordial relations between the two orders of government.

Federal–Provincial Policy Relations

Since the movement away from constitutional reform, there have been important policy developments involving the two orders of government. In some instances, these developments have witnessed a transfer of responsibility to the provinces, while in others the federal government has made clear its intention to remain a major force:

- The federal government has always sought to reduce barriers that restrict trade between the provinces and regions of Canada.[19] The thinking was that freer internal trade would produce economic benefits for the country and also act to bring Canadians closer to together. In 1995, Ottawa and the provinces entered into an agreement that seeks to prevent the introduction of new trade barriers in Canada and endeavours to reduce present obstacles in designated areas of trade. Though it has some weaknesses (e.g. exceptions, non-binding nature), the Agreement on Internal Trade has been seen by many as an important step toward eliminating trade barriers within Canada. Similar success has also been achieved in the negotiation of international trade agreements. The federal government has provided a role for the provinces in the negotiation and implementation of such agreements, including the Free Trade Agreement with the United States and the North American Free Trade Agreement with Mexico and the United States.

- In response to pressures emanating largely from Quebec, the federal government agreed to devolve much of its responsibility for labour market training to the provinces.[20] For provinces ready and able to assume full responsibility for this area, the transfer left only a smaller role for Ottawa in the training and preparation of people for work. Other provinces were unable to assume such a responsibility, and the result has been a shared management relationship with the federal government.

- In 1998, the two levels of government (except Quebec) agreed to the Canada-Wide Accord on Environmental Harmonization.[21] The Accord gives the provinces a role in setting environmental standards—heretofore a responsibility of the federal government—and also places them in the forefront of developing plans for satisfying the standards. As can be seen, the Accord represents an enlargement of the role of the provinces in managing the environment. Lately, the federal government has reasserted itself in this area of public policy by ignoring provincial objections and ratifying the international Kyoto Protocol on climate change (and its commitment to reduce greenhouse gas emissions).

- The two orders of governments have negotiated a series on health care accords through which the provinces have received additional federal funding on condition that they move ahead with key health care reforms. The reform areas include primary health care, home care, and prescription drugs. A separate fund has also been set up to deal with the important issue of waiting lists for care. For some, these accords represent an attempt by the federal government to play a major role in the renewal of medicare.

- The federal government has most recently signed individual agreements with many of the provinces for the purpose of implementing an early childhood education and care program for young children. As with the health care accords, Ottawa has used the lure of federal dollars to shape a national day care program for Canada. In this case, the provinces have committed themselves to ECEC programs that respect conditions relating to quality, universality, accessibility, and development. However, the new government of Stephen Harper has stated its intention to end these agreements and put in their place direct tax benefits to families with children under six.

- In 1999, the federal, provincial, and territorial governments (save for Quebec) signed the Social Union Framework Agreement (SUFA). Though it was not directed at any policy area, SUFA committed all signatories to collaborate more often and to give prior notice of any major changes to their social policies. Most importantly, the federal government agreed that it would launch no new federal–provincial fiscal arrangements without the consent of the majority of the provinces; it also agreed to provide for greater flexibility in the use of monies made available under any new fiscal arrangement between the two orders of government. SUFA served to recognize a legitimate role of the federal government in major areas of social policy, but also to reiterate provincial control over these areas.

Machinery for Intergovernmental Relations

The expansion of the activities of all governments and the increased interdependence of federal and provincial responsibilities has led to a need to design and operate machinery to manage contacts between governments. What has resulted is a hierarchical network of intergovernmental structures (see Figure 15.3). At the top are found "peak" institutions, which are "central to determining the direction of Canadian federalism in a wide variety of policy areas, including federal–provincial financial relations, trade, health care and social policy."[22] Easily the most important peak institution is the First Ministers Conference (FMC), where Canada's prime minister and premiers (including territorial ones) meet to discuss and resolve the most important intergovernmental issues. Also included in this category are the Annual Premiers Conference (APC) and the yearly meetings of both the western premiers and those in Atlantic Canada. The most senior elected officials in government are associated with these peak institutions, but appointed officials located in intergovernmental departments and secretariats also play an important advisory role here. Immediately below the peak institutions are the councils, conferences, forums, and meetings populated by departmental ministers. The task of these intergovernmental bodies is to act on directives issued by FMCs and other peak organizations, and to manage the daily relations with their counterparts in other governments. Federal

| Figure 15.3 | Hierarchical Network of Intergovernmental Structures |

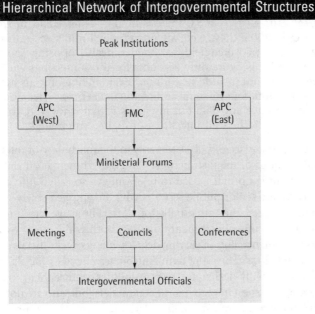

Chapter 15 / Intergovernmental Administrative Relations

and provincial ministers of health, for instance, will get together to arrange for the implementation of accords formulated by the first ministers and to deal with any health issues that may arise which concern both orders of government (such as building the capacity of governments to deal with a possible influenza pandemic).

The last basic piece of intergovernmental machinery is the variety of intergovernmental institutions and interactions involving appointed officials exclusively. As in any area of public administration, administrators and analysts must complement and support the work of the country's elected representatives. In many policy areas, formal arrangements have been made to facilitate bureaucratic dealings on intergovernmental matters. In the field of fiscal relations, for example, a permanent committee of the deputy ministers of finance from the federal, provincial, and territorial governments (called the Continuing Committee of Officials) carries out the necessary preparation for meetings of finance ministers and resolves issues not requiring ministerial attention. Federal and provincial ministries of finance also participate in a number of joint committees whose job is "to produce technical analyses and policy options with respect to budget planning, the tax system, and fiscal transfer arrangements."[23] Informal interactions are also a crucial part of intergovernmental relations at this level. Appointed officials emphasize the "importance of being able to connect with their counterparts in other governments on the phone or via email, sometimes on an almost daily basis."[24] The respect and trust among officials developed during formal contacts pave the way for frank and productive discussions outside of, and between, formal meetings. During these discussions, officials exchange a great deal of information about their government's position on matters of continuing concern and negotiation. An essential attribute of intergovernmental officials is their ability to obtain current information about the perceptions and positions of other governments. This information is crucial in determining the officials' advice to their political and administrative superiors.

Together, the pieces of intergovernmental machinery add up to a multitude of federal–provincial–territorial committees of varying degrees of importance. Some of these committees meet more than once, while some do not meet at all during a particular year. A senior Quebec intergovernmental specialist below tries to convey the quantity of intergovernmental contacts arising out of the various conferences, committees, councils, and other bodies:

> [A]ccording to the numbers provided by the Canadian intergovernmental conference secretariat (the CICS), there were 117 federal and provincial–territorial conferences in 2003; these were attended by first ministers, ministers and deputy ministers and they covered fields as varied as health, housing, sports, and feminine condition. And this figure only accounts for those meetings where the CICS was involved. It does not include senior nor lower ranking officials meetings, nor does it include the numerous bilateral and regional meetings . . . let alone the conference calls! I do not have any data but my guess is that if we were to add up all these instances we would be well into the four digits . . . annually![25]

In looking at the place of public servants in the machinery of intergovernmental relations, it is difficult to distinguish between "intergovernmental officials" and other public servants. The term is normally used to refer only to so-called intergovernmental affairs specialists. These are senior public servants who are engaged solely or primarily in intergovernmental business. They are usually found in central agencies and are responsible for the coordination of intergovernmental matters both within their own government and with other governments. But, in varying degrees, many other officials are involved in intergovernmental relations. Thus, the term "intergovernmental officials" also refers to those officials whose formally designated responsibilities require them to spend the majority of their working hours on intergovernmental matters, but who are not normally described as intergovernmental affairs specialists. The most prominent among these are senior public servants in operating departments who look after intergovernmental issues affecting their departments. In addition, there are officials, notably in senior positions, who devote relatively little time to intergovernmental issues but whose occasional involvement has a major influence on the outcome of intergovernmental negotiations.

Intergovernmental affairs specialists play a central role in government both in the organizational sense and in the development and implementation of policy. They must be adept in *intra*governmental as well as *inter*governmental bargaining. Their influence is based to a large extent on their ability to wind their way skilfully through the labyrinth of intergovernmental affairs in search of agreement with officials in their own government and in other governments. An important element of their expertise is in the appreciation of the various processes of intergovernmental relations. In a survey of intergovernmental officials in Canada, Inwood and his colleagues found that liaising and constructing networks, managing disputes, forging agreement, and other process-related matters were central to their duties.[26] Intergovernmental officials must also be knowledgeable about the substance of a broad range of policy fields. This is especially so with officials located in line departments, for they may be assigned to propose or carry out solutions to policy problems. In general, intergovernmental officials located in central agencies tend to be more concerned about process, while those in departments concentrate more on matters of substance.

In the past, intergovernmental officials mostly dealt with their counterparts in other governments. But increasingly "intergovernmental officials have felt pressures to expand their interactions beyond the federal–provincial framework."[27] This more inclusive world of intergovernmental affairs includes line department officials, municipal governments, representatives of the public, and even international actors. The consequences of federal–provincial relations touch many more now, and the result is a much more crowded world of intergovernmental affairs. This development has contributed to a sense among intergovernmental officials of being overwhelmed with duties and responsibilities. Even though the federal government and all ten provinces have either departments or secretariats in central agencies assigned to deal with intergovernmental affairs (and some departments have intergovernmental units), it appears that this is insufficient.

Interprovincial Administrative Relations

Interprovincial relations are broadly similar to federal–provincial relations in their organization and participants. Interprovincial interactions occur on both a formal and informal basis; they involve both political executives (premiers and ministers) and public servants, and they cover virtually all provincial policy fields. Most of the intergovernmental bodies created during the formalization of federal–provincial relations are also used to coordinate interprovincial relations.

Provincial political leaders and public servants meet to discuss problems of mutual concern and, when appropriate, to work out joint or common solutions. Among the formal interprovincial mechanisms for collaboration is the Premiers' Conference, which is the provincial version of the First Ministers' Conference. The Premiers' Conference is held annually and is usually attended by all ten premiers and their senior advisors (and territorial leaders). There are also important interprovincial meetings organized on a regional basis, notably meetings of the Western Premiers' Conference and the Council of Maritime Premiers.

Ministers of most provincial departments also meet regularly with their counterparts in other provinces, not only to exchange information and ideas but also to seek interprovincial coordination. For example, the Council of Ministers of Education, Canada permits provincial ministers of education to consult one another on issues of interest and to oversee such initiatives as standardized testing across the provinces and the collection of data crucial to education reform. Probably the most effective interprovincial interactions for seeking coordination are the meetings of public servants from both the senior administrative and the professional/technical level of various departments. Aside from the interprovincial meetings, the many federal–provincial meetings provide opportunities for provincial officials to get together informally outside the meeting room. Moreover, many of the same political and bureaucratic officials participate in both types of meeting. These personal contacts are subsequently utilized, via telephone, fax, and letter, to seek interprovincial policy coordination.

Recently, provincial and territorial premiers agreed to a new formal interprovincial mechanism called the Council of the Federation. The purposes of the new body are to fortify interprovincial–territorial cooperation, improve intergovernmental relations, and supply leadership in addressing issues of national significance.[28] The new council has generated some controversy, with some fearing that it amounts to "the erection of a parallel national government, intended to displace the federal cabinet as the place where important national decisions are made."[29] Others contend that the council represents a sensible response to "unsatisfying federal–provincial dynamics" in which the federal government is too often able to get its way with woefully unprepared provinces.[30] Only time will tell how the council will fit into the field of intergovernmental relations.

Models of Intergovernmental Administrative Interaction

As has been shown, intergovernmental affairs largely involves the interaction of senior elected representatives and their officials. The term **executive federalism** has been coined to identify these interactions because the participants are to be found in the executive branch of government. In turn, three distinct but complementary models have been used to explain the role and power of officials in the operation of executive federalism at the administrative level. These are the cooperation, bargaining, and bureaucratic politics models.

The cooperation model refers to intergovernmental relations concerning, to a great extent, program specialists from each order of government. Harmonious and productive interaction is facilitated, because these program specialists share a body of knowledge and skills and possess a common set of professional attitudes and values relating to their particular policy fields (e.g., welfare officials, foresters).[31] In this model, program specialists are permitted to exercise a large measure of autonomy from control by political and administrative superiors, especially those in intergovernmental relations units, treasury boards, and finance departments. The value of this model for explaining policy development and implementation in certain areas of federal–provincial relations has been demonstrated in the 1960s and earlier. However, more recent developments reveal the continuing value of the model. In looking at the formulation of major trade agreements, Skogstad states that the "fact that a number of trade officials across the two tiers of government have worked together on these issues over several years facilitates the trust ties that … promote effective intergovernmental relations."[32] Similarly, Bakvis and Aucoin observe that important aspects of the labour market development agreements of the late 1990s depended on the rapport between program officials located in the relevant line departments of the two orders of government.[33]

The bargaining model refers to intergovernmental relations involving primarily ministers and central-agency officials in the two levels of government. Interaction takes the form of a bargaining process in which these ministers and officials present and defend their government's position on specific public policy issues. Intergovernmental conflict is more prevalent, because ministers and central agency officials tend not to share values, attitudes, and skills to the same extent as program specialists; their interests lie less in resolving technical program issues and more in achieving broader policy and political goals. The focus of attention here is on political resources, strategies, and tactics used by participants in the process. This model gained prominence in the 1970s as decision making in governments became more centralized, and it remains important as a tool for understanding intergovernmental interactions, especially with high-profile issues in which the political stakes are high. A good example of the bargaining process at work now can be seen in federal–provincial (and territorial) meetings relating to the reform of the Canadian health care system. Health care involves a number of technical issues, but it also represents a symbol of basic Canadian values and beliefs and thus attracts the interests of first ministers and their close advisors.

A third model, which complements both the cooperation and bargaining models, is the bureaucratic politics model.[34] This model refers to the bargaining over intergovernmental matters among ministers and officials in departments and agencies within each order of government; it is *intra*governmental rather than *inter*governmental bargaining that is involved. Despite the use of the term "bureaucratic politics," the model is concerned with interaction among both ministers and officials. The bureaucratic politics approach (which has been mentioned in earlier chapters) suggests that it might be more productive to consider each government as a loose coalition of organizations and the negotiating positions of the governments as outcomes of an internal negotiating process. Typically, governments are treated as single actors, because they usually present a united front in negotiations with other governments. This united front may, however, be a mask that conceals conflict among ministers and officials within governments. Neither departments and agencies nor whole governments are homogeneous entities. Federal–provincial relations in the area of the environment, for instance, have witnessed the importance of bureaucratic politics, as environment departments have struggled with other departments and central agencies over responsibility for the development of policy.[35] This instance of intragovernmental conflict also reveals that bargaining occurs not only over the substance of intergovernmental policy but also over the distribution of resources between intergovernmental programs and other, competing government activities.

The Power and Responsibility of Intergovernmental Officials

The Power of Intergovernmental Officials

It has been suggested that there has been a politicization of intergovernmental affairs specialists. "Politicization" refers here to the process by which officials become increasingly involved in politics, either in the partisan sense or in the broader sense of the authoritative allocation of values for society. Public servants in general have become more politicized as a result of departures from some aspects of the traditional doctrine of political neutrality. The question is whether intergovernmental officials have become politicized and, if so, whether this politicization has taken different forms and emphases from that of other officials.

The overriding objective of intergovernmental relations is the determination of policy. Like other public servants, intergovernmental officials use their knowledge, experience, and discretionary authority to exercise power in the formation and administration of public policy; they engage in consultation and bargaining with other political actors; and their ministers rely heavily on them for advice on complex issues. Thus, in the intergovernmental field, as in other areas of government, the line between the policy contributions of ministers and officials is blurred.

However, the role of intergovernmental officials in the policy process can be distinguished from that of other officials in two significant ways. First, intergovernmental officials cannot exercise control, in the sense of authority, over their counterparts in other governments; rather, they must exercise influence through a process of bargaining. Compared with bargaining with pressure groups, for example, where government officials retain ultimate authority to decide or recommend a course of action, bargaining between governments requires give-and-take among negotiators of roughly equal status.

Second, intergovernmental officials, especially those who participate in formal meetings, enjoy more discretionary power in the bargaining process than most other officials. They are, therefore, more involved in politics in the broad sense than many of their colleagues. In the intergovernmental policy process, usually several governments, and often all eleven governments, are involved in a complicated bargaining process. The outcome of negotiations is frequently a tentative agreement representing a delicate balancing and accommodation of numerous and diverse interests. The federal and provincial cabinets, individual ministers, and even legislatures are sometimes reluctant to force a renewal of these intricate negotiations unless they have substantial objections to the agreement worked out by their officials.

Both scholars and practitioners of intergovernmental relations have perceived a tendency among intergovernmental officials to become somewhat more politicized than other public servants. A distinguishing feature of the doctrine of political neutrality is that public servants explain policy and ministers defend it. But in the course of intergovernmental negotiations, the line between explanation and defence becomes blurred. As a result, intergovernmental officials tend to be more involved in politics in the broad sense of that term.

Moreover, some intergovernmental officials occasionally develop an especially intense commitment to the objectives of their own government or their own minister that goes beyond the loyalty expected from public servants. This strong sense of loyalty appears primarily among senior intergovernmental specialists whose working environment is often highly political in the partisan sense, and whose duties require the management of conflict with other governments. They may be motivated both by pressure "not to let the minister down" and by personal commitment to government policies. It is natural for such loyalty and commitment to result from the obligation to continually explain and defend those policies. Vigorous defence by intergovernmental officials of the policies of the government of the day is not usually prompted by partisan support for the governing party, but it does on occasion have that appearance.

The Responsibility of Intergovernmental Officials

In the sphere of intergovernmental relations, it is difficult to pinpoint those who are actually, rather than formally, responsible for government decisions, because an important locus of decision making is an intergovernmental body of ministers or officials. There is no space here to examine the broad range of controls and influences that may promote responsible behaviour by intergovernmental officials. Therefore, attention will focus on relations between intergovernmental officials in different jurisdictions and between these officials and cabinet members and legislators.

The increased influence of the provinces in federal–provincial relations rests on several factors, including the constitutional distribution of responsibilities, the relative wealth of a province, and the electoral success of its political leaders. However, a major reason for the growth of provincial power has been the heightened expertise of their intergovernmental officials. The expertise of federal officials, which explained to a large extent the federal government's dominant influence in intergovernmental relations during the 1950s and early 1960s, is now more closely matched by the expertise of their provincial counterparts.

In the intergovernmental policy process, officials exercise significant power, in the sense of influence, over cabinet members and legislators. They exercise significant influence over policy development before, during, and after interministerial conferences. Moreover, as noted earlier, officials exert much policy influence in connection with the very large number of intergovernmental meetings below the ministerial level. This influence arises both from their expertise and from the formal and informal bargaining, often on a multilateral basis, in which they engage on behalf of their ministers. The demands of intergovernmental relations also work to give influence to appointed officials. As Inwood and his colleagues observe, "The sheer volume of federal–provincial interactions within the context of executive federalism underlines the necessity of officials' prominent place."[36] However, the influence of intergovernmental officials in relation to ministers should not be exaggerated. Cabinet members, both individually and collectively, possess ultimate control over the government's stance on all intergovernmental matters. Officials must be highly sensitive to the desires of the cabinet as a whole, and of individual ministers, in regard to both the substance and strategy of negotiations. Also, cabinet members are the central actors in making decisions on major and politically sensitive intergovernmental issues and in much of the negotiation leading to those decisions. In general, officials involved in intergovernmental affairs recognize "the authority of their minister or government" and are quick to state that their purpose is "to serve the minister."[37] This suggests that elected officials are largely in charge of intergovernmental relations in Canada.

Compared to cabinet members, legislators have little control or influence over intergovernmental activities. Indeed, legislators do not exercise much power over the executive in general or officials in particular in any area of government activity. There appears to be agreement in the scholarly community with the observation that the "business of the federation [in Canada] is currently carried out via the fluid processes and lightly institutionalized organizations of executive federalism" and that is made possible by "the strength and autonomy of the executive branch" and the inability of legislatures "to impose accountability on governments and leaders."[38] Yet, according to the principle of collective ministerial responsibility, the cabinet is responsible to the legislature—the legislature ought to have some say, indeed the final say. Nevertheless, there is normally much more discussion of intergovernmental matters in conferences than in the federal Parliament or provincial legislatures. There are few opportunities for legislators to examine intergovernmental policy issues before legislation incorporating agreements reached at conferences is presented to the legislature. Since this legislation is often the outcome of complicated and protracted negotiations among governments, ministers are understandably reluctant to make changes at the legislative stage with which other governments may disagree.

This lack of accountability of the results of intergovernmental affairs has led to proposals for strengthening the legislature so that it may play a more pivotal role in relations between the two orders of government. Some are well known—less party discipline, more powerful standing committees, more free votes—and recently the federal government had introduced some of these reforms in an effort to address the "democratic deficit" in Canadian politics. It remains to be seen whether these changes will have the desired effect and change the dynamics of intergovernmental affairs. More intriguing is a proposal for "inter-legislative federalism" in which legislatures would get together (in various ways) to create a decision process that parallels executive federalism.[39] For instance, a legislature considering a matter whose effects spill into other jurisdictions would invite legislators of affected areas to debate and discuss the issue. The aim is not to make changes within legislatures, but rather between and among them.

Conclusion

Intergovernmental management involves, to a very large extent, the management of conflict and complexity. Alan Cairns has observed that "intergovernmental coordination is not a simple matter of agreement between a handful of political leaders and their staff advisors. It requires . . . the containment of ineradicable tendencies to conflict between the federal vision of a society and economy, and ten competing provincial visions."[40] The key role of intergovernmental officials in seeking to harmonize these diverse perspectives ensures that the handling of intergovernmental relations will remain a dominant concern of students and practitioners of Canadian public administration.

1. Richard Simeon, "The Federal–Provincial Decision Making Process," in Ontario Economic Council, *Issues and Alternatives—1977: Intergovernmental Relations* (Toronto: Ontario Economic Council, 1977), 26.

2. Adapted from M.J.C. Vile, *The Structure of American Federalism* (London: Oxford University Press, 1961), 199.

3. Daniel Elezar quoted in Douglas M. Brown, "Getting Things Done in the Federation: Do We Need New Rules for an Old Game?" *Constructive and Co-operative Federalism?* (Montreal: Institute for Research on Public Policy, 2003), 2. Available at Policy.ca, www.policy.ca/policy-directory/Detailed/890.html. Retrieved July 11, 2006.

4. The territories have now achieved a status almost equal to federal and provincial governments in intergovernmental relations, so increasingly we refer to federal–provincial–territorial relations (FPT relations) when discussing federalism in Canada. However, this chapter will sometimes revert to the traditional practice of using federal–provincial relations, especially when relations literally apply only to the two orders of government (e.g., the Equalization program).

5. K.C. Wheare, *Federal Government*, 4th ed. (London: Oxford University Press, 1963), 10.

6. Quoted in Edwin R. Black, *Divided Loyalties: Canadian Concepts of Federalism* (Montreal: McGill-Queen's University Press, 1975), 43.

7. Donald V. Smiley, "The Rowell-Sirois Report, Provincial Autonomy, and Post-War Canadian Federalism," *Canadian Journal of Economics and Political Science* 28 (February 1962): 54.

8. David Cameron and Richard Simeon, "Intergovernmental Relations in Canada: The Emergence of Collaborative Federalism," *Publius: The Journal of Federalism* 32(2) (spring 2002): 51.

9. Richard Simeon and Ian Robinson, "The Dynamics of Canadian Federalism," in James Bickerton and Alain-G. Gagnon, eds., *Canadian Politics*, 4th ed. (Peterborough: Broadview Press, 2004), 113. This period is often given the name "executive federalism."

10. Ibid., 117.

11. David Cameron and Richard Simeon, "Intergovernmental Relations in Canada," 54.

12. Gerard Boismenu and Peter Graefe, "The New Federal Tool Belt: Attempts to Build Social Policy Leadership," *Canadian Public Policy* XXX (2004): 71–89.

13. And just to make things more complicated, the government of Stephen Harper shows signs of wishing to pursue something that most federal–provincial experts say is impossible: the disentanglement of the two orders of government—an outcome that would leave the provinces alone to pursue their social policy responsibilities without the intervention of the federal government (or possibly of federal money). See Department of Finance Canada, *Restoring Fiscal Balance in Canada: Focusing on Priorities, Budget 2006* (Ottawa: Her Majesty the Queen in Right of Canada, 2006), ch. 6.

14. Frances Abele and Michael J. Prince, "Aboriginal Governance and Canadian Federalism: A To-Do List for Canada," in François Rocher and Miriam Smith, eds., *New Trends in Canadian Federalism*, 2nd ed. (Peterborough: Broadview Press, 2003), 145.

15. Neil Bradford, "Canada's Urban Agenda: A New Deal for the Cities?" in Bickerton and Gagnon, eds., *Canadian Politics*, 431, 435.

16. Peter Leslie, Ronald H. Neumann, and Russ Robinson, "Managing Canadian Fiscal Federalism," in J. Peter Meekison, Hamish Telford, and Harvey Lazar, eds., *Canada: The State of the Federation 2002: Reconsidering the Institutions of Canadian Federalism* (Montreal & Kingston: McGill-Queen's University Press, 2004), 224.

17. For more on the fluid nature of fiscal relations, see Department of Finance Canada, *Restoring Fiscal Balance in Canada: Focusing on Priorities*, Annexes 1–3.

18. Peter Russell, *Constitutional Odyssey: Can Canadians Become a Sovereign People?* 3rd ed. (Toronto: University Press, 2004), 228.

19. See Mark R. MacDonald, "The Agreement on Internal Trade: Trade-Offs for Economic Union and Federalism," in Herman Bakvis and Grace Skogstad, eds., *Canadian Federalism: Performance, Effectiveness, and Legitimacy* (Toronto: Oxford University Press, 2002).

20. See Herman Bakvis, "Checkerboard Federalism? Labour Market Development Policy in Canada," in Bakvis and Skogstad, eds., *Canadian Federalism*.

21. See Mark S. Winfield, "Environmental Policy and Federalism," in Bakvis and Skogstad, eds., *Canadian Federalism*.

22. J. Peter Meekison, Hamish Telford, and Harvey Lazar, "The Institutions of Executive Federalism: Myths and Realities," in Meekison, Telford, and Lazar, eds., *Canada: The State of the Federation 2002*, 16.

23. Leslie, Neumann, and Robinson, "Managing Canadian Fiscal Federalism," in Meekison, Telford, and Lazar, eds., *Canada: The State of the Federation 2002*, 234.

24. Gregory J. Inwood, Carolyn Johns, and Patricia L. O'Reilly, "Intergovernmental Officials in Canada," in Meekison, Telford, and Lazar, eds., *Canada: The State of the Federation 2002*, 268.

25. Marc-Antoine Adam, "The Creation of the Council of the Federation," *Democracy and Federalism Series* (Kingston, Ont.: Institute of Intergovernmental Relations, Queen's University, 2005), 1. Available at the Institute of Intergovernmental Relations site, www.iigr.ca/pdf/publications/382_The_Creation_of_the_Coun.pdf. Retrieved July 11, 2006.

26. Inwood, Johns, and O'Reilly, "Intergovernmental Officials in Canada," 257.

27. Ibid., 267.

28. Council of the Federation, *Founding Agreement*, December 5, 2003. Available at the Canadian Intergovernmental Conference Secretariat site, www.scics.gc.ca/cinfo03/850095003_e.pdf. Retrieved July 11, 2006.

29. Andrew Coyne, "Ten Premiers, One Bad Idea," *National Post*, July 12, 2003. Available at Andrew Coyne's personal site, http://andrewcoyne.com/columns/NationalPost/2003/20030712.html. Retrieved July 11, 2006.

30. Marc-Antoine Adam, "The Creation of the Council of the Federation," *Democracy and Federalism Series* (Kingston, Ont.: Institute of Intergovernmental Relations, Queen's University, 2005), 1.

31. This model is elaborated in Donald V. Smiley, "Public Administration and Canadian Federalism," *Canadian Public Administration* 7 (September 1964): 371–88; and Smiley, *Constitutional Adaptation and Canadian Federalism Since 1945* (Ottawa: Queen's Printer, 1970), ch. 7.

32. Grace Skogstad, "International Trade Policy and Canadian Federalism: A Constructive Tension?" in Bakvis and Skogstad, eds., *Canadian Federalism*, 172.

33. Herman Bakvis and Peter Aucoin, *Negotiating Labour Market Development Agreements* (Ottawa: Canadian Centre for Management Development, 2000), 15, 32, 35.

34. See Richard Schultz, *Federalism, Bureaucracy and Public Policy* (Montreal: McGill-Queen's University Press, 1980), and Kim Richard Nossal, "Bureaucratic Politics in Canadian Government," *Canadian Public Administration* 22 (winter 1979): 610–26.

35. Kathryn Harrison, *Passing the Buck: Federalism and Canadian Environmental Policy* (Vancouver: University of British Columbia Press, 1996), 121.

36. Gregory J. Inwood, Carolyn Johns, and Patricia L. O'Reilly, "Intergovernmental Officials in Canada," in Meekison, Telford, and Lazar, eds., *Canada: The State of the Federation 2002*, 261.

37. Ibid., 261, 258.

38. David Cameron, "Inter-Legislative Federalism," in Meekison, Telford, and Lazar, eds., *Canada: The State of the Federation 2002*, 465–66.

39. See Cameron, "Inter-Legislative Federalism."

40. Alan Cairns, "The Governments and Societies of Canadian Federalism," *Canadian Journal of Political Science* 10 (December 1977): 722.

16

Nongovernmental Actors and the Bureaucracy

The most significant relations involving appointed officials are usually thought to be those that involve either one of the three branches of government or another level of government. Appointed officials exist in a governmental setting, so it is natural to infer that other entities within government will be central to public administration. This line of thinking has an element of truth to it, for the interactions of public servants with ministers, cabinet, the legislature, the courts, and other orders of government are important. Nevertheless, the world of public administration includes entities that exist outside of government. We must appreciate that nongovernmental actors also form part of the world of the public servant. To believe otherwise is to miss a significant part of the study of bureaucracy and the public service in Canada.

The key nongovernmental actors for the study of public administration are pressure groups, the media, the interested public, and political parties. These entities all interact with public servants in part because they contribute to the goal of serving the public interest. Pressure groups, for example, can help the government administer public initiatives, and the media can assist the government in supplying the citizenry with information about important public programs. Similarly, consultations with the public can contribute to the design of better public policy. However, these interactions are not always a product of civility and common interests. The media may target a particular program for extensive criticism, or pressure groups might attempt to force senior elected officials to make a decision inconsistent with the mandate of the government in office. When this happens, governments and their appointed officials need to respond and in so doing engage nongovernmental actors.

This chapter seeks to provide an understanding of the relations between the public bureaucracy and the major nongovernmental actors. The chapter outlines the nature of each of the nongovernmental actors and reveals how they affect the political process. It also discusses the often strategic or game quality of the relationship between nongovernmental actors and government—the interaction between the two sometimes appears as a contest in which all sorts of tactics are employed to secure preferences and interests.

Pressure Groups

Pressure groups (or *interest groups*)[1] are organizations composed of persons who have joined together to further their mutual interest by influencing public policy. These groups do not have hierarchical or legal authority over government officials and are without any desire to secure public office. They do, however, exercise influence over both the development and the implementation of public policy. A large part of their efforts are commonly described as **lobbying**. This particular pressure-group activity can encompass informal meetings between interest group leaders and their counterparts in government, access to cabinet and senior party members at fundraising gatherings, arranged meetings with government officials, and the employment of professional lobbyists to make the case of pressure groups to government.[2] To some Canadians, the term "lobbying" has unsavoury connotations of illegal, immoral, or inappropriate means of influencing government decision makers. This perception has its origins in the 19th-century United States, when "lobbyists" would frequent the lobbies and corridors of legislative buildings to influence legislators, sometimes with offers of bribes. The passage of legislation to regulate the behaviour of professional lobbyists also speaks to concerns about lobbying activities—something can hardly be seen in a positive light if it requires limiting laws.[3] It is important to emphasize, however, that lobbying is now a legitimate means of attempting to influence government decisions through individual or collective action.

Every policy field and every policy issue attracts the attention of one or more pressure groups and their lobbying efforts. These groups are thus numerous and pervasive in the political system. They include business, labour, agricultural, professional, social welfare, and public interest organizations. Examples of each of these types of organization are the Canadian Manufacturers' Association, the Canadian Labour Congress, the Canadian Federation of Agriculture, the Canadian Bar Association, and the Canadian Council on Social Development.

Though lobbying is important, the activities of pressure groups include more than influencing public officials in order to affect a government decision. Pressure groups also engage in what might be called "representation activities," which entail such actions as presenting briefs to government commissions or appearing before legislative committees. This activity seeks not to influence a particular decision—typically the concern of lobbying—but rather to shape the broad policy agenda and to influence overall thinking in a particular area of public policy. Pressure groups also take part in "governance" or "problem solving" exercises.[4] This activity involves pressure groups lending their expertise and other resources to address issues that go beyond their immediate interests. For example, Greenpeace, an influential environmental pressure group, may hold back on some lobbying efforts in support of their specific demands and instead participate in collective efforts to address broader environmental problems. The significance of this activity is to reveal that immediate self-interest is not the only motivating factor influencing the behaviour of interest groups (though one might argue the problem solving is linked to a group's long-term interest in a particular outcome). Other activities include litigation or the use of the courts, the employment of public protests, and interventions into elections.[5]

In looking at the activities of pressure groups, it is important to understand that pressure groups are usually part of a larger system of decision making for each sector of public policy. The terms "**policy community**" or "**policy network**" have been used to identify this system. Figure 16.1 shows that each policy community consists of an inner circle or "sub-government" of key players—cabinet, the lead department or agency, and major pressure groups—who make the actual decisions and an outer circle (or "attentive public") that indirectly influences policy through discussion and debate of the issues of the day. The political activities of pressure groups take place in relation to these policy communities.

Figure 16.1 | The Policy Community

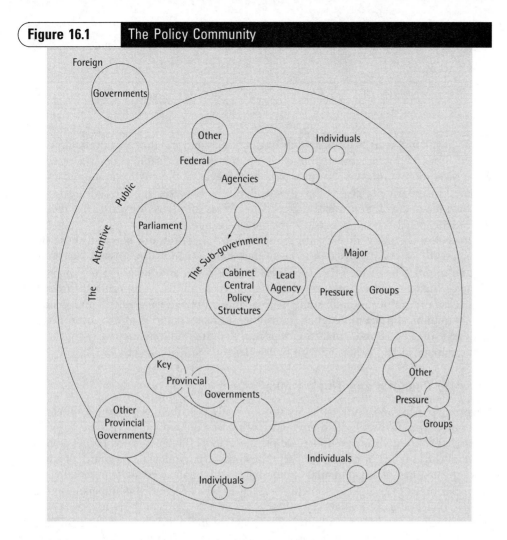

Source: Adapted from Paul Pross, *Group Politics and Public Policy*, 2nd ed. (Toronto: Oxford University Press, 1993), 123.

Types of Pressure Groups

Pressure groups have been classified into a variety of types according to such criteria as their objectives, activities, and structure, but a broad distinction can be made between "institutionalized groups" and "issue-oriented groups."[6] Institutionalized groups are characterized by organizational continuity and cohesion. They are highly knowledgeable about the policy-making process and about how to get access to public officials, in part because they usually employ a professional staff; their membership is stable; they have concrete and immediate operational objectives, but their ultimate aims are sufficiently broad that they can bargain with government over achieving particular concessions; and their long-term credibility with government decision makers is more important than any single issue or objective. Examples of institutional groups are the Canadian Medical Association, the Canadian Chamber of Commerce, the Canadian Bankers Association, and the Canadian Labour Congress.

Issue-oriented groups tend to be less organized, and to have less knowledge of government and of how to contact public officials; there is a constant turnover in their

Figure 16.2 | **Continuum of Types of Pressure Groups**

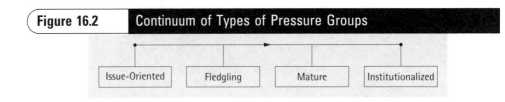

membership; they usually focus on only one or two issues; and they are not usually concerned about their long-term credibility with public officials. Examples of issue-oriented groups are those concerned about a particular threat to the environment and those opposed to specific projects of developers. Recently, however, the policy influence of certain issue-oriented groups has increased greatly, as they have learned to use the fax, the Internet, and access to the media and outside expertise.

In reality, virtually all pressure groups fall on a continuum between these two extremes, and can be discussed in terms of the extent to which they possess the characteristics of one type or the other (see Figure 16.2). A few additional types of pressure groups—"fledgling" and "mature"—can be placed along the continuum in order to emphasize this point.[7] As well, some issue-oriented groups may gradually move along the continuum, shifting to fledgling status, then to mature, and finally to institutionalized (and some of the more mature groups may at times find it necessary to adopt some of the extreme tactics associated with issue-oriented and fledgling groups).

Advisory Councils and Think Tanks

Advisory councils and think tanks are not normally described as pressure groups, but they do play an advocacy role by trying to influence public policy decisions.

Advisory councils are composed of private citizens that are created by the government, outside of the normal bureaucracy. They provide an independent source of advice to a minister, free of any potential laundering by the public service. Representatives of particular pressure groups are sometimes asked to serve as council members. Appointment to such bodies as the National Advisory Council on Aging or the Nova Scotia Advisory Council on the Status of Women gives pressure group members an opportunity to advance their group's interests. Advisory councils are in a difficult position because they receive most of their funding from government; they must tread a middle course so that they retain credibility with the government while avoiding being captured by it. They must also be skilful in balancing the interests of their constituents so that they are not captured by any one group. There is often disagreement among these constituents as to whether the best way to maximize their influence on government is to use friendly persuasion or to "go public" in order to bring about overt pressure.

Think tanks (often called research institutes) are nonprofit organizations outside of government that are primarily involved in producing research and holding conferences and workshops designed to inform or to influence public policy, or both. Think tanks vary considerably in their size, activities, and influence. They include, for example, the Institute for Research on Public Policy, which provides reports (and a magazine) on a wide range of public policy issues; the Public Policy Forum, which publishes reports based on roundtable discussions as part of its effort to improve policy-making by fostering business–government collaboration; the Fraser Institute, which, through such means as publications and symposia, applies market principles to public policy problems; the Canadian Centre for Policy Alternatives, which applies social-democratic principles in research papers directed to unions and other social organizations; and the Conference Board, which is a large, well-financed organization that produces research and holds conferences on a wide range of public policy issues.

Some are critical of the quality of their research and describe the resulting reports as "bland"[8] and with little real direct impact on policy outcomes. Not surprisingly, the think tanks themselves believe differently and contend that they have an important impact on public policy.[9] However, there appears to be no disagreement on the contention that the policy process has opened up and provided an opportunity for think tanks to play a greater role. This has occurred in larger part because of the disappointment of senior elected officials in the value of policy advice proffered by public servants and the feeling that public servants wield too much influence.[10] The result is that the provision of policy advice has become a much more complicated process, in which career officials no longer hold a monopoly over proceedings.

Functions of Pressure Groups

Pressure groups perform a number of functions crucial to the operation and performance of the political system. By looking at these functions, we can not only better understand the role of pressure groups, but also gain a view of their relations with government officials.

Communication. Given that an important objective of pressure groups is to influence the development and execution of public policies, it is not surprising that their main function is two-way communication between their members and public officials. The content of this communication ranges from detailed, technical data on existing or proposed policies, programs, and regulations to irate demands for government action on particular issues. Public servants and, to a lesser extent, cabinet ministers also use pressure group contacts to communicate with the groups' members. Many pressure groups regularly pass along to their members, through newsletters and other internal means of communication, information about government policies and programs. This practice is mutually beneficial in that the groups provide a service to their members and the public servants get their message to the groups' membership.

Legitimation. The communication function of pressure groups is closely related to another important function they perform in the political system—legitimation. Through consultation with pressure groups whose members will be affected by proposed policies, government officials can assess the probable effects of adopting these policies and can seek support for them. Such consultation gives these policies a measure of legitimacy in that groups representing those likely to be affected by the policies have had their views heard and ostensibly taken into account by government decision makers. Certainly, government officials are well advised to consult any group whose opposition to policies might weaken the legitimacy of the policies in the eyes of the public. The importance of the legitimation function is evident in the efforts of public servants and government in general to promote the creation and maintenance of particular pressure groups. This activity serves the legitimation function by ensuring outside support for the government's policies, facilitating group input into the policy process that might not otherwise take place, and promoting the representation of disadvantaged groups.

Regulation and Administration. Pressure groups sometimes assist governments by regulating their members and administering programs. For example, the governing bodies of the legal, medical, and accounting professions regulate their members by such means as restricting entry to the profession and imposing penalties for unethical behaviour. Pressure groups also conduct research and collect information that assists government's regulatory and legislative activities.

Targets of Pressure Group Activity

It is critical to the success of pressure groups that, in their interactions with government, they identify and aim at the right targets. They must decide first whether to direct their efforts to the federal, provincial, or local spheres of government—or to all of them. The federal nature of Canada has important effects on the organization and operations of pressure groups. Many Canadian pressure groups are federations—that is, they are composed of provincial bodies that lobby provincial governments and a national organization that focuses its efforts on Ottawa. Many other groups are not large enough to have provincial components or affiliates of a national organization, and are therefore obliged to channel their limited resources to those governments where the resources will do the most good. Another impact of federalism on pressure group activity is that, in order to be effective on issues that involve more than one level of government, groups may be required to lobby federal, provincial, and local governments simultaneously.

Whether pressure groups lobby federal or provincial governments, the usual targets of their activity are cabinet ministers, public servants, and legislators, all of whom play important roles in the public policy process. This process may be divided into pre-legislative, legislative, and post-legislative stages. Public servants are influential in the pre- and post-legislative stages, making them entities to which pressure groups will address many of their efforts. In the pre-legislative stage, the temptation for interest groups may be to concentrate their attention on cabinet and the prime minister, who are formally responsible for proposing legislative enactments to Parliament. However, at this stage public servants play a key role:

> [T]he prime minister does not draft legislative or regulatory initiatives alone. The prime minister, along with cabinet, enjoys important administrative support. Consequently, civil servants are in a position liable to give them significant influence over government projects. In such a setting, rather than direct their efforts towards Parliament, Canadian interest groups are more likely to aim at the government bureaucracy.[11]

The power of public servants does not, of course, give them the final say on major public policy issues; that authority belongs to cabinet ministers. Therefore, pressure groups are frequently obliged to lobby ministers to influence both the decisions of individual departments and those of cabinet committees and cabinet as a whole. Moreover, ministers are often the ultimate target of lobbying aimed at public servants and legislators by pressure groups striving to influence those who can influence ministers.

Cabinet ministers have enormous power in all three stages of the policy process—if they decide to exercise that power. In practice, they have neither the time nor the inclination to participate actively in the post-legislative stage; rather, they tend to leave policy implementation to the public servants. Because of this decision, pressure groups will be encouraged to direct most of their attention in this last stage to appointed officials. In this post-legislative stage, pressure groups know that public servants have some discretion in the carrying out of government policies and programs. Though some may believe that the policy process ends with the passing of proposed legislation into law, knowledgeable actors in the political process appreciate that the truth is something quite different.

Compared with cabinet ministers and public servants, legislators and legislative committees are a secondary target of pressure group activity. Nevertheless, legislative support for pressure groups can be extremely important, especially on issues of widespread public concern, and can complement a group's efforts to influence officials in the executive–bureaucratic arena. Government backbenchers have opportunities to influence government decisions in party caucus meetings and in formal and informal meetings with ministers and public servants. Opposition members are anxious to receive representations from pressure groups so as to understand better the groups' problems and to obtain ammunition to be used against the government. If individual legislators and legislative committees had more influence on the formulation and implementation of public policy, pressure groups could usefully spend more time and effort trying to influence public policy during the legislative stage of the policy process.

Recognition of Pressure Groups

Pressure group access to public officials, particularly to public servants, depends largely on the extent to which the group has resources which can further the policy and political interests of government. A major concern of appointed officials is the availability of the knowledge and expertise necessary to ensure the efficient formulation and administration of public programs. Thus, a pressure group which can supply usually unavailable to government will be recognized favourably by appointed officials and their superiors:

> It is simply the case that the more an interest group has the resources to move beyond communicating demands, to become instead a source of knowledge (and thereby a potential source of effective administration), the more it becomes of interest to civil servants.[12]

An instance of this at work can be seen in government regulation of assisted reproductive technologies. In this area, the federal government has relied on the knowledge of medical experts and so gave valuable access to groups representing physicians. Moreover, the success of medical groups in securing their interests in this policy area reveals that "government decision makers may defer to groups possessing expertise related to the subject matter at hand."[13] In other words, expertise and knowledge can buy more than access—it can produce victories for pressure groups.

Certain pressure groups gain access and maintain recognition more easily than others, because they constitute the sole clientele, or a large part of the clientele, of a specific department. A department can rely on a clientele group as a source of information and as a channel of communication to the group's members. It can also use the group to gain support for its policies from other departments and, indeed, from the general public by claiming to speak for the interests of the major group affected by the department's policies. To do this, the department must maintain good relations with the group and take special pains to avoid open conflict with it. Similarly, the group can benefit in the way of access and influence by receiving such departmental recognition. But if a group is tied too closely to a single department, it may have nowhere else to go, with the result that the department may be able to influence its activities unduly. So far as possible, therefore, a group will usually cultivate support in other departments so that all of its lobbying eggs are not all in one basket.

Another important basis of pressure group access and recognition is the group's political clout. Ministers, legislators, and public servants are interested in the political impact pressure group activity can have on the next election and on the overall fortunes of the party in power. While public servants are expected to be nonpartisan, they are at the same time supposed to be politically sensitive. They should be able to advise the minister as to the likely effects of proposed policies on various segments of society, including those represented by influential pressure groups. Thus, public servants should strive to be aware of the possible effects of government decisions on the voting behaviour of a pressure group's membership. Similarly, public servants should be aware of the capacity of pressure groups to shape public opinion on an issue. Accordingly, public servants are more likely to grant access to groups that have the resources to influence the political fortunes of their minister or of the government as a whole. Moreover,

Chapter 16 / Nongovernmental Actors and the Bureaucracy

they will be more favourably disposed toward groups that can help them help the minister.

A primary function of interest groups is the provision of legitimacy to government actions. A pressure group can therefore gain access to government if it can serve to increase the acceptability of public initiatives in the mind of the public. Public servants and other actors in government seek out those groups that can facilitate legitimating government initiatives.[14] The importance of pressure groups in this regard is revealed in the fact that governments actively support the creation of groups who have the potential to support public initiatives.

Pressure Group Tactics

The success of pressure groups depends partly on gaining access to government, but it also requires that they develop tactics appropriate for achieving their interests:

- Groups are well advised to attempt to influence policy at the earliest possible stage of its development and to follow the progress of that policy all the way through the policy-making process, including the post-legislative or implementation stage. Groups can perform this task more successfully if their contacts with government officials are sufficiently cordial and continuous to allow them to anticipate or learn quickly about policy initiatives. As can be seen, a group's tactics are determined significantly by the extent of its recognition.
- Both common sense and the present nature of the policy process suggest that pressure group representations to government should, where feasible, be framed in terms of the public interest. The requests of pressure groups are more likely to be met if they are attuned to the priorities and plans of the government than if they amount to blatant, self-interested pleading. For example, in a time of high inflation and high unemployment, officials are likely to look favourably on proposals that may reduce these. Similarly, proposals that require the expenditure of substantial public funds during a time of severe economic restraint are unlikely to receive a sympathetic hearing. In short, pressure groups can advance their own interests by demonstrating that these interests enhance, or at least complement, the broader public interest.
- Pressure groups typically rely on quiet, behind-the-scenes consultations rather than media campaigns and public demonstrations designed to influence decision makers indirectly. Aside from the fact that public protests and the like may embarrass the government—and hence reduce the receptivity of the latter—the quiet approach allows pressure groups to more effectively convey their concerns and offer any possible help to government. Certainly, groups within the inner circle of the policy community rely on the more discrete manner of approaching government. But those in the outer circle may find that a less discrete approach is the only way to make known their views. Groups in support of additional funding of AIDS research and assistance or environmental groups have found that protest marches and road blockades can have the desired effect.
- One effective and frequently used tactic is cooperative lobbying. This requires groups to create formal or informal alliances with other groups who share their views on a particular policy issue. Cooperative lobbying enables several groups to present a united front to government as an indication of widespread concern. At the same time, the groups profit from this cooperative arrangement by sharing information and contacts. Even competing pressure groups may benefit from consultation with one another, because they can learn the content and strength of their opponents' arguments, even if they cannot work out a common position to present to government.

Media

Like pressure groups, the media act as intermediaries between the government and the public. The term "media" includes traditional transmitters of mass communication—radio, television, newspapers, magazine—and new purveyors of information to the public—the Internet, satellite radio, and cell phone technology. The two are also similar in the sense that each wields more and more influence in the political process and therefore have increasing relevance for appointed officials. The two, however, have their differences as well. Pressure groups seek directly to influence public policy while the media are more focused on servicing customers and generating economic returns for their owners and shareholders. As well, pressure groups tend to represent well-defined interests to carefully identified officials. On the other hand, the media's audience inside and outside governments tends to be broader and more diffuse.

Operation of the Media

The media perform a number of important public functions. They provide the information necessary for a citizenry to become informed about the operation of its government—in a way, they constitute democracy's oxygen. Without this information, a political system committed to democratic norms would be hard pressed to truly represent the people and their wishes. The media also offer analyses of political events, and in so doing give greater sense to the large amount of information available on the political process. It is also appreciated that newspapers, television, radio, and other forms of media investigate and uncover serious abuses of power in government (and elsewhere).

These are all important duties, but arguably more important for government officials and their interaction with the media is how the latter go about making news concerning government and politics. There are a number of theories about the newsmaking activities of the media. The theory with the greatest resonance is that "journalists and news organizations are not passive, neutral, and objective reflectors of reality but active agents that change the reflection in various ways."[15] Moreover, the media use various techniques to mould their stories and to develop an audience for their work. It is these techniques that public servants must always keep in mind when dealing with the media.[16]

1. Simplicity. In reporting on events, the media look for events that are straightforward and easy to explain and understand. If an important event fails to reflect these qualities, the media will be tempted to simplify it even at the risk of losing some meaning or distorting the truth.

2. Dramatization. "The story" is central to the journalistic enterprise. Accordingly, the media look to provide drama in their reports. Conflict, surprise, and juxtaposition are highlighted to make the story work.

3. Personalization. Successful media reports rely on personalities. A news event without identifiable individuals is more likely than not to be rejected in favour of one that includes people. These people can be both elected and appointed officials, which makes this technique especially crucial for public servants and their superiors.

4. Preformed storylines. Journalists usually frame an event in a particular way and interpret any developments in accordance with this interpretation. Facts which conflict with the storyline can be ignored, downplayed, or made to fit the storyline.

5. The unexpected. News reports thrive on the unexpected, especially if it involves a serious error on the part of government. The unexpected event can form part of the preformed storyline—the surprise development becomes an expected event.

There are some additional qualities of the operation of the media that government officials must respect. The advent of new technology and the increasingly competitive nature of the media business "has placed enormous pressure on government to make decisions quickly, for fear of appearing indecisive and not in control."[17] Similar forces have also made the media much more willing to challenge ministers and their senior officials. The old days when inkstained newspaper reporters dutifully recorded the announcements of government are over:

> The role of the media [in the past] was to be a narrator or an independent observer reporting and commenting on political events. It is now, of course, a major political actor in its own right. Television and its tendency to offer a ten- or thirty-second clip on the evening news to sum up major issues, or, more often, to report on something gone awry in government, have changed government operations. The media have become far more aggressive and less deferential to political power.[18]

Government and the Media

Like the media, governments also seek to shape reality and to present information in a manner that meets their goals. Most government contacts with the media are handled by public servants (and other appointed officials) who strive to use the media to support their political superiors, to publicize their department's activities, to obtain favourable comment on these activities, and to measure public reaction to proposed policies and programs. To meet these goals, attempts will be made to satisfy the needs of the media. Information will be available to meet tight deadlines, and sources within government will work hard to ensure that journalists have something important to report. This category of interaction between the media and government typically involves an exchange of largely factual information on the content and administration of government programs. Another category of interaction entails an exchange of views on controversial issues. In this instance, partisan officials in the central agencies and public servants will have to rely on their own set of techniques to please their political superiors. Sometimes the techniques are used directly to counter those of the media. Other times the government will take the offensive and use the techniques in an endeavour to shape the story:

- One thing public servants must do is to be prepared for the media, especially in relation to possible crises that can do great damage to the political fortunes of government. Here are the words of a senior federal official lamenting his failure to read correctly the signs of serious trouble:

  > ...I did not know that a crisis was in the making. Despite the extensive media coverage Thursday and Friday, and a foreshadowing of the issues that could play out over the course of the next ten months, when I left the office late Friday evening, I believed that the matter would "blow over." In retrospect, I should have read the media reports in a more pessimistic manner to prepare myself, and my staff, for what lay ahead.[19]

- How a government is perceived or "framed" will help determine the attitude of the public. Studies show that the media actively engage in framing exercises and that these exercises can have a large effect. Accordingly, government has to compete with the media in the shaping of issues. Sometimes this activity of government is associated with the term "spin doctors"—government officials who put a policy, program, or event in just the right light. Often these officials will be the media officers in departments or political operatives found in the Prime Minister's Office.

Box 16.1   The Prime Minister and the Press

One day, in the spring of 2006, Prime Minister Stephen Harper met with the Parliamentary press gallery to answer questions about an important piece of government legislation. To facilitate questions, the press supplied two microphones so that any journalist could line up and make one query or another of the prime minister. But this conflicted with the prime minister's practice of choosing journalists to ask questions. So he left and set up the press conference in another room, but again the journalists lined up to speak into a mike. Initially, the prime minister relented and answered queries from a journalist in the lineup, but then asked a journalist who was sitting down whether he had any questions. The journalists who had lined up complained that the prime minister was ignoring them. So, again, the prime minister relented and took some additional questions from the first reporter in the lineup. Then he suddenly vacated the room.

Source: Gloria Galloway, "PM Fires Another Salvo at the Press," *The Globe and Mail*, April 12, 2006, A4.

- Mistakes in government often form an important part of any storyline in the media. Public servants thus must be sensitive to the making of errors and make every effort to limit them—mistake-free government is the goal of any political leader and his or her government. When mistakes do happen, ministers and their subordinates may be well advised to hide or bury them. Alternatively, they may provide so much information on the alleged mistake that the media and others find it difficult to sort out the issue and pinpoint the nature of the error. This last technique is sometimes called a "paper dump."[20]

- Politicians and public servants may provide privileged access to journalists in return for favourable coverage. All media types require sources who can provide scoops on forthcoming government initiatives and who more generally can provide a sound basis for a story. Government officials can put this basic truth to great use.

- To deal with the media, communication directors in government may try to limit media access to public officials and to set up strict rules when journalists and government representatives do interact. PMO officials in the Harper government have directed ministers to be less accessible to the media and have directed both elected and appointed officials to speak to the media only about the stated priorities of the government. As well, the PMO has instructed all that it would "have final approval for all communication products—even Notes to Editors or Letters to the Editor."[21] The Prime Minister's Office also tried to determine where questions would be asked on Parliament Hill and which journalists could ask these questions.[22]

The foregoing techniques—combined with those employed by the media—suggest an almost Machiavellian-type interaction or game between government and the media. The two sides have differing aims and each at times may have to use morally questionable tactics in order to prevail over the other. However, it also has to be appreciated that each requires the other and hence they must learn to cooperate as well:

While the media crave politicians and need them to generate their texts, the reverse is also true. The relationship can be described metaphorically as symbiotic. Politicians need the media in order to disseminate their views. Consequently, politicians [and public servants] must work within the parameters of news value and according to media schedules and preferences in order to be noticed.[23]

The commonalities between government and media can also go beyond cooperation based on shared interests. Ultimately, each seeks to contribute to a functioning political system premised on democratic norms and public initiatives which contribute to the well-being of the citizenry.

Public Participation and Consultation

Another type of interaction important to public administration in Canada revolves around public servants and their consultations with the public. The traditional mechanisms for allowing public participation in the governmental process—elections, political parties, pressures groups, and the media—also represent accepted aspects of the democratic process. Nevertheless, there is a demand for a more direct relationship between those responsible for designing government initiatives and individual members of the public. Part of this demand arises from a desire on the part of government to enhance the legitimacy or acceptability of public programs. In its effort to achieve efficiency and effectiveness in their offerings, government sometimes fails to appreciate sufficiently that legitimacy "is conferred upon policies when a large public feels it has been consulted and heard."[24] A force complementary to this first one is the wish of the public to be more actively involved in the design of public actions. Canadians appear less willing to defer to experts in government and increasingly express their desire to be a more direct part of the policy-making process. This particular force also brings to the surface the fear that too often appointed officials—not elected representatives—direct the design of public policy. The demand for public consultation also springs from the belief that it may lead to better public policy. Not only will government initiatives be more readily accepted if they are the product of public consultation, but they will also constitute a more effective response to the problem at hand. There is also a prevailing sentiment in Canada that a "democratic deficit" exists and that every effort ought to be made to give individual Canadians a greater opportunity to give input to their elected representatives. The political process offers access to those belonging to a political party or pressure group, but the same cannot be said of unattached Canadians who are without membership in a stakeholder group.

The push for greater public consultation and citizen engagement has special relevance for public servants. The focus of this push is typically on the design of public programs. Most forms of public participation—be they town hall meetings, advisory groups, round tables—seek a capacity to intervene before governments make a final decision. And in the Canadian political process appointed officials play a large role in the formulation or design of public programs:

> The Westminster parliamentary system confers a central role in the design process upon the state bureaucracy, normally a ministry for which a Cabinet minister is held responsible. Indeed, the prime responsibility for drafting policies before their presentation to Cabinet, and possibly Parliament, falls upon civil servants.[25]

Accordingly, much of the consultation process entails relations between appointed officials and the public.[26] Politicians are eager to see the public play a greater role in designing policies, but more often than not it is the civil servant—not the cabinet minister or parliamentary member—who represents government.

Mechanisms of Public Participation

Public participation can take a number of forms distinguished by the purpose of the consultation and the accompanying degree or level of citizen involvement. One way to conceptualize public consultation is to see it as comprising five levels of interaction with the citizenry (see Figure 16.3).[27] Level 1 involves a "low level of public involvement

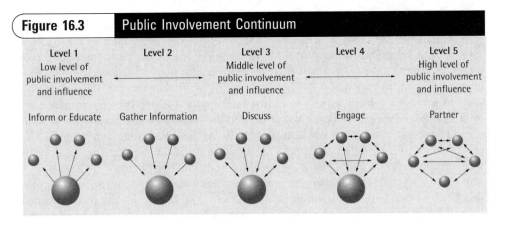

Figure 16.3 Public Involvement Continuum

Level 1	Level 2	Level 3	Level 4	Level 5
Low level of public involvement and influence		Middle level of public involvement and influence		High level of public involvement and influence
Inform or Educate	Gather Information	Discuss	Engage	Partner

Source: Adapted from *Health Canada Policy Toolkit for Public Involvement in Decision Making*, page 12, Health Canada, 2000. Reproduced with the permission of the Minister of Public Works and Government Services Canada, 2006.

and influence," because the purpose here is merely to "inform or educate" the public on an issue of importance. The mechanisms used with this level of consultation include fact sheets, backgrounders, press releases, information fairs, open houses, and the use of 1-800 numbers to convey information to the public (the large ball in the figure is government). Level 2 represents an attempt on the part of government to "gather information" and a corresponding rise in the intensity of citizen involvement. An important distinction between this level and the preceding one is that at Level 2 government has typically not made a final decision on a matter. To gather information, ministers may instruct their officials to arrange for a public or town hall meeting at which members of the public express their sentiments about a proposed public initiative. Public hearings or seminars constitute another mechanism for gathering information. This mechanism involves selecting a panel of individuals—public servants, experts, informed members of the public—to conduct an open forum on a specific topic. Royal Commissions are another method of securing information on a public issue at this second level. Level 3 moves beyond the gathering of information and toward the discussion of issues. For this purpose, advisory boards or councils may be employed. These mechanisms of participation typically entail government selecting public representatives to offer input on a matter and to hold conferences that lead to the provision of helpful advice to government. Various forms of computer assisted participation—televoting, online discussion groups, electronic conferencing—may also be used to permit the public to comment on public matters. To gain public views on how to address its budget deficit, the City of St. John made it possible for citizens to submit their views electronically and to participate in electronic or online discussion groups relating to the city's budgetary problems.[28]

The first three levels are usually considered to be fairly traditional forms of participation and are linked with the rather passive involvement of the public in government decision making. The next two levels endeavour to involve the public more actively in government affairs, a shift signified by the substitution by some of the term "citizen engagement" for "public participation" or "public consultation."[29] Citizen engagement means that the consultation process—the agenda, the invitees, and the use of generated information—will be less controlled by government. With regard to the role of public servants, they assume a more open stance with respect to public input and effectively change from "substantive policy experts to public consultors."[30] Mechanisms used at Level 4 include joint working groups, retreats, round tables, and citizen dialogues. Each is distinguished by the fact that active deliberation takes place among the participants and that the results of the deliberation will play an important part in the final resolution of the issue at hand. Level 5 represents the ultimate in participation, because it allows the public to manage the consultation process and to put forward solutions that government will seriously consider. Citizen juries represent one kind of mechanism found at this level. This mechanism involves the selection of community representatives who hear expert evidence on a particular matter and who then make a decision for government to consider seriously. Deliberative polling is another mechanism that can be used to achieve a relatively high level of citizen participation. The government first polls a sample of the population on an issue, and then selects a small portion of the sample to hear expert opinion on the issue and to discuss the matter among themselves. The process ends with a polling of the selected group in an effort to gauge the opinions of well-informed citizens and to use these opinions in the making of policy. In 2003, Transport Canada engaged in a deliberative polling exercise to help determine the most appropriate way to deal with new technological devices in cars. Departmental officials learned from the process and "are using the results to inform their decision on the strategy the department will pursue."[31] Citizen panels, search conferences, and study groups are other modes of participation that may be used at this level. The modes are different in the way they operate, but similar in the sense that all they involve citizens actively deliberating a matter and recommending a clear course of action for government.

Effectiveness of Public Consultation

There are various concerns about the effectiveness of exercises in public consultation. One is that the participating public is unrepresentative of the general public. For public participation to achieve its various purposes—to produce better policy, to engage Canadians from all walks of life, to contribute to civil literacy—it must ensure that more than just select portions of the Canadian population take part in the interaction between government and individual residents. The attraction of public participation is that ordinary Canadians—those unattached to any formal group or cause—are provided with an opportunity to influence their government. However, this attractiveness quickly dissipates if we realize that only the well-organized and the well-off participate. A related concern is that the number and quality of participants is often disappointing to public officials. The latter expect many citizens to grasp the opportunity to participate in the decision-making process, but inevitably the actual numbers fall short of expectations. Government also expects participants to have a good understanding of the issues, but "some participants have limited policy knowledge, engendering skepticism about the practical value of their contributions."[32]

There is also concern that the methods of consultation rarely go beyond the first three levels of consultation. It appears that government has developed a standard operating procedure that discourages citizen engagement. It circulates an information document for discussion, holds a series of stakeholder meetings, sets up a website for citizen responses, makes available a workbook for the interested to complete, and includes many people to protect itself against claims of insufficient consultation. Nowhere in this process is there an opportunity for informed discussion and an assurance that the consultation is integrated into the government decision process. For some, what is happening is a process fated to be ineffective:

> Public consultation normally occurs quite late in policy processes, once problems have been defined in concrete terms and a preferred policy option has been developed. Reaction to these is being sought. By the time a consultation is concluded, there is usually considerable pressure to move decision-making along, so there is seldom enough time for an in-depth analysis of the knowledge acquired or the opportunity to go back to citizens to discuss particular matters further. In general, then, such practices greatly limit the ability of consultation to inform public policy or to satisfy the other dimensions of citizen involvement.[33]

A final weakness with public consultation is the resistance of the policy communities or policy networks to open themselves up to new players. The discussion of pressure groups revealed that sectors of public policy tend to be shaped by a rather close-knit group of public servants, senior politicians, and pressure-group leaders. This group may feel that the inclusion of the public may disturb carefully crafted policy compromises or make it more difficult for established members of the policy communities to secure their preferences. Even if policy communities are motivated largely by serving the public interest, they may still believe that widening the boundaries of the policy community to include members of the public will hinder exercises in problem solving; in the eyes of the policy community, the public may have neither the expertise nor the experience necessary to make a contribution.

The various concerns with public consultations suggest that more work needs to be done with this aspect of public administration, and it is even suggested that elected officials should rethink the value of including citizens in the decision-making process. But the larger societal forces pushing for greater public participation indicate that government should at least face the challenge of providing for greater citizen engagement in public affairs. The mushrooming of public-participation activities also point toward some progress in meeting this challenge.

Political Parties

The functions of political parties are usually described as interest aggregation and articulation, the recruitment and training of political leaders, and the education and socialization of the public on political matters; control or influence over the public service is rarely mentioned. In brief, political parties are organizations that seek to get their members elected to political office and to gain and maintain control of the government. They pursue this objective both inside and outside government. The internal and external components of a political party are often referred to as the *parliamentary* and the *extraparliamentary party*. Earlier chapters discussed relations between the public service and the parliamentary party—that is, the parties' elected members in the legislature and in party caucus. The brief treatment of political parties provided here is concerned with the impact on the public service of the extraparliamentary parties—the parties' national and provincial executives and offices and the constituency associations—that exist outside government proper. There are two general types of interaction between political parties and public servants. The first involves the public servant as citizen; the second involves the public servant as government employee.

The most direct contacts between public servants and political parties take the form of public servants' participation in the activities of political parties. Restrictions have been placed on the partisan political activities of public servants so as to preserve their political neutrality. Within the bounds of these restrictions, public servants do seek nomination and election to public office and provide various forms of support for individual candidates and political parties. The right of public servants to participate in partisan political activities has gradually been extended over the past thirty years, and there are strong pressures for further relaxation of the constraints on such activities. Through the limited opportunities to contribute directly to political parties, public servants can have some direct influence on the policy positions adopted by parties, but their participation is usually circumspect. The most senior public servants and those in sensitive positions are usually excluded, or deliberately exclude themselves, from any kind of partisan political activity. However, some senior public servants are political appointees—that is, they are appointed by the governing party because they have been involved in partisan politics.

The influence of the extraparliamentary wing of political parties on the public servant as government employee is indirect and difficult to assess. This influence is exercised in the form of policies, proposals, and promises that have implications for the public service as a whole or particular parts of it, and that are made during party meetings, leadership conventions, and election campaigns. Political candidates and political parties, especially if they are in Opposition, frequently join in the bureaucrat bashing that generally falls on such fertile ground among the electorate. Charges of inefficient, ineffective, and unresponsive bureaucratic behaviour are usually accompanied by promises of cutbacks in the number of public servants and in the amount of money they spend. It is understandable that political parties that have been in Opposition for a long time should become antagonistic toward the public service and view some public servants as being too close to the governing party. This leads to threats that many senior public servants will be turfed out with a change in government, and to unhappiness among many of the party faithful when these threats are not carried out.

Aside from attacks on the general performance of the public service, political parties and their leaders adopt party platforms that have implications for public servants working in particular policy fields, which can range from broad promises to reduce expenditure on social policy to specific promises to abolish certain programs or agencies. While experience has shown that once in office, political leaders often deviate substantially from their party's platform, policies set by political parties can be very influential, especially through the publicity received in the news media.

There are often significant differences among political parties in the ways they view the public service. In the federal sphere, for example, the Conservative Party is more likely than the Liberal Party to lament the size and expenditures of government and to propose such solutions as privatization of Crown corporations and deregulation. The New Democratic Party, which favours policies likely to require a larger governmental apparatus and which is affiliated with the trade-union movement, generally avoids broad attacks on the public service and gives greater support than other parties to collective bargaining in the public sector.

It is difficult for public servants to separate completely their role as citizen or voter from that of government employee, and it is therefore reasonable to assume that sympathy for a political party will carry over into decisions or recommendations on the job. Equally problematic is assessing the effect of the ideological commitments of public servants. These commitments need not be manifested by a formal or emotional attachment to a particular political party; the public servant who is politically neutral in the partisan sense still has ample opportunity to inject personal ideological preferences into the policy-making process. These preferences will obviously affect the public servant's views on major policy issues involving such social values as the redistribution of income and the protection of human rights.

Access to Information

Access-to-information laws are certainly not actors in the same sense as pressure groups, the media, the public, and political parties. But they are important to consider at this point, because they facilitate the operation of these nongovernmental actors. As Savoie says of access-to-information legislation, it is probably right to conclude that such laws "may have enabled the media, the general public, interest groups, and opposition parties to open up the private space of government and career officials."[34] In so doing, the legislation has significantly changed the functioning of government in many different ways.

The *Access to Information Act*

The government of Canada has traditionally operated on the principle that all government information is secret unless the government decides to release it. Many proponents of freedom of information contend that this principle should be reversed so that all government information will be released unless the government can make a good case for keeping it secret. Under this latter approach, the burden on the public of justifying requests for the disclosure of information is lifted and the burden of justifying nondisclosure of information is imposed on the government, specifically on ministers and public servants. The federal *Access to Information Act* permits the government to keep a great deal of information confidential, but, in general, the act follows the second approach. The *ATI Act*'s stated purpose is

> to provide a right of access to information in records under the control of a government in accordance with the principles that government information should be available to the public, that necessary exceptions to the right of access should be limited and specific and that decisions on the disclosure of government information should be reviewed independently of government.[35]

People seeking information under the federal Act must write to the appropriate department and must identify as precisely as possible the information they require. Assistance in this regard is available in the *Access Register*, which contains a description of the records held by each department. Copies of the register and of access request forms can be obtained in public libraries and government information offices in major population centres, as well as in postal stations in rural areas. Each department has an access coordinator to assist applicants to identify the records required. The department has thirty days either to produce the information requested or to provide reasons why a request has been denied. If the request is for a large number of records or is complicated, the department can extend the time limit, but it must inform the applicant of the situation. Eventually, the department will accede to the request or deny it. In the latter case, the person seeking the information may enter into a review process in an attempt to overturn the denial. A nominal fee is charged for each request for information. Applicants must pay an extra amount if excessive time is needed to process a request and for copying and computer processing time.

The federal access-to-information legislation has had a fairly substantial effect on supplying more information about government activities to nongovernmental actors. In 2004, for example, there were over 25,000 requests for information made under the *ATI Act*, and the number of requests has been growing annually.[36] Nongovernmental actors have benefited from the legislation. Thanks to the access-to-information legislation, the media are much more knowledgeable about the workings of government and are better able to pinpoint administrative problems in government.[37] The data on information requests also show that pressure groups, Opposition parties, and the public also take advantage of the legislation, and the fact that public servants now appear as if they work in a "glass house" also reveals the transforming effect of the federal legislation and comparable acts at the provincial level.[38] However, there is concern about the legislation's effect on important doctrines of governance, especially individual ministerial responsibility and the anonymity and neutrality of public servants.

Ministerial Responsibility and Political Neutrality

Discussion of freedom-of-information legislation has centred on the issue of whether such legislation would unduly encroach on ministerial responsibility. Somewhat less

Box 16.2   **Whistle-Blowing**

Through the practice of whistle-blowing, public servants can make public some of the sensitive information exempted or excluded from disclosure by the access-to-information legislation. In the context of public administration, whistle-blowing refers to making available confidential information to someone not in the government in order to draw attention to an action that causes serious harm. The kind of wrongdoings that usually provoke whistle-blowing are illegal activity, gross waste of public funds, and threats to public health or safety. Canadian public servants who engage in whistle-blowing may be subject to disciplinary action for violating their oath of office and secrecy or such statutes as the *Official Secrets Act* and the Criminal Code. But the *Public Servants Disclosure Act* was passed into law in late 2005 in order to give statutory protection to whistle-blowers at the federal level. And in early 2006, the new government of Stephen Harper indicated its intention to strengthen protections for whistle-blowers.

concern has focused on the possible reduction in the political neutrality and anonymity of public servants.

It is easy to understand why ministers and senior public servants do not share the enthusiasm of people outside government for freedom-of-information legislation and for access to material on the decision-making process in particular. The release of information revealing ministerial and public service contributions to, and debates over, policy has important consequences for both ministerial responsibility and political neutrality. Documents that expose disagreement among ministers or between ministers and public servants might be exploited by the government's opponents to the ministers' political disadvantage. To take a relatively small example of this at work, the media used the federal access-to-information law to uncover a seeming disagreement between officials in the federal Department of Finance and the new Conservative Party Finance minister about the wisdom of reducing the GST tax in the 2006 budget.[39] It is natural that ministers—especially new ministers in a new government—should not want to answer to the legislature and the public for the content of documents that are likely to be controversial and that should in their minds be kept secret. Ministers do not deliberately seek trouble.

Similarly, senior public servants generally resist the expansion of public access to official documents that disclose their personal views and values on policy issues. If public servants are drawn into public debate over their contributions to policy development, their anonymity will decline. Moreover, to the extent that a public servant's written advice is at odds with his or her minister's decision, both may be publicly embarrassed. As the events in the sponsorship scandal show, public servants may respond to freedom-of-information laws in two ways. One is simply not to write down information that may be contentious, an action that can lead to a decline in the quality of advice provided to senior political officials. Another response is to put on paper information of little substance or value.[40] Both responses were used in the process that eventually led to the mismanagement of the sponsorship program.

Clearly, access-to-information legislation has produced an element of "adversarialism" in relations between government officials and nongovernmental actors.[41] The hope had been that the introduction of legislation would usher in a culture that supported access to government information as a matter of right, but this has not been realized. This is not to say that this policy of opening up government has been a failure, for many requests for information have been fulfilled to beneficial effect. However, more attention will have to paid to the adversarial nature of access-to-information legislation in an attempt to ensure that all actors are satisfied.[42]

Conclusion

This chapter has examined the interactions of government officials with entities that exist outside the three branches of government. At one time, public servants could afford to pay little attention to such actors as the pressure groups, the media, and the public. However, these times are gone, and in their place a political process has emerged that is more populated and more complex.

Notes

1. For our purposes, these two terms can be used interchangeably. Often, however, the term *interest group* is used when the broad range of functions performed by these groups is under consideration, whereas the term *pressure group* is used when the focus of discussion is primarily on the exercise of political pressure.

2. Lisa Young and Joanna Everitt, *Advocacy Groups* (Vancouver: UBC Press, 2004), 88–95.

3. Events associated with the sponsorship program have done little to change the largely negative view of lobbying and lobbyists. See Commission of Inquiry into the Sponsorship Program and Advertising Activities, *Restoring Accountability: Recommendations* (Ottawa: Her Majesty the Queen in Right of Canada, 2006), 171–74.

4. See Éric Montpetit, "Public Consultations in Policy Network Environments: The Case of Assisted Reproductive Technology Policy in Canada," *Canadian Public Policy* XXIX (2003): 95–110, and Éric Montpetit, "Governance and Interest Group Activities," in James Bickerton and Alain-G. Gagnon, eds., *Canadian Politics*, 4th ed. (Peterborough: Broadview Press, 2004).

5. Young and Everitt, ch. 7.

6. Paul Pross, *Group Politics and Public Policy* (Toronto: Oxford University Press, 1986), ch. 5; Paul Pross, "Pressure Groups: Adaptive Instruments of Political Communication," in Paul Pross, ed., *Pressure Group Behaviour in Canadian Politics* (Toronto: McGraw-Hill Ryerson, 1975), 9–18.

7. Pross, *Group Politics and Public Policy*, 122.

8. Leslie A. Pal, *Beyond Policy Analysis: Public Issue Management in Turbulent Times*, 3rd ed. (Toronto: Thomson Nelson, 2006), 320.

9. Donald J. Savoie, *Breaking the Bargain: Public Servants, Ministers and Parliament* (Toronto: University of Toronto Press, 2003), 113.

10. Ibid., 115–16.

11. Montpetit, "Governance and Interest Group Activities," 316.

12. Ibid., 317.

13. Young and Everitt, 134.

14. Ibid., 99.

15. David Good, *The Politics of Public Management* (Toronto: University of Toronto Press, 2003), 61.

16. See ibid., 63.

17. Savoie, 75.

18. Ibid., 65.

19. Good, 211.

20. Ibid., 78.

21. Campbell Clark, "Harper Restricts Ministers' Message," *The Globe and Mail*, March 17, 2006, A1.

22. Don Martin, "Even Orwell Couldn't Have Made This Up," *National Post*, April 13, 2006, A6.

23. Paul Nesbitt-Larking, *Politics, Society, and the Media: Canadian Perspectives* (Peterborough: Broadview Press, 2001), 362.

24. Montpetit, "Public Consultations in Policy Network Environments," 97.

25. Ibid, 96.

26. Susan D. Phillips and Michael Orsini, *Mapping the Links: Citizen Involvement in Policy Processes* (Ottawa: Canadian Policy Research Networks, 2002), 22.

27. Health Canada, *Health Canada Policy Toolkit for Public Involvement in Decision Making* (Ottawa: Minister of Public Works and Government Services, 2000), 12.

28. Keith Culver and Paul Howe, "Calling All Citizens: The Challenges of Public Consultation," *Canadian Public Administration* 47 (spring 2004): 52–75.

29. See, for example, Phillips and Orsini, 3, or Health Canada, 14–16.

30. Montpetit, "Public Consultations in Policy Network Environments," 97.

31. David Taylor, "Transport Canada's Deliberative Democracy Experiment," *Optimum Online* 34(2) (July 2004): 2.

32. Culver and Howe, 55.

33. Phillips and Orsini, 19.

34. Savoie, 52.

35. *Access to Information Act*, R.S. 1985, c. A-1, s. 2(a).

36. Alasdair Roberts, "Two Challenges to Administration of the Access to Information Act," in Commission of Inquiry into the Sponsorship Programs and Advertising Activities, *Restoring Accountability: Research Studies, Volume 2: The Public Service and Transparency* (Ottawa: Her Majesty the Queen in Right of Canada, 2006), 116. It should be noted, however, that this number falls well short of expectations (which were about 100,000 requests annually). Available at the Commission of Inquiry into the Sponsorship Program and Advertising Activities site, http://www.gomery.ca/en/phase2report/volume2/CISPAA_Vol2_4.pdf. Retrieved July 11, 2006.

37. Savoie, 51.

38. Ibid., 164.

39. Steven Chase, "Finance Department at Odds with Government over GST Cut," *Globe and Mail*, April 24 2006, B1, B3.

40. Roberts, 127. There are additional instances of public servants failing to write down the appropriate information in the administration of programs. See Jeff Sallot, "Decisions Lack Proper Paper Trail, Watchdogs Complain," *The Globe and Mail*, May 22, 2006, A4.

41. Roberts, 117.

42. For suggestions on how this might be done, see Roberts, 2006.

The Management of Organizational Resources

The Management of Human Resources

The last part of the book strives to offer a close-up view of how public servants go about managing organizational resources in the public sector. This purpose might encompass the examination of a number of activities—engaging in strategic planning, meeting the information technology requirements of the organization, structuring procedures for collective bargaining—but Part 5 focuses on two central challenges facing appointed officials: the management of human resources and the management of financial resources. This chapter and the next consider the first test, and the final two chapters discuss the second.

One of the most important aspects of the management of organizational resources, if not the most important, is addressing the human resources needs of the organization. To carry out this task, it is necessary first of all to determine an underlying principle or philosophy that guides the terms and conditions for employment in the public sector. In Canada, and other countries, the merit principle—the notion that employees must be qualified to do the job—has come to be accepted as the foundation for human resources systems. However, other principles, such as a public bureaucracy that is broadly representative of the society it serves, ought to be considered as well. The management of human resources also includes the creation of a process that allows for, among other things, the classification of jobs and the training and evaluation of employees. We must also provide for the organizations necessary to this managerial effort and do so in a way that facilitates respect for the merit principle and other principles while allowing managers to tend to the personnel needs of the organization without facing a web of rules and regulations.

In this chapter, we explore the processes, structures, principles—and frustrations—integral to the management of human resources. Appropriately, the chapter commences with a consideration of the merit principle and the evolution of the human resources system. The chapter then examines the legislative and organizational framework for managing federal employees, and follows this with a discussion of the separate steps—job classification, human resources planning, staffing, training, and performance evaluation—that make up the actual management of people in the public service. The following chapter offers a detailed review of a crucial issue in the management of human resources, namely the concern for a public bureaucracy which includes representation from the many different groups in society.

The Concept of Merit

Merit is the most pervasive and enduring theme in human resources management. To understand the concept of merit, one must distinguish between the merit principle and the merit system. The **merit principle** has often been explained as requiring that public service appointments be based exclusively on merit, in the sense of fitness to do the job, and that citizens have a reasonable opportunity to be considered for public service employment. Yet this definition allows for considerable interpretation as to what is meant by "reasonable"; moreover, fitness for the job does not necessarily require that the most qualified person be chosen. The merit principle is often interpreted solely in terms of appointing the best-qualified person—that is, the "reasonable opportunity" component is omitted. For their part, the courts in Canada have consistently interpreted merit to mean "best qualified."

In practice, the meaning of the merit principle is worked out through the **merit system**, which is the mechanism, consisting of policies, procedures, and regulations, by which the merit principle is pursued. The merit system is a dynamic concept in that it can be adapted to changing circumstances. The federal Public Service Commission, which is responsible for safeguarding the merit principle through implementation of the merit system, is obliged to reconcile the merit principle with several other important principles. These other principles include a public service which is representative of the larger population, a process of staffing which is fair and transparent, and appointees who are competent and able to work in both of the official languages. A further principle is that the merit system itself should be flexible and conducive to the efficient staffing of positions; but there have been concerns expressed about the operation of the merit system—that its procedures are inflexible and that the rigidity of system actually impedes the satisfaction of the merit principle. The oft-expressed wish of many is a merit system that gives managers a better opportunity to use their own judgment in the selection of personnel while still working within a framework of general policies and procedures. In 2003, the federal government passed legislation that provided a definition of merit that attempts to introduce more flexibility into the merit system, for it allows managers to move away from the idea of locating the best-qualified candidate and instead to hire people on the basis of the requirements of the agency and any qualifications deemed necessary for the performance of the work (the chapter discusses this in more detail later).[1]

There have been few significant events, developments, or reforms in the public service that have not affected human resources management in general and merit in particular. Merit has been pursued within the broader context of the traditional public service values, namely neutrality, accountability, efficiency and effectiveness, responsiveness, representativeness, integrity, fairness, and equity. The priority that public servants assign to each of these values at any given time is a reflection of the desires and expectations of the various actors in the political system who control or influence public servants. Among the most important of these actors are political superiors. The uniqueness of human resources management in the public, as opposed to the private, sector can be explained in large part by the political environment within which public servants work. Evidence of the importance of the politics of human resources management has been provided in earlier discussions of such matters as political appointments, political partisanship, public comment, anonymity, permanence in office, and ministerial responsibility. Additional evidence can be seen in the evolution of the human resources management system in Canada.

Evolution of Human Resources Management

The development of human resources management in Canada may be viewed in terms of the effect on merit, and to a lesser degree on motivation, of the shifting importance of the dominant administrative values. In the federal sphere of government, this evolution may for analytical purposes be divided chronologically into six periods. In each of these periods, human resources management has been affected by a different mix of administrative values as the priority of the various values has risen and declined.

The Patronage Era (Pre-1918)

This period was dominated by efforts to promote political neutrality by eliminating, or at least minimizing, political patronage in the appointment of public servants.[2] Indeed, between 1867 and 1918, as many as five royal commissions and a judicial inquiry on the federal public service devoted considerable attention to the evils of patronage. In relation to the staffing of the public service, patronage took several forms. The most common form was appointments based on party affiliation, which occurred at the level of the local constituency and which involved both the member of Parliament and the local party members. Most of these appointments were to lower-level positions in the public service, and many of the positions were of a seasonal nature. A second form was appointments made by the cabinet to senior-level positions, largely on the basis of partisan political considerations. A third form of appointments related to positions to be filled from within the public service; since many deputy ministers were political appointees themselves, it is not surprising that some "bureaucratic" patronage occurred. Lastly, there were a greater number of appointments following a change of government when some appointees of the outgoing governing party were dismissed and replaced by supporters of the incoming party.

The first major step toward the abolition of patronage was the *Civil Service Amendment Act* of 1908, which established the Civil Service Commission. The Act also provided for appointment on the basis of merit and for heavy penalties for partisan political activities by public servants. However, the Act applied only to the "inside service" or public servants working in Ottawa.

From Patronage to Merit (1918–45)

This period began with the passage of the *Civil Service Act* in 1918. The search for political neutrality was supplemented by concern for efficiency. The major objective of the Act was the "promotion of economy and efficiency in the non-political public service." Merit was to be achieved through "selection and appointment without regard to politics, religion or influence," and through "the application of methods of scientific employment to maintain the efficiency of these selected employees after they enter the service." The Act applied to both the "inside" and "outside" services. Severe restrictions in this Act on partisan political activities remained virtually unchanged until 1967.

Continued pursuit of political neutrality and efficiency had important effects on human resources management. The emphasis during the 1920s on eradicating patronage rather than on improving efficiency led to a significant decline in patronage appointments and partisan political activities by 1930. In the 1930s, the Civil Service Commission, with its persistent focus on merit in terms of selection of the best qualified candidates, lost ground to the Treasury Board, which emphasized economy and efficiency, not only in the human resources area but throughout government. This emphasis continued during the war years.

The Roots of Reform (1946–66)

This postwar period provided a strikingly different environment for human resources management. The rapid expansion of government activities in an increasingly complex and technological society required a much larger number of employees and a greater proportion of employees with professional, technical, and managerial skills. By the end of this period, public service unions had won the right to bargain collectively and to strike. Efficiency remained the paramount public service value as the Royal Commission on Government Organization (the Glassco Commission)[3] examined human resources management as part of its task to recommend changes to "promote efficiency, economy and improved service in the dispatch of public business." Political neutrality was a continuing, but secondary, concern. Also, representativeness emerged as a primary public service value, specifically in regard to remedying the longstanding discrimination in the public service against French-speaking Canadians.

The Fruits of Reform (1967–78)

This period was an especially momentous one in the evolution of human resources management. Public service managers in general and human resources managers in particular felt the full effects of reforms generated in the previous period. Among the most important reforms were collective bargaining, language training, new management techniques, and departmental reorganizations.

A larger number of public service values contended for precedence during this period. The former emphasis on economy and efficiency was supplemented by vigorous concern for effectiveness. Disclosures of mismanagement and of inefficient and ineffective use of public funds led to widespread anxiety about the accountability of public servants. Revelations of numerous incidents of unethical conduct involving government officials aroused unprecedented concern about their integrity. The representativeness of the public service also became a major issue as the claims of women, aboriginal peoples, and the disabled were added to those of French-speaking Canadians. The Trudeau government's promises of participatory democracy gave responsiveness a higher place among the public servants' value priorities. Finally, the importance of political neutrality was renewed with the increased recognition of the changing role of public servants in the political system.

The Failure to Reform (1979–89)

It was evident by the end of the 1970s that the traditional concept of merit would have to be reinterpreted to take account of important public service values. Since that time, the federal government has consistently argued that the principles of the merit system noted earlier in this chapter (e.g., fairness, equity, efficiency) should govern all aspects of human resources management. These principles are very similar to the public service values discussed in earlier chapters. During the 1980s, the values of efficiency and accountability had an especially important impact on human resources management.

In 1979, the Special Committee on Personnel Management and the Merit Principle[4] (the D'Avignon Committee) reported that the basic human resources problems were a lack of leadership, excessive and inflexible regulation, managers who were ill equipped for managing, and an absence of accountability for the proper management of human resources. The report rejected "authoritarian, non-participative, uncommunicative and centralized systems" and proposed "a flexible, entrepreneurial, professional and participative style of management."[5] Other studies documented the deficiencies of human resources management,[6] including low morale caused in part by staff and expenditure reductions. Since the government's efforts to remedy these problems during the 1980s enjoyed little success, in 1989 the government launched Public Service 2000 (PS 2000), an initiative to revitalize the public service, especially in the sphere of human resources management.

The Road to Renewal? (1990–Present)

By the time PS 2000 reported in late 1990,[7] human resources management was being affected by the emergence of new values that had arisen from extensive public service reform. Notable among these new values were innovation, service, quality, and

Box 17.1   The Merit Principle

In the *Public Service Modernization Act*, the merit principle is defined in law for the first time. The act states that an appointment has respected the merit principle when "the person to be appointed meets the essential qualifications for the work to be performed, as established by the deputy head. ...." The deputy head also has the authority to consider other qualifications that might be considered an "asset" to the organization now or in the future, and may as well take into account "the current or future operational requirements [and] needs of the organization." The definition has some important implications. One is that there is no longer any need to show that the chosen candidate is the "best" in comparison to others; it only has to be demonstrated that the appointed person has the necessary qualifications. Another is that merit criteria can be quite broad and aware of the needs of the organization.

teamwork. There was also continuing emphasis on the traditional values of efficiency and accountability. PS 2000, which viewed people as the main asset of the public service, recommended the pursuit of such human resources objectives as the empowerment of employees, enhanced career planning and professional development, and improved union–management relations.

In 1996, to reinforce the actions taken to achieve these objectives, the government launched La Relève, an initiative designed to a address a kind of malaise in the public service brought on by downsizing, pay freezes, and minimal recruitment and thereby build a modern and efficient public service able to take on the challenges of the 21st century. This ambitious initiative endeavoured to go beyond structural adjustments and to change the very culture of the public service, but assessments of La Relève suggest that its reach may have exceeded its grasp.[8] More recently, legislation has been introduced to address precise concerns about the inefficiency of the merit system and the alleged absence of an effective definition of the merit principle. The *Public Service Modernization Act*, of 2003, equates merit with meeting "essential qualifications" necessary for the position in question and any "additional qualifications" or needs of the organization (see Box 17.1). The definition acts to broaden the traditional conception of merit "to allow departments to meet multiple considerations when hiring and promoting staff, such as the ability to work in teams and enhancing diversity."[9] The Act also leaves much of the determination of qualifications and needs of the department to senior department officials and thus "underscores the closer alignment of staffing with the business needs of an organization."[10] In general, the legislation seeks to build greater flexibility into the human resources management process.

The Legislative and Organizational Framework

The function of human resources management pervades government, but the development and administration of human resources policy in the federal government is determined largely by a few key statutes and organizations. The scope and objectives of human resources activities and their allocation among these organizations are set out in three major statutes. The *Financial Administration Act* states that the Treasury Board is charged, among other things, with broad responsibility for "personnel management in the federal public administration, including the determination of the terms and conditions of employment of persons employed therein." The *Public Service Employment Act* grants the Public Service Commission authority to appoint persons to and within the public service according to merit and to handle matters relating to political partisanship and principles concerning layoffs and priorities for appointments. The *Public Service*

Box 17.2   Collective Bargaining

Collective bargaining refers to the process by which parties negotiate the pay, hours of work, and other conditions of employment, and it is an important part of the operation of the public sector. As noted earlier, at the federal level there are laws and structures set up to manage the collective bargaining process, and the same can be found at the other levels of government. The process of bargaining requires, among other things, the establishment of **bargaining units**, the determination of the scope of bargaining, the identification of **bargaining agents**, and the manner of resolving differences within and between parties in the bargaining process. Given the nature of collective bargaining, it should not be surprising that it represents one of the more controversial issues in human resources management. Disputes over such matters as pay, benefits, and the right to strike can lead to acrimony and work stoppages.

Labour Relations Act sets out the responsibilities of the Public Service Labour Relations Board (recently renamed) and provides for the structure and operation of the collective bargaining process and for the resolution of disputes and grievances.[11]

Until very recently, the Treasury Board Secretariat and the Public Service Commission constituted the two major bodies in the area of human resources management at the federal level. Acting on behalf of the Treasury Board, the TBS's responsibilities in the human resources field traditionally included the development and interpretation of policies, programs, and procedures in regard to the organization of the public service; positions; compensation; training and development; official languages; discipline; working conditions; human resources needs and their utilization; classification of employees and employee benefits; and other terms and conditions of employment necessary for effective human resources management. In addition, the secretariat represented the government as employer in the collective bargaining process. As for the Public Service Commission, it had the responsibility to recruit, select, promote, transfer, demote, and dismiss public servants; to provide staff development and training, including language training, within the framework of Treasury Board policies; to hear and decide appeals relating to appointments or to demotions and dismissals for incompetence or incapacity; to investigate allegations of discrimination in public service employment practices; and to administer regulations on political activities by public servants, including decisions on requests for leave of absence to seek political office.

The aforementioned *Public Service Modernization Act* and complementary decisions, however, have caused a realignment of roles and responsibilities in the area of human resources management. As Figure 17.1 shows, a new body called the Public Service Human Resources Management Agency of Canada, which reports to the Treasury Board, has assumed many of the human resources responsibilities of the Treasury Board Secretariat (follow the arrow from the Treasury Board Secretariat under "Previous" to the Public Service Human Resources Management Agency of Canada under "New"). The secretariat's duties in the area of human resources now concern only collective bargaining and related matters (plus reporting to Parliament). Similarly, the new Canada School of Public Service now provides all training of public service members, leaving the Public Service Commission to focus on the application of the merit principle. (Another new body, the Public Service Staffing Tribunal, now manages complaints concerning such matters as layoffs, cancellation of appointments, and general abuse of authority in the appointment process—once a responsibility of the Public Service Commission.) Finally, the new definition of merit contained in the *Public Service Modernization Act* has resulted in deputy heads of departments taking on more responsibility for determining departmental needs and policies relating to learning, training, development,

Previous	New
Treasury Board Secretariat • Collective bargaining and compensation • Labour relations • Pension and benefits • Implementation of *Public Service Modernization Act* (*PSMA*) • Values and ethics • Official languages • Employment equity • Human resources policy and planning • Leadership development • Classification	**Treasury Board Secretariat** • Collective bargaining and compensation • Labour relations • Pension and benefits • Treasury Board report to Parliament on human resources management*
	Public Service Human Resources Management Agency of Canada • Implementation of *PSMA* • Values and ethics • Official languages • Employment equity • Human resources policy and planning • Leadership development • Classification • Management development policies and programs
Public Service Commission • Management development policies and programs • Redress on staffing disputes • Staffing • Investigations and audits • Reporting to Parliament • Training for all employees • Language training	**Public Service Staffing Tribunal*** • Redress on staffing disputes
	Public Service Commission • Staffing • Investigations and audits • Reporting to Parliament
	Canada School of Public Service* • Training for all public service employees • Language training
Canadian Centre for Management Development • Training for managers	**Public Service Labour Relations Board** • Administer the collective bargaining and grievance adjudication systems for the public service • Increased mediation services* • Compensation research and analysis*
Public Service Staff Relations Board • Administer the collective bargaining and grievance adjudications systems for the public service	
Deputy Heads • Delegated responsibilities from Treasury Board • Delegated responsibility for staffing from Public Service Commission (PSC)	**Deputy Heads** • Delegated responsibilities from Treasury Board • Delegated responsibility for staffing from PSC • Establish learning, training, and development needs* • Provide awards* • Set standards of discipline* • Release for unsatisfactory performance*

▨ Transfer

*New

Source: *Report of the Auditor General of Canada*, Chapter 3, page 8, Auditor General of Canada, 2005. Reproduced with the permission of the Minister of Public Works and Government Services Canada, 2006.

discipline, and dismissal for unsatisfactory performance. Also, the Public Service Commission delegates much of its authority for making appointments to deputy ministers, who in turn give this responsibility to managers within the organization.[12] The task of the PSC, as noted, will be more to monitor the application of the merit principle and the values accompanying the appointment process (fairness, transparency, and access).[13]

In addition to these bodies, other federal organizations with important roles in human resources management include the Deputy Ministers Human Resource Management Advisory Committee (MAC), the External Advisory Committee on Senior Level Retention and Compensation, the Human Resources Council, and the Privy Council Office. Set up to oversee the introduction of the *Public Service Modernization Act*, the MAC now has an expanded mandate that encompasses the review of all major reforms in human resources management in the federal government. The External Advisory Committee on Senior Level Retention and Compensation, created in 1997, provides advice to the president of the Treasury Board on the management and compensation of senior executives. The Human Resources Council, which is composed of senior human resources personnel in departments and central agencies, "provides advice and leadership in strategic resources management for the Federal Public Service."[14] For its part, the Privy Council Office exercises a major influence on human resources policy and appointments for the most senior ranks of the public service. It is the prime minister's prerogative to make a large number of order-in-council appointments, including deputy ministers, heads of Crown agencies, and federal judges. The clerk of the Privy Council, who is also secretary to the cabinet, advises the prime minister on the qualifications of existing and prospective order-in-council appointees. The PCO also assumes a leadership position in advancing the agenda for public service management and the clerk speaks for the public service.

Major Human Resources Management Processes

In practice, the distribution of responsibilities for human resources management among the key organizations discussed above and the many other administrative bodies within government is very complex. A comprehensive examination of the entire field of human resources management in Canadian government cannot be provided here, but an explanation of the major human resources processes—classification, human resources planning, staffing, training and development, and performance evaluation—is provided.

Job Classification

Job classification is the process by which jobs are assigned to an occupational group within an occupational category and to a level within that group. Both logically and chronologically, classification usually precedes the other main human resources processes. It supplies an essential basis for effective human resources management in general and appropriate wage and salary administration in particular.

An **occupational category** includes a broad range of occupations of the same type, distinguished by the nature of the duties performed and the education required. The six occupational categories in the federal public service and the number of full-time employees in each category in 2004 were as follows: Executive Group (4,322), Scientific and Professional (23,920), Administrative and Foreign Service (69,868), Technical (17,567), Administrative Support (31,736), and Operational (18,563).[15] An occupational group within a category includes occupations that require similar types of work involving similar skills (e.g., the actuarial science group within the Scientific and Professional category or the firefighters group within the Operational category) and that are often related to the labour market outside the public service.

The primary task in classification is **job evaluation**, which consists of the following:

- The analysis of a job in terms of its duties and responsibilities, its physical and mental demands, the knowledge and skills it requires, and the conditions under which it is performed

- The writing of a job description that explains the duties, working conditions, and other aspects of the job
- The assessment of these job characteristics against the classification standard established for the relevant occupational group

Each occupational group has a classification standard, which contains a definition of the category within which the group falls, the groups within each category, the job evaluation plan, and the descriptions of benchmark positions to be used as guides for assessing jobs and rating them according to their level in the group. Jobs at the same level are assigned the same salary range. Since classification is essentially a matter of judgment, it is common practice to obtain more than one person's judgment by having jobs evaluated and rated by committees who advise the official responsible for the final decision.

Human Resources Planning

Human resources planning is the process through which a government strives to ensure that it has—and will continue to have—the appropriate quantity and quality of employees to carry out its responsibilities. This process aims to eliminate the gap between the existing supply of qualified employees and the current and anticipated demand. There is a close relationship between this planning and virtually all other areas of human resources management.

The precise structure of human resources planning in government may vary, but it can be seen as including the following steps.[16]

Step 1. Determine the overall goals and priorities of the organization to ensure that the human resources plan is developed in light of the purposes of the department or agency.

Step 2. Appreciate the workforce of the organization, which means the demographic makeup, the skills mix, and the climate or culture of the agency. This provides an overall appreciation of the current state of the employee structure.

Step 3. Forecast and plan for expected changes in the work of the organization. This step seeks to anticipate the human resources implications of possible adjustments in the responsibilities of the department. For example, what are the possible effects for employees if it is anticipated that the organization will no longer be providing a certain service?

Step 4. Identify the personnel needs of the organization and pinpoint any gaps on the basis of this needs assessment. As an example, a planned expansion of the department combined with an aging employee structure may suggest the need for an aggressive recruitment program.

Step 5. Be aware of efforts of others in the human resources field. The appropriate response to a certain challenge may already be evident in the human resources strategies of other departments.

Step 6. Make sure that the human resources plan includes the capacity to measure its success in achieving the goals of the plan. Benchmarks may, for example, be set to gauge the performance of the plan, and various methodologies may be employed to reveal financially how human resources planning contributes to the organization.

Staffing

The integral link between attracting capable employees and attaining program objectives suggests that staffing may well be the key element of human resources management. We have already seen that determining staffing needs and the means of meeting these needs is a central feature of human resources planning. At the beginning of this chapter, we also saw the importance in the staffing system of balancing the merit principle with other principles. The Public Service Commission sets out the following guiding principles to which the entire staffing system should conform:

- **Fairness.** Staffing decisions must be made objectively and be without favouritism and political interference.
- **Access.** Interested persons must have a reasonable opportunity to apply for positions and to be considered for employment.
- **Transparency.** Any information about decisions, policies or procedures relating to staffing must be communicated to the public openly and in a timely fashion.[17]

Staffing is a complex process, especially in government, where account must be taken of policy and procedural considerations absent in most private sector organizations (e.g., language requirements). However, the staffing process in Canadian governments is normally characterized, and to some extent simplified, by a number of policy and program components (e.g., delegation of staffing authority, open and closed competitions) and of sequential and interrelated steps (e.g., written tests, interviews). Moreover, these policies, programs, and procedures are usually spelled out in a human resources management manual.

The central activities in staffing are recruitment, promotion, and deployment. *Recruitment* involves identifying candidates for public service positions from outside the public service by such methods as inviting job applications from within and from outside the public service and using a human resources inventory system. Figure 17.2 shows how the new definition of merit at the federal level would be applied to the recruitment activity for a senior position in international trade. The merit criteria include the essential qualifications of the job, which are those skills and knowledge required to do the job; the criteria also include the "asset qualifications"—qualifications which are unnecessary for the job but might improve performance—and overall "organizational needs."[18] *Promotion* involves the appointment of an employee from within the public service to a position for which the maximum rate of pay is greater than that of the employee's current position. **Deployment** involves the appointment of an employee to another position at the same level as his or her existing position, or to a higher or lower level, provided that there is no change in the employee's personnel classification. In turn, all of these activities involve **selection**—that is, the screening of candidates through such means as application forms, written examinations, interviews, and a review of the candidate's credentials and past performance. The activities of recruitment and selection are followed by appointment to a specific position or level in the public service.

It is difficult to design and operate a staffing system that will fully satisfy all the parties affected. In a report, the Office of the Auditor General of Canada found that "managers continue to view staffing as unduly complex, inflexible and inefficient, and [that] many employees still are not confident that the system is fair."[19] A major concern expressed in the report related to the slowness of the staffing system, especially when compared with the staffing decisions made in Crown corporations and other government agencies existing outside the core public service. The proposed solution to this problem (and others) was to give individual departments and their managers more leeway in the appointment of officials, a proposal that has been acted upon in the *Public Service Modernization Act*.

Training, Development, and Learning

Training, development, and learning are related activities centred on the desire to ensure that employees are properly equipped and disposed to successfully implement present duties and any future requirements that might arise from the needs of the organization.

Figure 17.2

Position: Senior Policy Officer in International Trade

Merit Criteria

Essential Qualifications	Asset Qualifications
• Language requirements: bilingual imperative CBC/CBC	• Master's degree in international trade
• Degree from a recognized university in business, economics, or political science	• Experience in developing policies on international trade
• Experience in developing policy	• Knowledge of international law related to international trade
• Experience with international trade agreements	• Ability to speak and write in one of the following languages: Russian, Mandarin, Cantonese, Italian, and German
• Knowledge of international trade issues	
• Knowledge of Canada's policy on international trade	**Organizational Needs**
• Ability to develop policy	• Increase Aboriginal representation
• Ability to analyze complex agreements	
• Ability to communicate orally and in writing	
• Effective interpersonal skills	
• Leadership	
• Adaptability	

Source: *Making it Work for You: Staffing Toolkit for Managers,* page 39, Government of Canada, 2006. Reproduced with the permission of the Minister of Public Works and Government Services Canada, 2006.

For the federal government, training refers to "the transfer of knowledge and know-how that is required for the successful performance in a job, occupation or profession," while development represents "an activity that assists employees further their careers and is aligned with departmental priorities and management objectives of the government." Learning involves the process of acquiring "new knowledge and ideas that change the way an individual perceives, understands or acts."[20] At the national level, the recently established Canada School of Public Service (CSPS) is the lead agency in providing overall direction in training, development, and learning and offering various services to ensure that employees of the federal public service have the requisite skills and knowledge. It is also understood that individual departments will develop training and development programs to suit their specific needs and to complement CSPS's efforts.

A great many activities are associated with training, development, and learning. CSPS, for instance, offers the following services:

- Conferences and special events to assist employees in appreciating issues confronting the government
- Classroom and online courses to meet training and development needs of departments and agencies
- Research publications to offer accessible research on government and public management

Chapter 17/The Management of Human Resources

- Language training to support a bilingual working environment and the provision of services in two official languages
- Career development programs to ensure that employees at various stages of their career are provided with an opportunity to build upon their skills and knowledge. Such programs include the Management Trainee Program, the Accelerated Executive Development Program, and Living Leadership: The Executive Excellence Program
- Learning services to help organizations to discover their learning needs and to shape the appropriate responses to these needs[21]

The varied activities of the CSPS reveal a trend in human resources management away from simply providing courses to supplying a rich menu of services. The underlying aim of this shift is to support a culture of continuous learning and education within organizations so that training and development become a natural part of public agencies.

Performance Evaluation

Performance evaluation (often called employee appraisal) is a process involving the systematic collection and analysis of information about the performance of employees over time. It is integrally linked to the other human resources processes discussed above. Employees must not only be recruited, selected, trained, and paid; they must also be evaluated in terms of their overall performance. Effective employee appraisal must be preceded by the process of performance review, which is "a continuous process in which a supervisor and an employee consider the duties to be performed by the employee, the achievements expected, the evaluation criteria and the results actually achieved."[22] Employee appraisal, which is based on this performance review, "identifies an employee's various qualifications, estimates potential, identifies and proposes responses to training and development needs, and indicates future assignments."[23] This employee appraisal is contained in a formal, written report that often includes a summary of the performance review.

The overriding purpose of performance evaluation is to improve the contribution and motivation of each employee. More specifically, it provides a means of assessing the advisability of pay increases and promotion, the strengths and weaknesses of an employee's present performance, and his or her potential for advancement and need for training and development. In addition, performance evaluation gives supervisors a regular opportunity to communicate with and motivate their employees and to check the effectiveness of such other human resources processes as selection and training.

A formal appraisal report is typically prepared once each year for permanent employees and more frequently, usually quarterly, for probationary employees. To facilitate comparison of employees within a single department and with employees in other departments, a common set of evaluation categories is normally used across the government as a whole. For example, the federal government has used the five categories of outstanding, superior, fully satisfactory, satisfactory, and unsatisfactory.

Performance evaluation, like job classification, is a difficult undertaking, because it involves a substantial measure of personal judgment. It is widely recognized that the objectivity, validity, and reliability of rating systems are often questionable. That one supervisor's "superior" is another supervisor's "satisfactory" raises questions about the fairness of the process. Thus, employees, aware of the impact of performance evaluations on their compensation and career prospects, frequently view evaluations with trepidation. If the process and the outcome of the evaluation are seen as unfair, they may actually reduce the employees' motivation to perform at his or her current level.

The matter of fairness is complicated by the reality that many employees have an inflated perception of their performance and may well resent even a "satisfactory" rating.

Supervisors, in turn, are sensitive to these high expectations and to the career impact of evaluation decisions; they are therefore reluctant to assign low ratings that they must then explain and defend in face-to-face meetings with employees. Supervisors are especially reluctant to assign ratings that may get them involved in the time-consuming process of grievances and appeals, and are understandably tempted to rate every employee as at least satisfactory. The annual employee appraisal tends to be easier when supervisors provide employees with an informal, ongoing assessment of their performance rather than storing up the good and bad points of performance for discussion at a single session.

Conclusion

In this chapter, we looked closely at the merit principle—the foundation of the process of recruiting and retaining public servants—and examined the evolution and elements of the human resources management system. This represents the core of the system of ensuring that the public service has the personnel necessary to carry out the duties assigned to appointed officials. However, there are other aspects of managing human resources, the two most important of which are providing for a public bureaucracy that is broadly representative of the society it serves and the commitment to pay equity. These are the concerns of the following chapter.

1. Public Service Commission, *Annual Report 2004–2005* (Ottawa: Her Majesty the Queen in Right of Canada, 2005), 11–12.

2. Valuable information and analysis on the nature and extent of patronage from the pre-Confederation period to the mid-1930s are provided by R. McGregor Dawson in *The Principle of Official Independence* (London: P.S. King and Son, 1922), ch. 3; *The Civil Service of Canada* (Oxford: Oxford University Press, 1929); and "The Canadian Civil Service," *Canadian Journal of Economics and Political Science* 2 (August 1936): 288–300. For a detailed treatment of the evolution of merit in the Canadian federal public service, see J.E. Hodgetts, William McCloskey, Reginald Whitaker, and V. Seymour Wilson, *The Biography of an Institution: The Civil Service of Canada, 1908–1967* (Montreal: McGill-Queen's University Press, 1974).

3. Royal Commission on Government Organization, *Report*, 5 vols. (Ottawa: Queen's Printer, 1962–63).

4. D'Avignon Committee, *Report of the Special Committee on the Review of Personnel Management and the Merit Principle* (Hull, Ont.: Supply and Services Canada, 1979), 5.

5. Ibid., 46.

6. See, notably, David Zussman and Jak Jabes, *The Vertical Solitude: Managing in the Public Sector* (Halifax: The Institute for Research on Public Policy, 1989).

7. Brian Mulroney, *Public Service 2000: The Renewal of the Public Service of Canada* (Ottawa: Supply and Services Canada, 1990).

8. Jonathan Malloy, "The Next Generation? Recruitment and Renewal in the Federal Public Service," in G. Bruce Doern, ed., *How Ottawa Spends 2004–2005: Mandate Change in the Paul Martin Era* (Montreal & Kingston: McGill-Queen's University Press, 2004), 279.

9. Evert Lindquist, Ian Clark, and James Mitchell, "Reshaping Ottawa's Centre of Government: Martin's Reforms in Historical Perspective," in Doern, ed., *How Ottawa Spends 2004–2005*, 333.

10. Public Service Commission of Canada, *Annual Report 2004–2005*, 12. Available at www.psc-cfp.gc.ca/centres/annual-annuel/2005/index_e.htm. Retrieved July 12, 2006.

11. Some other pieces of legislation might be mentioned, including the *Official Languages Act* and the *Canadian Human Rights Act*.

12. Government of Canada, *Making It Work for You: The Government of Canada Tool-Kit for Managers* (Ottawa: Her Majesty the Queen in Right of Canada, 2006), 20.

13. For a good overview of these changes, see Auditor General of Canada, *Report of the Auditor General of Canada* (Ottawa: Department of Public Works and Government Services, February 2005), ch. 3.

14. Public Service Human Resources Management Agency of Canada, "Welcome to HR Council Online." Available at the Human Resources Council site, www.hrma-agrh.gc.ca/hr-rh/hrc-crh/index_e.asp. Accessed July 12, 2006.

15. Public Service Human Resources Management Agency of Canada, *Employment Equity in the Federal Public Service* (Ottawa: Her Majesty the Queen in Right of Canada, 2005), 25–27.

16. Public Service Human Resources Management Agency of Canada, *Introduction to HR Planning—A Reference Tool for HR Specialists in the Public Service of Canada*. Available at www.hrma-agrh.gc.ca/hr-rh/hrp-prh/ihp-ipr_e.asp. Accessed July 12, 2006. The text modifies slightly the presentation of the steps outlined in this document.

17. Public Service Commission, *Annual Report 2004–2005*, 12.

18. Government of Canada, *Making It Work for You*.

19. Auditor General of Canada, *Report of the Auditor General of Canada* (Ottawa: Department of Public Works and Government Services, April 2000), ch. 9, "Streamlining the Human Resource Management Regime," 9–20.

20. Treasury Board of Canada Secretariat, *Policy on Learning, Training and Development* (January 1, 2006), 9–11. Available at www.tbs-sct.gc.ca/pubs_pol/hrpubs/TB_856/ltd-afp02_e.asp. Retrieved July 12, 2006.

21. See the website of the Canada School of Public Service at http:// myschool.gc.ca/main-html.

22. Treasury Board of Canada Secretariat, *Personnel: A Manager's Handbook*, 49.

23. Ibid.

18

Representative Bureaucracy and Employment Equity

When we look at public bureaucracies in Canada or elsewhere, sometimes we can see that the composition of the organization is not representative of the population it serves. A society may be highly multicultural, for example, but have a public service which has seemingly recruited only from one or two segments of the society. This result may arise from a very strict application of the merit principle, or it might be a consequence of discrimination inherent in the system of human resources management. Whatever the reasons, governments—and their societies—are usually unhappy with this situation, because they understand it is unfair and most likely detrimental to the responsive delivery of services. Accordingly, governments will take action to correct it. In Canada, the actions taken to provide for a more representative bureaucracy constitute an effort typically called employment equity. Another unsettling aspect of the public bureaucracy is evidence that there may be discrimination in the payment of public servants. Even though women may carry out a job comparable to one carried out by men, they may find that they are paid less than men. Pay equity is the program in Canada established to address this problem.

This chapter first examines the philosophical and logical underpinnings of representative bureaucracy. We will see that representative bureaucracy has its supporters, but that it is not without its critics. The chapter also considers the employment equity efforts at the federal level and their effects. These efforts are for the benefit of four groups: women, visible minorities, the disabled, and aboriginals. There is also an effort at ensuring that the distribution of jobs broadly reflects the presence of francophones in the larger population. The chapter ends with a discussion of pay equity.

Representative Bureaucracy

Representative bureaucracy is a difficult concept that has been interpreted in a variety of ways. A strict interpretation would require that the public service be a microcosm of the total society in terms of a wide range of variables, including race, religion, language, education, social class, and region of origin. Most governments would probably see this interpretation as too literal and probably impossible to achieve. But these same governments would most likely accept the following sentiment as the foundation for their efforts in this area: that a public service that is representative of the larger society will be responsive to the needs and interests of the public and will thus be more responsible. This belief in turn would be based on several propositions:

1. If the values of the public service as a whole are similar to those of the total population, the public service will tend to make the kinds of decisions the public would make if it were involved in the decision-making process.
2. The values of public servants are molded by the pattern of socialization they experience before they enter the public service. This pattern includes such socializing forces as education, social class, occupational background, race, family, and group associations.
3. The values arising from this socialization will not be modified by prolonged exposure to bureaucratic values.
4. The values arising from socialization will be reflected in the behaviour of public servants and, therefore, in their recommendations and decisions.
5. Thus, the various groups in the general population should be represented in the public service in approximate demographic proportion so that public servants will be responsive to the interests of these groups both in policy development and in program delivery.

For many, this set of propositions makes sense; but there are some who believe that the theory of representative bureaucracy and its supporting propositions are vulnerable. The critics of representative bureaucracy contend, for instance, that it is insufficient for the public service as a whole to be broadly representative of the total population; for all interests to be represented in the decision-making process, each major administrative unit must be representative of the total population, especially at its senior levels where the most important recommendations and decisions are made. It is also pointed out that a public servant with certain social and educational origins will not necessarily share the values of those outside the public service with similar origins. The lifelong process of socialization continues after entry to the public service in the form of re-socialization to the values of the service as a whole or of particular administrative units. Moreover, representatives of a specific group in the population, particularly if they achieve high office in the public service, are likely to be upwardly mobile and may well share the socioeconomic and other values of those with whom they work, rather than of the group from which they came. It is also possible that an *un*representative bureaucracy may successfully represent the various groups in a society, and indeed some claim that this has happened in some civil services. All in all—and somewhat ironically—it is possible to have a representative public service that is not responsive and a responsive public service that is not representative.

Canadian Writings

The major points of contention in the historical debate on representative bureaucracy in Canada involve the extent to which the values of efficiency, effectiveness, neutrality, and responsiveness conflict with, or complement, that of representativeness.[1] In this debate,

Donald Rowat objects to John Porter's sacrifice of representativeness for the sake of efficiency and suggests that both values can be achieved. He argues that representativeness "is essential to the efficiency of the bureaucracy, in the sense of the latter's effectiveness in a democratic, pluralistic society."[2] Porter asserts that people of various social origins will be found in the bureaucracy in roughly the same proportion as in the population as a whole *if* government recruitment and promotion policies do not discriminate against particular groups, *if* educational facilities to qualify persons for public service appointments are equal among these groups, and *if* these groups are equally motivated to join the public service. He contends that "in the theoretically ideal bureaucracy, the candidate for office neither gains nor loses as a result of ethnic, religious or regional origins."[3]

Rowat, who is more concerned with what can be realized in practice than with a search for a theoretically ideal bureaucracy, observes that Porter's conditions of equality do not exist and cannot be easily achieved. He contends that representativeness must be actively sought, even at the expense of technical efficiency and neutrality. Intelligent people with the potential to rise to higher levels in the service could be recruited and provided with the required in-service education and training. Moreover, competent members of underrepresented groups could be brought into the public service from outside. Porter opposes the recruitment of outsiders on the grounds that this practice threatens the neutrality of the service and the concept of the bureaucratic career. He states that "since the basis of power associations are frequently ethnic, regional, or religious, the idea that these groups should be represented in the bureaucracy contradicts the notion of the official as the servant of the state."[4] Rowat does not agree that the appointment of "bureaucratic outsiders" would endanger political neutrality, and he argues that a public service that complemented career public servants with outsiders would be more responsive, since a career bureaucracy tends to "lose contact with and lack understanding of the changing feelings, needs and desires of the great variety of people and groups found in our dynamic, pluralistic society."[5]

Rowat does not suggest that underrepresented groups should be represented in precise proportion to their presence in the total population, and he rejects the use of quotas for recruitment and promotion as unworkable. He does suggest, however, that recruitment to the public service should be guided by the principle of representation.

Porter objects on several grounds to Rowat's plea for representativeness. He first poses the basic question as to which of the many groups in society should be represented in the public service. He then contends that Rowat's proposals for recruiting members of underrepresented groups and providing them with in-service training serve the principle of equal opportunity rather than representativeness. He states also that "in a society of classes, the upwardly mobile are seldom representative of the social interests from which they originated."[6] Finally, he notes the assumption in the theory of representative bureaucracy that political institutions are inadequate to cope with modern demands and questions the view that "ways can be found for governmental bureaucracy to make up for the deficiencies in our representative political institutions."[7]

The Representativeness of the Canadian Bureaucracy

Data on several aspects of the current composition of the Canadian public service in relation to the total population are unavailable, but the available data indicate that the service is not a microcosm of Canadian society. Moreover, it is not the policy of the federal government to establish in the public service a microcosm of the Canadian mosaic by pursuing exact demographic representation of all groups in society; rather, the government's aim is to achieve a more proportionate representation of a limited number of politically significant, but underrepresented, groups. In this regard, the government has argued that the underrepresentation of such groups as francophones, women, and aboriginal peoples may diminish the sensitivity of the public service to the needs of certain segments of the population. Thus, a prime motivation underlying efforts to represent these groups more adequately is to make the public service more responsive, in both the provision of policy advice and the delivery of services. As explained above, the assumption that representativeness will promote responsiveness is central to the theory of representative bureaucracy. The government also presumes that members of underrepresented groups who join the public service will remain sensitive to the needs and claims of these groups.

In view of the deficiencies of the theory of representative bureaucracy outlined earlier, the benefits of representation in terms of increased responsiveness are likely to be less than anticipated. However, we know little about the extent to which the expanded representation of members of underrepresented groups has had a policy impact by advancing the substantive interests of these groups.

Increased representation has effects that are not covered by the theory of representative bureaucracy. Representation has a symbolic impact that helps to promote quiescence and stability in the Canadian political system and explains, in part, its appeal to government officials. The statutes, regulations, and administrative units designed to increase the representation of underrepresented groups evoke symbols of equality of opportunity and upward mobility for members of these groups. In the name of equal opportunity, the government has instituted programs to recruit and train group members who have not enjoyed equal access to the public service. Also, recruitment to senior posts from outside the service and post-entry training geared to promotion to the higher ranks of the service demonstrate the opportunities for group members to attain senior policy-making posts. Thus, group members who are appointed to, and promoted in, the public service provide role models for other members of their group.

Government actions to increase the representativeness of the public service serve a partisan political purpose in that they help to sustain or increase electoral support for the governing party. Evidence of partisan motivation can be seen in the fact that the groups for whom increased representation has been sought have mobilized for political action and are highly visible and vocal in their demands for greater participation in the political and administrative systems. The government's efforts on behalf of underrepresented groups have brought about a more representative public service. It is not viable, however, to attempt to represent proportionately all the myriad groups that make up the Canadian mosaic. Experience to date suggests that future government measures toward a more representative public service will be directed primarily to underrepresented groups that become politically influential.

Equal Opportunity and Employment Equity

The issues of representative bureaucracy and equal opportunity are closely linked: the attainment of a representative public service depends largely on the extent to which various groups in society have equal access to employment in the public service. The federal, provincial, and municipal governments have adopted a wide range of programs to promote equal opportunity in the public service for segments of the population that have historically been underrepresented. As explained above, the federal government is committed to improving the representation of certain "target" or "designated" groups, namely women, members of visible minority groups, persons with disabilities, and aboriginal peoples. In the federal sphere, francophones are not treated as one of the target groups; rather, they are treated separately as part of the government's efforts to ensure equitable participation in the public service of Canada's two official language communities.

The term "equal opportunity" was largely displaced in the early 1980s by "affirmative action," which was in turn soon displaced by **employment equity**. "Affirmative action" and "employment equity" are often used interchangeably; both can usefully be viewed as means to the end of equal opportunity. In June 1983, the government announced its continued commitment to a bureaucracy that is representative of and responsive to the people it serves,[8] and introduced an affirmative action program to accelerate the participation in the public service of the target groups. Affirmative action was defined as "a comprehensive systems-based approach to the identification and elimination of discrimination in employment. It makes use of detailed analyses to identify and systematically remove employment policies, practices, and procedures that may exclude or place at a disadvantage the three target groups"[9] (which at that time included women, aboriginal peoples, and disabled persons).

The government stressed that the merit principle would be preserved, and that the numerical goals being set were not quotas but "an estimate of what can be achieved when systemic barriers are eliminated and some temporary special measures are put in place to accelerate training and development experience."[10] The president of the Treasury Board announced that implementation of the affirmative action program would be viewed as a major consideration in the performance of deputy ministers. Thus, while this program did not establish quotas, it moved in that direction by using temporary special measures, numerical goals, and pressure on senior public servants to achieve these goals.

The legal basis for affirmative action programs was laid in 1977 by the *Canadian Human Rights Act*, which also established the Canadian Human Rights Commission. Section 16(1) of the Act provides in effect that measures taken to redress historical imbalances in the participation of certain groups do not amount to reverse discrimination. More recently, the recommendations of the Royal Commission on Equality in Employment[11] (the Abella Commission) and the coming into force of Section 15—the equality rights section—of the Canadian Charter of Rights and Freedoms have supported the federal government's affirmative action programs.

It is important to note that employment equity programs are protected under the Charter. Section 15 guarantees "equal protection and equal benefit of the law without discrimination," and then goes on to say that this guarantee "does not preclude any law, program or activity that has as its object the amelioration of conditions of disadvantaged individuals or groups including those that are disadvantaged because of race, national or ethnic origin, colour, religion, sex, age or mental or physical disability." In other words, preferential treatment for groups that have historically been disadvantaged does not constitute reverse discrimination.

As noted, the term employment equity, which came into frequent use in 1985, is very similar in meaning to affirmative action. The *Public Service Employment Act*, as amended in 1992,[12] defines an employment equity program as a "policy or program established by the Treasury Board to improve employment and career opportunities in the Public Service for groups of persons that are disadvantaged, including women, aboriginal peoples, persons with disabilities, and persons who are, because of their race or colour, in a visible minority in Canada, and to correct their conditions of disadvantage experienced by such groups in their employment."

In March 1986, the House of Commons passed the federal *Employment Equity Act*, which required federally regulated employers with 100 or more employees (primarily in the banking, transportation, and communication industries) and Crown corporations to report annually to the government on the extent to which they have achieved results in promoting employment equity programs for designated groups. In the same year, the Treasury Board issued an employment equity policy for the public service that required departments and agencies, among other things, to identify systemic barriers to equitable participation by designated groups, adopt special measures to remedy imbalances in the public service workforce, and meet numerical objectives for the representation and distribution of the designated groups.[13]

The term "systemic barriers" (or "systemic discrimination") refers to an employment policy, practice, procedure, or system that excludes, or has a negative effect on, the designated groups, whether or not that effect was intended, and that cannot be justified as being job-related. For example, if 15 percent of geologists in Canada are women but only 6 percent of the geologists in a particular department are women, the burden is on the department to show that this is not the result of discrimination. The explanation might be that the department requires all the geologists it hires to have ten years of work experience and that relatively few female geologists have that experience. Consideration would be given to removing this requirement, because it penalizes women more than men, even though no discrimination was intended.

In early 1991, the Treasury Board announced a new approach to setting employment equity targets on the basis of rates of recruitment, promotion, and separation, not just on representation. "This reflects the principle that the workplace should be conducive to attracting and retaining designated group members, that they should receive a fair share of recruitment and promotion opportunities, and that their rate of separation from the Public Service should be no higher than that of other employees."[14] In 1995 a new *Employment Equity Act* replaced the 1986 Act. The new Act applies to public servants as well as the previously covered Crown corporations and federally regulated industries; it also authorizes the Canadian Human Rights Commission to audit employers to verify their compliance with the Act.

In the federal government, the Treasury Board Secretariat and the Public Service Commission have played the leading roles in developing, implementing, and monitoring employment equity programs. The two agencies devised programs for francophones and women in the 1960s that were strengthened and supplemented by programs for aboriginal peoples, visible minorities, and the disabled during the 1970s and 1980s. Table 18.1 shows the distribution of employees by designated group and occupational category as of March 2004.

Employment equity programs can be grouped into three categories: training and development (e.g., special training opportunities for women); new or modified administrative units and practices (e.g., a special office for aboriginal employment); and vigorous recruitment (e.g., various programs to recruit qualified persons from every target group). Departments and agencies are required to run employment equity programs to promote representativeness and fairness in the public service.

Programs to overcome artificial institutional barriers to public service employment are of limited use in overcoming attitudinal barriers—notably prejudice against the target groups—that exist in the public service and in Canadian society as a whole. There is, however, an ongoing effort in government to sensitize public service managers to the importance of removing obstacles to equal access to public service employment. To ensure that managers are sensitive to this effort, success in enhancing the participation of these groups is now deemed to be one element of the managers' performance evaluation.

There have been complaints from public servants and from their unions that equal opportunity programs violate the merit principle and discriminate against candidates outside the designated groups for appointment and promotion. The Public Service Commission has responded by explaining that merit is a dynamic principle; its application must be reconciled with such other values as responsiveness, representativeness, fairness, equity, and economy. Moreover, according to the commission, the equal opportunity program does not amount to reverse discrimination, because individual abilities, rather than group characteristics, are emphasized in appointments and promotions.

To assess the extent to which the federal government's employment equity programs have been successful, it is useful to examine briefly the experience of five

Table 18.1 — Distribution of Public Service Employees by Designated Group, Occupational Category, and Workforce Availability as of March 31, 2004

OCCUPATIONAL CATEGORY	WOMEN (%)	ABORIGINAL PEOPLES (%)	PERSONS WITH DISABILITIES (%)	PERSONS IN A VISIBLE MINORITY (%)
Executive	34.9	2.9	4.9	4.8
Scientific and Professional	41.4	2.4	3.7	11.9
Administrative and Foreign Services	59.7	4.1	6.0	7.7
Technical	31.4	3.0	4.4	5.2
Administrative Support	82.7	5.2	8.0	9.3
Operational	17.6	5.3	4.7	3.8
Total % in public service	53.1	4.1	5.7	7.8
Availability in workforce	52.2	2.5	3.6	10.4

Source: Adapted from Public Service Human Resources Management Agency of Canada, *Employment Equity in the Federal Public Service 2003–04* (Ottawa: Her Majesty the Queen in Right of Canada, 2005), 23–27.

major groups that, historically, have been underrepresented in the public service: francophones, women, aboriginal peoples, members of visible minorities, and disabled persons.

The Representation of Francophones

Barriers to equal opportunity for French-speaking people existed both in the government and in the francophone community itself for much of this century. During the post-Confederation period before the 1918 *Civil Service Act*, francophones were numerically well represented in the public service. They were not, however, as well represented as anglophones at the senior levels. Also, many of the francophone appointments rested on patronage, whereas the 1918 Act emphasized merit and efficiency. Especially after 1918, the public service was pervaded by an anglophone linguistic and cultural bias. Merit and efficiency were linked to formal education and technical qualifications. French-language, or bilingual, competence was not considered a component of merit or likely to enhance efficiency. Furthermore, written examinations and interviews for recruitment and promotion reflected anglophone values and the anglophone educational system, to the disadvantage of francophones. Finally, the view was widely held that the Quebec educational system was a significant barrier to francophone representation, because it emphasized education for such occupations as law, medicine, and the priesthood, and did not, therefore, provide its graduates with the technical, scientific, and commercial skills required for appointment to the public service.

All these factors combined to reduce the motivation of francophones to seek or retain positions in the federal public service. The result was a decline in the proportion of francophones from 21.58 percent in 1918 to 12.25 percent in 1946, and a decline at the deputy minister level during the same period from 14.28 percent to zero.[15]

During the early 1960s, the so-called Quiet Revolution in Quebec focused national attention on francophone grievances about their inadequate participation in the public service. The Glassco Commission reported in 1963 that francophones were poorly represented in the service. The commissioners noted that public confidence in the public service will depend on "how representative it is of the public it serves," and that to achieve representativeness, "a career at the centre of government should be as attractive and congenial to French-speaking as to English-speaking Canadians."[16]

Then, in 1966, Prime Minister Pearson promised that the "linguistic and cultural values of the English-speaking and French-speaking Canadians will be reflected through civil service recruitment and training."[17] The Royal Commission on Bilingualism and Biculturalism, which reported in 1967, gave enormous impetus to this objective. Prime Minister Trudeau, in his comments on the commission's report, stated that "the atmosphere of the public service should represent the linguistic and cultural duality of Canadian society, and ... Canadians whose mother tongue is French should be adequately represented in the public service—both in terms of numbers and in levels of responsibility."[18] Then, in keeping with the aim of the *Official Languages Act* passed in 1969,[19] the Treasury Board established the Official Languages Program, with three major objectives—providing services to, and communicating with, the public in both official languages; enabling public servants to work in the official language of their choice; and achieving the full participation in the service of members of both the anglophone and francophone communities.

In a concerted effort since the late 1960s to increase francophone representation in the public service, the major strategies adopted by the government have included more active recruitment of francophones, the designation of language requirements for public service positions, and the development of an extensive language training system. The latest strategy, released in 2003, is the *Action Plan for Official Languages*, whose purpose is to supply additional financial assistance to language training services, the recruitment of bilingual personnel, the study of the administration of language training and testing, and innovative programs designed to support official languages.[20]

These strategies have helped to reduce institutional barriers in the government to francophone representation. Francophones now represent 32 percent of employees in the federal public service, which comprises people working in government departments (but not Crown corporations and separate agencies). Also, as Table 18.2 shows, their presence in each of the occupational categories in the public service either equals or exceeds their representation in the population of Canada (which is 24 percent); for example, francophones constitute 29 percent of those in the management category and 37 percent in the administrative and foreign service category.[21] At the very highest peak of the public service, francophones are doing better as well. During the period 1987–97, francophones represented 23 percent of the deputy minister appointments; in the ensuing period 1997–2003, they constituted 40 percent of the appointments.[22] If we look at the entire number of people working in the federal government (which incorporates those left out the public service proper), and those in privatized organizations, francophones represent 27 percent of the total number, again higher than their representation in the general population.[23]

The Representation of Women

The underrepresentation of women in Canada's public services, especially at the middle and senior levels, resulted from obstacles to equal opportunity, both in the government

Table 18.2	Participation of Anglophones and Francophones in the Public Service by Occupational Category	
	1984	2004
Canada:		
Anglophones	72%	68%
Francophones	28%	32%
Total	227,942	165,679
Management:		
Anglophones	80%	71%
Francophones	20%	29%
Total	4,023	3,872
Scientific and professional:		
Anglophones	78%	74%
Francophones	22%	26%
Total	22,826	23,772
Administrative and foreign service:		
Anglophones	71%	63%
Francophones	29%	37%
Total	56,513	68,033
Technical:		
Anglophones	79%	76%
Francophones	21%	24%
Total	27,824	16,828
Administrative support:		
Anglophones	67%	67%
Francophones	33%	33%
Total	72,057	32,888
Operational:		
Anglophones	75%	76%
Francophones	25%	24%
Total	44,699	20,286

Source: Adapted from Public Service Human Resources Management Agency of Canada, *Annual Report on Official Languages 2003–04* (Ottawa: Her Majesty the Queen in Right of Canada, 2004), 53.

and in society generally. By 1885, only 23 of 4,280 public servants were women and more than one-third of these were junior clerks in the Post Office Department. The proportion of women in the service rose gradually to 14 percent in 1928 and to 18.7 percent in 1937. It accelerated during the war years, reaching 35 percent in 1943, but declined after the war and remained at about 27 percent during the 1960s. Since, by 1970, women constituted about 30 percent of the total labour force, they were not badly underrepresented in the public service compared to the private sector. However, they were poorly represented at senior levels of the service. In 1971, only 14.1 percent of officer positions were held by women, whereas women made up 29.3 percent of the service as a whole.[24]

Before 1970, the government took little action to promote female representation in the public service. It was not until 1955 that the restriction against hiring married women for government employment was abolished. The Royal Commission on Government

Chapter 18 / Representative Bureaucracy and Employment Equity

Organization (the Glassco Commission) called upon the government in 1963 to show "creative leadership in providing equal opportunities for women."[25] In the 1967 *Public Service Employment Act*, sex was included with race, national origin, colour, and religion as a basis on which it was forbidden to discriminate. Then the Royal Commission on the Status of Women reported in 1970 that women do not enjoy equal opportunity to "enter and advance in Government Service, and that their skills and abilities are not being fully used there. Attitudes and practices seem to be at fault."[26] The commissioners made numerous recommendations to ensure equality of opportunity for women in the public service, and the government implemented most of these recommendations.

Barriers to equal opportunity for women have been similar in the public and private sectors of society. The underutilization of women has generally been attributed to differences between men and women in formal education and work experience, and to low career expectations, high absenteeism, and high turnover among female employees. Studies on the role of women in the public service conclude that these factors are not sufficient to explain fully the lower salaries and subordinate positions received by women. Additional factors include attitudes that militate against women advancing and developing, corporate cultures which women find stultifying, and the sheer difficulty of balancing work and family duties.

As with francophones, the government has used a variety of strategies to remove barriers to female representation, including new administrative structures, active recruitment, and training. The impact of these activities leads one to be cautiously optimistic about the efficacy of employment equity. As Table 18.1 shows, women now represent more than half of all employees (53.1 percent) in the core federal public service, and they constitute 35 percent of those in the Executive occupational category—double the percentage of ten years ago.[27] Women have also made impressive gains in other occupational categories (Administration and Foreign Service, and Scientific and Professional) that require higher levels of education, and these gains should only increase in light of the fact that the representation of women in these categories is inversely related to age (e.g., women represent 44 percent of all employees in the Executive category in the age cohort 30–39).[28] Not all the signs, however, are positive. Women still represent the vast majority of employees in Administrative Support, the occupational category that encompasses most of the low-paying and low-skilled positions. Also, about 55 percent of all federal employees earn $50,000 or more, yet only 44 percent of women have attained this salary figure (though controlling for age might change this situation).[29] Women also remain underrepresented in occupational groups relating to computers and engineering—areas with high hiring potential in an increasingly technological world. Lastly, it appears that progress in the deputy ministerial ranks has slowed. During the period 1987–97, women represented 19 percent of the deputy-minister appointments, an increase of seven percentage points over the preceding ten-year period. But between the years 1997 and 2003, the percentage of female appointments to the most senior departmental position has increased only to 22 percent.[30] Projections based on historical increases have shown that women would constitute nearly half of all deputy-minister appointments by 2011, which seems most unlikely in light of the recent slowdown in female appointments.

The Representation of Aboriginal Peoples

The underrepresentation of aboriginal peoples reflects the lack of effective aboriginal participation in the Canadian labour force as a whole and results from a formidable array of institutional and attitudinal barriers to representation, both in the government and in the aboriginal community. Aboriginal peoples have been isolated culturally and geographically from the mainstream of Canadian society. Inadequate educational facilities and opportunities have made it difficult for them to obtain the academic qualifications required for entry into the public service, especially at the senior levels. As a result of their small numbers in the public service and of their concentration in the lower ranks, they are not sufficiently aware of career opportunities in the more senior echelons. There is no visible cadre of aboriginal public servants whose achievements they are motivated to emulate. Furthermore, the government's recruitment practices tend to emphasize formal academic qualifications rather than practical experience, and to stress competence in the French or English languages rather than in an aboriginal language. Discriminatory attitudes toward aboriginal peoples that are widespread in Canadian society have in the past been found also in the public service.[31] In addition, some aboriginals choose not to work for the Canadian government because they do not recognize this government as their government.

These various governmental and societal factors have combined to discourage aboriginal peoples from seeking positions in the service and to confine those who do enter primarily to lower-level positions. To overcome these obstacles, the federal government has adopted strategies similar to those used to increase the representation of francophones and women; new administrative units have engaged in active recruitment and training of aboriginal peoples, and these efforts appear to have had some effect. Aboriginal peoples constitute 2.5 percent of the labour force, but they make up 4.1 percent of the public service (in 2004), a doubling of the percentage since 1994.[32] Moreover, aboriginal representation in the important Executive category has increased in the past years, from 1.7 percent in 1997 to the present figure of 2.9 percent.[33] However, as with women, aboriginals are overrepresented in the Administrative Support category.

The Representation of Visible Minorities

Visible minorities make up an increasing percentage of the Canadian population, and thus of the labour force. However, they are significantly underrepresented in the federal public service. In 2004, visible minorities represented 10.4 percent of the labour force of Canada, but constituted only 7.8 percent of federal government employees.[34] Representation of visible minorities in federal public service has admittedly grown over the years—in 1994, the percentage of federal employees designated as visible minorities was a little lower than 4.0.[35] Nevertheless, it was hoped that visible minorities could enjoy the same sort of progress achieved by other designed groups.

The federal government has made various efforts to address this lack of progress. In 1995, it announced that special measures would be taken to increase the presence of visible minorities in the national public service. The special measures included revising employment application forms to allow members of visible minority groups to so identify themselves, providing estimates of the availability of qualified members of these groups in the labour market to help public service managers establish targets for hiring such members, and incorporating a special section on visible minorities in training courses for public service managers. Five years later, in 2000, the federal government adopted a task force report that posited a number of goals in relation to fixing the underrepresentation of visible minorities in the federal public service.[36] One of the most significant goals was to set and meet "one-in-five" benchmarks in various staffing areas (e.g. recruitment, entry into executive levels) by a certain time. So, for example, 20 percent of new recruits to the public service in 2005 would be visible minorities. The goals also included a commitment to make the culture of the public service more appreciative of diversity and to provide the necessary financial resources for successfully meeting the recommendations of the task force.

Early evaluations of this most recent effort of the federal government reveal mixed results. The relevant data show an increased presence of visible minorities in the public service overall and in targeted occupational categories, but most of the benchmarks have not been met. The federal government, however, has taken actions to change the culture of the public service—training courses on diversity, managerial tools to help senior officials gauge their work on corporate culture—and additional monies have been made available to support the action plan.

The Representation of Disabled Persons

The federal government has been more successful in increasing the representation of disabled persons as compared to members of visible minorities. As Table 18.1 shows, the representation of disabled persons in every occupational category and for the public as a whole surpasses the percentage of disabled persons in the Canadian labour force (at 3.6 percent). The same table in the preceding edition of this text (for the year 1997) showed the exact opposite—that representation of disabled people in the federal public service and its occupational categories fell well short of their participation in the overall labour force of Canada. Additional information also confirms the success with disabled persons in the federal public service. For instance, in 1994, disabled persons represented a little under 3 percent of all employees in the federal government, a percentage that has doubled over the past ten years.

Pay Equity

Over the past decade, **pay equity**—or equal pay for work of equal value—has been an issue of considerable importance in the management of human resources in both the public and private sectors of the economy. It is one component of the broader concept of employment equity already discussed (though employment equity supports movement into new occupational categories, pay equity accepts differences in representation in occupations and seeks to eliminate pay differences among these occupations).

Pay equity is a shorthand term for equal pay for work of equal value. This concept must be distinguished from that of equal pay for equal work, which requires that men and women be paid the same for doing the same job, or for a job that is very similar. The concept of equal pay for work of equal value permits comparisons of different jobs performed for the same employer. For example, if one job classification, such as public health nurse, is of equal value to another, such as public health inspector, employees in these two categories should receive the same base pay.

A primary purpose of pay equity programs is to ensure that women receive equal pay for doing work that has the same value as that done by men. Historically, women have been segregated into certain low-paying jobs (e.g., clerical, sales, and service jobs); these jobs have received lower rates of pay than those of equivalent value traditionally performed by men. Pay equity programs strive to devise a job evaluation method that removes sex bias from job classifications. If the requirements of a female-dominated job category, such as secretary, were found to be equivalent in terms of skill, effort, responsibility, and working conditions to those of a higher-paid job category in which males predominated, a pay adjustment would be made for the female-dominated category.

The implementation of pay equity usually involves three steps. The first step is the identification of jobs that are mostly female or male; gender dominance can be defined, for example, as 70 percent or more of either sex. The second step is evaluation of jobs by a job assessment procedure that is gender-neutral and that awards points for various criteria found in a job. For example, a certain job may be given a certain number of points for decision-making responsibility or quality of the working conditions. The third step is the identification of jobs of comparable value (as determined by the awarding of a similar number of points) and any necessary upward pay adjustments to ensure that the pay is the same in the female- and the male-dominated jobs. Luciani nicely sums up the operation of the three steps:

> In order to evaluate two totally different jobs, pay equity legislation relies on a point system assigned to various criteria, such as skills, efforts, experience, responsibility, and working conditions. These points are added up to see which jobs are comparable, and then wages are set accordingly.[37]

Among the concerns about pay equity programs are that "all evaluation techniques are fundamentally arbitrary and can at best only estimate the comparable value between one job and another" and that both the pay adjustments and the administration of pay equity programs are very costly.[38] It is also argued that higher wages mean higher prices for the affected jobs, which in turn may lead to less demand for these positions. Despite these and other concerns about pay equity, most governments in Canada are convinced that the benefits outweigh the disadvantages. Several provinces have enacted pay equity legislation for their employees based on a "proactive" system-wide approach that requires employers to implement pay equity regardless of whether a complaint has been made or whether there is solid evidence of wage discrimination.

In the federal government, and in most provincial governments (only Alberta has no pay equity law or framework), the battle for pay equity legislation has been won, but the issue is still very much alive, because pay equity settlements are so costly. Recently, the Canadian Human Rights Tribunal, which is responsible for adjudicating pay equity claims, ruled that Canada Post must pay $150 million to 6,000 clerical workers because of pay discrimination committed more than two decades ago.[39] As with many cases relating to pay equity, the government had decided to appeal the order to the Federal Court. The challenges now lie in implementing and enforcing the legislation effectively, and in evaluating the extent to which the goals of pay equity are achieved in practice and the extent to which pay equity contributes to the broader objective of employment equity. In 2004, a federal task force released an extensive report on pay equity, and it may provide the basis for achieving a truly effective regime for eliminating wage discrimination in Canada.[40]

Conclusion

In this chapter, we have examined the attempt of the federal government to create a more representative public service. Though it is difficult to gain a true picture of the effects of employment equity efforts, it appears that some success has been achieved. However, it seems equally clear that additional advances need to be made, especially in relation to the participation of visible minorities in the public service. As for pay equity, this complex area requires more discussion and attention.

Notes

1. John Porter, "Higher Public Servants and the Bureaucratic Elite in Canada," *Canadian Journal of Economics and Political Science* 24 (November 1958): 483–501; Donald C. Rowat, "On John Porter's Bureaucratic Elite in Canada," *Canadian Journal of Economics and Political Science* 25 (May 1959): 204–7; and John Porter, "The Bureaucratic Elite: A Reply to Professor Rowat," *Canadian Journal of Economics and Political Science* 25 (May 1959): 207–9.

2. Rowat, "On John Porter's Bureaucratic Elite," 204.

3. Porter, "Higher Public Servants," 490–91.

4. Ibid., 490.

5. Rowat, "On John Porter's Bureaucratic Elite," 207.

6. Porter, "The Bureaucratic Elite," 208.

7. Ibid., 209.

8. Treasury Board of Canada Secretariat, "Affirmative Action in the Public Service," news release, June 27, 1983.

9. Ibid.

10. Ibid.

11. Royal Commission on Equality in Employment, *Report* (Ottawa: Minister of Supply and Services, 1984).

12. Department of Justice, "Public Service Reform Act," *Statutes* (1992), ch. 54, s. 5.1 (5).

13. Treasury Board of Canada Secretariat, *Employment Equity in the Public Service: Annual Report 1992–93* (Ottawa: Minister of Supply and Services, March 1994), 6.

14. Paul Tellier, Clerk of the Privy Council and Secretary to the Cabinet, *Public Service 2000: A Report on Progress* (Ottawa: Minister of Supply and Services, 1992), 59–60.

15. V. Seymour Wilson and Willard A. Mullins, "Representative Bureaucracy: Linguistic/Ethnic Aspects in Canadian Public Policy," *Canadian Public Administration* 21(4) (winter 1978), 520.

16. Royal Commission on Government Organization, *Report*, vol. 1 (Ottawa: Queen's Printer, 1963), 27–29.

17. House of Commons, *Debates*, April 6, 1966, 3915.

18. Ibid., June 23, 1970, 8487.

19. A new *Official Languages Act* was proclaimed in September 1988. Among other things, the new act recognizes that the participation rates of anglophones and francophones may vary from one department to another, depending on such considerations as the department's mandate, clientele, and location.

20. Public Service Human Resources Management Agency of Canada, Government of Canada, *Annual Report on Official Languages 2003–04* (Ottawa: Her Majesty the Queen in Right of Canada, 2004), 9–11.

21. Ibid., 53.

22. Jacques Bourgault, *Profile of Deputy Ministers in the Government of Canada* (Ottawa: School of Public Service, 2004), table 2.

23. Public Service Human Resources Management Agency of Canada, 58.

24. Calculations based on Public Service Commission, *Annual Report 1971* (Ottawa: Information Canada, 1972), 44–45.

25. Royal Commission on Government Organization, *Report*, 275.

26. Royal Commission on the Status of Women, *Report* (Ottawa: Information Canada, 1970), 138.

27. Public Service Human Resources Management Agency of Canada, Government of Canada, *Employment Equity in the Federal Public Service 2003–04* (Ottawa: Her Majesty the Queen in Right of Canada, 2005), 3.

28. Ibid., 28. Author's calculation.

29. Ibid., 17.

30. Jacques Bourgault, *Profile of Deputy Ministers in the Government of Canada* (Ottawa: Canada School of Public Service 2003), 1.

31. See "Native People and Employment in the Public Service of Canada," a report prepared by Impact Research for the Public Service Commission, October 1976, 40–44.

32. Public Service Human Resources Management Agency of Canada, *Employment Equity in the Federal Public Service 2003–04* (Ottawa: Her Majesty the Queen in Right of Canada, 2004), 4. Available at www.hrma-agrh.gc.ca/reports-rapports/ee-04-1_e.asp. Retrieved July 12, 2006.

33. Ibid., 28. For a more critical look at employment equity efforts in relation to aboriginals, see Pay Equity Task Force, *Final Report: Pay Equity: A New Approach to a Fundamental Right* (Ottawa: Her Majesty the Queen in Right of Canada, 2005), 41–42. This report also takes a more critical stance on the other designated groups under the employment equity program.

34. Ibid., 6–7.

35. Ibid., 7 (discerned from Figure 4).

36. Ibid., ch. 2.

37. Patrick Luciani, *Economic Myths: Making Sense of Canadian Policy Issues* (Toronto: Pearson Education Canada, Inc., 2004), 11.

38. Ibid., 11–12.

39. Gloria Galloway, "Canada Post Workers Win Lengthy Battle for Pay Equity," *Globe and Mail*, October 8, 2005, A4.

40. Pay Equity Task Force, *Final Report: Pay Equity*.

19

The Budgetary Process

Political scientists like to say that money is what motivates and structures business and the private sector, but that in politics and public administration it is power which underlies all activities and operations. The interactions and relations between public servants and others in the political process show that there is an element of truth in this assertion; power shapes the activities of government and represents a resource eagerly sought by all in the political process. However, this should not be taken to mean that money is unimportant in the public sector. Without money and financial resources, there would be no programs to administer, no regulations to make, no Crown corporations to run, no public servants to hire, and no public administration or even government to study and consider. Thus, one of the major duties of political officials and their advisors is the management of money and financial resources. This particular task involves generating the necessary public revenues (another term for "money" in government), and then making plans for the allocation of these revenues to government agencies and their programs. Budgeting is the mechanism used to carry out these twin activities. The management of financial resources also entails gaining approval from elected representatives of the budgetary plans; in parliamentary governments, no money can be collected or expended without the assent of the legislative branch. The resources also have to be administered, which means that procedures must be put in place to distribute the money to government bodies and to ensure that the resources are used wisely and in accordance with the law.

This chapter concerns itself with an examination of the first step in the management of financial resources, which is the making of the budget. The chapter considers the two types of budgets, revenue and expenditure, and the various styles or ways in which the expenditure budget can be structured. We also look at the expenditure budgetary cycle for the government of Canada in an attempt to see budgeting in action. Sometimes it is forgotten that budgeting is a supremely political act, so the chapter concludes with a review of some of the strategies used by government actors to achieve their goals in the budgetary process. The last part reminds all those interested in public administration that factors other than the public interest may motivate participants in the political process.

The Budget

Integral to the management of financial resources in government is the preparation of a budget. The budgetary process forces public officials to establish priorities and to set out their major plans for the provision of services to the citizenry of the country. It also requires that government make decisions concerning the raising of funds to finance these plans and to allocate monies to programs consistent with priorities of government. Another aspect of this phase of the financial management process is that it takes place in a politicized environment because budget decisions involve attempts to please various interests and to resolve policy differences. Because of all these qualities and others, it seems fair to say that budgeting is the "quintessential act of governing."[1]

The significance of the budget presents its makers with many difficulties. One of the great difficulties in preparing a government budget is that the budget typically has many specific objectives, not all of which are consistent with one another. In preparing a personal budget, one usually thinks in terms of the fairly one-dimensional problem of adjusting expenditures to fit a relatively fixed income. The complicating factor in the preparation of government budgets is that they must address at least three objectives.

First is the setting of macroeconomic policy or at least that part of it that is influenced by fiscal instruments—that is, levels of aggregate revenue, expenditure, and surplus or deficit. Governments set total revenue and expenditure targets so as to stimulate the economy or slow it down.

The second objective involves influencing behaviour at a more micro level. Governments frequently use tax provisions, not just to raise revenue but also to encourage people to do, or refrain from doing, certain things. For example, customs duties raise a sizable portion of government revenue, but their main objective is to protect domestic industry. Budgets may also contain provisions that reduce the tax liability of citizens who engage in designated actions; a budget might lessen the tax load of young families who place their children in non-parental care arrangements or do the same for taxpayers who invest their money in retirement savings plans. The third objective of a budget is simply to raise the resources needed to fund expenditures. This involves estimating the amounts to be received from various tax and nontax sources of revenue, and adjusting those under the control of the government so that adequate funds are raised. Thus, the mark of a good tax system is that it produces reasonably stable amounts of money from year to year, but, even more important, the amount ought to be predictable well in advance, so that the government knows where it will stand as the year progresses.

The most difficult aspect of these three objectives is that not all point toward the same action at the same time. For example, in difficult economic times, government will need more revenue to fund employment insurance and social assistance plans. However, macroeconomic principles suggest that it is desirable to reduce taxes to stimulate spending in hard economic times. The continuing adjustment of these seemingly irreconcilable factors makes government budgeting a most challenging task.

Revenue Budget

There are two basic types of budgets, one of which is the revenue budget. At least once each year, the federal Minister of Finance and all provincial treasurers prepare their revenue budgets that contain, among many other things, a request to their respective legislatures to impose new taxes or modify existing ones. The revenue budget may accomplish other purposes, such as providing overviews of the economy and announcing changes in expenditures, but the primary intent is to give a picture of the revenue structure and to announce changes in taxes and other means of raising revenue.

The fiscal year of the federal and provincial governments begins on April 1 and ends the following March 31, so the practice is to present the revenue budget shortly before the beginning of the fiscal year, usually around February. But there is no set rule for this timing; budgets are sometimes presented at other times of the year and more than one budget can be presented in the same year. These deviations stem from either political considerations (e.g., the desire to present an attractive budget on which to fight an election), or from volatile economic conditions such as changing international trade situations or energy prices. The arrival of new governments, as in the case of Stephen Harper and the Conservative Party, can also throw the budgetary schedule off its usual track.

The revenue budget is presented as a part of the minister's budget speech. There is no set format for this speech, but it usually contains most of the following elements:

- A review of economic conditions and problems based on information from a paper tabled a few days earlier (or at the same time as the budget)
- A statement of government revenues and expenditures over the past year and a comparison with the previous budget's estimation
- An estimation of government expenditures and revenues for the upcoming year and the surplus or deficit
- Notice of any ways and means motions—that is, motions to introduce bills to amend various tax acts[2]

The last two items are usually given the most attention. In recent years, the emergence of sizable surpluses and their proposed allocation has made this part of the revenue budget even more prominent. The notice of ways and means motions holds the greatest interest for most taxpayers, because this is the announcement of changes in tax structure or rates, which means that new taxes will be introduced, new items taxed, or tax loopholes opened or closed.

The minister's budget speech is given much more attention than other speeches in the legislature. Because it says so much about the government's financial situation, it can be regarded as a sort of "mini Throne Speech." The date and time are set several weeks in advance at an hour when stock markets are closed so that the contents of the speech will not affect stock prices precipitously. The media focus on this event, and it is usually broadcast live on radio and television, followed by analyses by learned economists, representatives of interest groups, and the inevitable interviews with the "average family." Several days of the legislature's time are set aside for what is euphemistically called debate on the budget speech. Actually it is a time for the opposition parties to criticize the minister for past mistakes and anticipated future mistakes.

After this debate, there is a vote of confidence concerning the overall budget. Assuming that the government does survive the initial vote of confidence, the Minister of Finance will then introduce, over the next few months, a series of motions implementing the specific taxation measures presented in the budget. Votes on these motions can be matters of confidence if the specific measure is central to the total budget package, but they are not ordinarily considered matters of confidence. However, defeat of a major tax measure can pose a serious problem for a government, because alternative sources of revenue will have to be found.

Budget Making

Traditionally, it has been difficult to discuss the making of the revenue budget in great detail; it is very much the personal work of the minister of finance or provincial treasurer and her or his senior public servants. The secrecy of the revenue budget has usually been considered important, because some taxpayers with advance information about revenue provisions might profit unfairly or evade the intended effects of the provisions. The parliamentary tradition is that a minister of finance must resign if there is any leak of information about the budget. However, in the past decade the secrecy has abated somewhat, with changes introduced in the budgetary process by the government of Jean Chrétien. The process now typically includes an economic and fiscal outlook preceding the actual budget, which gives the appropriate context in which the budget will be prepared. Following this are a series of formal and informal consultations with stakeholders or groups interested in the contents of the budget. At this point, the government may even hint at its intentions, either because of a desire to gauge reaction to some proposals or to move the debate about revenue provisions in the desired direction. The process ends with the budget speech, whose contents by now are largely known but which usually still has a few surprises.[3] Despite these changes, there is still concern about leaks about one planned revenue provision or another. In late 2005, a minister in the Paul Martin government casually mentioned to an acquaintance in the financial sector that he might be happy with the tax treatment of a particular investment vehicle in a forthcoming announcement on the budget. The action precipitated an RCMP investigation—and rather active trading in the investment vehicle the day following the conversation between the minister and his friend.

The relaxation of secrecy surrounding the preparation of the revenue budget has helped address concerns about the old budgetary process. The consultations have reduced the uncertainty for business people and others about the plans of the government, an important benefit, and government officials are now better able to talk with those who might supply valuable assistance to the devising of tax measures. But the new openness has generated some new concerns, one of which is that the consultation might be uneven and favour some groups who are better prepared to participate in the new process. Another concern—one seemingly well founded in light of the aforementioned leak of information—is that there will be a greater chance of people gaining inside information about the budget before its release. Nevertheless, the consensus seems to be that the lessening of budget secrecy is on balance a positive step.

Expenditure Budget

The preparation of the expenditure budget is a much more open process. It usually involves almost everybody in the organization and actively seeks the views of interested groups and the general public. The remainder of the chapter will discuss some of the different styles of preparation of the expenditure budget, provide a step-by-step illustration of how a budget is prepared, and finish with a discussion of some of the strategies and tactics employed by organizations to maximize their budgetary allocation.

Styles of the Expenditure Budget

Many different styles of budgeting are in use in different jurisdictions. There is no general agreement about the ideal approach to the expenditure budget; each organization seems to adopt a slightly different style. Regardless of the approach employed, the ideal budgeting system should serve three purposes: control, management, and planning and policy choice.[4] "*Control* refers to the process of binding operating officials to the policies and plans set by their superiors."[5] A satisfactory budgeting system must have some method of ensuring that managers do not overspend their budgets or spend money on programs that have not been properly authorized.

A sound system of management goes beyond simply guaranteeing that subordinates are following orders; it also ensures that work is organized so as to achieve efficiency and effectiveness. The ideal budget would provide some method of evaluating the quality of the management of an organization. Of course, control would ensure that managers do not overspend their budgets, but more than that is expected of a competent manager.

The budget should allow for comparisons between the operating costs of similar organizations and/or the comparison of costs from previous years. These comparisons would provide an insight into the quality of the organization's management. "*Planning* involves the determination of objectives, the evaluation of alternative courses of action and the authorization of select programs."[6] If planning is part of the budgetary system, the system can be used to provide information about the future, which can be used in making tradeoffs among policies. The perfect budgeting system will combine all three factors, but attaining that ideal has been somewhat elusive.

In searching for this ideal style, a number of innovations have been introduced over the years. It is sometimes difficult to find precise dividing lines between approaches, but it is possible to identify three major styles of budgeting that have been employed in recent years: line-item, performance, and program. It is important to understand that these different styles are not mutually exclusive. There are many examples of organizations creating hybrid systems by borrowing from different styles.

Line-Item Budgeting

Line-item budgeting was the first style of budgeting employed in modern public administration, and is usually considered the most rudimentary. Table 19.1 illustrates a page from a line-item budget; it covers the entire budget of one department and shows how the requested funds will be spent by object of expenditure. This illustrates the fact that the line-item budget focuses on inputs used rather than outputs achieved.

The key person in the preparation of this type of budget is the accountant, because the process basically involves reviewing last year's budget and making revisions on the basis of inflation and changes in the size of the population served. This process is usually carried out on an annual basis; there is ordinarily no attempt at long-range planning. The key agency is the operating department because the budget is prepared on a "bottom-up" basis. This means that the process begins with the operating department preparing a request for funds that it then passes upward to decision makers who,

Table 19.1	Expenditure Budget of Hypothetical City Fire Department	
OBJECT OF EXPENDITURE	2007 BUDGET ($000s)	2006 ACTUAL ($000s)
Salaries—regular	120,000	110,000
Salaries—overtime	10,000	9,000
Casual labour	9,000	8,000
Employee benefits	12,000	11,000
Equipment	11,000	10,000
Uniforms	6,000	5,000
Building rent	24,000	22,000
Stationery	6,000	5,000
Cleaning supplies	3,000	2,000
Travel	5,000	4,000
Vehicle maintenance	4,000	3,000
Miscellaneous expenses	3,000	3,000
Total	213,000	192,000

frankly, have a great deal of difficulty making any revisions in the original request because of the very detailed manner in which it is prepared. This leads to a decentralized style of decision making, because decisions are made in operating departments with little opportunity for meaningful review by politicians.

The use of line-item budgeting makes it somewhat awkward to evaluate a manager's performance. The main sign of a good manager in this system is that he or she does not overspend the assigned budget; clearly, this is a minimal requirement for good management, but there is simply too little information available to make any other kind of judgment. All of this adds up to a style of decision making on budgetary allocations that can only be incremental; that is, this year's budgetary allocation is determined by making incremental changes in last year's allocation. This usually means uniform, across-the-board increases (or decreases) in the allocations to all departments. Everyone involved in the process recognizes that this is inferior to a thoughtful process that seriously considers the needs of each department separately and provides more funding to agencies with greater needs. However, because of the dearth of meaningful information generated in a line-item budgeting system, there is no alternative to the incremental approach.

Line-item budgeting emphasizes the control aspect of the budget. It makes it very easy to prevent overspending or to determine who is responsible if it does occur. It also limits some of the conflict found in other styles of budgeting because it tends to compartmentalize spending rather than emphasize tradeoffs. This characteristic is also a political defect in line-item budgeting. The limited information about output that it generates makes it difficult for decision makers to make tradeoffs about the quality of programs. Therefore, line-item budgeting does not lend itself to the management and planning and policy choice orientations that were discussed earlier.

Performance Budgeting

The basic difference between line-item and **performance budgeting** was the output orientation of performance budgeting. Line-item budgeting measured only inputs used; performance budgeting established a relationship between inputs employed and outputs attained. The basic building-block of performance budgeting was the unit cost of providing a service (inputs) and the number of units of service provided (outputs). Thus, the line-item budget in Table 19.1 would be adjusted to include information on the cost of fighting fires or other activities of fire departments, and a budgetary allocation would be established by multiplying units of service (fires fought, emergencies attended to) by the unit cost of providing each service.

The key budgetary expert now became the cost accountant, because he or she possessed the esoteric skills needed to collect and calculate information about unit costs. The unit-cost information created an additional method of evaluating a good manager besides looking for overspending. Managers performing similar duties could be evaluated by comparing the unit costs of their operations.

In making budgetary allocations, it was possible to escape from incrementalism in a limited way. Reasonable estimates could usually be made about changes in the demand for the service, although, even here, incrementalism frequently had to be used as an aid in calculation. The unit cost could be influenced somewhat by experience in other jurisdictions, but, in the final analysis, incrementalism was a frequent guide here as well.

The strong point of performance budgeting was that it added a management improvement focus to the control focus of line-item budgeting. It provided decision makers with enough information to consider management improvement and cost-minimization techniques. However, performance budgeting did not provide any techniques for future planning; nor did it provide enough information to make tradeoffs between programs. These techniques would come later.

Program Budgeting

In proceeding chronologically through the various budgetary styles, one can see a steady ascendancy in the basic building block from the object of expenditure, to the unit of service, to the entire program. But many changes came with program budgeting that involved more than just the emphasis on program.

In general, **program budgeting** was an attempt to adapt the rational decision-making techniques to the budgetary process. Program budgeting concepts included

- The setting of specific objectives
- The systematic analysis to clarify objectives and to assess alternative ways of meeting them
- The framing of budgetary proposals in terms of programs directed toward the achievement of the objectives
- The projection of the costs of these programs a number of years in the future
- The formulation of plans of achievement year by year for each program
- An information system for each program to supply data for the monitoring of achievement of program goals, and to supply data for the reassessment of the program objectives and the appropriateness of the program itself[7]

In practice, the implementation of program budgeting involved the division of the activities of each department into discrete units called programs and the preparation of multiyear budgetary forecasts for each program. The purpose of the multiyear estimates was to alert decision makers to the full future costs of programs, particularly in cases in which programs started with a limited use of resources and expanded in future years. The program budget would also make some provision for measuring the efficiency and performance of the programs over time.

Program budgeting is frequently described as a "top-down" system, because it encourages a centralization of decision making by allowing decision makers to escape the excessive detail contained in line-item and performance budgets. Decision makers are usually provided only with information about total levels of expenditure, not the details of the objects of expenditure. This should encourage them to focus on making choices among programs rather than becoming mired in details. They could communicate messages such as "we need to hold the line on social services," or "this is the year to provide a bit more to defence," by simply allowing smaller increases in social programs and greater increases in defence ones. This sort of movement of macrolevers is possible only because of the emphasis on broad programs instead of details of expenditure.

Program budgeting brought with it a large set of rational economic tools such as cost-benefit analysis, cost-effectiveness analysis, and systems analysis. These tools could maximize government performance by providing a rational, economic comparison of different methods of attaining goals and even comparing the worth of trying to attain different goals. The most extreme proponents of this kind of thinking argued that the ultimate purpose of government was to maximize human well-being—economic, physical, social, psychological—and that this well-being could be measured and rational techniques employed to determine which government programs would best attain its maximization. Others stopped somewhat short of these beliefs, but all practitioners of program budgeting argued that there were rational, economic tools that could be used to make tradeoffs between programs.

Since the economist was the primary person who employed these kinds of techniques, program budgeting caused the mantle of key expert to pass from the accountant to the economist. The other structural change that occurred at the same time was the ascendancy of central agencies, in particular the Treasury Board Secretariat. If decision making is more centralized and tradeoffs between departments are more important, there is an obvious need for a central agency to deal with these various elements.

The strength of program budgeting is that it includes all three of the factors that are important for an ideal budgeting style—control, management, and planning and policy choice. In evaluating the worth of a manager, program budgeting emphasizes not just avoiding overspending or minimizing cost but also maximizing program performance. In the example of the fire department, one might track the change in expenditure and the change in demand for the service over time. If these seem to be out of line, the manager should be asked for an explanation. One might also compare the unit cost of providing fire department services in this city with similar costs in other cities. Also, performance indicators in program budgets for fire departments, such as response times to fires, might allow for future planning. It may be determined that the location of fire stations hinders quick responses to fires in certain parts of the city, or that the colour of the fire trucks is not striking enough for motorists get out of the way quickly.

Notwithstanding the obvious attractions of this third style of expenditure budgeting, it is not without its failings. One is the high cost, in both dollars and time, of implementing this ambitious and complex style of budgeting. It is difficult to specify goals, measure benefits achieved, and predict future conditions—all requirements of program budgeting. Take, for example, the challenge of measuring quantitatively the benefits derived from government action. Everyone agrees that it is beneficial for the garbage to be picked up or for property to be saved from fire, but how is this value determined objectively in dollars and cents so that costs and benefits can be compared? Some of the core benefits might be measured, but what about the esthetic, practical, and other benefits?

Arguably the most serious failing of program budgeting is its inability to appreciate sufficiently the political nature of the budgeting process. Program budgeting foresees the possibility of major adjustments to the list of government expenditures, yet interests negatively affected by these proposed changes will fight them. This third style of expenditure budgeting assumes that budgeting is a rational or technical process in which all participants can agree on the best course of action. The reality is otherwise. Budget allocations represent substantial benefits to various societal groups, and these groups will fight to maintain and enhance these benefits. A program might be shown to be inefficient or unfair, but this may matter little to parts of the electorate who benefit from it and to the public servants who administer the program.

Government Expenditure Budgeting System

The process for preparing and adopting the expenditure budget at the federal level is outlined in the Expenditure Management System (EMS). The EMS, introduced in 1995, reflects many of the principles inherent in program budgeting styles of expenditure budgeting. For example, it provides for strategic planning and encourages the use of performance information for the purpose of reallocating revenues to more appropriate areas. Since its inception, some adjustments have been made to the EMS, but the basic elements remain basically the same:

- The process begins a little less than one year before the presentation of the budget, with cabinet and its committees meeting in the spring to consider plans and priorities that can be used to guide the allocation of revenues in the forthcoming budget. Around this same time, departments lay out multiyear plans on their future operations and priorities within their area. These plans are assessed by the Treasury Board.
- In the summer period, central agencies and departments work together to bring together the planning done in the first stage in order to come up with some expenditure proposals which can be employed in the forthcoming public consultation process. The Department of Finance also drafts a report on the financial and economic

outlook for the budget period. This is essentially a report on the condition of the government's finances and the economy, and provides a backdrop to decisions about spending (or cutbacks) in the budget.

- In the fall and early winter, the minister of finance releases the consultation papers and begins meeting with parliamentary committees, provinces, groups, and the interested public. Within the government, central agencies and departments will continue their work on fine-tuning proposals, and eventually cabinet committees will propose expenditure priorities to cabinet. This part of the cycle ends with the minister of finance developing a budgetary strategy that takes into consideration recommendations and decisions flowing from the various actors and processes involved in the budgetary cycle up to this point (e.g., public consultation, central agencies and departments, cabinet committees).

- In the few months preceding the budget, cabinet examines the budgetary strategy, and the prime minister and the finance minister make the final decisions on the contents of the budget. In February, the finance minister concludes the budgetary cycle by the presentation of the budget in the House of Commons. At this time, the Treasury Board Secretariat tables documents called the "Main Estimates," which lay out the allocation of resources to departments for the forthcoming fiscal year and constitute a request of House of Commons for authority to expend these resources. The Main Estimates are referred automatically to various parliamentary committees for review, and by the end of May the committees report back on their consideration of the Estimates (more on this in the following chapter).[8]

The budgetary process depicted here is considerably more static and one-dimensional than it is in practice. For example, the Department of Finance will most likely revise its report on the economic outlook, and this in return may cause cabinet and other actors to revise their thinking on budgetary items and priorities. It is unfortunate that the real world of budgeting cannot be as neat as the above description, but everyone must be alert to changes in the external environment. A more realistic depiction would also reveal the various political and bureaucratic strategies and tactics used to achieve aims in the process. The standard approach to decision making in government, including the preparation of the budget, is to believe that all players carry out their assigned duties—public servants advise, elected officials decide, each group acting in the public interest and moving toward the same goal. However, an alternative approach envisions both elected and appointed officials involved in a kind of game in which all participants use various tactics to achieve their specific interests. The object of departments, for example, is often to increase spending in their area, or at least to defend themselves against cutbacks, because they wish to accumulate a large budget to satisfy their clientele and their own inherent instinct to grow. Accordingly, departments may use a well-known tactic: they pad their budgets to ensure departmental revenues remain the same even with cutbacks. If no cutbacks take place, so much the better, because the department now has a larger budget. Departments may also mobilize interest groups in favour of additional spending in order to the give the minister more clout at the cabinet table when it comes to allocating scarce public revenues: "My hands are tied, I have to respond to the demands of my clients." Another favourite departmental tactic is to generate a crisis that demands attention—and more money; still another is to propose a program or policy that requires few funds initially but has the potential to grow into something quite large in the future.

Departments represent the "spenders" in the budgetary game of strategy, but there are also players who serve as "guardians" of the public purse.[9] Spenders score points in the budgetary game when they operate attractive, well-funded programs, but guardians do well when avoiding deficits and holding the line on spending and taxes. Two major guardians are the minister of finance and the secretary of the Treasury Board.

Box 19.1	The Musical Ride

When asked for cutbacks in their spending, departments sometimes respond with proposals to eliminate programs that are well liked by the electorate. To entertain tourists, RCMP officers ride their horses around in a series of configurations to the accompaniment of music. This is called the "Musical Ride." It is, as stated, very popular with the crowds. Apparently, one year, the federal police service was asked to reduce its spending. The RCMP put forward a proposal to eliminate the Musical Ride. No cuts took place. The story, as with many good stories, may be apocryphal. But it nicely demonstrates one of the more effective tactics of departments in the budgetary battles.

To serve their aims, these two ministers and the advisors located in the Department of Finance and the Treasury Board Secretariat can employ their own tactics. For example, they can counter the padding strategy by automatically cutting departmental spending, or they may underestimate purposely the amount of revenue available or exaggerate expenses in order to reduce departmental pressure on the public purse. In recent years, the Department of Finance has been accused of using this last tactic, as annual revenue projections have fallen well short of actual revenues.[10] Partly in an attempt to limit the possibility of the use of this tactic, the government of Stephen Harper has proposed establishing a new position of parliamentary budget officer, whose holder would be responsible for, among other things, providing fiscal forecasts independently of the Department of Finance.[11]

For some, this strategic or gaming side of the budgetary process may be dispiriting and exasperating. However, it is important to understand that overarching the seemingly deceptive strategies is a concern for maintaining mutual trust. The complexity of budgeting means that, for the most part, participants in the budgeting process must rely upon one another, for there is simply not enough time and energy to deal with all aspects of the allocation of public money. There are also well-understood limits to how far one can go with the strategies and the tactics, and a failure to appreciate these limits usually leads to censure of the offender. If all this still fails to satisfy those disgruntled with the sometimes strategic nature of budgeting, it should be remembered that often competitive relations in any situation—including those found in the creation of an expenditure budget—can be a good way of finding the best possible outcome.

Alternative Budgeting Process

The formal budgetary cycle includes a wide range of people engaged in various duties (and strategies) for the purpose of preparing a budget. The cycle also places the cabinet

Box 19.2	Games and Public Money

The Institute of Public Administration of Canada sponsors a case program in Canadian public administration. One of its most notable cases was written by the late Douglas Hartle, who attempts to convey the strategic nature of public administration when public monies are at stake. In the case, a minister, without the approval of cabinet, proposes an expensive new program that requires no new funds—a seeming impossibility. It is up to a senior public servant in the minister's department to make the impossible very possible, and to do so he engages in a number of strategic games with his bureaucratic counterparts. Hartle was a former senior official in a federal central agency, so his insights are based on actual experience.

Source: Douglas G. Hartle, *The Draft Memorandum to Cabinet*, 2nd rev. ed. (Toronto: Institute of Public Administration of Canada, n.d.).

at the centre of the process (along with the prime minister and the finance minister) in that it determines the initial budgetary plans and priorities and signs off on the minister of finance's budgetary strategy. But some scholars claim that the prime minister and the finance minister (with some advisors) now strongly control the cycle and at times feel little need to consult cabinet on certain budgetary initiatives.[12] The explanation for this development is the fear that cabinet and its committees might fail to recognize the significance of certain initiatives and allocate public funds to less important proposals. When confronted with the absence of cabinet approval for certain budget actions, finance officials have simply replied that their minister had checked with the prime minister. A further difference in this alternative budgetary process is the seeming end of the departmental role as "spender" or advocate of budgetary expenditure initiatives. Now, the prime minister and the finance minister function as both guardian and spender. Savoie explains this development:

> It appears that the prime minister and his courtiers have become convinced that ministers are not capable of establishing priorities, that they lack the ability to look at spending proposals from a broader perspective than their respective department or region.[13]

Publications of the federal government still refer to the Expenditure Management System when discussing financial management, which means that cabinet, cabinet committees, and departments play a role in the budgetary process. Moreover, it does seem difficult to accept that the prime minister and senior ministers effectively run the budget system. As with the reaction to the thesis of prime ministerial government (discussed in Chapter 11), the concentration of power proposed in the alternative budgetary system appears unlikely—budgeting is just too complicated and expansive to put into the hands of a few. Nevertheless, this different conception of the budgetary process urges us to be always on the lookout for changes in how government manages its financial resources.

Conclusion

This chapter has attempted to provide a close-up view of the first stage in the management of financial resources at the federal level in Canada. It revealed that there are two types of budgets in the budgetary process, and that one of these—the expenditure budget—can be created through the use of various styles. The chapter also examined the budgetary process at the federal level, and the various gaming strategies employed to secure preferences in the final document. At the end, it was suggested that an alternative budgetary process has been established as a response to the shortcomings in the formal process.

1. Allan Maslove, "Introduction: Budgeting in Provincial Governments," in Allan M. Maslove, ed., *Budgeting in the Provinces: Leadership and the Premiers* (Toronto: Institute of Public Administration of Canada, 1989), 1.

2. Douglas G. Hartle, The Revenue Budget Process of the Government of Canada: Description, Appraisal, and Proposals (Toronto: Canadian Tax Foundation, 1982), 31. Footnotes omitted.

3. Communication with Geoffrey Hale, an expert on government budgeting in Canada. For more on these developments, see Geoffrey Hale, *The Politics of Taxation in Canada* (Peterborough: Broadview Press, 2002), 238–39, and Geoffrey E. Hale, "Priming the Electoral Pump: Framing Budgets for a Renewed Mandate," in Leslie A. Pal, ed., *How Ottawa Spends 2001–2202: Power in Transition* (Toronto: Oxford University Press, 2001).

4. Donald Gow, *The Process of Budgetary Reform in the Government of Canada* (Ottawa: Information Canada, 1973), 1.

5. Allen Schick, "The Road to PPB: The Stages of Budget Reform," *Public Administration Review 26* (December 1966): 244. (Emphasis in original.)

6. Ibid. (Emphasis in original.)

7. Honourable C.M. Drury, *Planning-Programming-Budgeting Guide* (Ottawa: Queen's Printer, 1969), 8.

8. Treasury Board of Canada, *The Expenditure Management System of Canada* (Ottawa: Minister of Supply and Services, 1995).

9. Hugh Heclo and Aaron Wildavsky, *The Private Government of Public Money*, 2nd ed. (London: The Macmillan Press Ltd., 1981), ch. 4.

10. Paul Vieira, "Ottawa Urged to Get Its Budgeting Right," *National Post*, March 30, 2006, FP1. See also Geoffrey E. Hale, "Trading Up or Treading Water? Federal Fiscal and Budgetary Policies in Search of a New Mandate," in G. Bruce Doern, ed., *How Ottow Spends, 2006–07: In from the Cold-the Tory Rise and the Liberal demise* (Montreal & Kingston: McGill Queen's University Press, 2006).

11. Government of Canada, *Canada's New Government: Federal Accountability Action Plan: Turning a New Leaf* (Ottawa: Her Majesty the Queen in Right of Canada, 2006), 13–14.

12. Donald Savoie, "The Federal Government: Revisiting Court Government in Canada," in Luc Bernier, Keith Brownsey, and Michael Howlett, eds., *Executive Styles in Canada: Cabinet Structures and Leadership Practices in Canadian Government* (Toronto: University of Toronto Press, 2005).

13. Savoie, "The Federal Government," 36.

Management of Financial Resources

As we saw in the preceding chapter, the preparation of the budget is key to the financial management of public resources. In fact, for many it is *the* most significant event of the year, the time when government reveals its plans and strategies for the generation and allocation of money. But this is hardly the end of the process of managing financial resources. In any democracy, adoption or acceptance of the budget requires the approval of the people's representatives. A society cannot allow a government to tax the incomes of citizens or corporations, for example, and spend the results of this effort without securing the agreement of the legislature. We also want to make sure that this money is allocated to the departments and other agencies as designated in the budget, and there is as well an understandable desire to know whether the funds are expended sensibly and in compliance with the law. All of these requirements lead to a process involving a number of executive and legislative bodies whose job is to ensure the prudent management of public resources. The federal government has recently been rocked by the sponsorship scandal and evidence of misuse of government monies, an event that only underscores the importance of paying attention to the issue of financial management in the public sector.

In this chapter, we examine the manner in which Parliament approves of the government's plans for the expenditure of public funds. This entails looking at how legislative entities undertake their perusal of the Main Estimates. The chapter also reviews the procedures for the transfer of monies from the fund which holds the government's revenues to departments and other agencies. The role of the Auditor General of Canada has received a lot of attention recently, and the duties of this sometimes controversial participant in the financial management process are considered. The chapter concludes with some comments on the effectiveness of the financial management process, especially in relation to the ability of Parliament and its committees to oversee the expenditure of public resources.

Figure 20.1 — Process of Financial Administration

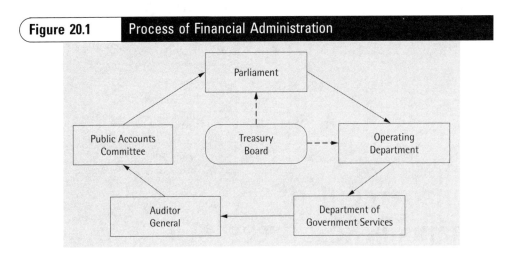

Financial Administration of Resources

As with the preparation of the budget, the adoption and execution of the budget can be seen as a related process or cycle involving various government agencies. This may also be called the financial administration process, and its working in the government of Canada is outlined in Figure 20.1.

Parliament

It is important to remember that it is a basic tenet of parliamentary government that the legislature must approve the expenditure of any funds before the expenditure occurs. This is the first step in the financial administration cycle (as shown at the top of Figure 20.1). The President of the Treasury Board begins the process, usually in February or March of each year, by tabling a series of documents in the House of Commons known as the **Estimates** (or Main Estimates at this point).[1] These documents list the overall budget allocations requested by each department for the fiscal year, as well as some supporting detail about the operation of the programs for which funding is requested. More recently, this supporting information has expanded so that the Main Estimates consist of several volumes, with a separate volume for each department providing supplementary information about the priorities of the department and its strategies in pursuing those priorities (see Box 20.1).

Table 20.1 is a page taken from Part II of the Estimates, and it summarizes the estimated expenditures on various programs administration by the Department of National

---

Box 20.1   Main Estimates

The Main Estimates are split into three parts:

- **Part I.** The "Government Expense Plan" offers an overview of federal expenditures and shows how key aspects of the Main Estimates relate to the Expense Plan.
- **Part II.** The "Main Estimates" detail the amounts to be allocated to the various government agencies and departments.

- **Part III.** The "Departmental Expenditure Plan" itself is divided into two parts. "Reports on Plans and Priorities" presents the expenditure plans and expected results for the individual departments and agencies. "Departmental Performance Plans," as the title suggests, examines the performance of the government organizations.

Table 20.1 Main Estimates of Department of National Defence, 2005–06 (thousands of dollars)

PROGRAM BY ACTIVITIES	2005–2006 MAIN ESTIMATES						2004–2005 MAIN ESTIMATES
	Operating	Capital	Grants	Contributions and Other Transfer Payments	Less: Revenue Credited to the Vote	Total	
Maritime command	616,807	89,649	10	–	40,612	665,854	619,034
Land forces command	1,050,903	99,653	–	–	75,898	1,074,658	1,089,524
Air command	820,850	93,298	1,137	2,457	118,113	799,629	805,743
Operations	480,646	58,091	–	–	17,870	520,867	470,580
Communications security	160,926	74,266	–	–	4,057	231,135	182,585
Research and development	249,081	12,929	–	–	6,995	255,015	257,994
Information management	349,355	27,808	–	–	5,559	371,604	388,125
Human resources	5,421,688	37,076	–	–	39,493	5,419,271	5,442,307
Infrastructure and environment programs	249,062	92,270	–	5,450	83,864	262,918	250,022
Material acquisition and support	1,979,258	1,662,890	–	–	8,528	3,633,620	3,595,646
Transfer payments and specifically allocated*	–	–	3,113	187,347	–	190,460	185,956
	11,378,576	2,247,930	4,260	195,254	400,989	13,425,031	13,287,516

*This represents the grants and contribution programs that cannot be attributed to any one activity.

Source: *Main Estimates 2005–2006*, pages 20–25, Treasury Board of Canada, 2005. Reproduced with the permission of the Minister of Public Works and Government Services Canada, 2006.

Defence in the fiscal year 2005–06. It shows that the planned expenditures for the fiscal year 2005–06 are about $13.4 billion, and that these monies will be spent on such programs as the marine, land, and air operations. It also reveals that the department is asking for a small increase in spending over the previous year's estimates of $13.3 billion. All other departments and agencies have the same delineation of expenditures by program activity in this part of the Main Estimates.

The Estimates and all other "money bills," as they are called, are always tabled and approved in the House of Commons before going to the Senate. This is a long tradition stemming from the fact that the House of Commons is the elected body of Parliament and is, therefore, the only body directly responsible to the electorate.

After the Estimates documents have been tabled in the House of Commons, they are sent to the various committees of the House for further consideration. Each committee specializes in a department or a related group of departments so that the Estimates are divided up and sent to the appropriate committees for more in-depth consideration. Since this usually takes some time, and since the Estimates are not tabled until a rather short time before the beginning of the fiscal year on April 1, it is unlikely that Parliament will approve the Estimates before the beginning of the fiscal year. Obviously, this creates a serious problem, because departments cannot begin to spend money until Parliament has appropriated it. To circumvent this problem, Parliament provides **Interim Supply** before the beginning of the fiscal year, a piece of legislation that provides for the operation of the government for the period from April 1 to June 30 by appropriating approximately one-fourth of the total budget requested. This allows departments to continue operating even though the full budget has not yet been considered. It is customary that Interim Supply should include funds only for the continuation of existing programs. Funding for new programs must usually await the approval of the Estimates.

Shortly after the Estimates are tabled, the various parliamentary committees begin to hold hearings on the part of the Estimates that most closely concern them. Usually, ministers and senior officials will appear before these committees to explain and defend their budget requests. The committees also like to hear from clientele groups and interested experts. The committees then recommend to Parliament what the appropriate budgetary allocation ought to be. Since these committees usually operate along highly partisan lines, it is unusual for the committee recommendation to deviate from the government's request. But that should not be taken as a sign of the committees' impotence: these budget hearings are an excellent place for Opposition members to learn about the activities of departments, and can also provide an important forum for holding ministers and public servants accountable.

After the committee reports have been received by the House of Commons, there is a vote on the full budget as contained in the Estimates. This vote is very important, because the expenditure budget is always a matter of "confidence," meaning that if the budget were defeated it would be an indication that the government no longer had the "confidence" of the House and, therefore, as a matter of convention, ought to resign. The rules of the House provide that if a budget has not been acted upon by the House before June 30, it is voted upon on that date. This means that the Opposition is free to defeat a budget, but it cannot hamstring the government by merely delaying its passage. In fact, the Estimates legislation is almost always passed in exactly the form proposed. When it becomes law, it is known as the *Appropriation Act* for that year.

The government usually attempts to estimate its needs as accurately as possible when it prepares its Estimates at the beginning of the year, but it is not surprising that sometimes these beginning-of-the-year estimates do not prove completely accurate. Since all expenditures require parliamentary approval, the government cannot unilaterally shift funds from one program to another or spend more than was allotted by Parliament in the original *Appropriation Act*. In order to meet unforeseen circumstances, the government presents

Supplementary Estimates to the House at various times during the fiscal year. The Supplementary Estimates are pieces of legislation that request either additional funds beyond those originally approved or a shift in funds between programs. In recent years, governments typically have presented Supplementary Estimates from three to five times each year.[2]

The role of Parliament and its committees in financial administration is crucial. Legally, it is Parliament—and only Parliament—that can start the process by appropriating funds. Still, there have been criticisms of Parliament's role. Some members of Parliament have complained that they have very limited time to consider the lengthy and complex Estimates before they are passed. A House of Commons Committee report captures some of the frustration and disappointment associated with this part of the financial management process:

> Parliamentary committees were intended to be the bodies where detailed scrutiny of government spending and performance would occur. But with some notable exceptions, these committees continue to provide relatively cursory attention to the main spending estimates and explanatory reports provided by government departments each year. Each year, some 87 departments and other government organizations provide parliamentary committees with separate spending estimates and related reports, and many of these receive no formal attention in committee meetings.... Consideration of the supplementary estimates, which allow departments to obtain additional funding at specified intervals during the year, has been even less satisfactory. With only a few exceptions, committees regularly fail to examine them at all.[3]

To address this concern, it has been proposed that Parliament focus on particular programs instead of trying to address the full range of information contained in the Estimates. This would permit a close examination of a selected public initiative, and put an end to just touching upon the plethora of government activities. It has also been noted that Parliamentarians have little incentive to examine the Estimates thoroughly because the workings of party discipline ensure that few changes can be recommended in the process.[4] Thus, the provision of some capacity to Parliamentary committees to make suggestions relating to a moderate shifting of funds within departmental budgets might lead to more attention being paid to the Estimates.[5] But the challenges facing this part of the process—for example, the complexity of the material and the absence of time for review—most likely require something more thorough or drastic.[6]

The Treasury Board

With the passage of the annual *Appropriation Act*, the departments are now able to seek access to the funds necessary for carrying out their programs and policies. In preparing to undertake this action, departments are aware of the central role of the Treasury Board in financial management. The Treasury Board, as shown earlier, participates in the formulation of the expenditure budget, but its involvement carries over into the process of managing the finances of government. The *Financial Administration Act* defines the general framework for financial and administrative management in the federal government, and as a part of that framework it gives authority to the Treasury Board to make regulations in most areas of general administrative and financial management. Some examples of the Treasury Board's authority are:

- Establishing allotments or subdivisions of parliamentary appropriations that cannot be varied without Treasury Board approval
- Prescribing rules and procedures to be followed before a cheque can be issued
- Prescribing rules for the receipt and control of funds paid to the government and for the safeguarding of public property
- Ensuring coordination of administrative functions and services within departments and within government as a whole

- Prescribing the form and manner in which government accounting records will be maintained
- Establishing regulations for entering into contracts and for purchasing

An overview of these activities indicates that the main role of the Treasury Board is to ensure prudence and probity in government, and to ensure uniformity in administration between operating departments. In a small organization, this kind of function would not be necessary, but this role is frequently found in large organizations. It is necessary to have some central agency to ensure that all the diverse and decentralized units of the total organization are conducting their administrative activities in an appropriate and reasonably uniform manner.

As with many aspects of the operation of the federal government, the reports of the auditor general on the sponsorship program in Quebec have affected the role and structure of the Treasury Board. In 2003, it was announced that the Treasury Board and its secretariat would focus more on the overseeing of public expenditures. It was also announced that the Office of the Comptroller General would be set up within the Treasury Board Secretariat "to help ensure that departments comply with the Treasury Board's spending and stewardship policies and to provide direction to departmental comptrollers."[7] Finally, the TBS would provide the necessary assistance to a new expenditure review committee of cabinet dedicated toward the control of spending and ensuring the best allocation of the government's expenditures. What this all meant was that the board and the secretariat—especially the latter—would pay greater attention to tracking funds as they moved to the departments.

Operating Departments

The line departments are involved in actually operating most large government programs, so this is where the bulk of government expenditure takes place. These departments are clearly in the front line, in terms of making expenditure decisions, but the above discussions about the role of the Treasury Board should make it clear that the authority of a department to act unilaterally is somewhat limited.

Departments are required to establish pre-audit procedures—procedures to confirm that appropriate conditions have been met before payment is approved. These procedures must ensure that the expenditure has been authorized by Parliament, that adequate funds still remain in the appropriation, that appropriate goods or services have been received, and that these were in line with the contract. If the payment is a grant or transfer payment, obviously the specific procedure is different, but the general idea is the same. The department must establish procedures to ensure that the person receiving the payment is entitled to it. These procedures are called a pre-audit because they are required, by Treasury Board guidelines, to occur before any public funds are paid out. These same guidelines specify similar rules for the protection of revenue received and the safeguarding of noncash assets such as inventories.

Departments are also responsible for establishing an internal audit group with free access to the deputy minister. The purpose of this is to provide the deputy with objective information about the adequacy and effectiveness of the management framework that each department has established for

- The achievement of its operational and program objectives
- The reliability and integrity of the information
- The economical and efficient use and safeguarding of resources
- Compliance with policies and regulations

In the wake of the scandal over the sponsorship program, departments have strengthened their efforts in the area of financial management. The independence of the internal audit function within departments has been enhanced to ensure that auditing of records is clearly separated from the daily operations of the department. The new position of Chief Audit Executive has also been created for all departments and agencies for the same purpose of enhancing the objectivity and thoroughness of auditing activities.

Department of Public Works and Government Services

The Department of Public Works and Government Services is responsible for many common services provided to all departments and agencies, such as accommodation, purchasing, and central accounting. It is this latter function that will be discussed in this chapter.

The department is the central accounting agency of the Government of Canada. This means that the Receiver General for Canada, which is another title that the minister of public works and government services always holds, is responsible for the receipt and disbursement of all public funds and for accounting for those funds in the Consolidated Revenue Fund. The *Consolidated Revenue Fund* is the one large cash account that the government maintains for all federal funds not earmarked for some specific purpose. The name comes from the fact that at one time there was a large number of cash funds held by a variety of different agencies and used largely for their own purposes. This created some confusion and raised the possibility of inappropriate use of, or accounting for, government funds. For this reason, it was felt desirable to consolidate all government funds in one account under the control of one minister—the receiver general—and his or her department—the Department of Public Works and Government Services.

The department receives cheque requisitions from operating departments and agencies and then issues cheques as requested. Before the cheque is issued, the Department of Public Works and Government Services ensures that the department will not be overspending its appropriation, but it undertakes no other reviews beyond that, because it assumes that the department has conducted a proper pre-audit. The Department of Public Works and Government Services handles all receipts and deposits of public funds and acts as a central accounting agency; it shares with the Treasury Board the responsibility for the establishment of the government accounting system.

The department is also responsible for the preparation of the government's year-end financial statements, referred to as the **Public Accounts**. These statements contain the government's balance sheet, which lists assets owned and liabilities owed, the Statement of Revenue and Expenditure, and certain other financial statements. The Public Accounts also contain a great deal of detailed information about sources of revenue and objects of expenditure by program and activity. This makes it a valuable source of information for researchers.

The Department of Public Works and Government Services is responsible for preparing the government's financial statements, but these statements must bear the scrutiny of an audit by an independent agency.

Auditor General

The Office of the Auditor General (OAG), which includes the Auditor General of Canada and over 600 audit professionals, is one of the most visible and well-known actors in the financial management system. With the appearance of the OAG, the financial management process moves away from the spending of monies to the examination of how these monies have been spent. The auditor general can be seen as having two roles—one narrow and one much broader. The narrow role is the least contentious and requires the **auditor general** to act in the same manner as an auditor would in the private sector. The auditor general's more contentious, broader role requires her or him to be something of a watchdog of government spending.

In the auditor general's narrow role, he or she performs an *attest audit*—one performed to ensure that the financial statements accurately reflect the financial position and activities of the government. The outcome of the attest audit is the auditor's opinion, which becomes a part of the Public Accounts. To fulfil this function, the staff of the OAG must undertake a post-audit of a random selection of financial transactions that occurred during the year. This means that these selected transactions are traced through the accounting process to evaluate the adequacy of the pre-audit performed within departments and to determine the accuracy of the accounting records. This is how the auditor general forms an opinion as to whether the financial statements contained in the Public Accounts, and prepared by the Department of Public Works and Government Services, accurately reflect the financial position of the government.

In addition to the attest audit, the auditor general is also responsible for the performance of a compliance audit. A *compliance audit* is one performed to ensure that all legislative enactments and government regulations have been complied with in the operation of programs. It goes beyond the attest audit in ensuring not just that transactions have been recorded correctly, but also that there was appropriate statutory authority for all expenditures and, further, that the regulations specified by the Treasury Board have been followed. This role of the auditor general has never been very contentious, because it can usually be objectively established if rules have been violated.

The broader—and more controversial role—of the auditor general flows from his or her authority to report to Parliament on cases in which government has spent money without considering economy or efficiency. Under this power, the auditor general may conduct value for money or **comprehensive audits**, which seek to determine the extent to which both accountability mechanisms are respected and the management of financial, human, and physical resources is conducted efficiently, effectively, and economically.[8]

Comprehensive auditing is more extensive than the traditional forms of auditing, because it goes beyond a concentration on financial activities to consider how the organization uses all its resources and is managed. This more encompassing type of audit can produce three kinds of reports

One type reports on the comprehensive audits of specific programs. A second kind of audit deals with government-wide reviews of a general nature, commenting on the value of program evaluation or the use of computers. These provide an overview of how well these resources are used and offer some advice for improvement. The third type, and in many ways the most interesting and useful, is more broadly philosophical. It addresses such matters as constraints on productivity in government, the effects of public service reform on accountability, and values, services, and performance in the public service.

This broader or expanded role of the auditor general has provoked a great deal of controversy. In the first place, comprehensive auditing is, by its nature, a more personal exercise than attest or compliance auditing; it is, as Aucoin says, "based on methodologies and evidence that are prone to a much greater degree of subjectivity than is the case with traditional audits."[9] Determining whether a government program has performed well is a great deal more difficult than determining whether monies for the same program have been expended properly. The practice of government evaluation is not nearly as developed as the rules of accounting.

The second element of controversy in the auditor general's expanded role stems from the heavily political content sometimes involved in assessing effectiveness. It is within the appropriate sphere of the auditor general to comment on economy and efficiency, but a consideration of effectiveness frequently requires some comment on government objectives that clearly goes beyond the mandate of the auditor general and may venture into political territory. The auditor general must exercise care lest at some point he or she

Box 20.2   Schizophrenia in the Office of the Auditor General?

A further concern about the OAG is that it suffers from a case of organizational schizophrenia. On the one hand, the office, in its reports, concentrates on the importance of accountability and the need for more controls and rules in government administration—the mechanist approach to organizations. But on the other, it urges agencies to experiment with greater decentralization and other reforms associated with the new public management. Is the auditor general an advocate of managerialism or a "control freak" or both?

Source: Denis Saint-Martin, "Managerialist Advocate or 'Control Freak'? The Janus-Face Office of the Auditor General," *Canadian Public Administration*, 47(2) (summer 2004).

usurp the role of the leader of the Opposition. Already, some believe the office of the auditor general has become a kind of "government in exile" whose purpose is to ensure that Parliament and the Canadian people are well aware of the shortcomings of government actions.[10] Where once the auditor general's office limited itself to supplying accounting reports to the House of Commons Committee on Public Accounts, it now—according to its critics—seeks to bypass elected representatives and almost on its own make government accountable to the citizens of Canada. In the process, some say that "[r]epresentative government is either being brushed to the side or deemed illegitimate."[11]

The auditor general must be careful about getting involved in political controversies. The audit function derives its credibility from its objectivity. While it is very tempting to move into controversial areas, this constitutes a movement away from pure objectivity to greater subjectivity, which could weaken the credibility of the office. Nevertheless, the activities connected with the sponsorship scandal suggest that the higher profile of the auditor general makes it difficult for the office to escape controversy. Its involvement in the scandal began with a request from the government to examine three contracts awarded by the Department of Public Works and Government Services to an advertising agency. The OAG had thus not initiated the audit itself, but it did on the basis of the investigation of the three contracts decide to conduct a full audit of the sponsorship program and related advertising activities. The result was a report that revealed severe failings in the administration of the program—and that served to weaken the government. It was also a report whose findings were corroborated by the commission set up to inquire into the workings of the sponsorship program. The Office of the Auditor General had done its job; it had also generated much controversy and ensured its prominence for the foreseeable future.[12]

The controversial nature of the Office of the Auditor General naturally leads to questions about the independence of its senior officer. The auditor general is an officer of Parliament. In practice, this means that he or she can deliver all reports directly to Parliament without intervention by the government; he or she can appeal directly to Parliament if he or she feels that the office is not being funded appropriately; and he or she can be dismissed only for cause after an address of both Houses of Parliament. This last point means that an auditor general can be dismissed only for inappropriate behaviour, and even then only after a majority vote of the House of Commons and Senate and the concurrence of the governor general. This is the same procedure that is followed for the dismissal of a judge, which certainly suggests that the auditor general is well protected against vengeful governments.

Public Accounts Committee

The Public Accounts Committee (PAC) is a committee of the House of Commons charged with the responsibility for reviewing public accounts of the government and the auditor general's annual report, but nearly all of its inquiries are directed toward the latter function.[13] In most ways, it functions just like any other parliamentary committee, with the exception that, by tradition, the chair of the committee is a member of the Opposition. It is quite possible that the committee will be composed of a majority of members from the government party, but this does not make the chair powerless. The chair establishes agendas and provides leadership to the committee. The presence of an Opposition member as chair ensures that important topics will be on the agenda and will be discussed in the presence of interested members of Parliament and the media. This high visibility does much to ensure accountability even if the contents of the committee's reports are dominated by government input.

The committee reviews the auditor general's annual report on a section-by-section basis. Usually, it considers the comprehensive audits of each program separately. Relevant ministers and/or senior public servants are invited to appear before the committee to comment on the findings of the auditor general and possibly explain what steps have been taken to solve the problems. Throughout the process, the members of the PAC are advised by staff of the auditor general's office. In all, the auditor general and the public accounts committee must work together to make a contribution to the sound management of government finances. The auditor general supplies the committee with the "fodder for discussion," while the committee "provides a public forum for the further examination of government activities."[14]

During the course of hearings, the committee sends a series of short reports to Parliament, providing its recommendations for what ought to be done as a result of the auditor general's observations. This series of reports closes the loop set out in Figure 20.1. Parliament will have the comments of the Public Accounts Committee before it when deciding what to do about the continued funding of a particular program in the next budget.

Effectiveness of Financial Administration

In recent years, and especially since the sponsorship scandal, there has been a great deal of concern about financial accountability and the quality of financial management and administration in the federal government. The scandal and its aftermath pinpointed some of problems in the system set up to provide financial management. Departments sometimes fail to comply with—or evade or ignore—Treasury Board directives relating to the expenditure of money, and the audit procedures within departments sometimes fall short of expectations. Parliament, too, may come up short in its duty to be the keeper of the public purse. In its investigation of the sponsorship program, the Public Accounts Committee "filled a clear public need for information and explanation," but "did not dig into the issues as deeply as the later judicial inquiry, and did not yield greatly new findings beyond the Auditor General's Report."[15] With its heavy turnover of membership and lack of staff—combined with elected officials' traditional lack of interest in accountability issues—the Public Accounts Committee might be considered a weak link in the process of financial administration. This perception of weakness has led to recommendations which call for more stable membership on the committee, additional staff to aid in analysis and handling of witnesses, and elected officials giving more attention to the issue of accountability.[16]

There are other problems in the financial management process. For example, parliamentary committees, as mentioned, are hard pressed to give the Estimates the kind of serious consideration deemed necessary, and any reforms to fix this situation may fly in the face of the historical lack of interest of parliamentarians in the Estimates.[17] As with members of the Public Accounts Committee, those who sit on committees reviewing the Estimates may see little political gain in poring over figures and numbers that no one in the electorate really cares about. Yet, while the sponsorship scandal and other pieces of evidence reveal the weaknesses in the financial management of government finances, it is also true that there are indications of effectiveness. The sponsorship scandal became a scandal in large part because the auditor general—an integral component of financial administration—reported on and documented wrongdoings in expenditures of public money. Moreover, the Treasury Board works diligently to come up with programs and procedures that make it more difficult for abuse to occur in government (though some complain of excessive frameworks and procedures). As well, reforms have been made to enhance the effectiveness of the financial management system. The House of Commons Standing Committee on Government Operations and Estimates was created to address concerns about the consideration of the Estimates, and audit procedures have been strengthened within departments.

Conclusion

Because of the attractions of money, any attempt to manage financial resources must be detailed and rigorous. This chapter and the preceding one have shown that the federal government has endeavoured to ensure that the generation and expenditure of public revenues are done properly and under the watchful eye of concerned authorities. Indeed, we might say that the procedures and policies for accomplishing the prudent management of public revenues are almost overwhelming. Notwithstanding this feeling, the chapter has shown that improvement can be made in this specific exercise of public management.

Notes

1. The term "Main Estimates" is sometimes used at this point to distinguish these estimates from ones that might be submitted that are called "Supplementary Estimates."

2. There is one other way of dealing with these unforeseen circumstances. "Governor General's Warrants" can be issued to meet an unforeseen need at a time when Parliament is not in session. In this case, the president of the Treasury Board notifies the governor general that funds must be spent even though there has been no parliamentary appropriation. The governor general then issues a warrant authorizing the expenditure of these funds.

3. House of Commons, Canada, *Meaningful Scrutiny: Practical Improvements to the Estimates Process*, Report of the Standing Committee on Government Operations and Estimates (September 2003), 1. Available at the Parliament of Canada site, www.parl.gc. ca/InfocomDoc/Documents/37/2/parlbus/commbus/house/reports/og-gorp06-e.htm. Retrieved July 13, 2006.

4. John A. Chernier, Michael Dewing, and Jack Stillborn, "Does Parliament Care? Parliamentary Committees and the Estimates," in G. Bruce Doern, ed., *How Ottawa Spends 2005–2006: Managing the Minority* (Montreal & Kingston: McGill-Queen's University Press, 2005), 215–16.

5. See David A. Good, "Parliament and Public Money: Players and Police," *Canadian Parliamentary Review* (September 2005): 17–21.

6. For more on the weaknesses in this part of the financial management process, see Peter Dobell and Martin Ulrich, "Parliament and Financial Accountability," in Commission of Inquiry into the Sponsorship Program & Advertising Activities, *Restoring Accountability: Research Studies, Volume 1: Parliament, Ministers and Deputy Ministers* (Ottawa: Her Majesty the Queen in Right of Canada, 2006).

7. Auditor General of Canada, "Managing Government: A Study of the Role of the Treasury Board and Its Secretariat," in Auditor General of Canada, *Report of the Auditor General of Canada to the House of Commons* (Ottawa: Minister of Public Works and Government Services, March 2004), ch. 7, 16.

8. Canadian Comprehensive Auditing Foundation, *Comprehensive Auditing in Canada: the Provincial Legislative Audit Perspective* (Ottawa: Canadian Comprehensive Auditing Foundation, 1985), 8.

9. Peter Aucoin, *Auditing for Accountability: The Role of the Auditor General* (Ottawa: The Institute on Governance, 1998), 14.

10. S.L. Sutherland, *The Officer of the Auditor General: Government in Exile?* (Kingston: School of Policy Studies, Queen's University, 2002).

11. Ibid., 16–17.

12. Despite this controversy, one person seems to have been impressed with the work of the auditor general, and that is Prime Minister Stephen Harper, who has introduced legislation to expand the reach of the auditor general and to ensure that its office is sufficiently funded to carry out its duties. It remains to be seen whether the proposed legislation (part of a larger package of changes) will receive the approval of Parliament. See Government of Canada, *Canada's New Government: Federal Accountability Action Plan: Turning a New Leaf* (Ottawa: Her Majesty the Queen in Right of Canada, 2006), 27–29. Available at the Government of Canada site, www.faa-lfi.gc.ca/docs/ap-pa/ap-pa_e.pdf. Retrieved July 13, 2006.

13. Jonathan Malloy, "The Standing Committee on Public Accounts," in Commission of Inquiry into the Sponsorship Program and Advertising Activities, *Restoring Accountability: Research Studies, Volume 1: Parliament, Ministers and Deputy Ministers* (Ottawa: Her Majesty the Queen in Right of Canada, 2006), 81.

14. Jonathan Malloy, "An Auditor's Best Friend? Standing Committees on Public Accounts," *Canadian Public Adminstration* 47(2) (summer 2004): 175.

15. Malloy, "The Standing Committee on Public Accounts," 89.

16. Ibid., 99–100.

17. Chernier, Dewing, and Stillborn, "Does Parliament Care? Parliamentary Committees and the Estimates," 202, 205.

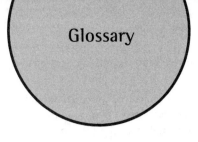

Glossary

Note: The numbers in parentheses following each item refer to the page(s) on which further elaboration on that item can be found.

A

accountability See *administrative accountability*.

administrative accountability The obligation of public servants to answer for fulfilling responsibilities that flow from the authority given them. Similar in meaning to the concept of *objective responsibility*.

administrative ethics Principles and standards of right conduct in public organizations. Normally used interchangeably with the term "administrative morality."

administrative law The branch of public law concerned with relations between the government and individual citizens. It deals with the legal limitations on the actions of governmental officials and on the remedies that are available to anyone affected by a transgression of these limits.

advisory council An organization composed of private citizens created by the government to provide an independent source of advice to a minister. It is established outside the normal departmental *bureaucracy* and does not ordinarily have responsibility for administering *programs*.

alternative service delivery The trend in recent years for governments to search for more innovative and efficient ways to deliver services than through traditional departments and agencies.

auditor general The officer of Parliament who performs an annual audit of the *public accounts* and prepares an annual report to Parliament on the government's financial stewardship.

B

bargaining agent An employee organization (a union) that has been certified—for example, by the federal Public Service *Staff* Relations Board—as the organization responsible for bargaining on behalf of a particular *bargaining unit*. Examples are the Public Service Alliance of Canada and the Professional Institute of the Public Service of Canada.

bargaining unit A group of two or more employees designated as constituting a unit of employees appropriate for *collective bargaining*.

bureaucracy A form of organization characterized by hierarchical structure, *unity of command*, hiring and promotion by merit, and specialization of labour.

bureaucratic politics An approach to the study of policy-making that focuses on interactions among individuals, in the form of conflict, bargaining, compromise, and persuasion, as determinants of the actions of a government.

C

captive agency theory A theory that holds that regulatory agencies eventually become captive of, or controlled by, the interests they were established to regulate.

central agency An agency that has a substantial amount of continuing legitimate authority to intervene in and direct the activity of departments.

citizen participation The direct involvement of individual citizens and citizens' groups in government decision making.

classical federalism A concept according to which the powers of government are divided so that the general and regional governments are each, within a sphere, coordinate and independent.

collective bargaining A method of determining wages, hours, and other conditions of employment through direct negotiations between the employer and the union.

collective ministerial responsibility The responsibility of ministers as a group (i.e., as members of the cabinet) for the policies and management of the government as a whole.

comprehensive audits A review of a *program* that considers its *economy*, *efficiency*, and *effectiveness*.

conflict of interest A situation in which a public employee has a private or personal interest sufficient to influence or appear to influence the objective exercise of his or her official duties.

contingency theory A theory that suggests that there is no one ideal type of organizational structure. It argues that organizational structure should be contingent on such factors as predictability of the task performed, the technology employed, and the size of the organization.

control That form of *power* in which A has authority to direct or command B to do something. Sometimes referred to as "authority of position" or "position power."

cooperative federalism A term used to describe federal–provincial relations when the constitutional division of powers is preserved but federal and provincial ministers and public servants engage in consultation and *coordination* to reach joint decisions on matters of mutual concern.

coordination The process by which two or more parties take one another into account for the purpose of bringing their decisions and/or activities into harmonious or reciprocal relation.

Crown corporation A corporation in the ordinary sense of the term, whose mandate relates to industrial, commercial, or financial activities but that also belongs to the state.

D

decentralization A system of organization that involves placing actual decision-making power in the hands of units outside the centre of power, either geographically or organizationally.

Department of Finance A central agency responsible for advising cabinet on economic matters. The Department also formulates fiscal and tax policies.

deconcentration The physical dispersal of operating units with only limited delegation of decision-making authority.

deployment The appointment of an employee to another position at the same level as his or her existing position, or to a higher or lower level, provided there is no change in the employee's personnel classification.

deputy minister The administrative head of a government department. Appointed by the prime minister or premier. Also referred to as the deputy head.

deregulation The elimination of government regulatory control over an industry so that it can operate through the dictates of the private enterprise system.

E

economy The acquisition of goods and services at the best possible price.

effectiveness A measure of the extent to which an activity achieves the organization's intended outcomes or objectives. To be distinguished from the related concept of *efficiency*.

efficiency A measure of performance that may be expressed as a ratio between input and output. The use of administrative methods and resources that will achieve the greatest results for a specific objective at the least cost. To be distinguished from the related concept of *effectiveness*.

emergency federalism A term used to describe federal–provincial relations during the two world wars and the Depression; these relations were characterized by a growth in federal power vis-à-vis the provinces.

employment equity An approach or *program* designed to identify and systematically remove employment policies, practices, and procedures that exclude or place at a disadvantage certain groups that have been historically underrepresented in the public service.

Estimates The series of documents containing the government's request for an annual appropriation and the necessary supporting documentation. When approved by Parliament, this becomes the *Appropriation Act*.

executive federalism A term used to describe federal–provincial relations characterized by the concentration and *centralization* of authority at the top of each participating government, the control and supervision of *intergovernmental relations* by politicians and officials with a wide range of functional interests, and the highly formalized and well-publicized proceedings of federal–provincial diplomacy.

F

federalism A political system in which the powers of the state are formally divided between central and regional governments by a written constitution but in which these governments are linked in a mutually interdependent political relationship.

Financial Administration Act The statute that governs the regime of financial *accountability* for federal departments and agencies.

G

governor general The representative of the Queen in Canada; functions as the head of state when the Queen is not in Canada.

Governor General in Council Refers to the *governor general* acting on the formal advice of the cabinet.

H

hierarchy of needs A concept developed by Abraham Maslow that suggests workers can be motivated by the satisfaction of a number of different needs ranging from basic shelter and food to self-actualization. As workers' lower-level needs are satisfied, they are motivated by desires to satisfy higher-level needs.

horizontal management A type of management process that involves two or more departments and, increasingly, nongovernmental bodies.

human relations school An approach to management and motivation that emphasizes the dignity and needs of workers in the workplace. Usually associated with social psychologists such as Mayo, Roethlisberger, and Dickson.

human resources planning The process through which a government strives to ensure that it has the appropriate quantity and quality of employees to carry out its responsibilities.

I

independent regulatory agency A body that administers, fixes, establishes, controls, or regulates an economic, cultural, environmental, or social activity by regularized and established means in the public interest and in accordance with policy guidelines specified by the government.

individual ministerial responsibility The responsibility of the minister, as the political head of the department, to answer to the legislature and through the legislature to the public both for his or her personal acts and for those of departmental subordinates.

influence That form of *power* in which B conforms to A's desires, *values*, or goals through suggestion, persuasion, emulation, or anticipation. A more general and pervasive form of power than *control*. Sometimes referred to as "authority of leadership" or "personal power."

intergovernmental relations The interactions between and among the federal, provincial, and municipal governments in the Canadian federal system.

Interim Supply A limited appropriation of funds provided by Parliament at the beginning of the fiscal year until the full *Estimates* have been approved.

J

job classification The process by which jobs are assigned to an occupational group within an *occupational category* and to a level within that group.

job evaluation The analysis of a job in terms of its duties, its physical and mental demands, the knowledge and skills it requires, and the conditions under which it is performed; the writing of a job description that explains the duties, working conditions, and other aspects of the job; and the assessment of these job characteristics against the classification standard established for the relevant occupational group.

L

lieutenant governors The representatives of the Queen in the provinces.

Lieutenant Governor in Council The lieutenant governor acting on the advice of a provincial cabinet.

line The part of an organization directly involved in producing the organization's output.

line-item budgeting A style of budgeting that emphasizes the object of expenditure (salaries, stationery) rather than the purpose of the expenditure.

lobbying A legitimate means by which groups and individuals try to influence government decisions by direct contact with politicians or public servants. Usually associated with the activities of *pressure groups* or interest groups.

M

managerialism A theoretical perspective on organization that emphasizes setting clear organizational goals and giving employees the flexibility and autonomy to pursue these goals.

Memorandum to Cabinet The key mechanism by which policy proposals are brought forward by ministers for consideration and approval by their cabinet colleagues. The formal means by which *deputy ministers* provide confidential policy advice to their ministers.

merit principle A principle according to which (1) all citizens should have a reasonable opportunity to be considered for employment in the public service and (2) *selections* must be based exclusively on qualification or fitness for the job. To be distinguished from the *merit system* (see).

merit system The mechanism in use at any time by which the goals of the *merit principle* are achieved. An administrative device that can and should be adapted to changing circumstances.

N

new public management (NPM) A style of management that borrows heavily from private sector principles and focuses on *values* like customer service, flexibility in delivery, entrepreneurship, and empowerment.

NPM See *new public management.*

O

objective responsibility The responsibility of a person or an organization to someone else, outside of self, for some thing or some kind of performance. Similar in meaning to *accountability* or answerability.

occupational category A broad range of occupations of the same type, distinguished by the nature of the duties performed and the education required. Examples in the federal public service are the Executive Group and the Operational categories.

Ombudsman An official authorized by statute to investigate complaints from citizens about improper, unfair, or discriminatory treatment by public servants. Reports to the legislature and is independent of the political executive and the *bureaucracy.*

open systems theory An approach to the study of organizations that emphasizes that organizations are a part of, and must interact with, their environment.

operating department An administrative unit comprising one or more organizational components over which a minister has direct management and control.

order in council An official proclamation made by the *Governor General in Council*; usually a government regulation.

organization development A participative approach to management that emphasizes team development and allows members of the organization to work together to identify and correct problems.

organizational humanism See *human relations school.*

organizational socialization The process through which individuals learn the expectations attached to the position they occupy in the organization and through which they selectively internalize as *values* some of the expectations of those with whom they interact.

P

participatory management A style of management emphasizing the desirability of workers actually being involved in decision making.

patronage The appointment of persons to government service or their advancement within the service on the grounds of contributions, financial or otherwise, to the governing party rather than of merit.

pay equity A system that permits comparisons to be made between different jobs performed for the same employer. A shorthand term for equal pay for work of equal value. To be distinguished from equal pay for equal work, which requires that men and women be paid the same for doing the same job.

PCO See *Privy Council Office.*

performance budgeting A style of budgeting that relates expenditure to specific activities to determine unit costs of providing services.

performance evaluation The process whereby information about the performance of employees over time is systematically collected and analyzed. Also referred to as "employee appraisal."

performance measurement The process of comparing the level of a government service provided against some standard to see whether it meets that standard or is at least improving.

PMO See *Prime Minister's Office.*

policy See *public policy.*

political neutrality A constitutional doctrine or convention according to which public servants should not engage in activities that are likely to impair or appear to impair their impartiality or the impartiality of the public service.

politics–administration dichotomy The idea that a clear distinction can be made between the responsibilities of elected executives, who make policy decisions, and the responsibilities of public servants, who execute these decisions.

policy community A cluster of interested groups (government organizations, interest groups, international agencies, interested companies and individuals, and journalists) organized around a particular policy. This group has a strong influence on the making of that policy.

policy network The interconnections among actors in a *policy community.*

post-bureaucratic organization A type of organization that eschews the qualities of traditional bureaucracies and stresses flexibility, *decentralization*, and citizen-centred delivery of services.

power The capacity to secure the dominance of one's *values* or goals. There are two forms of *power—control* and *influence.*

pressure groups Organizations composed of persons who have joined together to pursue a mutual interest by influencing government decisions and actions. Often referred to as "interest groups."

Prime Minister's Office (PMO) The *central agency* providing partisan policy advice to the prime minister. It is most concerned with relations between the prime minister and the media and the party.

privative clauses Statutory provisions designed to prevent judicial review of the decisions of administrative tribunals.

Privy Council Office (PCO) The *central agency* providing policy advice and administrative support to cabinet and its committees.

program A set of activities selected to carry out a policy chosen by government.

program budgeting A style of budgeting that allocates funds by *program* and attempts to measure the impact of expenditures on the goals and objectives of programs.

public accounts The series of documents containing the government's year-end financial statements.

public bureaucracy The system of authority, people, offices, and methods that government uses to achieve its objectives. The means by which the practice of public administration is carried on.

public choice theory The use of economic principles to analyze political activity. It suggests that people take political action to further their self-interest.

public enterprise *Crown corporations* and mixed enterprise.

public participation A broad range of direct and indirect forms of participation by members of the public in government decision making. Includes such forms of participation as membership in political parties, *pressure groups*, and advisory bodies. A broader concept than *citizen participation*.

public policy A course of action chosen by government to address a societal problem.

Public Service Commission An independent agency that serves Parliament as the guardian of the *merit principle* in human resources management. It is responsible for *recruitment*, staffing, and promotion in the public service.

public service ethics See *administrative ethics*.

Q

quasi-federalism A term used to describe the early decades of the Canadian federation during which the federal government dominated the provincial governments, in part by making frequent use of the federal constitutional powers to disallow and reserve provincial legislation.

R

representative bureaucracy The idea that the social composition of the *bureaucracy* should reflect that of the population as a whole. Also that larger numbers of persons from certain underrepresented groups (e.g., women, minority groups) should be brought into the public service.

S

scientific management A management style that emphasizes tailoring the physical nature of work to the physical abilities of workers. Characterized by time-and-motion studies and precise work standards. Usually associated with Frederick W. Taylor.

selection The process through which candidates for public service positions are screened by such means as application forms, written examinations, and interviews.

span of control The number of subordinates reporting to a particular supervisor.

special operating agency An organization structure that provides the unit with some autonomy from its department, but not as much autonomy as a *Crown corporation* has.

staff The part of the organization that supports the *line* function but that is not directly involved in producing the organization's output (e.g., accounting or personnel).

subjective responsibility The responsibility a person feels toward others. Often described as personal or psychological responsibility. Similar in meaning to identification, loyalty, and conscience.

Supplementary Estimates A request for funds in addition to the original *Estimates*. Usually requested toward the end of the fiscal year.

T

TB See *Treasury Board*.

Theory X/Theory Y Developed by Douglas McGregor to describe different managers' views of workers. Theory X holds that workers are basically lazy and need to be closely watched. Theory Y holds that workers are highly motivated and will voluntarily work hard.

total quality management (TQM) A style of participative management popularized in the 1980s and early 1990s. It requires changing an organization's culture to focus on establishing and maintaining high standards of quality, especially with respect to meeting "customer" expectations.

TQM See *total quality management*.

Treasury Board (TB) A cabinet committee consisting of the President of the Treasury Board, the Minister of Finance, and four other cabinet ministers. Responsible for preparation of the expenditure budget and for administrative management in departments.

Treasury Board Secretariat (TSB) The *central agency* that assists the *Treasury Board* in carrying out its responsibilities.

TBS See *Treasury Board Secretariat*.

U

unity of command The bureaucratic principle that holds that all employees must report to one, and only one, supervisor in order to minimize confusion and misdirection.

V

values Enduring beliefs that influence the choices made by individuals, groups, or organizations from among available means or ends.

visible minority A person (other than an aboriginal person) who is non-white in colour/race, regardless of place of birth.

W

whistle-blowing The overt or covert disclosure of confidential information to persons outside the organization about real or anticipated wrongdoing.

Bibliography

Chapter 1

Canadian Tax Foundation. *Finances of the Nation 2005.* Toronto: Canadian Tax Foundation, 2005.

Dunn, Christopher. (Ed.) *The Handbook of Canadian Public Administration.* Toronto: Oxford University Press, 2002.

Hodgetts, J.E. *The Canadian Public Service: A Physiology of Government, 1867–1970.* Toronto: University of Toronto Press, 1973.

Inwood, Gregory J. *Understanding Canadian Public Administration: An Introduction to Theory and Practice* 2nd. ed. Toronto: Pearson Education Canada, Inc., 2004.

Johnson, David. *Thinking Government: Public Sector Management in Canada.* 2nd ed. Peterborough: Broadview Press, 2006.

Kernaghan, Kenneth, Brian Marson, and Sandford Borins. *The New Public Organization.* Toronto: Institute of Public Administration of Canada, 2000.

Nevitte, Neil. *Decline of Deference.* Peterborough: Broadview Press, 1996.

Pal, Leslie A. *Beyond Policy Analysis: Public Issue Management in Turbulent Times.* 3rd ed. Toronto: Thomson Nelson, 2006.

Peters, B. Guy, and Jon Pierre. *Handbook of Public Administration.* London: Sage Publications, 2003.

Rainey, Hal G. *Understanding and Managing Public Organizations.* 3rd ed. San Francisco: Jossey-Bass, 2003.

Rosen, Harvey S., Bev Dahlby, Roger S. Smith, and Paul Boothe. *Public Finance in Canada.* 2nd ed. Toronto: McGraw-Hill Ryerson.

Savoie, Donald J. *Thatcher, Reagan, Mulroney: In Search of a New Bureaucracy.* Toronto: University of Toronto Press, 1994.

———. *Breaking the Bargain: Public Servants, Ministers and Parliament.* Toronto: University of Toronto Press, 2003.

Wilson, James Q. *What Government Agencies Do and Why They Do It.* New York: Basic Books, 1989.

Chapter 2

Albrow, Martin. *Bureaucracy.* London: The Macmillan Press, 1970.

Beetham, David. *Bureaucracy.* 2nd ed. Minneapolis: University of Minnesota Press, 1996.

Copley, Frank Barkely. *Frederick W. Taylor: Father of Scientific Management.* 2 vols. New York: Augustus M. Kelley, 1969.

Fry, Brian R. *Mastering Public Administration: From Max Weber to Dwight Waldo.* Chatham, N.J.: Chatham House Publishers, Inc., 1989.

Gulick, Luther, and L. Urwick, eds. *Papers on the Science of Administration.* New York: Augustus M. Kelley, 1969.

Harmon, Michael M., and Richard T. Mayer. *Organization Theory for Public Administration.* Boston: Little, Brown, 1986.

Heffron, Florence. *Organization Theory and Public Organizations: The Political Connection.* Englewood Cliffs, N.J.: Prentice-Hall, 1989.

Hodgetts, J. E. *The Canadian Public Service: A Physiology of Government, 1867–1970.* Toronto: University of Toronto Press, 1973.

McLaren, Robert I. *Organizational Dilemmas.* Chichester, U.K.: John Wiley and Sons, 1982.

Merton, Robert K. "Bureaucratic Structure and Personality." *Social Forces* 18 (May 1940): 560–68.

Mitzman, Arthur. *The Iron Cage: A Historical Interpretation of Max Weber.* New York: Knopf, 1970.

Rainey, Hal G. *Understanding and Managing Public Organizations.* 3rd ed. San Francisco: Jossey-Bass, 2003.

Simon, Herbert. *Administrative Behavior.* 2nd ed. New York: The Free Press, 1957.

Taylor, Frederick Winslow. *The Principles of Scientific Management.* New York: W. W. Norton, 1967.

Weber, Max. *From Max Weber: Essays in Sociology.* Ed. and trans. H.H. Gerth and C. Wright Mills. New York: Oxford University Press, 1946.

Chapter 3

Argyris, Chris. *Personality and Organization: The Conflict Between System and Individual.* New York: Harper and Row, 1957.

———. *Integrating the Individual and the Organization.* New York: John Wiley and Sons, 1964.

Barnard, Chester. *The Functions of the Executive.* Cambridge, Mass.: Harvard University Press, 1962.

Beckhard, Richard. *Organization Development: Strategies and Models.* Reading, Mass.: Addison-Wesley, 1969.

Caropreso, Frank. (Ed.). *Making Total Quality Happen.* New York: The Conference Board, 1990.

Cohen, Steven, and Ronald Brand. *Total Quality Management in Government.* San Francisco: Jossey-Bass Publishers, 1993.

Deming, W. Edwards. *Quality, Productivity, and Competitive Position.* Cambridge, Mass.: Massachusetts Institute of Technology, Center for Advanced Engineering Study, 1982.

Denhardt, Robert B. *Public Administration: An Action Orientation.* Pacific Groves, Calif.: Brooks/Cole Publishing Company, 1991.

Drucker, Peter F. *The Practice of Management.* New York: Harper and Row, 1954.

Etzioni, Amitai. *Modern Organizations.* Englewood Cliffs, N.J.: Prentice-Hall, 1964.

Follett, Mary Parker. *Creative Experience.* New York: Peter Smith, 1951.

———. *Dynamic Administration: The Collected Papers of Mary Parker Follett.* Elliot M. Fox and L. Urwick, eds. London: Pitman, 1973.

———. *The New State.* Gloucester, Mass.: Peter Smith, 1965.

Fry, Brian R. *Mastering Public Administration: From Max Weber to Dwight Waldo.* Chatham, N.J.: Chatham House Publishers, Inc., 1989.

Galbraith, Jay. *Designing Complex Organizations.* Reading, Mass.: Addison-Wesley, 1973.

Garvin, David A. "Quality on the Line." *Harvard Business Review* 61 (September-October 1983): 64–75.

Garvin, David A., and Artemis March. "A Note on Quality: The Views of Deming, Juran, and Crosby." In *Unconditional Quality.* Boston: Harvard Business School Press, 1991.

Golembiewski, Robert T. *Humanizing Public Organizations.* Mt. Airy, Md.: Lomond Press, 1985.

Golembiewski, Robert T., and William B. Eddy, eds. *Organization Development in Public Administration.* 2 vols. New York: Marcel Dekker, Inc., 1978.

Harmon, Michael M., and Richard T. Mayer. *Organization Theory for Public Administration.* Boston: Little, Brown, 1986.

Heffron, Florence. *Organization Theory and Public Organizations: The Political Connection.* Englewood Cliffs, N.J.: Prentice-Hall, 1989.

Herzberg, Frederick. *Work and the Nature of Man.* Cleveland, O.: The World Publishing Company, 1966.

Herzberg, Frederick, Bernard Mausner, and Barbara Bloch Snyderman. *The Motivation to Work.* New York: John Wiley and Sons, 1959.

Hodgetts, J., William McCloskey, Reginald Whitaker, and V. Seymour Wilson. *The Biography of an Institution.* Montreal: McGill-Queen's University Press, 1972.

Huse, Edgar F. *Organization Development and Change.* 2nd ed. St. Paul, Minn.: West Publishing Company, 1980.

Jablonski, Joseph R. *Implementing Total Quality Management: An Overview.* San Diego: Pfeiffer and Company, 1991.

Katz, Daniel, and Robert L. Kahn. *The Social Psychology of Organizations.* New York: John Wiley and Sons, 1966.

Laframboise, H. L. "Administrative Reform in the Federal Public Service: Signs of a Saturation Psychosis." *Canadian Public Administration* 14(3) (fall 1971): 303–25.

Marson, Brian. "Building Customer-Focused Organizations in British Columbia." *Public Administration Quarterly* 17(1) (spring 1993): 30–47.

Maslow, A. H. *Eupsychian Management.* Homewood, Ill.: Dorsey Press, 1965.

———. *Motivation and Personality.* New York: Harper and Row, 1970.

McGregor, Douglas. *The Human Side of Enterprise.* New York: McGraw-Hill, 1960.

McLaren, Robert I. *Organizational Dilemmas.* Chichester, U.K.: John Wiley and Sons, 1982.

Miner, John B. *Organizational Behavior: Foundation, Theories, and Analysis.* New York: Oxford University Press, 2002.

———. *Organizational Behavior I: Essential Theories of Motivation and Leadership.* Armonk, N.Y.: M.E. Sharpe, 2005.

Miner, John B. *Organizational Behavior II: Essential Theories of Process and Structure.* Armonk, N.Y.: M.E. Sharpe, 2006.

Mintzberg, Henry. *The Structuring of Organizations.* Englewood Cliffs, N.J.: Prentice-Hall, 1979.

Mintzberg, Henry. *Structure in Fives: Designing Effective Organizations*. Englewood Cliffs, N.J.: Prentice-Hall, 1983.

Morse, John J., and Jay W. Lorsch. "Beyond Theory Y." *Harvard Business Review* 48 (May/June, 1970): 61–68.

Perrow, Charles. *Complex Organizations: A Critical Essay*. Glenview, Ill.: Scott, Foresman, 1972.

Rahnema, Saeed. *Organization Structure: A Systemic Approach*. Toronto: McGraw-Hill Ryerson, 1992.

Roethlisberger, F. J., and William J. Dickson. *Management and the Worker*. Cambridge, Mass.: Harvard University Press, 1964.

Sashkin, Marshall, and Kenneth J. Kiser. *Putting Total Quality Management to Work*. San Francisco: Berrett-Koehler Publishers, 1993.

Chapter 4

Aucoin, Peter. *The New Public Management: Canada in Comparative Perspective*. Montreal: Institute for Research on Public Policy, 1995.

———. "Beyond the 'New' in Public Management Reform in Canada: Catching the Next Wave?" in Christopher Dunn, ed., *Handbook of Canadian Public Administration*. Toronto: Oxford University Press, 2002.

Barzelay, Michael, with collaboration of Babak J. Armajani. *Breaking Through Bureaucracy: A New Vision for Managing in Government*. Berkeley: University of California Press, 1992.

Carroll, Barbara Wake, and David I. Dewar. "Performance Management: Panacea or Fools' Gold?" in Christopher Dunn, ed., *The Handbook of Canadian Public Administration*. Toronto: Oxford University Press, 2002.

Denhardt, Robert B. *The Pursuit of Significance: Strategies for Managerial Success in Public Organizations*. Belmont: Wadsworth Publishing Company, 1993.

Denhardt., Janet V., and Robert B. Denhardt, *The New Public Service: Serving, Not Steering*. Armonk: M.E. Sharp, 2003.

Dunleavy, Patrick, Helen Margetts, Simon Bastow, and Jane Tinkler, "New Public Management Is Dead—Long Live Digital-Era Governance," *Journal of Public Administration Research and Theory* 16: 467–94.

Dunn, Christopher. (Ed.) *The Handbook of Canadian Public Administration*. Toronto: Oxford University Press, 2002.

Fountain, Jane E. *Building the Virtual State: Information Technology and Institutional Change*. Washington, D.C.: The Brookings Institution, 2001.

Frederickson, H. George, and Kevin B. Smith. *The Public Administration Theory Primer*. Boulder: Westview Press, 2003.

Good, David A. *The Politics of Public Management: The HRDC Audit of Grants and Contributions*. Toronto: Institute of Public Administration and the University of Toronto Press, 2003.

Government of Canada. *Public Service 2000: The Renewal of the Public Service of Canada*. Ottawa: Minister of Supply and Services, 1990.

Hood, Christopher. "A Public Management for All Seasons?" *Public Administration* 69 (spring 1991): 3–19.

Hood, Christopher, and Michael Jackson. *Administrative Argument*. Aldershot: Dartmouth, 1999.

Kernaghan, Kenneth. Brian Marson, and Sandford Borins. *The New Public Organization*. Toronto: Institute of Public Administration of Canada, 2000.

Kettl, Donald. *The Global Public Management Revolution*. 2nd ed. Washington, D.C.: The Brookings Institution, 2005.

Organisation for Economic Co-operation and Development. *Governance in Transition: Public Management Reforms in OECD Countries*. Paris: OECD, 1995.

Osborne, David, and Ted Gaebler. *Reinventing Government: How the Entrepreneurial Spirit Is Transforming the Public Sector*. London: Penguin, 1993.

Pal, Leslie A. "New Public Management in Canada: New Whine in Old Battles?" In James Bickerton and Alain-G. Gagnon, eds., *Canadian Politics*. 4th ed. Peterborough: Broadview Press, 2004.

———. *Beyond Policy Analysis: Public Issue Management in Turbulent Times*. 3rd ed. Toronto: Thomson Nelson, 2006.

Peters, B. Guy, and Donald J. Savoie, eds. *Governance in the Twenty-First Century: Revitalizing the Public Service*. Montreal and Kingston, 2000.

Peters, Thomas J., and Robert H. Waterman Jr. *In Search of Excellence: Lessons from America's Best-Run Companies*. Cambridge: Harper and Row Publishers, 1982.

Politt, Christopher, and Geert Bouckaert. *Public Management Reform: A Comparative Analysis*. New York: Oxford University Press, 2000.

Savoie, Donald J. *Thatcher, Reagan, Mulroney: In Search of a New Bureaucracy*. Toronto: University of Toronto Press, 1994.

———. *Breaking the Bargain: Public Servants, Ministers and Parliament*. Toronto: University of Toronto Press, 2003.

West, Darrell M. *Digital Government: Technology and Public Sector Performance*. Princeton, N.J.: Princeton University Press, 2005.

Chapter 5

Aucoin, Peter, "Organizational Change in the Machinery of Canadian Government: From Rational Management to Brokerage to Brokerage Politics." *Canadian Journal of Political Science* 19(1) (March 1986) 3–27.

Axworthy, Thomas S. "Of Secretaries to Princes." *Canadian Public Administration* 31(2) (summer 1988): 247–64.

Bernier, Luc, Keith Brownsey, and Michael Howlett, eds. *Executive Styles in Canada: Cabinet Structures and Leadership Practices in Canadian Government*. Toronto: University of Toronto Press, 2005.

The Sponsorship Program and Advertising Activities. *Restoring Accountability: Recommendations* Ottawa: Her Majesty the Queen in Right of Canada, 2006.

———. *Who is Responsible?* Fact Finding Report. Ottawa: Her Majesty the Queen in Right of Canada, 2005.

Doern, G. Bruce. "Horizontal and Vertical Portfolios in Government." In G. Bruce Doern and V. Seymour Wilson, eds., *Issues in Canadian Public Policy*. Toronto: Macmillan, 1974.

Dunn, Christopher. "Changing the Design: Cabinet Decision-Making in Three Provincial Governments," *Canadian Public Administration* 34(4) (winter 1991): 621–40.

———. *The Institutionalized Cabinet: Governing the Western Provinces*. Montreal and Kingston: McGill-Queen's University Press and Institute of Public Administration of Canada, 1995.

Lalonde, Marc. "The Changing Role of the Prime Minister's Office." Canadian Public Administration 14(4) (winter 1971): 509–37.

Osbaldeston, Gordon. *Organizing to Govern*. 2 vols. Toronto: McGraw-Hill Ryerson, 1992.

Robertson, Gordon. "The Changing Role of the Privy Council Office." *Canadian Public Administration* 14(4) (winter 1971): 487–508.

Sutherland, S.L. "The Role of the Clerk of the Privy Council." In Commission of Inquiry into the Sponsorship Program and Advertising Activities, *Restoring Accountability: Research Studies, Volume 3: Linkages: Responsibilities and Accountabilities*.

Ottawa: Her Majesty the Queen in Right of Canada, 2006.

Chapter 6

Borins, Sandford F. "World War Two Crown Corporations: Their Wartime Role and Peacetime Privatization." *Canadian Public Administration* 25(3) (fall 1982): 380–404.

Garant, Patrice. "Crown Corporations: Instruments of Economic Intervention—Legal Aspects." In Ivan Bernier and Andre Lajoie, eds., *Regulations, Crown Corporations and Administrative Tribunals*, 1–79. *Research Study for the Royal Commission on the Economic Union and Development Prospects for Canada*, vol. 48. Toronto: University of Toronto Press, 1985.

Laux, Jeanne Kirk. "How Private Is Privatization?" *Canadian Public Policy* 19(4) (December 1993): 398–411.

Luciani, Patrick. *Economic Myths: Making Sense of Canadian Policy Issues*. 4th ed. Toronto: Pearson Education Canada, Inc., 2004.

Neu, Dean, Duncan Green, and Alison Taylor. "Privatizing the ALCB: Ideology and Symbolism or Efficiency and Equity?" *Policy Options* 18 (April 1997): 28–31.

Perl, Anthony. "Public Enterprise as an Expression of Sovereignty: Reconsidering the Origin of Canadian National Railways." *Canadian Journal of Political Science* 27(1) (March 1994): 23–52.

Prichard, J. Robert S. (Ed.) *Crown Corporations in Canada: The Calculus of Instrument Choice*. Toronto: Butterworths, 1983.

Stevens, Douglas F. *Corporate Autonomy and Institutional Control: The Crown Corporation as a Problem in Organizational Design*. Montreal: McGill-Queen's University Press, 1993.

Treasury Board of Canada Secretariat. *Crown Corporations and Other Corporate Interests of Canada*. Annual. Ottawa: Her Majesty the Queen in Right of Canada.

———. *Review of the Governance Framework for Canada's Crown Corporations*. Ottawa: Her Majesty the Queen in Right of Canada, 2005.

Tupper, Allan, and G. Bruce Doern. *Privatization, Public Policy and Public Corporations in Canada*. Halifax: Institute for Research on Public Policy, 1988.

———. (Eds.) *Public Corporations and Public Policy in Canada*. Montreal: The Institute for Research on Public Policy, 1981.

West, Douglas S. "Alberta's Liquor Store Privatization: Economic and Social Impacts." *Policy Options* 18, April 1997: 24–27.

Chapter 7

Doern, G. Bruce. "'Smart Regulation', Regulatory Congestion and Natural Resources Regulatory Governance." In G. Bruce Doern, ed., *How Ottawa Spends 2004–2005: Mandate Change in the Paul Martin Era*. Montreal and Kingston: McGill-Queen's University Press, 2004.

Doern, G. Margaret M. Hill, Michael J. Prince, and Richard J. Schultz. *Changing the Rules: Canadian Regulatory Regimes and Institutions*. Toronto: University of Toronto Press, 1999.

External Advisory Committee on Smart Regulation. *Smart Regulation: A Regulatory Strategy for Canada*. September 2004.

Government of Canada. *Regulatory Process Guide: Developing a Regulatory Proposal and Seeking Its Approval*. June 2004.

Hartley, Sarah, and Grace Skogstad, "Regulating Genetically Modified Crops and Foods in Canada and the United Kingdom: Democratizing Risk Regulation." *Canadian Public Administration* 48(3) (fall 2005): 305–27.

Johnson, David. "Regulatory Agencies and Accountability: An Ontario Perspective." *Canadian Public Administration* 34(3) (autumn 1991): 417–34.

Luciani, Patrick. *Economic Myths: Making Sense of Canadian Policy Issues*. 4th ed. Toronto: Pearson Education Canada, Inc., 2004.

May, Peter J. "Social Regulation." In Lester M. Salamon (with special assistance of Odus V. Elliott), ed., *The Tools of Government: A Guide for the New Governance*. New York: Oxford University Press, 2002.

Organisation for Economic Co-operation and Development. *Canada: Maintaining Leadership Through Innovation*. Paris: OECD, 2002.

Privy Council Office. *A Guide Book for Heads of Agencies*. August 1999.

———. *Government of Canada Regulatory Policy*. November 1999.

Schultz, Richard. *Federalism, Bureaucracy, and Public Policy: The Politics of Highway Transportation Regulation*. Montreal: McGill-Queen's University Press, 1980.

Strick, John C. "Regulation and Deregulation." In Christopher Dunn, ed., *The Handbook of Canadian Public Administration*. Toronto: Oxford University Press, 2002.

———. *The Economics of Government Regulation: Theory and Canadian Practice*. 2nd ed. (Toronto: Thomson Educational Publishing Inc., 1994).

Chapter 8

Borins, Sandford. "On the Frontiers of Electronic Governance: A Report on the United States and Canada." *International Review of Administrative Sciences* 68 (2002): 199–211.

De Bettignies, Jean-Etienne, and Thomas W. Ross. "The Economics of Public-Private Partnerships." *Canadian Public Policy* XXX(2) (June 2004): 135–154.

Ford, Robin, and David Zussman, eds. *Alternative Service Delivery: Sharing Governance in Canada*. Toronto: KPMG Centre for Government Foundation and Institute of Public Administration of Canada, 1997.

Fyfe, Toby. "Alternative Service Delivery—Responding to Global Pressures." *International Review of Administrative Sciences* 70(4): 637–44.

Kernaghan, Kenneth. Brian Marson, and Sandford Borins. *The New Public Organization*. Toronto: Institute of Public Administration of Canada, 2000.

———. "Moving Towards the Virtual State: Integrating Services and Service Channels for Citizen-Centred Delivery." *International Review of Administrative Sciences* 71(1): 119–31.

McKenzie, Judith I. "Walkerton: Requiem for the New Public Management in Ontario?" *International Journal of Environment and Pollution* 21 (2004): 309–24.

Mylvaganam, Chandran, and Sandford Borins. "'If You Build It . . .': Business, Government and Ontario's Electronic Toll Highway*. Toronto: University of Toronto Press, 2004.

Treasury Board of Canada Secretariat. "Policy on Alternative Service Delivery." Available at www.tbs.sct.gc.ca/pubs_pol/opepubs/tb_B4/information_e.asp. Retrieved November 14, 2005.

———. "Alternative Service Delivery." Available at www.tbs-sct.gc.ca/asd-dmps/index_e.asp. Retrieved November 14, 2005.

———. "Becoming a Special Operating Agency." Part 1. Available at www.tbs-sct.gc.ca/pubs_pol/opepubs/TB_B4/bsoa-doss_e.asp. Retrieved July 14, 2006.

———. "Scope of ASD." 5. Available at www.tbs-sct.gc.ca/asd-dmps/soa_e.asp. Retrieved November 14, 2005.

Vining, Aidan R., Anthony E. Boardman, and Finn Poschmann. "Public-Private Partnerships in the U.S.

and Canada: 'There Are No Free Lunches.'" *Journal of Comparative Policy Analysis* 7, (September 2005) 199–220.

Wilkins, John K. "Conceptual and Practical Considerations in Alternative Service Delivery." *International Review of Administrative Sciences* 69 (2003): 173–89.

Winfield, Mark S., David Whorley, and Shelley Beth Kaufman. "Public Safety in Private Hands: A Study of Ontario's Technical Standards and Safety Authority." *Canadian Public Administration* 45(1) (spring 2002): 24–51.

Zussman, David. "Alternative Service Delivery." In Christopher Dunn, ed., *The Handbook of Canadian Public Administration*. Toronto: Oxford University Press, 2002.

Chapter 9

Blakeney, Allan, and Sandford Borins. *Political Management in Canada*. 2nd ed. Toronto: University of Toronto Press, 1998).

Government of Canada, Deputy Minister's Task Force. *Discussion Paper on Values and Ethics in the Public Service*. Ottawa: Privy Council Office, 1996.

Kernaghan, Kenneth. "East Block and Westminster: Conventions, Values, and Public Service." In Christopher Dunn, ed., *The Handbook of Canadian Public Administration*. Toronto: Oxford University Press, 2002.

———. "Politics, Policy and Public Servants: Political Neutrality Revisited." *Canadian Public Administration* 21 (fall 1976): 432–56.

———. "Shaking the Foundation: Traditional Versus New Public Service Values." In Mohamed Charih and Arthur Daniels, eds., *New Public Management and Public Administration in Canada* (Toronto: Institute of Public Administration of Canada, 1997), 47–65.

———. *The Future Role of a Professional Non-partisan Public Service in Ontario*. Brock University, June 2003.

Savoie, Donald J. *Breaking the Bargain: Public Servants, Ministers and Parliament*. Toronto: University of Toronto Press, 2003.

———. *Thatcher, Reagan, Mulroney: In Search of a New Bureaucracy*. Toronto: University of Toronto Press, 1994.

Simpson, Jeffrey. *Spoils of Power: The Politics of Patronage*. Toronto: Collins, 1988.

Wilson, Woodrow. "The Study of Administration." Reprinted in Peter Woll, ed., *Public Administration and Policy*. New York: Harper and Row, 1966.

Chapter 10

Canada, Royal Commission on Financial Management and Accountability. *Final Report*. Ottawa: Supply and Services, 1979.

Commission of Inquiry into the Sponsorship Program and Advertising Activities. *Who is Responsible? Fact Finding Report*. Ottawa: Her Majesty the Queen in Right of Canada, 2005.

Commission of Inquiry into the Sponsorship Program and Advertising Activities. *Restoring Accountability: Recommendations* Ottawa: Her Majesty the Queen in Right of Canada, 2006.

Finer, Herman. "Administrative Responsibility in Democratic Government." *Public Administration Review* 1 (summer 1941): 335–50.

Friedrich, Carl J. "Responsible Government Service Under the American Constitution." In Carl J. Friedrich, William Carl Beyer, Sterling Denhard Spero, John Francis Miller, and George A. Graham, *Problems of the American Public Service*. New York: McGraw-Hill, 1935, 3–74.

———. "Public Policy and the Nature of Administrative Responsibility." In Carl J. Friedrich and Edward S. Mason, eds., *Public Policy*. Cambridge, Mass.: Harvard University Press, 1940, 3–24.

Government of Canada. Privy Council Office. *Values and Ethics in the Public Service*. Ottawa: Privy Council Office, December 1996.

Kernaghan, Kenneth. (Ed.) *Do Unto Others: Ethics in Government and Business*. Toronto: Institute of Public Administration of Canada, 1991.

———. "Encouraging 'Rightdoing' and Discouraging Wrongdoing: A Public Service Charter and Disclosure Legislation." In Commission of Inquiry in the Sponsorship Program and Advertising Activities, *Restoring Accountability: Research Studies, Volume 2: The Public Service and Transparency* (Ottawa: Her Majesty the Queen in Right of Canada, 2006.

———. "The Emerging Public Service Culture: Values, Ethics and Reforms." *Canadian Public Administration* 37(4) (winter 1994): 614–30.

———. "Towards a Public-Service Code of Conduct— and Beyond." *Canadian Public Administration* 40(1) (spring 1997): 40–54.

———. "Values, Ethics and Public Service." In Jacques Bourgault et al., eds., *Public Administration and Public Management: Canadian Experiences* (Quebec: Les Publications du Qubec, 1997): 101–11.

Kernaghan, Kenneth and John Langford. *The Responsible Public Servant*. Toronto: Institute of Public

Administration of Canada, and Halifax: Institute for Research on Public Policy, 1990.

Osbaldeston, Gordon. *Keeping Deputy Ministers Accountable*. Toronto: McGraw-Hill Ryerson, 1989.

Privy Council Office. *Values and Ethics in the Public Service*. Ottawa: Privy Council Office, December 1996.

Tait, J. "A Strong Foundation: Report of the Task Force on Public Service Values and Ethics (the Summary)." *Canadian Public Administration* 40(1) (spring 1997): 1–22.

Thompson, Dennis F. *Political Ethics and Public Office*. Cambridge, Mass.: Harvard University Press, 1987.

Treasury Board of Canada Secretariat. *Values and Ethics Code for the Public Service*. Ottawa: Her Majesty the Queen in Right of Canada, 2003.

Chapter 11

Bakvis, Herman. "Prime Minister and Cabinet in Canada: An Autocracy in Need of Reform"? *Journal of Canadian Studies* 20(4) (Winter 2001): 60–79.

Bernier, Luc, Keith Brownsey, and Michael Howlett, eds. *Executive Styles in Canada: Cabinet Structures and Leadership Practices in Canadian Government*. Toronto: University of Toronto Press, 2005.

Campbell, Colin. *Governments Under Stress: Political Executives and Key Bureaucrats in Washington, London and Ottawa*. Toronto: University of Toronto Press, 1983.

Campbell, Colin, and George J. Szablowski. *The Superbureaucrats: Structure and Behaviour in Central Agencies*. Toronto: Macmillan, 1979.

Clark, Ian. "Recent Changes in the Cabinet Decision-Making System in Ottawa." *Canadian Public Administration* 28(2) (summer 1985): 185–201.

———. "Restraint, Renewal and the Treasury Board Secretariat." *Canadian Public Administration* 37(2) (summer 1994): 209–48.

Dunn, Christopher. "Changing the Design: Cabinet Decision-Making in Three Provincial Governments," *Canadian Public Administration* 34(4) (winter 1991): 621–40.

———. "The Central Executive in Canadian Government: Searching for the Holy Grail." In Christopher Dunn, ed., *The Handbook of Canadian Public Administration*. Toronto: Oxford University Press, 2002.

French, Richard. *How Ottawa Decides: Planning and Industrial Policy Making, 1968–1984*. 2nd ed. Toronto: James Lorimer, 1984.

Lalonde, Marc. "The Changing Role of the Prime Minister's Office." *Canadian Public Administration* 14(4) (winter 1971): 509–37.

Lindquist, Evert A., and Graham White. "Analyzing Canadian Cabinets: Past, Present and Future." In Mohamed Charih and Arthur Daniels, eds., *New Public Management and Public Administration in Canada*. Toronto: Institute of Public Administration of Canada, 1997, 113–38.

Lindquist, Evert A., Ian Clark, and James Mitchell. "Reshaping Ottawa's Centre of Government: Martin's Reform in Historical Perspective." In G. Bruce Doern, ed., *How Ottawa Spends 2004–2005: Mandate Change in the Paul Martin Era*. Montreal and Kingston: McGill-Queen's University Press, 2004.

Matheson, W. A. "The Cabinet and the Canadian Bureaucracy." In Kenneth Kernaghan, ed., *Public Administration in Canada: Selected Readings*. 5th ed. Toronto: Methuen, 1985, 266–80.

———. *The Prime Minister and the Cabinet*. Toronto: Methuen, 1976.

Nossal, Kim Richard. "Allison Through the (Ottawa) Looking Glass: Bureaucratic Politics and Foreign Policy in a Parliamentary System." *Canadian Public Administration* 22(4) (winter 1979): 610–26.

Osbaldeston, Gordon. *Organizing to Govern*. 2 vols. Toronto: McGraw-Hill Ryerson, 1992.

Robertson, Gordon. "The Changing Role of the Privy Council Office." *Canadian Public Administration* 14(4) (winter 1971): 487–508.

Savoie, Donald J. *Breaking the Bargain: Public Servants, Ministers and Parliament*. Toronto: University of Toronto Press, 2003.

———. *Governing from the Centre: The Concentration of Power in Canadian Politics*. Toronto: University of Toronto Press, 1999.

———. "The Rise of Court Government in Canada." *Canadian Journal of Political Science* 32(4) (December 1999): 635–64.

Van Loon, R. "The Policy and Expenditure Management System in the Federal Government: The First Three Years." *Canadian Public Administration* 26(2) (summer 1983): 255–84.

White, Graham. *Cabinet and First Ministers*. Vancouver: UBC Press, 2005.

Zussman, David. "Walking the Tightrope: The Mulroney Government and the Public Service." In Michael J. Prince, ed., *How Ottawa Spends 1986–87: Tracking the Tories*. Toronto: Methuen, 1986.

Chapter 12

Auditor General of Canada. *Report of the Auditor General to the House of Commons*, ch. 4. Ottawa: Minister of Public Works and Government Services, November 2005.

Bakvis, Herman, and Luc Juillet. *The Horizontal Challenge: Line Departments, Central Agencies and Leadership*. Ottawa: Canada School of Public Service, 2004.

Benoit, Liane E. "Ministerial Staff: The Life and Times of Parliament's Statutory Orphans." In Commission of Inquiry into the Sponsorship Program and Advertising Activities, *Restoring Accountability: Research Studies, Volume 1: Parliament, Minister, and Deputy Minister*. Ottawa: Her Majesty the Queen in Right of Canada, 2006.

Bourgault, Jacques. *The Contemporary Role and Challenges of Deputy Ministers in the Federal Government of Canada* (Ottawa: Canadian Centre for Management Development, January 2003).

———. "The Deputy Minister's Role in the Government of Canada: His Responsibility and His Accountability." In Commission of Inquiry into the Sponsorship Program and Advertising Activities, *Restoring Accountability: Research Studies, Volume 3: Linkages: Accountabilities and Responsibilities*. Ottawa: Her Majesty the Queen in Right of Canada, 2006.

Bourgault, Jacques, and Rene Lapierre. *Horizontality and Public Management, Final Report to the Canadian Centre for Management Development, the Leadership Network, the Federal Regional Council—Quebec and the École nationale d'administration publique*. Ottawa: Canadian Centre for Management Development, December 2000.

Canadian Centre for Management Development, Roundtable on the Management of Horizontal Initiatives. *Moving from the Heroic to the Everyday: Lessons Learned from Leading Horizontal Project*, 2001.

Commission of Inquiry into the Sponsorship Program and Advertising Activities. *Restoring Accountability: Recommendations*. Ottawa: Her Majesty the Queen in Right of Canada, 2006.

Flemming, Jeanne M. "The Role of Executive Assistant to a Federal Minister." *Optimum* 27 (1997): 63–68.

Hurley, James Ross. "Responsibility, Accountability and the Role of Deputy Ministers in the Government of Canada." In Commission of Inquiry into the Sponsorship Program and Advertising Activities, *Restoring Accountability: Research Studies, Volume 3: Linkages: Accountabilities and Responsibilities*. Ottawa: Her Majesty the Queen in Right of Canada, 2006.

O'Connor, Loretta J. "Chief of Staff." *Policy Options* 12 (April 1991): 23–26.

Osbaldeston, Gordon. "Dear Minister." *Policy Options* 9 (June/July 1988): 3–11.

———. "Job Description for DMs." *Policy Options* (January 1988): 33–38.

Savoie, Donald J. *Breaking the Bargain: Public Servants, Ministers and Parliament*. Toronto: University of Toronto Press, 2003.

———. *Governing from the Centre: The Concentration of Power in Canadian Politics*. Toronto: University of Toronto Press, 1999.

Thomas, Paul G. "The Role of Central Agencies: Making a Mesh of Things." In James Bickerton and Alain-G. Gagnon, eds., *Canadian Politics*. 3rd ed. Peterborough: Broadview Press, 1999.

Treasury Board of Canada Secretariat. *Guidelines for Ministers' Offices*. Ottawa: Her Majesty the Queen in Right of Canada, 2006.

Chapter 13

Aucoin, Peter, Jennifer Smith, and Geoff Dinsdale. *Responsible Government: Clarifying Essentials, Dispelling Myths and Exploring Change*. Ottawa: Canadian Centre for Management Development, 2004.

Aucoin, Peter, and Mark D. Jarvis. *Modernizing Government Accountability: A Framework for Reform*. Ottawa: Canada School of Public Service, 2005.

Canada. House of Commons. Special Committee on Reform of the House of Commons. 3rd Report. Ottawa: June 1985.

Canada. Royal Commission on Financial Management and Accountability. Final Report. Ottawa: Supply and Services, 1979.

Commission of Inquiry into the Sponsorship Program and Advertising Activities. *Who Is Responsible? Fact Finding Report*. Ottawa: Her Majesty the Queen in Right of Canada, 2005.

Franks, C. E. S. "Putting Accountability and Responsibility Back into the System of Government." *Policy Options* 25(9) (October 2004): 64–66.

———. "The Respective Responsibilities and Accountabilities of Ministers and Public Servants: A Study of the British Accounting Officer System and Its Relevance for Canada." In Commission of Inquiry into Sponsorship Program and Advertising Activities, *Restoring Accountability: Research Studies, Volume 3: Linkages: Accountabilities and Responsibilities*. Ottawa: Her Majesty the Queen in Right of Canada, 2006.

———. "Not Anonymous: Ministerial Responsibility and the British Accounting Officers." *Canadian Public Administration* 40(4) (winter 1997): 626–52.

Government of Canada. *Accountable Government: A Guide for Ministers*. Ottawa: Her Majesty in Right of Canada, 2006.

———, Special Committee on Reform of the House of Commons. *3rd Report*. Ottawa: June 1985.

———, Royal Commission on Financial Management and Accountability. *Final Report*. Ottawa: Supply and Services, 1979.

House of Commons, Standing Committee on Public Accounts. *Governance in the Public Service of Canada: Ministerial and Deputy Ministerial Accountability*. May 2005.

Savoie, Donald J. *Breaking the Bargain: Public Servants, Ministers and Parliament*. Toronto: University of Toronto Press, 2003.

Smith, Alex. *The Accountability of Deputy Ministers Before Parliament*. Ottawa: Library of Parliament, 2006.

Smith, David E. "Clarifying the Doctrine of Ministerial Responsibility As It Applies to the Government and Parliament of Canada." In Commission of Inquiry into the Sponsorship Program and Advertising Activities, *Restoring Accountability: Research Studies, Volume 1: Parliament, Ministers, and Deputy Ministers*. Ottawa: Her Majesty in Right of Canada, 2006.

Sossin, Lorne. "Speaking Truth to Power? The Search for Bureaucratic Independence in Canada," *University of Toronto Law Journal* 55 (2005): 1–59.

Thomas, Paul G. "The Past, Present and Future of Officers of Parliament." *Canadian Public Administration* 46(3) (fall 2003): 287–314.

Chapter 14

Blake, Sara. *Administrative Law in Canada*, 3rd ed. Markham: Butterworths, 2001.

Braverman, Lisa. *Administrative Tribunals: A Legal Handbook*. Aurora: Canada Law Book, Inc., 2001.

Evans, J. M., H. N. Janisch, and David Mullan. *Administrative Law: Case, Text and Materials*, 4th ed. Toronto: Emond Montgomery Publications Ltd., 1995.

Hogg, Peter W. *Constitutional Law of Canada*. Toronto: Carswell, loose-leaf edition.

Gall, Gerald. *The Canadian Legal System*, 5th ed. Toronto: Thomson Carswell, 2004.

Jones, David P., and Anne de Villars. *Principles of Administrative Law*, 4th ed. Toronto: Thomson Carswell, 2004.

Kelly, James B. *Governing with the Charter: Legislative and Judicial Activism and Framers' Intent*. Vancouver: UBC Press, 2005.

Macaulay, Robert W., and James L. H. Sprague. *Practices and Procedures Before Administrative Tribunals*. Toronto: Thomson Carswell, loose-leaf edition.

MacIvor, Heather. *Canadian Politics and Government in the Charter Era*. Toronto: Nelson Thomson, 2006.

Mullan, David. *Administrative Law*. Toronto: Irwin Law, 2001.

Savoie, Donald J. *Breaking the Bargain: Public Servants, Ministers and Parliament*. Toronto: University of Toronto Press, 2003.

Yates, Richard A., Ruth Whidden Yates, and Penny Bain. *Introduction to Law in Canada*, 2nd ed. Scarborough: Prentice-Hall Canada Inc., 2000.

Chapter 15

Abele, Frances, and Michael J. Prince. "Aboriginal Governance and Canadian Federalism." In Francois and Miriam Smith, eds., *New Trends in Canadian Federalism*. 2nd ed. Peterborough: Broadview Press, 2003.

Adam, Marc-Antoine. "The Creation of the Council of the Federation." *Democracy and Federalism Series*. Kingston: Institute of Intergovernmental Relation, Queen's University.

Bakvis, Herman. "Checkerboard Federalism? Labour Market Development Policy in Canada." In Herman Bakvis and Grace Skogstad, eds., *Canadian Federalism: Performance, Effectiveness and Legitimacy*. Toronto: Oxford University Press, 2002.

Bakvis, Herman, and Peter Aucoin. *Negotiating Labour Market Development Agreements*. Ottawa: Canadian Centre for Management Development, 2002.

Black, E. R. *Divided Loyalties: Canadian Concepts of Federalism*. Montreal: McGill-Queen's University Press, 1975.

Boismenu, Gerard, and Peter Grafe. "The New Federal Tool Belt: Attempts to Rebuild Social Policy." *Canadian Public Policy* XXX(1) (March 2004): 71–89.

Bradford, Neil. "Canada's Urban Agenda: A New Deal for the Cities?" In James Bickerton and Alain-G. Gagnon, eds., *Canadian Politics*. 4th ed. Peterborough: Broadview Press, 2004.

Brown, David M. "Getting Things Done in the Federation: Do We Need New Rules for an Old Game?" *Constructive and Co-operative Federalism? A Series of Commentaries on the Council of the Federation*. Montreal:

Institute of Intergovernmental Relations, Queen's University, and Institute for Research on Public Policy, 2003. Available at www.irpp.org/miscpubs/archive/federation/brown.pdf. Retrieved July 14, 2006.

Cairns, Alan. "The Governments and Societies of Canadian Federalism." *Canadian Journal of Political Science* 10 (December 1977): 695–725.

Cameron, David. "Inter-legislative Federalism." In J. Peter Meekison, Hamish Telford, and Harvey Lazar, eds., *Canada: The State of the Federation 2002: Reconsidering the Institutions of Canadian Federalism.* Montreal and Kingston: McGill-Queen's University Press, 2004.

Cameron, David, and Richard Simeon. "Intergovernmental Relations in Canada: The Emergence of Collaborative Federalism." *Publius: The Journal of Federalism* 32 (spring 2002): 49–71.

Council of the Federation. *Founding Agreement.* December 5, 2003.

Doerr, Audrey. "Public Administration: Federalism and Intergovernmental Relations." *Canadian Public Administration* 25(4) (winter 1982): 564–79.

———. "Building New Orders of Government: The Future of Aboriginal Self-Government." *Canadian Public Administration* 40(2) (summer 1997): 274–89.

Elton, David, and Peter McCormick. "The Alberta Case: Intergovernmental Relations." In Jacques Bourgault, Maurice Demers, and Cynthia Williams, eds., *Public Administration and Public Management: Canadian Experiences.* Quebec: Les Publications du Qubec, 1997, 209–18.

Hobson, Paul A. R., and France St. Hilaire. *Reforming Federal-Provincial Fiscal Arrangements: Towards Sustainable Federalism.* Halifax: Institute for Research on Public Policy, 1994.

Inwood, Gregory J., Carolyn M. Johns, and Patricia O'Reilly. "Intergovernmental Officials in Canada." In J. Peter Meekison, Hamish Telford, and Harvey Lazar, eds., *Canada: The State of the Federation 2002: Reconsidering the Institutions of Canadian Federalism.* Montreal and Kingston: McGill-Queen's University Press, 2004.

Leslie, Peter, et al. "Managing Canadian Federalism." In J. Peter Meekison, Hamish Telford, and Harvey Lazar, eds., *Canada: The State of the Federation 2002: Reconsidering the Institutions of Canadian Federalism.* Montreal and Kingston: McGill-Queen's University Press, 2004.

———, et al. *A Partnership in Trouble: Renegotiating Fiscal Federalism.* Toronto: C.D. Howe Institute, 1993.

Lindquist, Evert A. "Recent Administrative Reform in Canada as Decentralization: Who Is Spreading What Around to Whom and Why?" *Canadian Public Administration* 37(3) (fall 1994): 416–30.

MacDonald, Mark R. "The Agreement on Internal Trade: Trade-offs for Economic Union and Federalism." In Herman Bakvis and Grace Skogstad, eds., *Canadian Federalism: Performance, Effectiveness and Legitimacy.* Toronto: Oxford University Press, 2002.

Meekison, J. Peter, Hamish Telford, and Harvey Lazar. "The Institutions of Executive Federalism: Myths and Realities." In J. Peter Meekison, Hamish Telford, and Harvey Lazar, eds., *Canada: The State of the Federation 2002: Reconsidering the Institutions of Canadian Federalism.* Montreal and Kingston: McGill-Queen's University Press, 2004.

Phillips, Susan D. "The Canada Health and Social Transfer." In Douglas Brown and J. Rose, eds., *Canada: The State of the Federation.* Kingston, Ont.: Queen's University, Institute of Intergovernmental Relations, 1995, 65–95.

Simeon, Richard, and Ian Robinson. "The Dynamics of Canadian Federalism." In James Bickerton and Alain-G. Gagnon, eds., *Canadian Politics.* 4th ed. Peterborough: Broadview Press, 2004.

Simeon, Richard. "The Federal-Provincial Decision Making Process." In Ontario Economic Council, *Issues and Alternatives—1977: Intergovernmental Relations.* Toronto: Ontario Economic Council, 1977.

Skogstad, Grace. "International Trade Policy and Canadian Federalism: A Constructive Tension?" In Herman Bakvis and Grace Skogstad, eds., *Canadian Federalism: Performance, Effectiveness and Legitimacy.* Toronto: Oxford University Press, 2002.

Smiley, Donald V., and Ronald L. Watts. *Intrastate Federalism in Canada.* Research study for the Royal Commission on the Economic Union and Development Prospects for Canada, vol. 39. Toronto: University of Toronto Press, 1985.

Winfield, Mark S. "Environmental Policy and Federalism." In Herman Bakvis and Grace Skogstad, eds., *Canadian Federalism: Performance, Effectiveness and Legitimacy.* Toronto: Oxford University Press, 2002.

Chapter 16

Abelson, Julia, et al. "Deliberations About Deliberative Methods: Issues in the Design and Evaluation of Public Participation Processes." *Social Science and Medicine* 57 (2003): 239–251.

Coleman, William D., and Grace Skogstad, eds. *Policy Communities and Public Policy in Canada*. Mississauga, Ont.: Copp Clark Pitman, 1990.

Culver, Keith, and Paul Howe. "Calling All Citizens: The Challenges of Public Consultation." *Canadian Public Administration* 47(1) (spring 2004): 52–75.

Fletcher, Frederick J., and Robert Everett. "The Media and Canadian Politics in an Era of Globalization." In Michael Whittington and Glen Williams, eds., *Canadian Politics in the 21st Century*. Toronto: Nelson Thomson, 2004.

Good, David A. *The Politics of Public Management: The HRDC Audit of Grants and Contributions*. Toronto: Institute of Public Administration and the University of Toronto Press, 2003.

Government of Canada, Health Canada. *Health Canada Policy Toolkit for Public Involvement in Decision Making* Ottawa: Minister of Public Works and Government Services, 2000.

Montpetit, Eric. "Public Consultations in Policy Network Environments: The Case of Assisted Reproductive Technology Policy in Canada." *Canadian Public Policy* XXIX(1) (March 2003): 95–110.

———. "Governance and Interest Group Activities." In James Bickerton and and Alain-G. Gagnon, eds., *Canadian Politics*. 4th ed. Peterborough, Ont.: Broadview Press, 2004.

Nesbitt-Larking, Paul. *Politics, Society, and the Media: Canadian Perspectives*. Peterborough: Broadview Press, 2001.

Phillips, Susan D. "Interest Groups, Social Movements and the Voluntary Sector: En Route to Reducing the Democratic Deficit." In James Bickerton and Alain-G. Gagnon, eds., *Canadian Politics*. 4th ed. Peterborough: Broadview Press, 2004.

Phillips, Susan D., and Michael Orsini. *Mapping the Links: Citizen Involvement in Policy Processes*. Ottawa: Canadian Policy Research Networks, 2002.

Pross, Paul. *Group Politics and Public Policy*. Toronto: Oxford University Press, 1986.

———. *Group Politics and Public Policy*. 2nd ed. Toronto: Oxford University Press, 1992.

Roberts, Alasdair. "Two Challenges in Administration of the Access to Information Act." In Commission of Inquiry into the Sponsorship Programs and Advertising Activities, *Restoring Accountability: Research Studies, Volume 2: The Public Service and Transparency*. Ottawa: Her Majesty in Right of Canada, 2006.

Savoie, Donald J. *Breaking the Bargain: Public Servants, Ministers and Parliament*. Toronto: University of Toronto Press, 2003.

Smith, Miriam. "Interest Groups and Social Movements." In Michael Whittington and Glen Williams, eds., *Canadian Politics in the 21st Century*. 6th ed. Toronto: Nelson Thomson, 2004.

Taras, David. *The Newsmakers: The Media's Influence on Canadian Politics*. (Scarborough: Nelson, 1990).

———. *Power and Betrayal in the Canadian Media*. Peterborough: Broadview Press, 1999.

Taylor, David. "Transport Canada's Deliberative Democracy Experiment." *Optimum Online* 34 (July 2004): 1–4.

Thomas, Paul G. "Debating a Whistle-Blower Protection Act for Employees of the Government of Canada." *Canadian Public Administration* 48(2) (summer 2005): 147–84.

Young, Lisa, and Joanna Everitt. *Advocacy Groups*. Vancouver: UBC Press, 2004.

Chapter 17

Auditor General of Canada. *Report of the Auditor General of Canada*, ch. 9. Ottawa: Department of Public Works and Government Services, October 2000.

———. *Report of the Auditor General of Canada*, ch. 20. Ottawa: Department of Public Works and Government Services, April 2000.

———. *Report of the Auditor General of Canada*, ch. 3. Ottawa: Minister of Public Works and Government Services, February 2005.

Government of Canada. *Public Service 2000: The Renewal of the Public Service of Canada*. Ottawa: Minister of Supply and Services, 1990.

———. *Making It Work for You: The Government of Canada Tool-Kit for Managers*. Ottawa: Her Majesty in Right of Canada, 2006.

Lindquist, Evert A., Ian Clark, and James Mitchell. "Reshaping Ottawa's Centre of Government: Martin's Reform in Historical Perspective." In G. Bruce Doern, ed., *How Ottawa Spends 2004–2005: Mandate Change in the Paul Martin Era*. Montreal and Kingston: McGill-Queen's University Press, 2004.

Malloy, Jonathan. "The Next Generation? Recruitment and Renewal in the Federal Public Service." In G. Bruce Doern, ed., *How Ottawa Spends 2004–2005: Mandate Change in the Paul Martin Era*. Montreal and Kingston: McGill-Queen's University Press, 2004.

Public Service Commission. *Annual Report 2004–2005*. Ottawa: Her Majesty the Queen in Right of Canada, 2005.

Public Service Human Resources Management Agency of Canada. *Introduction to HR Planning—A Reference Tool for HR Specialists in the Public Service of Canada*. Available at www.hrma-agrh.gc.ca/hr-rh/hrp-prh/ihp-ipr_e.asp. Retrieved July 14, 2006.

Treasury Board of Canada Secretariat. *Policy on Learning, Training and Development*. November 25, 2005.

Zussman, David, and Jak Jabes. *The Vertical Solitude: Managing in the Public Sector*. Halifax: The Institute for Research on Public Policy, 1989.

Chapter 18

Government of Canada. Public Service Human Resources Management Agency of Canada. *Annual Report on Official Languages 2003–04*. (Ottawa: Her Majesty in Right of Canada, 2004), 53.

———. Public Service Human Resources Management Agency of Canada. *Employment Equity in the Federal Public Service 2003–04*. Ottawa: Her Majesty in Right of Canada, 2005.

Leck, Joanne D. "Making Employment Equity Programs Work for Women." *Canadian Public Policy* XXVIII, supplement (2002): S85–S100.

Pay Equity Task Force. *Final Report: Pay Equity: A New Approach to a Fundamental Right*. Ottawa: Her Majesty the Queen in Right of Canada, 2005.

Weiner, Nan. "Effective Redress of Pay Inequities." *Canadian Public Policy* XXVIII, supplement (2002): S101–S115.

———. "Workplace Equity: Human Rights, Employment, and Pay Equity." In Christopher Dunn, ed., *The Handbook of Canadian Public Administration*. Toronto: Oxford University Press, 2002.

Chapter 19

Good, David A. *The Politics of Anticipation: Making Canadian Federal Tax Policy*. Ottawa: Carleton University, School of Public Administration, n.d.

Hale, Geoffrey E. *The Politics of Taxation in Canada*. Peterborough: Broadview Press, 2002.

———. "Trading Up or Treading Water? Federal Fiscal and Budgetary Policies in Search of a New Mandate." In G. Bruce Doern, ed. *How Ottawa Spends, 2006–2007: In From the Cold-The Tory Rise and the Liberal Demise*. Montreal: McGill-Queen's University Press, 2006.

Hartle, Douglas G. *The Revenue Budget Process of the Government of Canada: Description, Appraisal, and Proposals* (Toronto: Canadian Tax Foundation, 1982), 61–62.

Maslove, Allan. "Introduction: Budgeting in Provincial Governments." In Allan M. Maslove, ed., *Budgeting in the Provinces: Leadership and the Premiers*. Toronto: Institute of Public Administration of Canada, 1989.

Savoie, Donald J. "The Federal Government: Revisiting Court Government in Canada." In Luc Bernier, Keith Brownsey, and Michael Howlett, eds., *Executive Styles in Canada: Cabinet Structures and Leadership Practices in Canadian Government*. Toronto: University of Toronto Press, 2005.

———. *The Politics of Public Spending in Canada*. Toronto: University of Toronto Press, 1990.

Schick, Allen. "The Road to PPB: The Stages of Budget Reform." *Public Administration Review* 26 (December 1966): 244.

Treasury Board of Canada Secretariat. *The Expenditure Management System of the Government of Canada*. Ottawa: Minister of Supply and Services, 1995.

Wildavsky, Aaron. *The New Politics of the Budgetary Process*. 2nd ed. New York: HarperCollins Publishers, 1992.

Chapter 20

Aucoin, Peter. *Auditing for Accountability: The Role of the Auditor General*. Ottawa: The Institute on Governance, 1998.

Canada, House of Commons, Standing Committe on Government Operations and Estimates. *Meaningful Scrutiny: Practical Improvements to the Estimates Process*, September 2003.

Chernier, John, Michael Dewing, and Jack Stillborn, "Does Parliament Care? Parliamentary Committees and the Estimates." In G. Bruce Doern, ed., *How Ottawa Spends 2005–2006: Managing the Minority*. Montreal and Kingston: McGill-Queen's University Press, 2005.

Dobell, Peter, and Martin Ulrich. "Parliament and Financial Accountability." In Commission of Inquiry into the Sponsorship Program and Advertising Activities, *Restoring Accountability: Research Studies, Volume 1: Parliament, Ministers and Deputy Ministers*. Ottawa: Her Majesty the Queen in Right of Canada, 2006.

Good, David A. "Parliament and Public Money: Players and Police." *Canadian Parliamentary Review* 28(1) (spring 2005): 17–21.

Government of Canada. *Canada's New Government: Federal Accountability Action Plan: Turning a New Leaf.* Ottawa: Her Majesty the Queen in Right of Canada, 2006.

Madore, Odette. *Federal Government Spending: A Priori and A Posteriori Control Mechanisms.* Ottawa: Library of Parliamentary, 2006.

Malloy, Jonathan. "An Auditor's Best Friend? Standing Committees on Public Accounts." *Canadian Public Administration* 47(2) (summer 2004): 165–83.

———. "The Standing Committee on Public Accounts." In Commission of Inquiry into the Sponsorship Program and Advertising Activities, *Restoring Accountability: Research Studies, Volume 1: Parliament, Ministers, and Deputy Minister.* Ottawa: Her Majesty the Queen in Right of Canada, 2006.

Saint-Martin, Denis. "Managerial Advocate or 'Control Freak'? The Janus-Faced Office of the Auditor General." *Canadian Public Administration* 47(2) (summer 2004): 121–40.

Sutherland, S.L. *The Office of the Auditor General: Government in Exile?* Kingston: School of Policy Studies, Queen's University, 2002.

Treasury Board of Canada Secretariat. *The Expenditure Management System of the Government of Canada.* Ottawa: Minister of Supply and Services, 1995.

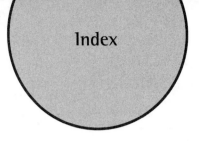

Index

The following notations have been used: b (box); f (figure); n (notes); and t (table).

Finer, Herman, 162–163
First Ministers' Conference (FMC), 243–244, 243f, 245
Follett, Mary, 33, 34
Food, inspection of, 4
Ford, Henry, 45
Foreign aid, delivery of, 4
Francophones, 291–292, 295–296, 297t
Friedrich, Carl, 162–163
The Functions of the Executive (Barnard), 35

G

Gaebler, Ted, 55–56
Gall, Gerald, 225
"A Garbage Can Model of Organizational Choice," 48
Gifts/entertainment, acceptance of, 166, 168
Gilbreth, Frank/Lillian, 22
Globalization, 3, 8–9
GOCO. *See* Government-owned-company-operated
Golembiewski, Robert T., 42
Good, David A., 61
Goodnow, Frank, 149
Government, Canadian
  access to, 9
  activities of, 4
  branches of, 70, 70f
  budget for, 10, 55, 70, 75, 130, 303
  centralization *v.* decentralization by, 29–31, 30f, 32nn24–25, 55, 60
  challenge to, 3
  characteristics of, 7
  CHT for, 239
  confidence in, 9, 129
  CST for, 239
  departmentalization of, 69
  downsizing in, 10, 15n11
  as federalism, 236
  federal/provincial fiscal relations for, 238–240, 239f
  hierarchy within, 42, 178–179, 193
  improvement in, 10, 55
  Increased Ministerial Authority and Accountability for, 62, 76
  Individual ministerial responsibility for, 75, 178, 207, 208, 209b, 217, 218–220
  judicial review of, 225–228
  managerialism in, 52
  minister/public servant relations in, 13
  monopoly by, 6
  NPM for, 61–64
  organization of, 70, 70f
  Parti Québécois as, 240
  patronage *v.* merit base for, 19, 23, 152–153, 222n2, 275–276, 277, 278, 284, 293
  policy development by, 129
  private *v.* public in, 104, 129
  PS 2000 program for, 42, 62
  public choice theory for, 52

Public Service Rearrangement and Transfer of Duties Act for, 73
  reform of, 10–11, 23, 42–43, 63
  relations between, 13, 87, 94–95, 235–240, 251n4
  reorganization of, by prime minister, 73–74
  research by, 4
  responsibility in, 162
  size of, 4, 11, 12, 130
  taxation for, 6, 238–240, 239f
  TQM for, 42
Government-owned-company-operated (GOCO), 133
Grants/loans, 4
Gulick, Luther, 17, 24–28, 29, 31, 33

H

Hackman, Richard, 47
Halperin v. the Attorney General of Canada et al., 233
Harper, Stephen, 73, 74, 81, 83f, 184, 184f, 186b, 202–203, 215, 218, 251n13, 263, 263b, 312, 326n12
Hartle, Douglas, 312b
Hawthorne effect, 35, 49n4
Hawthorne Works, 35, 38
Health care, responsibility/advances in, 4, 9
Herzberg, Frederick, 46, 47
Hierarchy
  Influence/control through, 17, 24–25, 24f, 45, 79
  as inoperable, 21
  between ministers, 178–179
  of needs, 36, 36f
  as protection, 170–171
  within public administration, 13, 18, 42, 131, 170, 193
  as pyramidal, 198
  as safeguard, 170–171
  span of control and, 17, 24–25, 24f, 45, 79
  unity of command for, 18
  violation of, 20
Highways. *See* Roads/highways, maintenance of
Hitler, Adolf, 18
Hodgetts, J.E., 71
Horizontal job loading, 47
Horizontal management, 192–195, 193f, 196f, 207
Housing, fair, 4
Humanistic perspective, 33
Human Resources Council, 282
Human resources, management of
  affirmative action in, 6–7, 292–293
  for employee quality/quantity, 283–286, 285f
  evolution of, 276–279
  job classification by, 282–283
  merit system for, 19, 23, 152–153, 222n2, 275–276, 278, 284, 293
  organizations for, 280–282
  pay equity for, 7, 287, 300–301
  prime minister/cabinet ministers and, 186
  private *v.* public administration of, 6–8
  Public Service Modernization Act for, 279b

Productivity, 8–9, 17, 21–22, 24–25, 24f, 28–29, 31, 34, 35, 45, 79
Profit, motive for, 38
Promotion, on merit, 19, 23, 152–153, 222n2, 275–276, 278, 284, 293
Protectionism, globalization and, 8–9
Provinces, government in, 10, 242–243, 245–246, 251n13
PS 2000. *See* Public Service 2000
PSC. *See* Public Service Commission
Public
  advisory boards/councils for, 265
  appointees' interaction with, 13, 52, 177, 208
  best interest of, 169–171, 253
  government participation by, 264–267, 265f, 266–267
  hearings/seminars for, 265
  protection for, 170–171
  Royal Commissions by, 265
  technology and, 13, 52
  trust/confidence by, 166
Public Accounts, 321–322
Public Accounts Committee (PAC), 202, 323–325
Public choice, theory of, 52, 66n2
Public enterprise, 91–92, 93–95. *See also* Crown corporations
Public goods, 96
Public hearing/seminars, 265
Public servants. *See also* Administration, public; Human resources, management of
  accountability by, 161, 165, 172
  achievement by, 46
  appointment of, 152–153, 158
  for ASD, 137
  as asset, 53
  authority of, 19, 151
  autonomy for, 33, 53, 54, 59
  characterization of, 25–26, 26f, 27f, 31
  conduct of, 21, 158–159, 161, 165–166, 208
  confidence of, 21
  confidentiality by, 166, 222n2
  conflict of interest by, 166
  contributions by, 35
  control/influence of, 34, 205
  cooperation by, 36
  deputy ministers as, 78, 208
  discipline for, 45
  education/in-service training for, 169, 242, 284–286, 294
  empowerment of, 56
  equity for, 7, 147–148, 275, 287, 289, 292–295, 295t
  financial incentives for, 22, 35, 36
  gifts/entertainment for, 166, 168
  goals of, 20
  as government representative, 264
  growth in, 11
  human resources for, 6–8
  hygiene factors *v.*, 46–47, 47f
  information leaking by, 166

  integrity of, 148, 161, 165–166, 172
  interaction between, 13, 144, 145–146
  interaction of, with public, 264
  interaction with executive branch by, 177
  intergovernmental relations by, 87, 94–95, 235–236, 251n4, 253
  job enrichment for, 47
  job interview for, 36
  judiciary interaction with, 223
  labor unions for, 45
  layoffs for, 38
  loyalty of, 159, 166, 208, 209b, 222n2
  management by, 60
  manipulation of, 38
  measurement of performance by, 59, 60, 212, 286–287
  media coverage of, 7, 156, 262–264, 263b, 271
  ministerial relations with, 198, 208
  moonlighting by, 166, 168
  motivation of, 34, 36, 37, 130–131
  neutrality by, 3, 4, 5, 51, 64, 147, 149, 151–159, 208, 209b, 211–212, 222n2, 269–270, 278
  as objective/subjective, 171–172
  Parliament and, 207
  in participatory management, 38–39
  pay equity for, 7, 287, 300–301
  performance evaluation of, 59, 60, 212, 286–287
  policies by, 3, 4, 5, 51, 64, 151–152
  political activities by, 153–154, 158, 166, 208, 222n2, 267–268
  political advice by, 6, 158, 222n2
  political *v.* moral responsibility of, 162–163
  politicization of, 247–248
  positive *v.* negative forms of, 45
  power by, 12, 19, 56, 150, 151, 157–158
  promotion of, 19, 152–153, 222n2, 284
  Public Service Employment Act for, 153–154, 200, 202
  questioning of, 207, 208, 211–212
  recruitment/retention of, 283–284, 285f, 287
  relations between ministers and, 13
  representativeness and, 147–148, 275, 289
  rotation of, 46
  rumour mill by, 41
  significance of, 45
  tenure for, 156–158, 209b
  training for, 169, 242, 284–286, 294
  types of, 4
  Values and Ethics Code for the Public Service for, 168–169
Public Servants Disclosure Act, 270b
Public Service 2000 (PS 2000), 42, 278
Public Service Commission (PSC), 152–153, 200, 202, 213, 214, 276, 280–281, 284, 294. *See also* Human resources, management of
Public Service Employment Act (1967), 153–154, 200, 202, 284, 293, 298. *See also* Public servants
Public Service Human Resources Management Agency of Canada, 280–281

Special Committee on Personnel Management and the Merit Principle, 278
Special operating agencies (SOAs), 131–132
Sponsorship Program, 73, 82, 100–101, 101f, 105, 213, 218–220, 270, 272n3, 320, 324–325
Statistical process control (SPC), 40
"The Study of Administration" (Wilson), 7, 149
Success, core values/practices for, 53, 56, 59, 66n22
SUFA. *See* Social Union Framework Agreement
Suresh v. Canada, 228
Sympathetic observer effect, 35, 49n4
Systemic barrier, 294, 298

T

Taxation, 6, 238–240, 239f
Taylor, Frederick Winslow, 21–23, 31, 33, 34, 41, 44, 48
TB. *See* Treasury Board
TBS. *See* Treasury Board Secretariat
Technology, 4, 9, 44–45, 132, 265
Tenure, 156–158, 209b
Terrorism, 73
Theory, organizational, 17
Theory X/Y, 37, 37t
Thomas, Paul G., 197
Thought, market-based, 56
Time-and-motion study, 22
Total Quality Management (TQM), 40–41
TQM. *See* Total Quality Management
Trade, barriers to, 242
Transparency, in private/public administration, 7
Transport Canada, organizational structure of, 76, 77f
Treasury Board (TB), 84–85, 181, 183, 200, 202, 203, 280, 293, 294, 296, 319–320
Treasury Board Secretariat (TBS), 84–85, 185–186, 189, 197–198, 280, 294, 309, 312, 320
Trebilcock, M.J., 95
Tribunals, 225–231, 301
Trudeau, Pierre Elliott, 79, 182, 185, 188, 241, 278
Turner, John, 182, 195

U

Ultra vires. See Judiciary, Canadian
United States, public administration in, 151
Unity of command. *See* Authority; Hierarchy
Urwick, Lyndall, 17, 24–28, 29, 31, 33

V

Values and Ethics Code for the Public Service, 168–169

W

War Committee, 182
Waste, minimization of, 21
Water, inspection of, 4
Waterman, Robert, 53
Waterways, coastal, 4
Weber, Max, 12, 17, 18–21, 23, 31, 33, 39, 41, 48, 52, 65
Welfare, 4
Western Premiers' Conference, 245
Whistle-Blowing, 270b
White, L.D., 149
Willoughby, W.F., 149
Wilson, Woodrow, 7, 149
Wolf, Charles, Jr., 97
Women, representation of, 10, 291–292, 296–298
Workplace
    autonomy in, 33, 53, 54, 59
    cooperation in, 36
    flexibility in, 33, 59
    harmony in, 22
    humanistic perspective for, 33
    informal system in, 20, 34, 36
    job classification within, 23–24
    monotony in, 22
    productivity in, 35
    rate-buster in, 34
    safety in, 4
    women in, 10, 291–292, 296–298
    worker control in, 34